FRAGMENTS OF THE AFGHAN FRONTIER

MAGNUS MARSDEN
BENJAMIN D. HOPKINS

Fragments of the Afghan Frontier

Columbia University Press
New York

Columbia University Press
Publishers Since 1893
New York
cup.columbia.edu
© Magnus Marsden and Benjamin D. Hopkins, 2011

Library of Congress Cataloging-in-Publication Data

Marsden, Magnus.
 Fragments of the Afghan frontier / Magnus Marsden
and Benjamin D. Hopkins.
  p. cm.
 Includes bibliographical references and index.
 ISBN: 978-0-231-70246-1 (cloth : alk. paper)
 ISBN: 978-0-231-80006-8 (ebook)
 1. Ethnology—Afghanistan. 2. Ethnology—Pakistan. 3. Afghanistan—
Relations—Pakistan. 4. Pakistan—Relations—Afghanistan. 5. Afghanistan—
Politics and government. 6. Pakistan—Politics and government.
 I. Hopkins, Benjamin D. II. Title.

 GN635.A3M37 2011
 306.09581—dc23

                   2011023869

∞

Columbia University Press books are printed on permanent and durable acid-free paper. This book is printed on paper with recycled content.
Printed in India

c 10 9 8 7 6 5 4 3 2 1

References to Internet Web sites (URLs) were accurate at the time of writing. Neither the author nor Columbia University Press is responsible for URLs that may have expired or changed since the manuscript was prepared.

To Our Parents

CONTENTS

LIST OF MAPS

ACKNOWLEDGMENTS

In the writing of this book we have accrued many debts. The research on which it is based has received generous support from Trinity College, Cambridge, Corpus Christi College, Cambridge, the School of Oriental and African Studies, University of London, the George Washington University, the Nuffield Foundation, the Leverhulme Trust, the British Academy, the Norwegian Institute of Foreign Affairs, the Smuts Fund (Cambridge) and the Carey-Robertson Fund (Cambridge). We have benefited from insightful conversations with Susan Bayly, Christopher Bayly, John Bowen, Joya Chatterji, Dale Eickelman, Jonathan Goodhand, Deniz Kandiyoti, Filippo and Caroline Osella, Anil Seal, Ben Soares, Matthew Carey, Humeira Iqtidar, Nile Green, Ed Simpson, Justin Jones, Seema Alavi and Abdul Iloliev, amongst others. Diana Ibañez-Tirado, in particular, has heard and read several drafts of this book, and deserves special thanks for patiently commenting on them. Lila Rabinovich has been unwavering in her support throughout this project. Parts of the book have also been the subject of welcome critique and discussion by seminar audiences at Anthropology, History, and South Asian studies departments and centers at the University of Cambridge, the London School of Economics, Brunel University, the School of Oriental and African Studies, Leeds University, University College London, University of California Los Angeles, the University of Edinburgh and the University of Pennsylvania. We have also benefited from the comments of anonymous reviewers for the *Journal of Asian Studies*, the *Journal of the Royal Anthropological Institute*, *Anthropology Today*, and the *Journal of Global History*, as well as for the Leverhulme Trust research awards scheme. A version of Chapter 5 was originally published as Marsden, M. (2009), A tour not so grand:

ACKNOWLEDGMENTS

mobile Muslims in northern Pakistan. *Journal of the Royal Anthropological Institute*, 15: S57–S75. It is reprinted here with kind permission from the *Journal of the Royal Anthropological Institute*. A version of Chapter 6 was originally published as Muslim Cosmopolitans? Transnational Life in Northern Pakistan, by Magnus Marsden, *The Journal of Asian Studies*, Vol. 67, No. 1 (February 2008), pp. 213–247 Copyright © 2008 Association of Asian Studies Inc. A revised and extended version is reprinted here with the permission of Cambridge University Press. The writing of this book would not have been possible without the support of numerous people in Afghanistan, Tajikistan and Pakistan, many of whose names we are unable to mention here. Amongst them, however, Ammanullah, Halim, Salehuddin, Sultan Mehmood, Zuhoor Aman, Nisar Ahmed, Ashraf Jan, Sarkar Baig, Hazar Baig, Haroon Ahmed, Sultan Rikweda, Allar Nizar, Mukhtar, 'Shahboye' and Mir Hussein Shah have all supported the research visits on which this book is based. We would like to thank Daisy Leitch for her tireless work with the proofs. Michael Dwyer has been a patient and always genial publisher whose support for this and our other endeavors we are delighted to gratefully acknowledge here. It goes without saying that all mistakes, substantive or otherwise, are our own.

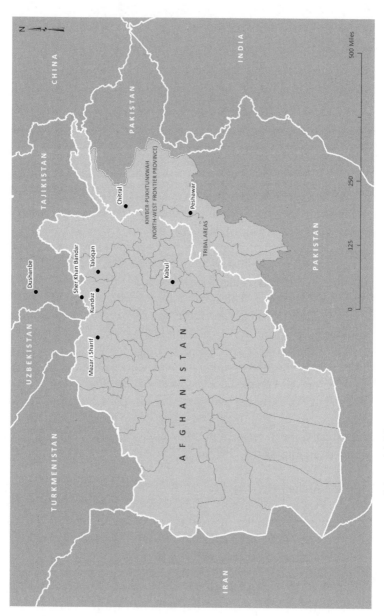

Map of Afghanistan © Naula Cowan, George Washington University

INTRODUCTION

The Afghan Frontier is a place beholden to imagination, myth and fiction. Defined for the consumption of Western audiences by the reporting of the likes of Winston Churchill and the fiction of Rudyard Kipling, it remains a place of profound mystery and alienation, despite its long and often intimate history of interaction with the West. Depictions of this space today generally evoke images of religious bigotry and primitive tribesmen. The inhabitants of this 'savage frontier'[1] remain fundamentally foreign and dangerously threatening to modern sensibilities and political order. These images, which claim definitive knowledge of the Frontier and its peoples, are steeped in ignorance, romanticism and conceptual lethargy. This work takes aim at them, and the structures of knowledge they rest upon, interrogating the multiple meanings of the Frontier and how they are continually constituted and reconstituted by a multifaceted spectrum of states and peoples. In doing so we hope to create a more dynamic, nuanced and sophisticated understanding of the Frontier which offers a picture of greater complexity.

Today, the Afghan-Pakistan Frontier is often depicted as the premier place of violence and lawlessness, an incubator of chaos and radicalism which threatens the stability of all who come into contact with it. Its power to pull within its orbit ideologically motivated 'jihadists' from as far afield as Algeria, America and Britain has become a regular fixture of the media trope. Even in much contemporary scholarly work, it is closely associated with images of Taliban fighters, powerful tribal leaders and roving gangs of foreign militants from Saudi Arabia, Chechnya and Uzbekistan. The region has come to be seen as a paradigmatic Islamist enclave central to wider developments in global

1

forms of violent Muslim militancy. Alternative, but no less negative images also define Western understandings of life in this borderland. The flow of refugees fleeing from or returning to Afghanistan, heroin trafficking, and the violence of continual conflict along the Frontier add to the sense of this as a place of instability and chaos.

These images mask far more than they reveal about the Frontier. This is a space that has been shaped powerfully by a poorly understood colonial legacy, as well as invisible histories of everyday movement that are rarely the focus of scholarship or popular reporting. Mobility has been a key feature of life on the Frontier, with its inhabitants employing movement as a strategy of survival and response to political pressure, as well as economic opportunism.[2] These histories of movement underline the complex dynamism of a space continually occupied, defined and redefined by the people, communities and political entities that claim it as their own. Yet the diverse ways in which the region's inhabitants perceive, act within and seek to understand this geopolitically divided and culturally discontinuous space remain poorly understood.

Fragments of the Afghan Frontier seeks to address these lacunae in the literature. It explores the ways in which the Frontier's inhabitants themselves register the social, religious and cultural patterns composing their region, and documents how those patterns are imprinted with a living history of colonialism, the after-life of which continues to shape life in the region today. Its central argument is that the Frontier has been too narrowly defined either as the territorially bounded tract of land that traverses what today constitutes the Afghan-Pakistan border or as a region that is distinct because of its social, or more pointedly 'tribal' composition. In contrast, we explore how the Frontier has been and continues to be perceived and experienced from a variety of different perspectives. These include the experiences and understandings of colonial states and interventionist powers active in the region, its modern nation-states, and its own diverse peoples. We are interested in the varying ways these actors relate to and clash with one another. By pairing a historical study of the high politics shaping the Frontier with a thick ethnographic account of the experiences and understandings of its inhabitants, this book explores the significant rupture between the way the Frontier has been conceptualized, mapped and deployed by local as well as colonial states, foreign powers and international organizations and the everyday modes of perceiving, interacting with and profiting from it by the region's people.

INTRODUCTION

This work is designed, at least in part, to rebut two powerful modes of understanding this space. First, central to our study is the acknowledgment that the Frontier's inhabitants are not now, nor have they historically been, a homogeneous group occupying a singular space. There is no clearer example of the contemporary tendency to treat the Frontier as a homogeneous and undifferentiated space than the use of the term 'Af-Pak'. 'Af-Pak' is today widely used to signal the need for an 'integrated' solution to the Taliban-insurgency in Afghanistan and its variants in Pakistan's settled and tribal areas. But the region's people widely consider the term 'Af-Pak' insulting; it ignores the complex multiple self-identifications maintained by the region's inhabitants. At the same time, it renders insignificant the very different types of states that have come to shape the region and the contrasting forms of the modernizing processes they have unleashed on local populations. The term 'Af-Pak' shows little in the way of historical sensitivity or cultural knowledge by amalgamating this space into a singular whole. Indeed, one of the striking features of this region is the extent to which very small distances signal major differences in culture, religious life and political disposition. We are interested in how political entities have sought to overcome this 'problem', as well as how populations have engaged actively with it.

The second dominant understanding of the Frontier we contest is that which characterizes it as a 'non-place', a chaotic buffer zone situated between 'real' regions such as Central and South Asia, and the Middle East. Such a reading of the Frontier traces its genealogy to the imperial ideas of British India and the so-called 'Great Game' it is supposed to have played with Russia for supremacy over Central Asia. Today, the idea of a 'buffer state' has been reincarnated in the Pakistan army's concept of 'strategic depth', an idea which like its colonial predecessor underlines the extent to which local actors consider the future of the region's nation-states as having little if anything to do with the integrity of their national borders. Equally, the Frontier has been mythologized as a space of freedom from and resistance against state authorities; anti-colonial nationalists, as well as anti-state regionalists or agitators for 'independence' and 'freedom', could find rebirth in the liberating air of the hills. To state authorities, this made this tract *yaghestan*, an ungovernable land of chaos. These tropes continue to be energized and embraced by popular studies and journalistic accounts, such as Rory Stewart's revealingly entitled work *The Places in Between*, as well as within policy circles. They also chime with recent attempts by anthropologists to theorize Asia's upland zones as anarchic spaces historically populated by state-evading peoples until they were inevitably incorporated within the all-seeing, all-knowing modern state.[3] But such images of disjuncture and marginality are problematic as they obscure the ways in which the Frontier was, and is, not only a space of uncontrolled freedom, but also one that binds, connects and thus helps to forge powerful forms of solidarity, community and collective identity that endure across time and space.

In contrast to the models that either homogenize or disintegrate the Frontier, we understand the Frontier as composed of a collage of interlinked and overlapping spaces. These spaces are inhabited by a diversity of often-fluid communities, as well as complex and shifting identity formations. We reject any single understanding or vision of the Frontier as paramount, but at the same time we recognize that those seeking to shape the region's future development want to impress their particular vision of the Frontier over that of others. Regardless of attempts to assert unity, a multiplicity of Frontiers coexist in time and space, simultaneously experienced by those inhabiting them. We hope a greater recognition of the complexity of these spaces and of the dynamism of their relationships with one another will enable a better understanding of the whole, as it has in other contexts.[4]

While we do not seek to openly intervene in policy debates, we hope to bring home to those engaged in them the dangers of talking in terms of a singular solution to the region's problems. The Frontier's multiple spaces are inhabited by, and nurture the existence of, multiple histories, communities, and lifeworlds: what we refer to as 'fragments'. One such fragment, for example, is the Khowar-speaking Chitrali or Khó people who are an important focus of this book's ethnographic chapters. It would be easy to think of these people as a distinct 'ethnic group', or a 'minority'. Yet, as we demonstrate in the following pages, such modes of conceptualizing difference fail to appreciate the heterogeneity inherent in such peoples' own histories and ways of being. Equally ignored is how they register what distinguishes them from other frontier dwellers in terms of complex and changing sensibilities rather than rigid forms of cultural difference or political affiliation. The coexistence of these fragments does not, however, signal the Frontier's inevitable fragmentation.[5] We seek to show, rather, how the vitality of each of these fragments, the ways in which they relate to one another as well as to a wider whole, is obscured by scholars and policy-makers who define the Frontier solely in terms of territories, social and ethnic groups, or political blocs locked in states of conflict or cooperation with one another. Far from simply eliding the existence of multiple fragments on the Frontier with its fragmentation, this work emphasizes that these fragments both repel and attract one another simultaneously. They are at the heart of the Frontier's heterogeneity, not its fracturing. Our call, thus, is for a greater recognition of the underlying dynamics and constantly evolving ties that simultaneously draw the Frontier's spaces and fragments together and also pull them apart.

Such a consciously plural approach runs contrary not only to the ways the Frontier is usually constructed or understood, but also to broader epistemologies of such places. The colonial and Western experiences of the Frontier, including those of many post-colonial states, persistently lay claim to an unjustified pedigree of knowledge about the Frontier. During a trip to Kabul in the winter of 2006, for example, NATO officers informed us that International Security Assistance Force (ISAF) was 'very keen' to learn from the past 'successes' of the British in the region. A number of these officers commented that the Pakistani army, which carried forward both the martial and intellectual traditions of the British Raj, knew how best to handle the Frontiersmen. This yearning for a return to colonial forms of knowledge is palpable on a number of fronts. Andrew M. Roe, a Company Commander in the Yorkshire Regiment, has recently published a monograph growing out of his work at the US Army Command and General Staff College about British colonial efforts in Waziristan, which self-consciously seeks to render utilitarian lessons from the past to guide current efforts in the region.[6] Colonial forms of knowledge have been reconstructed most invidiously in the form of the US Department of Defense's Human Terrain System. The program manufactures a highly reified version of Afghan society and makes claims of authenticity, often framed within a discourse of 'tribe' as an unchanging dimension of Afghan society.[7] The Human Terrain System is indeed the new incarnation of the 'ethnographic state', unashamedly harking back to the tradition of the 'scholar-administrator' which once defined and ruled the Frontier.[8]

Many anthropologists and historians have challenged the simplistic understandings that programs such as the Human Terrain System promote of dynamic societies like those along the Frontier. Some scholars have turned their attention to the debates concerning military strategy in Afghanistan and the wider region, showing how they depict Afghans as lacking civilization and humanity, rendering them both inherently incapable of self-government and the rightful subjects of civilizing violence.[9] Such language echoes that of Kipling in 'The Young British Soldier' where he admonished the maker of empire: 'When you're wounded and left on Afghanistan's plains, And the women come out to cut up what remains, Jest roll to your rifle and blow out your brains, An' go to your Gawd like a soldier'. The savagery of the Afghan persists. So too, then, does the moral imperative of the West's civilizing mission.

As part of that civilizing mission, policy makers ask how many troops are needed in Afghanistan, pondering how long these forces will remain in the country. Even those opposed to such a long-term strategy argue that it is 'Afghan corruption' that lies behind the failure of well-intentioned, if poorly thought out, Western plans. There is a rising chorus that Afghans ungrateful for Western efforts should be forced 'to look after themselves', while Western forces should focus solely on their own interests—the destruction of Al Qaeda and other terrorists. The premise, in short, of much 'security speak' about the Frontier continues to be that Afghans and frontier people more generally are uncivilized and incapable of self-rule, but that the cost of 'civilizing' them is prohibitively high.[10] In such an intellectual environment, we agree with other scholars that the role of the social science and humanities disciplines is above all to challenge 'the form of propaganda perpetuated by the most powerful members of society', and we hope this book makes a small contribution.[11]

In focusing on the heterogeneity of the Frontier, and the shifting modes of identity that its inhabitants navigate daily, this book forces the question of how policy-makers and institutions deal with a region marked by such fluidity. While much contemporary policy and security discourse homogenize the Frontier, the following chapters document how in the past political actors have recognized the Frontier's multiple faces. Yet many of those actors promptly ignored the Frontier's multiplicity, continuing to treat it as a unitary whole. Doing so better fit available resources, both mental and material, as political authorities found themselves overstretched and conceptually unfamiliar with the challenges the Frontier continually threw up. In policy terms, this often took the form of 'bribing' locals, a practice employed by the West since the US invasion in 2001. It is also a practice about which military chiefs often seek advice from anthropologists, enquiring about the meaning of money in Afghan society, and the nature and significance of 'the gift' in social life there.[12] But this schema, and attempts to call upon anthropologists to help with its execution, have had a doubly negative effect. First, new hierarchies of power and authority in local society have been created, based on external patronage. In the past, when such patronage disappeared, it left an unstable mix. This instability is visible now in the highly fractious forms of patron-client politics that have developed over the past decade across Afghanistan.[13] Second, belief in the 'buy-ability' of locals has negated their moral agency, or rather failed to recognize and take into account the complex normative worlds these people inhabit. What we are arguing for, then, is the need for policy-makers to recognize the sophistication of this region and its people, and in doing so to design commensurably sophisticated policy prescriptions and actions.

Local inhabitants and external authorities do not invest the Frontier with the same meaning, and that disjuncture is arguably the most significant one marking the Frontier. Time and again, external state authorities have attempted to construct alliances based on their understandings of the dispersal of power within Frontier communities. Yet these are often constructed on prefabricated expectations rather than in-depth local knowledge. But there is more going on than a simple mismatch between the ways in which states have viewed the region and the 'reality' of how people in the region experience it on the ground. Rather, multiple forms of mismatch and cross-communications have emerged. Both states and the region's peoples have held manifold, often competing understandings of the Frontier born of context, ignorance and knowledge. Different states—colonial, local and national—have conceptualized the Frontier in very different ways. Furthermore, the power of definition exerted by state actors has meant that rather than being expelled from the Frontier, their vision of its reality has gained traction through the coercive force of state sanction. The socio-political topography of the Frontier has therefore been shaped as much by the states' multiple understandings and misunderstandings as by the efforts of local inhabitants.

Although today the 'Frontier' usually refers to the Afghan-Pakistan boundary, historically it looped around and within the region, extending from the Afghan boundary in the west to the *de facto* border between Russia and the British India in the north. These boundaries were not considered discrete from one another, but rather were thought of as an intricately interlinked, yet concurrently discontinuous whole. The boundary between Iran and Afghanistan in the west, for example, mattered as much to the British as their own boundary with Afghanistan in the east. As important as how the Frontier has been conceived and defined spatially is how it has been envisaged and deployed socially. Frontier (*sarhad*) may refer to a political boundary, to 'uplands' in contrast generally to lowlands, as well as to contexts that are held by people to be 'urban' and 'civilized'. Thus, the significance of being designated a frontier person (*sarhadi*) assumes different meanings that are contextually dependent and defined. It is, nevertheless, a concept denoting particular types of space and people which is deployed by frontier dwellers from a variety of backgrounds who speak diverse languages across the region, including Pashto and Dari as well as Khowar. In the light of both this local usage and the changes in the way it has been approached by state officials and external actors, we employ the 'Frontier' in this book to denote not a bounded tract of territory but a space—part conceptual, part physical—fashioned both by the boundary-making designs of states, colonial and otherwise, and by local understandings of frontiers and frontier people.

Likewise, the Frontier cannot be conceived as the purview of a single ethnic or tribal group, no matter how large that group might be. Historically, the character of the Frontier was defined as much by its Baluch as by its Pukhtun inhabitants; as much by the princely states like Chitral as the area of *yaghestan* considered outside the control of any state authorities. As Shah Mahmoud Hanifi has recently argued, not only do different ethnicities (Pashtun-Baluch) and polities (princely state/tribal area) exist relationally to one another, but so too do Frontier languages.[14] These relationships are largely defined by the meanings carried by their different constituent fragments. Nowhere are these meanings more profoundly manifest than in the terms assigned to different ethnic groups inhabiting the Frontier. Terms such as 'Pukhtun', 'Pashtun', and even the British colonially-derived term 'Pathan', not to mention 'Afghan', 'Tajik', and 'Farsiwan', are the source of profound debate throughout the region, as well as the scholarship on it. These debates concern what constitutes the authentic use of these terms, their meanings and relationships to one another as well as to languages, linguistic groups and political territories.

It is easy to fall foul of such debates, by either pursuing a naming agenda or suggesting that conflicts over nomenclature are trivial and insignificant. On the contrary, debates about names are important to many of the region's own people, especially, though not exclusively to its intellectuals. While recognizing the importance, both emotional and intellectual, of these debates, we do not seek to intervene in them. We self-consciously use all of these terms throughout the manuscript, including the colonially-burdened 'Pathan', as appropriate to the context we discuss. Further, we bring into play alongside them a bewildering range of yet more names, such as 'Chitrali', 'Wakhi', 'Pamiri', 'Panjshiri' and 'Badakhshi'. Yet we do not use these terms interchangeably. Rather, we explore the processes through which naming has come to be central to the ways in which states have sought to map the Frontier and local populations respond to these processes of mapping and reassert their own spatial imaginings.[15] Such processes reflect the power disparities between different actors; the power to name is indeed a considerable one. Thus where we use the common term of contemporary convention, we do so fully aware that such usage is the manifestation of specific agendas and the ability to enforce them. In addition to signaling practices of spatial mapping, labels and names such as 'Pukhtun', 'Chitrali', and 'Tajik' are also identity markers that are contextually and performatively 'enacted'. They signal particular constellations of political, socio-economic, emotional and ethico-moral sensibilities, which might value resistance to the state, commitment to particular types of work, or balanced constellations of thought and emotion to peoples' attempts to live a good Muslim life. These sensibilities are often discursively connected to particular 'ethnicities', yet they are also central to people's strivings to understand the worlds they inhabit.

While we challenge the seemingly unthinking understandings of the Frontier as an undifferentiated, homogeneous whole, we do not deny that there are indeed ties that bind. This whole region bears the powerful imprint of colonial forms of boundaries and expectations regarding the constraints and possibilities of communal behavior. Not only is the Frontier divided by a colonial-imposed boundary, it is also made up of colonially-derived administrative districts, themselves subdivided in relation to the types of state penetration that extend within them. These range from 'tribal' to 'semi-tribal' to 'settled zones', defined by the type of state jurisdiction local communities are subject to. State-imposed or state-related markers are not the only ones simultaneously uniting and dividing this region. Identity registers, continually defined and redefined by local inhabitants, profoundly shape the Frontier. In some localities, so-called 'tribes' and ethnic communities stretch across the Afghan border, as do families and webs of kinship, while elsewhere the border marks important distinctions between ethno-linguistic groups. The Frontier is thus defined by forces that are simultaneously centrifugal and centripetal.[16] The geography of these patterns of difference and sameness is not static and unchanging. Instead, it reflects both state-led policies of resettlement and the constant movement of people across the region's numerous and overlapping internal, as well as international political boundaries, often in contravention of the state. As anthropologists have long demonstrated in the region, boundaries between ethnic groups and political spaces rarely coincide with the contours of the region's cultural forms or stand for the national identity of their respective nation-states in any simple sense.[17] Instead, the region is replete with ethno-linguistic groups that are minorities both within the Frontier and within their respective states. While projects of cultural identification are often associated with particular languages, they are also embarked upon by people with very different modes of personal and collective self-understanding. This level of sameness allows people to negotiate and navigate through the region's deeply contrasting spaces. At the same time, however, shared cultural values have also led ruling elites and powerful opinion makers to assert claims of ethnic or religious distinction, often underwritten in a language of authenticity and exclusive forms of collective, national identity.

The presence of different types of spaces, readily injected with emerging political and economic opportunities, nourishes important possibilities for the realization of social, moral and political forms. The opportunities latent in these differences have led to a rich variety of experiences within a relatively confined space. Yet while the Frontier may be unique in the particular constellation of differences that compose it, many of its component parts are readily discernable in other contexts. The experience of state actors, both colonial and post-colonial, in asserting authority over this 'periphery' is by no means exceptional. Likewise, the practices of mobility contouring the Frontier's social landscape are neither temporally or geographically singular. Indeed, amongst the most interesting aspects of the Frontier are the connections binding it together, as well as to the larger world. The discussion we embark upon here, therefore, is not simply about the Afghan-Pakistan frontier, but more generally about similarly situated frontier spaces.

INTRODUCTION

Frontier Perspective

It would be both disingenuous and irresponsible of us to leave the reader without any sense of the ties binding this work together. While we present a number of discrete episodes to illuminate the varied experiences of the Frontier, they are also selected to illustrate common themes that run along the Frontier geographically, historically and culturally. The central discursive theme of our work is that of representation. How have the Frontier and its inhabitants been depicted by state authorities, foreign media, scholars, and locals themselves? What do these representations tell us about that which is depicted, as well as those who depict? How are these representations conceived, practiced, experienced and imagined both collectively and individually by people living in the region? Each of the episodes that follow is laden with multiple representations projected for different purposes to different audiences. By exploring such representations we hope to both fracture their all-encompassing claims of truth, while at the same time reconstituting them in new ways to give assorted perspectives of the Frontier.

In addition to representation, a number of other themes further our discussion of the Frontier. One of these is mobility. The anthropological chapters trace the practices and patterns of mobility embarked upon by the region's inhabitants, while the historical chapters examine state efforts to control that mobility, through topographical delineation and cultural encapsulation wherein the colonial state bounded the tribesmen within a colonially mandated version of 'tradition'. Another theme is religion. Whether it is a language of legitimacy deployed by the state to justify its actions, or conversely used by its enemies to justify their resistance, or something that informs and is integrated into discussions and practices of everyday ethics, religion is a central part of the fabric of the Frontier. We are also interested in ideas of 'modernity'. What we mean by 'modernity' and how it is manifested differs for both authors. Historically, this is really about forms of state power. Anthropologically, it centers on ideas of 'globalization' and how the inhabitants of this region fit into the larger world they are part of. Yet we both recognize the many origins and manifestations of the multiple 'modernities' marking the Frontier.[18]

This book grows out of our previous work, both individual and joint, which has been concerned with the forms of political order and ethical sensibilities in the region. Hopkins' *The Making of Modern*

Afghanistan locates the evolution of alternative social formations in the geopolitical space which would come to form the state of Afghanistan in an economic, political and cultural world in flux.[19] It largely challenges and inverts the longstanding historical tropes defining the Frontier, most notably the so-called 'Great Game', which understand this area as, at one and the same time, the center of imperial strategic concerns and an afterthought in terms of its local complexity and importance. The failed efforts of the British to construct a 'modern' Afghan state have led Hopkins to a further consideration of the meaning and form of a 'modern state' in the colonial world of nineteenth-century South Asia. It has also raised questions about the importance of the 'periphery', the Frontier, in the formation of the norms and character of political authority for the imperial center.

Marsden's work has also been concerned by the relationship between the periphery and the center. *Living Islam* challenges commonplace models that treat 'village Muslims' in South Asia and elsewhere as the hapless recipients of Islamizing processes flowing out of Muslim urban centers, 'cores' of learning and knowledge. Instead, it demonstrates the intellectual significance of 'village Muslims' from Rowshan in Chitral, a remote region of Pakistan's North-West Frontier, to the dynamics of religious life in Pakistan.[20] The questions raised in *Living Islam* have forced Marsden to consider their implications in a world marked by ever-evolving practices of mobility and expanding forms of connectivity. Is Chitral a singularly unique space, or is it rather one of many interconnected unique fragments that are constantly reshaped by moving peoples and ideas, yet nevertheless depicted by the states of which they are a part as different from 'the mainstream'? And how does what Marsden refers to as a local 'culture of debate', concerning matters of ethics, morality and aesthetics that mark the lives of Chitrali people he interviewed and enrich their collective solidarities through explorations and discussions of meaning and significance, play out in the larger region? These questions are especially important and pressing given the simplistic and negative ways in which expressions of Islam and modes of being Muslim along the Frontier are often portrayed.

We have been exploring many of these questions together over the past few years, realizing the intimacy and immediacy of both the past and present. By asking each other the questions prompted by our separate works, we have been encouraged, cajoled and forced to think and engage more broadly with this area and the increasingly policy-dominated forms of knowledge that exist about it. It is this ongoing conversation that has set the agenda, and indeed the tone for this volume. We do not presume, nor desire to offer a panoptical gaze or comprehensive understanding of the Frontier. Rather, we seek to share some of the most striking and arresting episodes and ideas gathered from our own research. In doing so, we self-consciously present a disjointed picture, both for the reasons outlined above regarding our view of the Frontier, but also in order to leave space for a conversation to germinate in response to our silences.

It is also incumbent on us to reflect on the challenges and opportunities of working together on this book, as well as the larger inter-disciplinary project it is part of. While it has long been recognized that history and anthropology are intimately related, spawning a wide range of shared projects in a wide variety of genres, we feel our research is unique. This book is neither an ethnographically thick history of the Frontier nor a historically grounded ethnography. Indeed, the history and anthropology presented are not as closely intertwined as if this book had been written by a single author. The tensions between our differing disciplinary orientations and the ways in which these have shaped our writing strategies and research methods erupt, indeed, in the very language we use in the book. Whilst we have tried as far as possible to frame our findings as part of a joint 'we', there are moments when we have had to use the first person pronoun, above all else in order to capture the immediacy and proximity of encounters in the field. This might appear to some in places as if the book has not benefited from a final and thoroughgoing copy-edit, yet we have made active decisions on this issue and feel that tension and dissonance better reflect the difficulty of bridging disciplinary divides.

This work has been jointly conceived, researched and authored. We have traveled together to some of the places detailed in the following pages, meeting many of its characters in the process.[21] In doing so, we have experienced together many of the particular challenges presented by doing fieldwork in such a difficult environment. This has been infinitely helpful in grounding the history in the physical reality of the present. At the same time, we have likewise looked at some of the same archives, investigating the 'paper lives' of many of the people and families mentioned below. This, in turn, has helped root the present firmly in the past. Oddly, but at the same time reassuringly, we have found many of the difficulties of the field mirrored in the archives and vice versa. The silences of the archival record requiring a 'reading against the grain' were in many ways matched by the reticence of informants, inhabitants of an unstable environment sensitive to the potential dangers of talking too freely to visiting researchers. Nowhere is this more clearly seen in this manuscript than in its lack of detailed consideration of the role played by women's agency in the making of the Frontier. If the archives in which Hopkins has worked have thrown little light on this critical dimension of the Frontier's spatial organisation, then Marsden's ethnographic research, especially in the context of northern Afghanistan, has thus far also been largely unable to address questions concerning women's experiences of mobility in this space. While this represents a very significant lacunae in the findings presented in this book, we nevertheless hope that it is a work that embodies both the possibilities and limits of such an intellectual collaboration.

This volume is not only meant to be an extension of our own previous work, but is also a contribution to a wide body of literature that has influenced our thinking. Our approach to understanding the Frontier as a heterogeneous space, shaped by but transcendent of colonial boundary-making processes, owes a considerable debt to a wide and expanding body of work in anthropology and history which seeks to describe and theorise the making of expansive spaces such as nations, regions and transregional ecumenes. One such debt is to Susan Bayly's recent exploration of the ways Vietnamese socialist intellectuals locate the significance of their immediate lives within a wider 'supranational terrain' in an effort to understand the processes through which modern mapping operations and more affective, intimate geographies interact with rather than simply displace one another.[22] Bayly's anthropological work finds its historical counterpart in Thongchai Winichakul's seminal *Siam Mapped*.[23] Winichakul examines the relationship between different ways of conceptualizing political order and space, rejecting the idea that European colonialism heralded the wholesale displacement of local knowledges and understandings. Newer colonial conceptions of territoriality were grafted onto older local ones, sometimes knowingly and sometimes not. Just as important, local ideas of place and power were as fundamental in shaping European understandings of their empires as their ideas were in affecting indigenous social and political topographies. Nowhere is this more evident than on frontiers, and a number of innovative recent works have acknowledged this.

14

The literature on frontiers is indeed massive, and growing, especially when paired with mushrooming studies of 'borders' and 'borderlands' over the past decade. Much of the work on 'borders' and 'borderlands' conceives these spaces as areas of disjuncture and rupture. In contrast, we see them as centrally connective of diverse regions and peoples.[24] Further, despite Willem van Schendel's call for a comparative history of the borderlands, much of the material remains bounded by the concerns of area studies.[25] Some recent works transcend those concerns, offering both history and theorization of geographically disparate, yet situationally similar places. For example, the borderlands of South-East Asia are subject to the same dynamics and concerns as the Afghan Frontier, with issues of 'legality', trade and state power core concerns of recent scholarship.[26] Anthropologists and historians have recently theorized how 'equivalence' allows travelers across the Indian Ocean realm to 'recognise the shape and characteristics of their home society in the societies of the places they visit' while at the same time allowing them to be 'blind ... to the differences between home and the places they have travelled to', thus making their journeys easier.[27] Likewise, new work on the Sahara has demonstrated how this region has been historically constituted through the ethics and legal considerations of contract, infused with concerns of Islam.[28] Notably, too, an important body of work on 'bounding' of Central Asia's nation-states serves as a reminder of the dangers of emphasizing the fluidity and porosity of 'borderlands' without also exploring the implications that multi-million dollar international projects of 'border strengthening' have had for the shaping of people's lived worlds.[29] By engaging in dialogue with these emerging bodies of literature, we hope to foster a broader discussion about the meaning of 'frontiers' and the worlds they delimit.

There is also an expanding body of sophisticated scholarship that challenges depictions of the Frontier as an unruly geopolitical space locked into a historically durable grid of 'Islamic militancy'. The titles, if not content and arguments, of some works characterize the entirety of this space as being best defined in terms of its association with 'political religion'.[30] In contrast, David Edwards has explored the ways in which competing moral, religious and political Afghan social codes are often inscribed upon and expressed through spatial understandings of the region.[31] In his study of the 'global *jihad*', Faisal Devji has theorized the ways in which the Frontier's landscape has been invested in more recent times with global forms of political and, more aptly, ethical significance.

The Frontier's mountainous and caved terrain has played a critical role in the transmission of the ideas and values of the 'global *jihad*', now most often associated with Osama Bin Laden and Al Qaeda. Devji emphasizes the ways in which the Frontier has come to be seen and imagined by such people as a 'disordered mystical landscape', which stands as an important site of 'ethical practice' providing Muslims with the possibility of refuge from the 'hurly burly of worldly life'.[32]

Yet Devji's focus on the Frontier's current status as a space of *jihad* must also be paired with its ideologically complex past. Mukulika Banerjee's pioneering work on Khudai Khitmatgar has revealed the importance of this peaceful, anti-colonial and predominantly Pushtun movement to understanding the Frontier's ideological geography.[33] The legacy of the Red Shirts' interaction with Gandhian non-violence continues to shape the Frontier today, through the memories of the movement's activists as well as in the Awami National Party. Complementing Banerjee's work on a kind of secular Pashtun nationalism is Sana Haroon's examination of the politics of the *ulama* along the Frontier during the late colonial period.[34] Haroon demonstrates the political and ethical debates gripping men of religious learning during this time, and how those debates continue to echo along the Frontier today. Taken together, what these works underline in the ideological complexity marking the politics of the Frontier over at least the last eighty years, if not more.

In what follows, we build on these explorations of the complex configuration of moral values and ethical practices encoded within such spatial orderings of the Frontier. Yet we also seek to address the ways in which Frontier people themselves live, work and move across this space, as well as engaging with and creating their own geographies, which sometimes build on globally resonant stereotypes and at other times stand opposed or detached from them. Our emphasis is on the degree to which the Frontier's mobile Muslims strive to acquire and exchange knowledge about the Frontier, recognize the importance of understanding the diverse range of constantly changing influences found therein, and consider this dimension of their daily lives as being critical also to their attempts to successfully negotiate, move within and profit from their world. A consideration of these local, intimate alternative geographies points toward a plurality of spaces associated with forms of thought, selfhood and daily action, which suggest other important social dynamics than those of Islam, honor, state authority, or global *jihad*.

Organization and Structure

This book addresses the lived experience of the Frontier from two very different angles. The first section examines the history of how the Frontier was imagined, mapped and ruled by state administrators, colonial and indigenous, as well as the reactions this engendered amongst local populaces. What distinguishes this book's historical treatment of the Frontier is its consideration of this space's cultural and political heterogeneity. In contrast to much scholarly work that treats the Frontier as being homogeneously or dominantly Pukhtun,[35] this book explores the ways in which both states and their officials as well as the region's people themselves have constantly been called upon to engage with the cultural, religious, political and ethnic heterogeneity of the region. It was in this arena that the colonial state sought to regulate and encapsulate its subjects by imposing political boundaries, deploying military force and developing modes of control related to its own understanding of local cultural norms. While anthropologists have considered heterogeneity as a key issue defining the region, historians, as well as many contemporary commentators, have not. The following pages consider how the region's heterogeneity has shaped peoples' experiential worlds and what has happened when such indigenous heterogeneity comes into contact with more rigid exogenous orders of spatial organization, such as borders.[36] Thus rather than approaching the Frontier as a politically divided territory in any simple sense, we approach it as an encompassing yet internally differentiated arena where diverse polities, peoples and cultural influences have interacted with one another.

The second section of the book explores the ways in which the political boundaries, expectations of behavior and everyday experiences of cultural heterogeneity are negotiated, experienced and perceived by Muslims living in the region today. The chapters in this section, based on in-depth fieldwork in Chitral, Pakistan's northernmost district, and across a wide range of localities in northern Afghanistan and the southern regions of Tajikistan, all of which are connected to one another, are ethnographic. They focus on the ways in which Frontier Muslims seek to understand and act in relation to the rapidly changing and politically unstable world in which they live. Critical to this is the way people in the region challenge, subvert and identify with the ongoing persistence not merely of colonially-derived geographical boundaries and conceptions of acceptable behavior, but also a range of cultural, religious and social dynamics that exist alongside these.

By concentrating on the capillary-like networks connecting the region—Chitral, the cities and towns of Pakistan's Frontier province, Afghanistan, and the border regions of the Badakhshan Province of post-Soviet Tajikistan—the ethnographic chapters nuance many of the concepts raised in the historical ones. It would be tempting to treat Chitral as an exceptional case, a princely-state addendum to the 'real' Frontier of British India that was gradually incorporated into the Pakistan state. But this approach leads to certain boundaries in the region being treated as more 'authentic' than others, some being 'primordial' while others are merely the outcome of colonial policy. We are not interested in these debates. Instead, this book highlights the importance of distinctions among the region's people that are poorly captured by tropes of ethnic differences, religious distinctions or colonially-derived boundaries. It explores the ongoing vitality of values and modes of distinguishing between the region's people that transcend conventional ways of classifying frontier Muslims in relation either to sectarian identity or to ethnicity.

In the pages that follow, each chapter engages a discrete fragment of the Frontier, exploring how the effected and involved actors have both shaped and experienced those fragments. The historical chapters investigate how the state, colonial and indigenous, envisaged, understood and attempted to shape the Frontier, presenting arguments about territoriality, tradition and religion. The anthropological chapters, forming the book's second half, document the sacred and profane, trans-regional community and language, politics and emotion. Each chapter centers on a particular episode or cast of characters through which it draws out the larger themes of the work. In keeping with our notion of fragments, the links between these episodes are not always explicitly teased out.

Chapter 1 concerns a boundary dispute between the Afghan kingdom and Qajar Persia over their mutual border in Sistan. This frontier was long a source of tension between these powers, leading to wars and lesser conflicts on a number of occasions. The issue was not settled until well into the twentieth century and only after a number of attempted arbitrations. This chapter looks at the earliest of these arbitrations, the Goldsmid mission in the early 1870s. The British decided this part of the Frontier was too sensitive to be left in the hands of native powers. Yet this was not simply another episode of British imperialism. British Indian authorities were reluctantly drawn in as arbiter, 'invited' through treaty obligation by the Persians. The Afghans readily assented to this British inclusion, but not only for reasons of political leverage. Both the Persians and the Afghans used this opportunity to present to the British, as well as each other, the demands and competences of modern statehood. The chapter presents and analyses the efforts of indigenous polities coming to grips with and reconstructing alien forms of political order for their own purposes.

The second chapter examines an episode of British imperial management of the Frontier, and its lasting legacies in the region. The southern frontier is populated in the main by Baluch, rather than Pakhtun tribesmen. It was here that Sir Robert G. Sandeman developed his system of frontier governance known as the 'tribal levy' or 'Sandeman' system. Unlike his peers further north who kept the inhabitants of the hills at arm's length, Sandeman embraced them and 'went native' in order to better rule them through their own institutions. But the 'tribal traditions' that were the foundation of his system, far from having some 'objectively' identifiable and timeless content, were those that Sandeman and other Frontier administrators deemed 'authentic'. The colonial state thus served as the arbiter of tradition. In doing so—subsequently governing the 'tribes' through their 'traditions'—Sandeman cut them off from the modernizing influences of the colonial regime. They thus became encapsulated as tribesmen rather than integrated as subjects. In many ways, their offspring have remained in this anomalous position.

Chapter 3 continues the swing around the Afghan periphery and settles in the Swat Valley. The claims of authority forwarded by the likes of Sandeman were contested not only by the inhabitants of the Frontier but also by other segments of South Asian society. These disparate streams of protest morphed into a common agenda of resistance through a shared religious idiom, giving rise to what the British termed 'religious fanaticism'. This chapter examines the history of religious violence in the form of a colony of '*mujahidin*' whom the British termed 'Hindustani fanatics'. This colony, which traced its origins to the revolt of Sayyid Ahmed of Rai Bareilly against the Sikhs in the 1820s, endured on the Frontier through the remainder of British rule in South Asia. Its inhabitants used the idiom of religious resistance, calling for a *jihad* against the 'infidel *sarkar*'. Yet with rare exceptions, they were surprisingly ineffective, both in gaining the support of local inhabitants and in repulsing British control. What they were instrumental in facilitating, however, was an anti-Muslim panic in British India which culminated in a series of 'Wahabi' trials in the 1860s. The story of these 'fanatics' is itself worth exploration. More important, though, their story forces a reassessment of the legacy of official British anti-Muslim sentiment. Here, perhaps more clearly than anywhere else, the centrality of the 'periphery' in shaping the center becomes obvious.

Chapters 4 serves as a connective corridor between the book's historical and anthropological parts. It conceptually links the past to the present, discussing how colonial ways of imagining Frontier peoples' moral values have inflected the ways Chitralis are understood and represented in the context of the ongoing 'War on Terror'. Chapters 5, 6 and 7 are anthropological in content and argument. These chapters move northward, completing our semi-circle of the Frontier from west to east. They focus on one particular and distinctive region: the connected societies of the Frontier's northwestern fringes. This region incorporates the former princely state of Chitral, as well as the Panjshir valley, known for its anti-Soviet *jihadi* movement led by Ahmed Shah Massoud, and Badakhshan, an area that incorporates both a province of Afghanistan and part of Tajikistan—a post-Soviet Muslim majority state in Central Asia. This is very often a region considered so different from the rest of the Frontier that it bears little if any significance for its future, or wider developments. This section of the book, however, challenges such an assertion, showing instead the complex ways in which the Frontier is connected by the mobile lives of these people.

The focus of Chapter 5 is Chitral. Rather than documenting the distinctiveness of Chitral's society or culture in relation to other regions of the Frontier, the chapter shows how the people of this region inhabit multiple landscapes—moral, sacred, profane and historical—which bear the imprint of a diverse range of cultural influences. It explores a practice of mobility that forms a very important dimension of the everyday lives of many young Chitrali men: the tour. Tours involve Chitralis visiting villages and valleys of the region held to be especially interesting and distinctive. The chapter explores the ways in which such tours are important not only because they re-inscribe the Chitrali landscape with forms of diversity, but also because they are central to the ways in which Chitrali people fashion themselves as curious, self-reflective yet also pious persons.

Chapter 6 also focuses on Chitral's internal heterogeneity and connectivity to the wider world, although in a different way and using

INTRODUCTION

another set of ethnographic datum. Turning away from Khowar-speaking people who refer to themselves as Chitralis, the chapter investigates the lives of people who came to the region from their homes and towns in neighboring areas of Afghanistan and Tajikistan during the long years of civil and international conflict in these countries. Through a consideration of the varying types of relations and social locales held by people often referred to as Afghan and Tajik 'refugees' (*muhajir*), it demonstrates the active ways in which their presence in Chitral led to the reactivation of some, and repression of other, ties that unite these places with very different experiences of modernizing processes to one another. By examining the lives of the 'displaced', the chapter adds another fragment to our understanding of the Frontier.

The book's final chapter continues the narrative thread of the previous two, while at the same time moving to a different location, namely Afghanistan itself. Chapter 7 traces the everyday lives and the patterns of mobility of the Afghan and Tajiki refugees with long-term life experiences in Chitral after they made the difficult, fraught and contested decision to return to their home countries. Based on fieldwork in Afghanistan and Tajikistan, the chapter documents the role such people play in creating and sustaining important forms of regional interconnectedness as friends, relatives and traders. At the same time, it also brings attention to the ways in which they connect diverse parts of this region together, and also bind it, as migrants, travelers, and sojourners to other places beyond. Mobility, circulation and return thus constitute the final fragment our study offers.

Ultimately, our aim is to proffer a glimpse of the rich complexity of the Frontier through a detailed study of these temporally divided and geographically disjointed fragments. In the midst of this disjuncture, however, we are acutely aware that all of these episodes have been and continue to be integral to the ever-evolving, indeed often inchoate, nature of the Frontier as a place with singular meaning. Through this work, we hope to contribute to and improve an ongoing conversation of what that meaning is, and how it should shape present and future engagement with the Frontier.

1

THE PROBLEM WITH BORDERS[1]

The Afghan Frontier is first and foremost known for the border which today separates Afghanistan and Pakistan. This border, commonly referred to as the Durand Line, was delineated at the end of the nineteenth century and is often characterized as the core 'problem' of the Frontier. To local states and some local residents, the border has created an artificial and wholly negative division between common peoples, cultures and societies. It prevents the erection of common political projects, most notably Pashtunistan, which would unify the area in a more organically natural arrangement, or so its proponents argue. To policy-makers in Washington today, and previously in London, Calcutta and Delhi, it is not the border's impermeability that is the problem, but precisely the opposite. The border is a meaningless fiction people easily slip across at will, often to get up to no good as far as these powers are concerned. Neither of these images is particularly revealing of substance, and both are guilty of resting on a totalizing narrative of what, exactly, the border is. This chapter seeks to challenge and complexify that narrative.

Borders, as delineated physical frontiers both dividing and constituting states, represent a particular European understanding of space and separation. More simplistic formulations treat these understandings as having displaced indigenous conceptions, including Islamic ones, through the spread of formal and informal imperialism. In contexts where European powers could not assert their authority directly, they pressured 'native' polities to adopt Westphalian state forms, specifically through the construction of borders. These borders were central to the

23

construction of states by indigenous political communities, helping define 'them' as well as the 'other' that they confronted. The images and conceptions of space communicated by these practices partially colonized the local political imagination. Thus when indigenous agents shaped their political space, physically and politically, they did so with these European-inspired images firmly fixed in their imagination.

Yet this was not simply a process of mimicry, forced upon weaker indigenous polities by the power inequalities that marked relations between themselves and European empires. Although, in many instances, 'native' polities assumed the forms of European political intercourse, namely Westphalian states with delineated borders, they often imbued those forms with radically different substance. Further, the assumption of those forms, as this chapter argues, was at times both strategic and disingenuous. Indigenous kingdoms played the game according to European rules to assuage the interests and potential anger of imperial centers, but they did so in pursuit of their own goals. Just as such processes of 'colonization' were contested historically, though perhaps not openly, so too today Western political norms and forms are subject to local manipulation. Regional populations have developed practices to keep other, older and often Islamic modes of perceiving, imagining and experiencing space in play, even as 'the border' in the Westphalian sense has also exerted a powerful force on the physical and imagined worlds they inhabit.

Few places demonstrate both the assumption of Western political forms by local inhabitants and political actors under pressure from the supposed juggernaut of European imperialism and its subversion as well as Afghanistan. Afghanistan was one of the first political entities defined by this process of frontier making beyond direct colonial control. Although bordered by two European empires, its first modern frontier was its western border facing Persia.[2] It was thus against Persia, another polity of the *dar-al Islam*, that Afghanistan was first topographically delineated and physically defined.

As the Afghan and Persian political communities coalesced into modern states during the course of the nineteenth century, they attempted to strengthen their institutions through the demarcation of frontiers and the assertion of territorial sovereignty. Yet our understanding of this process is heavily colored by the story of Anglo-Russian rivalry, known as the 'Great Game'. The Perso-Afghan frontier represented the only one defined largely by indigenous actors themselves, rather than by the

Russians or British.[3] It therefore became the center of a definitional rivalry between the emerging Persian and Afghan states. In this arena of contestation, these powers faced an opponent of roughly equal strength, rather than the imperial juggernauts pressuring them from other directions. The contest over the Perso-Afghan frontier reveals a story fundamental to state construction for both protagonists, one that was repeated elsewhere in the world as European norms of political intercourse came to monopolize the expectations of the international community, as well as indigenous communities.

Central to the process of border creation on Afghanistan's western frontier in the late nineteenth century was the first delineation of the Sistan frontier by the Goldsmid mission between 1870 and 1872. This mission embodied a profound conceptual shift, redefining the Islamic and 'tribal' political worlds from which the Afghan and Persian states were emerging. It marked the point at which these political communities assumed, to differing degrees, the characteristics of modern West-phalian states in their rhetoric and aspirations. Rather than simply emphasizing the role of local interests in affecting the outcome of Anglo-Russian imperial rivalry, this chapter recasts the Perso-Afghan frontier dispute as a vehicle for the transformation of the region's political landscape into one contoured by 'native' states of recognizably European form. This transformation was not simply imposed by the region's colonial hegemon, British India, whose power was too ephemeral to warrant such an assertion. While the British may have originally framed the conceptual landscape of statehood, it was ulti-mately subverted by indigenous actors who populated it with local notions, creating a hybrid political order. The experience of the Afghan and Persian courts on their common frontier powerfully demonstrates the multifaceted hybridity of the Frontier's construction.

The Goldsmid mission occurred at a time when the influence of cen-tralizing Islamic states was at a low ebb. Both the Qajar and Durrani dynasties were relatively weak. Likewise, neither the British, still embracing their policy of 'masterly inactivity', nor the Russians, who had yet to secure their control of Central Asia, were particularly inter-ested in asserting their limited power in the region at this time. Conse-quently, the mission the British dispatched was charged with arbitrating between local states, rather than delineating the Frontier on behalf of the Empire, as would later be the case. The mission took place before our vision becomes blurred by the all-encompassing legend of the

Great Game.[4] It thus offers a window onto a vanishing world of indigenous polities adapting, and simultaneously succumbing, to the pressures of imperial conformity. Finally, the mission's introduction of Westphalian norms of statehood was expressed through the cartographic depiction of both political identity and control. Mapping the delineation of political authority in the area embodied a fundamentally different understanding of politics within it.

The experience of the Goldsmid mission encapsulates the contradictory pressures of modernization and traditionalization affecting the British colonial project in South Asia, and Western imperialism more generally. Yet, as neither Persians nor Afghans were directly ruled by colonial powers, their assumption of European ideas of statehood stands apart, even if it was driven by power disparities with neighboring empires. As happened in Siam, Persians and Afghans defined their own 'geo-bodies', in the absence of direct colonial control.[5] The demarcation of their common border thus gives rise not so much to a study of imperial domination as to an examination of the 'indigenization' of European norms and forms of political intercourse.

The Perso-Afghan contest was an expression of the hegemony of the European paradigm of political community, which colonized spaces beyond direct imperial control. It redefined the nature of the emerging Qajar and Durrani states by making them essentially territorial entities. While both Persian and Afghan polities adopted the norms and forms of European political intercourse through the demarcation of boundaries separating discrete physical and political spaces, their assumption of these remained distinct. Neither the Afghan nor the Persian experience followed the same course. The process of state formation in Afghanistan was largely driven and defined exogenously.[6] Further, the image of geo-bodies was initially central to the mapping and creation of a state rather than a nation. In contrast, the Persians, though prompted by Anglo-Russian pressures, had an indigenously authored cultural memory of statehood and political authority on which they could draw, even if it differed markedly from the new political project they were in the midst of constructing.[7]

Territoriality and the Meaning of Sovereignty

The issue of territoriality has elicited a sophisticated body of scholarship, examining the implications of the pre-eminence of European understandings of territory in the creation of the nation.[8] According to these authors, the creation of state boundaries through technological innovation, including mapping and surveying, gave birth to geopolitical shapes, or 'geo-bodies', which 'created nationhood spatially'.[9] As Thongchai Winichakul has argued, '[t]he geo-body, the territoriality of a nation as well as its attributes such as sovereignty and boundary, are not only political but also cultural constructs'.[10] The main thrust of this scholarship has focused on the role of territoriality in the construction of the nation, rather than that of the state. Yet the modern delineation of territory through boundaries is first and foremost an exercise of state power, and a prescriptive practice of state competence. While important in the definition and construction of the 'nation', territoriality must be understood as constitutive of the state itself. This is particularly true in the Afghan case where the territorial genesis of the state preceded the tentative emergence of an Afghan nation.

The dominance and entrenchment of European ideas of territoriality can be traced through the sharpening of frontiers during the nineteenth century. They were originally conceived as spaces of transition, regions of overlapping claims of suzerainty and control, and it was only with advancing survey technologies that conceptions of boundaries began to sharpen in the European imagination. This sharpening filtered into colonial spaces first, and then affected interstitial spaces by drawing the limits of the colonial state. Thus, boundaries moved from a zone of control to a line of control. In South Asia, what once had been a frontier zone separating East India Company (EIC) influence from that of Ranjit Singh became a textual line with the 1809 Treaty of Amritsar, and practical reality with Ranjit's establishment of a line of forts along the Sutlej.[11] Likewise, Franco-Thai competition for influence in Vietnam collapsed what had been a space of transition, where tributaries navigated the demands of multiple suzerains, into a discrete line, cartographically depicted and separating sovereign states.[12] It was not only changing ideas of political allegiance and power that were embodied in the mapping of frontiers, but also concepts of law and sovereignty which accompanied the jurisdictional delineation of spaces within imperial realms, such as the princely states of India.[13] As colonial regimes became more firmly established, and more convincingly monopolized political space, the political concepts that they represented gained traction in indigenous imaginations.[14] Territory thus became a central element of political identity, and its delineation a

constituent element of statehood. The representation of this understanding of political order took cartographic form, with an emphasis
on mapping, particularly by the colonial authorities.[15]

Pre-European states throughout the region conceptualized political
space and territoriality quite differently, stressing a relational rather
than territorial focus which existed in Islamic legal principles, as well
as in tribal concepts of use rather than land value.[16] The lands constituting the emerging Durrani and Qajar states had previously been subject to different administrative divisions. 'Feudal'-like estates, known
*tiyūl*s, in many cases served as units of administration, emphasizing the
power of local lords in a political universe defined largely by suzerain
relations.[17] Political authority, in the main, rested on tributary, segmentary relationships better mapped through genealogical tables than cartographic depictions. Tributary polities often formed relationships with
multiple overlords, creating overlapping layers of authority, and allowing them to play suzerains off against one another. Accepting multiple
tributary relationships as a fundamental part of the political order,
suzerains claimed paramountcy rather than exclusive allegiance.[18] The
overlords' concern focused on the obligations that tributary relationships entailed, rather than on land and its control. These relationships
had their symbolic, and submissive, expression in the confined physical
space of the court. Direct control could therefore be circumscribed, but
nonetheless effective. In this space, the visible bestowal of honor, visitation and expressions of mutual, albeit hierarchical obligation filled the
substance of these pre-modern political orders.[19]

In contrast, modern European ones were emphatically territorial,
with space judged not by relational proximity to centers of authority,
but by physical distance. European political ideas elevated the exclusive control of territory as a constituent element of sovereignty, wherein
the sovereign maintained a permanent and uncontested claim over territory alienable only by its consent. During the nineteenth century,
indigenous polities' sophisticated understandings of territory and its
relation to political authority were eclipsed and replaced by universal-
izing European norms, shaping legitimately recognizable expressions
of political community.[20]

While the territorialization of state boundaries and political authority ultimately represented the pre-eminence of European ideas of sovereignty, it was nonetheless the outcome of a lengthy and hotly disputed
process. Nowhere was this contestation, and the hybridity it produced,

more visible than in South Asia, and especially in the domains of the EIC. The establishment of Company power radically altered the political landscape, by challenging indigenous concepts of political order. Yet, while Company governance was in the main a modernizing phenomenon, it was also a uniquely 'Asian' polity. Although the Crown asserted sovereignty over Company lands as early as 1813, Company servants nevertheless recognized the suzerainty of the Mughal emperor in Delhi, presenting *nazr* (presents) to him until 1843.[21] The Company thus understood, and to a limited extent maintained, indigenous concepts of suzerainty and tributary relations, as well as European precepts of sovereignty and territoriality. After the imposition of Crown rule in 1858, however, the Government of India allowed such understandings to lapse, in favor of European norms of territoriality.

Much the same was true of the Russian Empire, as it expanded into the Central Asia from mid-century onwards, with its identity as a European or Asian power constantly contested. Imperial power was exercised not simply by local collaborators, but also through local channels, often predating the Russian conquest.[22] The Russians, as well as the British, were conservative imperial powers who sought to utilize pre-existing social structures rather than create new ones. Thus while colonialism ultimately displaced indigenous concepts and practices of power, it often did so by initially usurping them. This must be seen one of the key differences between the European imperial and national states.

The ascendance of the Westphalian political paradigm, and its indigenization, therefore took time. The emergent states of the nineteenth century were initially able to navigate a hybrid political universe with considerable success, due to their ability to speak both the old indigenous languages of political authority and the new European one. The Punjab of Ranjit Singh, the Gorkha kingdom, Awadh under Ghazi al-Din Haydar's rule, and the Thai kingdom all continued effectively to employ the language of suzerainty while at the same time perfecting the language of territorial sovereignty.[23] Yet the success of these states waned as European ideas of statehood became the only acceptable language of politics after mid-century. It remained, nonetheless, at least rhetorically important for indigenous polities to employ earlier idioms of authority, which resonated with ideas of political order that still shaped the communal imagination. This was particularly true in instances where indigenous Islamic polities faced off against one another, rather than against neighboring imperial powers. European imperial powers recognized the continuing resonance of these idioms and attempted to deploy them to their advantage through the re-creation and embellishment of indigenous political spectacle deployed for imperial aims, such as the imperial durbar of 1877.

Herat and the Great Game

Herat, on the margins of both the Persian and Afghan political projects for much of the first half of the nineteenth century, became a focus of dispute for these emerging states.[24] Qajar demands for Herat attempted to compensate for lands lost to Russia in Persia's northwest through conquests in Afghan Khorasan.[25] Their claims were commensurate with contemporary conceptions of suzerainty, notably the reading of the *khutba* in the *jame masjid* in the name of the shah, the minting of coins with the shah's inscription, and annual tribute dispatched to Tehran.[26] The British, in turn, sought to counter Russian pressure with a combination of incentives and threats, designed to dissuade Qajar attempts on Herat. Between 1830 and 1860, the Qajars attempted to conquer Herat three times, but were defeated by a combination of their own incompetence, Afghan resistance and the violence of British reaction.

The struggle for Herat has long been viewed primarily as part of the Great Game. According to this dominant narrative, indigenous actors had little say in the evolution of a complex political situation, shaped almost exclusively by the strategic calculations of London, Calcutta, and St Petersburg.[27] Some have challenged this account, arguing that considerations of indigenous powers affected regional events as much as colonial policies.[28] Yet both interpretations view this competition rather narrowly, as driven by state strategic imperatives, be they Russian, British or Persian. Such analysis overlooks the construction of European-like states as the expression of political order by indigenous communities. The contestation of Herat and its environs was not simply driven by calculations of state advantage, but by the very nature of the emerging states themselves.

Alternatively, Perso-Afghan competition for Herat has been understood under the rubric of a familiar and 'traditional' contest for suzerain allegiance to a monarch, whose authority remained distant and whose power rested on personal ties to his vassals. Both the Persians and the Afghans relied on the dynastic and tribal loyalties of local *sardār*s (lords) to assert their suzerain claims to the area. The demands of the Persian shah, for example, focused on the submission of the Herati ruler to Persian overlordship. To the Afghans, with a long collective memory of Persian political paramountcy, this possibility was not completely alien. Tehran repeatedly attempted to pull Herat into its orbit by exploiting the tribal rivalry between the Saddozai and Barakzai Durrani, promising aid against Kabul. The Persians buttressed their dynastic claims with cultural assertions, especially stressing the linguistic patrimony of Herat. The limited linguistic differentiation between Afghans and Persians, however, made such assertions fall rather flat.

Persian shahs also looked for religious sanction for their territorial expansion, persuading the *ulama* to declare a *jihad* against the Sunni Afghans. Yet the invocation of religious sanction by the Qajar state was ambivalent at best. Shi'i doctrine arguably did not allow for *jihad* in the absence of the Imam.[29] Further, the Qajars attempted to demarcate a fairly restricted political community, based on a combination of linguistic (Persian) and confessional (Shi'i) commonality.[30] Such efforts were complicated by the prevalence of both Persian-speaking Sunnis and Shi'i who did not speak Persian, both within and without the empire's territorial limits.

Likewise, the language of defiance chosen by Herat's *sardār*s remained the language of 'pre-modern' Islamic political communities, resting on religious as well as tribal bases, with declarations of *jihad* against the apostate Persians.[31] Such calls resonated with the 'ecumenical character of Islamic sovereignty', as opposed to rallying Heratis to defend the polity's territorial integrity.[32] Yet resistance in the name of Sunni Islam was complicated by the area's large Shi'i population, to whom the Persians presented themselves as protectors against the incessant slave raiding practiced by Sunni tribesmen.

Embedded in such religious discourses were ideals of community based on Islamic precepts, such as the *umma* (community of faith) and *watan* (homeland), as well as their limits marked by the *hodūd* (limit, or boundary) and *sarhadd* (frontier). The majority of Afghans were Sunni adherents of the Hanafi school, and thus theoretically belonged to a larger confessional community than the Shi'i. But Afghan tribal society greatly colored understandings of Islam, making it difficult for many to transcend lineage-based social identities in the name of religion, and thus circumscribing the community of faith. Sectarian differences therefore meshed with a divergence between the textually Islamic religious-politico universe of the Qajars and the largely non-textual, lived Muslim one of the Afghans. The religious space separating the Persians from the Afghans was as much a divide between 'Islamic' and 'Muslim' societies as between Shi'i and Sunni ones.

Yet this was a period of dramatic religious change for both Persians and Afghans, as movements of Islamic revival in Persia and South Asia transformed public debates about the meaning and content of religious community. Modernists tended to accept novel ideas about nation states, while at the same time advocating a textually-based Islam of universal applicability.[33] As part of their adoption of European norms of statehood, the Qajar and Durrani monarchies aspired to an increasing secularization of political space, in which religious leadership was to be subservient to the state. Such aspirations were clearly discernible in their efforts to subjugate offices of religious authority to state control.[34] Offices of Islamic authority, as well as ideas of Islamic community, were eventually subsumed within the political discourse and institutions of emerging states, at least until the late twentieth century.

Older political languages of Islamic suzerainty disguised the emergence of a new sovereign political order. European empires demanded the trappings of European political form from the polities that they dealt with, imposing these forms on those that they conquered or indirectly controlled. The direct involvement of British and Russian troops in the Herat dispute personified the reality of a European political universe stealthily inhabiting the space claimed by the old order. This was a process, as new norms first integrated with and then replaced those more familiar. Thus, while reading the *khutba* in the name of the Persian shah may have been an acceptable sign of submission in the early 1820s, it no longer was by the 1870s. While earlier Persian expeditions against Herat sought to extract the rituals of allegiance common to the Islamic political universe, the British boundary arbitration of 1872 sought to establish the physical demarcation of an order based on European sovereign statehood. The dispatch of the arbitration marked the reformulation of the political landscape as one defined largely by European-inspired, universal norms enacted by local actors.

While the parameters of the political stage were defined by imperial interests, the stage itself left great room for indigenous agency and ideological subversion. The Goldsmid mission authored this new sovereign universe through the language of respect for 'ancient custom and tradition', while both Persians and Afghans attempted to demonstrate their adept adoption of the norms of this universe through what the British would consider clearly established historical practice. Local actors thus made use of the narrative and discourse of the state to fashion their own space of political action, often at odds with those state-created discourses. This type of subversive dialogue continues today on the Frontier, as the later anthropological chapters illustrate. But it is not only state authored narratives that provide the old wine-skins for new wine. A similar phenomenon can be observed in the form of the so-called 'Islamic resurgence' in the region where old, familiar idioms of identity are vacated of their past meaning and reinvigorated with new significance.[35]

Herat's importance waned in the latter half of the nineteenth century. The Persian defeat by the British in 1856–57 effectively ended any hope of the realization of Qajar ambitions in the area, although it would be a number of years before Herat was firmly fixed within the emerging Afghan state. Repeated British interventions removed the issue of Herat's control from the acceptable realm of competition between these two indigenous polities. More pointedly, the city's economic importance, derived from its position as a caravan *entrepot*, sharply declined in the second half of the nineteenth century. Regional trade suffered from competition with seaborne trade routes, and many inland routes reoriented to adjust to new trade patterns with South and Central Asia, badly affecting Herat.[36] Its history of instability discouraged the resumption of trade through its gates. With Herat effectively neutralized as a plausible source of conflict, both Persians and Afghans looked elsewhere. By the late 1860s, their ambitions clashed with increased imperial interests in Sistan. It was there, in a rural, tribal 'backwater', that the next chapter of Perso-Afghan competition was set and that the modernizing process of border delineation physically took place.

The Goldsmid Mission, 1870–72

The Persians sensed an opportunity to assert claims over Sistan, never effectively controlled by them, as the Afghan kingdom again succumbed to internal distraction in the late 1860s. At their formal request, the British Government of India dispatched an arbitral mission headed by Major-General Sir Frederic Goldsmid to determine the Perso-Baluch frontier in Makran, and the Perso-Afghan frontier in Sistan. The Persians invoked Article VI of the Treaty of Paris of 1857, which ended the Anglo-Persian war of 1856–57. The article read in relevant part:

...in case of differences arising between the Government of Persia and the countries of Herat and Afghanistan, the Persian Government engages to refer them for adjustment to the friendly offices of the British Government...[who] on their part engage at all times to exert their influence with the states of Afghanistan to prevent any cause of umbrage being given by them or by any of them to the Persian Government....[37]

By defining the extent of Persian and Afghan sovereignty in this contested region, the British believed they could hold these states responsible for threats to their imperial interests. The Makran arbitration provided a vehicle for the settlement of British-Persian frontier in Baluchistan, where Britain's direct involvement was both expected and understandable.[38] In contrast, Sistan lay outside any formal British remit, so that British arbitration presented a less obvious case meriting imperial involvement. However, the British understood the benefit of a clearly delineated frontier between these emergent states, in terms of the assignation of both control and responsibility.[39]

As the frontier drew a clear line in the sand, effectively marking the geographical limit of Russian influence, British participation could also be understood within the logic of the Great Game. Yet such an interpretation misconstrues the character of, and motives behind, British involvement. While it has long been argued that British fears of Russian influence drove their actions in the area, the Russian menace at this time was more illusory than real.[40] In 1870, the Russians had yet to firmly establish their hegemony over northern Persia, complete their conquest of the Central Asian khanates, or secure financing for their Central Asian military railway. Russia's imperialist ventures into the Central Asian steppe were largely a consequence of its weakness on the European stage, clearly revealed in the Crimean War.[41] In contrast, the British were secure in their Indian possession, the 'Mutiny' notwithstanding. During this period of 'masterly inactivity' and weak Russian threat, British interests beyond the frontier were essentially intellectual rather than geo-strategic in nature. The British wanted to assert their authority over this region through the monopolization of knowledge and definition, delineating the reaches of properly recognized political authority, namely the Persian and Afghan buffer states. This was manifest through their dispatch of a mission whose chief aim was to collect and order information, and then deploy that information for the creation of a new political reality in the form of a delineated boundary.

Since the 'Mutiny' in 1857–58, the British had separated and transformed the government of their Indian possessions from the indigenous body politic. One consequence of such disengagement with local political culture was that when casting their gaze beyond the frontiers of their domains, the British looked not to the native polities occupying that space, but rather to the European empires coveting it. From the mid-nineteenth century onwards, the British steadily lost the ability to speak in the languages of local political cultures, and instead relied on 'colonial knowledge' to both order and understand the indigenous polities they dealt with. These polities were now understood in terms of their shortcomings *vis-à-vis* their European contemporaries. Rival European empires, particularly Russia, embodied familiar political order, allowing the British to conceptualize and define the intervening spaces in a way that they understood. This process of conceptual colonization had been developing since the early nineteenth century, leading up to the British defeat in Afghanistan in 1842.[42] In the post-1858 environment, it came to monopolize the 'official mind'. Competing understandings of the space separating the British and the Russians thus became homogenized in a conceptual landscape delimited by the language of European political precepts, cloaked in the rhetoric of Russian threat. British participation in frontier arbitration thus rested on a desire to transform these indigenous polities into a more familiar and thus malleable form.

The reasons propelling Persians and Afghans to avail themselves of British 'good offices' appear unremarkable, at least initially. As the regional imperial power, Britain repeatedly demonstrated that it would not tolerate a situation perceived to threaten its interests. This knowledge no doubt weighed heavily in the Qajars' minds, as it was they who suffered Britain's displeasure in 1838–42 and again in 1856–57. By invoking a treaty largely dictated by Britain, Tehran sought to portray its eastward ambitions in a more sympathetic light, untainted by shadowy Russian influence and encouragement. Conversely, the Afghans had little choice, once the British decided to arbitrate. Sher Ali Khan, ruler of the truncated Afghan kingdom, could not easily reject Lord Mayo's entreaties, especially at a time when he was cultivating an accommodating relationship with British India. Further, Sher Ali could feel assured that British interests in western Afghanistan probably complemented his own, as the British preferred the area to remain under Afghan overlordship.[43] Yet such explanations, focusing exclusively on the subjugation of indigenous interests to imperial imperatives, are rather unsatisfactory.

The British arbitration of their common frontier offered both the Persian and Afghan governments important advantages, which could not be obtained through direct conflict. In addition to placing the resolution of territorial claims in a matrix that Britain could accept, British delineation of this contested space accomplished what neither Tehran nor Kabul could achieve on their own: the recognition, both domestically and internationally, of their control of this hitherto recalcitrant region. Although both Qajars and Durranis put forward longstanding claims to Sistan, neither had been able to convincingly demonstrate the control that such claims entailed.[44]

The Sistanis, like the Heratis under whose overlordship they so often fell, had proven adept at navigating the region's segmentary political order, and had protected their autonomy through tributary relations.[45] To the British, the region's history was one of a constant tug of war between Persian and Afghan power.[46] They ignored the claims of local power-holders or the possibility that this was a contest for the preservation of Sistani independence, protected against the Persians through many open conflicts, and from the Afghans through the intricacies of tribal politics. This understanding inherently limited the universe of possible outcomes, with either the Persians or the Afghans as the ultimate winners, and the Sistanis as the inevitable losers. The way the British framed such disputes had important implications for the outcomes. Just as Goldsmid made the Sistan arbitration a dispute between the Persian and Afghan courts, so too did his contemporary Robert Sandeman on another part of the frontier frame the claims and contestants of local power disputes in such as way as to best benefit the imperial state.[47]

The willingness of both the Afghan and the Persian governments to submit this region to arbitration represented a desire to extend their sovereignty over the region with the help of British negotiating partners, a strategy that was not without precedent in the region. In South Asia's tumultuous eighteenth century, local intermediaries, unable convincingly to assert control over recalcitrant regions, had relied on *sanad*s (documents/deeds) from political overlords, with which they buttressed claims of authority.[48] Both Persians and Afghans mimicked this tradition during the course of the arbitration, attempting to establish their sovereign claims through a time-tested strategy of suzerain dispensation. The reliance on indigenous methodology to establish exogenous political substance underlines the hybridity central to the assimilation of European norms of political order and territoriality. Indigenous powers worked within a landscape of possible outcomes whose limits were defined by the imperial powers but whose contours were shaped by local agents. This interaction between the local and the imperial or indeed the global has been a central dynamic defining the Frontier throughout its history and into its present.

Strategies of Control: Persian Obstructionism

Qajar strategies for the arbitration partly reflected their position relative to the British as well as local centers of power. Goldsmid characterized the actions of the Persian commissioner, Mirza Maasum Khan, as duplicitous, insisting that he was playing a 'double game'.[49] The commissioner systematically used the presence of the British mission as a confirmation of Persian claims to the area, and his repeated obstructions of the mission's inquiries were more than simple attempts to sabotage British impartiality. Rather, they were calculated to make the British mission appear subservient to its Persian hosts, demonstrating Qajar sovereignty, in the face of its delimitation by the British. The Persian commissioner's lack of diplomatic etiquette towards the British mission signaled both the center's willingness and its supposed ability to stand against Britain's imperial ambitions. Yet Tehran's eventual disavowal of Mirza Maasum Khan's actions underlined its ultimate acquiescence to British demands.[50]

One of the most visible symbols of apparent British subservience was the Persian commissioner's insistence that while the mission was in Sistan, it could not fly the Union Jack. The commissioner argued adamantly that such a display would inflame local Muslim sensibilities, and was likely to provoke a 'general massacre'.[51] To underline Persian pre-eminence *vis-à-vis* the British, the commissioner placed a Persian banner in front of his residence on a 'flag-staff made at least two or three feet higher than that of the English Commissioner'.[52] By making the British mission appear in a visibly subservient status, Tehran set forth its unchallenged claims of sovereignty over the region to its inhabitants and local lords. The arbitration mission's procession evidenced Tehran's apparent triumph over London and Calcutta to the local populace, undoubtedly ignorant of the arbitration's true nature or purpose.[53]

The Persian commissioner's actions were, however, complicated by the relationship between central and local authorities. Tehran issued orders empowering the commissioner to demarcate the frontier with the British mission, but such orders could only be discharged with the cooperation of local officials.[54] Yet some governors were autonomous of Tehran, and had little to gain by cooperating with its representative.[55] The commissioner's presence personified an assertion of sovereignty by the Persian center, representing a radical break from the universe of tributary relationships hitherto shaping the Persian political landscape.[56] The Qajars' willingness to turn to Britain, their imperial nemesis, clearly demonstrated a desire to prevail in the face of *de jure* autonomous regional lords, who were sometimes *de facto* independent. Tehran thus walked a fine line, attempting to assert a territorial claim of sovereignty and central control over a distant borderland through the offices of tributaries ruling the region.

Indeed, the commissioner's reliance on the Amir of Kain, the Persian governor of the area abutting and potentially including Sistan, led Goldsmid to complain continually that he was in the Amir's pay.[57] According to Smith, the Amir 'pays no fixed revenue to the Shah, but supports the whole expenditure of troops and government servants located in his province...he, moreover, transmits from time to time presents or '*ta'arufs*', in money and kind, to Tehran'.[58] The Amir's virtual independence made him suspicious of central authority, so that he viewed the arrival of a Qajar official in the company of a British mission as an unwelcome development. While his distance inoculated him from Tehran's control, it also deprived him of its protection. Only the Qajars could protect him from the British, and this required some sort of accommodation with the center. His willingness to accede to central demands was thus commensurate with his perceived vulnerability to British ambitions.

The Persian commissioner's unambiguous brief was fundamentally compromised by a lack of material resources necessary to successfully complete it, underlining the wide discrepancy between the center's aspirations and its real authority. Tehran badly wanted to assert both control and sovereignty over areas in the political outlands.[59] To compensate for its weakness, Tehran ironically relied on the symbol of its impotence, namely British arbitration. The Persian court adopted the canny political strategy of using an imperial hegemon to assert its claims of authority over loosely controlled areas, but this did not come without risks or costs.

While Tehran attempted to use the British mission to forward its own political agenda, that agenda itself was permanently altered by the ideas of political order that the mission represented. The Sistan arbitration was not simply an attempt by Tehran to co-opt the Amir of Kain or Sistani *sardārs* into a tributary relationship, in which the Qajar shah stood as suzerain overlord in a segmentary political order. Rather, it was an attempt to territorially delimit the reaches of Persian sovereignty, or to territorialize the bounds of Tehran's authority, filling the intervening space with a new concept of political order based on that of the emerging modern state. It is worth quoting at length how the Persians themselves conceptualized that order, with the Nizam ul-Mulk writing:

According to an old custom, the greater number of Persian provinces were delivered, as a kind of inheritance, to the chiefs of those provinces; and this is even now the practice in some parts of Persia. The Govt of Seistan has also in this manner from the time of the Safavin kings until now, been usually vested in the local chiefs, especially the Kaianis.

In the commencement of Mohamed Shah's reign, the policy of Persia was to concentrate gradually into her own hands the power of her chiefs. This new policy changed wholly the former system of Govt. Those provinces which were formally quasi independent became thus absorbed within the centralising influence. Under this new policy a change also from the same period was applied to the govt of Seistan.[60]

The Goldsmid mission's failure to definitively delineate the Sistan border, and thus the limits of Tehran's sovereign authority, demonstrated that while European ideas of political order triumphed, their realization remained incomplete. A second British mission was dispatched in 1905, followed by a Turkish one in 1935.[61] The Persian commissioner's reliance on local acquiescence and negotiation in the early 1870s underlines the fact that the indigenous political order retained conceptual as well as practical vitality. Nonetheless, this mission represented a definitive break in the way the Qajar state conceived its own political power. Demands of sovereignty could no longer be satisfied by the ritual subjugation of local lords central to tributary relations. Instead, the Persian state, reified in the person of the shah, required the assertion and acknowledgment of its control.

The records of the British mission reflected, if they did not actually engender, this reification. In questioning a local *sardār*, Goldsmid recorded that 'Sardar Imam Khan...took the opportunity of saying that all the country from here to Rudbar...was the property of the

Shah'. According to Goldsmid, this constituted a *'complete acknowledgment of Persian sovereignty* [emphasis added]'.[62] Goldsmid's observation enunciated the transformation of political order from a suzerain to a sovereign one. Read literally, it equated the shah's ownership with state sovereignty. Regional political cultures had framed political suzerainty in a different language, envisaging obligations created through imperial dispensations. Yet in the British schema, obligation was incumbent upon the land, itself the object of ownership, an idea first fully articulated in British India in the Bengal Permanent Settlement of 1793.[63] The shah was transformed from the recipient of obligation to the sovereign of territory, and thus became the personification of the state. This transformation of his personage reflected a transformation in the political universe in which he operated. As suzerain, the shah was entitled to tribute as part of a segmentary relationship; as sovereign, he owned the land inalienably. This transition was precisely what the Qajar dynasty sought to accomplish, although neither their aspirations nor understandings accorded wholly with those of the British.

Strategies of Control: Afghan Acquiescence

While the Persian state was more advanced in its adoption of European norms of political order, the participation of the Afghan kingdom in the arbitration represented a no less profound change in its political culture. Like the Persians, the Afghans deputed a commissioner to the arbitration, Sayyid Nur Muhammad, who was accompanied by a representative of the Government of India, Major-General Henry Pollack.[64] They were to meet the Persian commissioner and Goldsmid, and then together proceed to the disputed areas of Sistan.[65] In the event, this journey never took place, largely because of the 'obstructionism' of the Persian commissioner.[66] The mission's full complement, together with both commissioners, assembled *in situ* for only three days, before Goldsmid decided to divide the parties and proceed to Tehran.[67]

Unlike his Persian counterpart, the Afghan commissioner evinced neither hostility nor duplicity towards his British companion, undoubtedly because British imperial interests paralleled the Afghans' own. Nor did he engage in similar attempts to visibly demonstrate Afghan superiority over the British representative to local people. Most of those encountered by Pollack and Sayyid Nur Muhammad willingly expressed allegiance to the Afghan Amir as overlord.[68] Nonetheless, the Afghan monarchy was in a considerably weaker position *vis-à-vis* local *sardār*s than its Persian cousin. Afghan claims of suzerainty were thus markedly less penetrative than Persian claims of sovereignty.

The relative weakness and immaturity of the Afghan state in the arbitration were apparent on a number of fronts. The Persians invited British participation by invoking a treaty conforming to European norms of international law, while the Afghan Amir was pressured by his personal relationship with the Viceroy.[69] Although both the Persians and the Afghans dispatched commissioners, only the Persian commissioner was accompanied by a survey officer, Ali Ashraf Khan, charged with producing a map of the disputed region.[70] Unlike his Persian counterpart, the Afghan commissioner was not a bureaucrat whose authority resided in his position within the institutions of the state.[71] Rather he was a personal confidant, 'one of the (probably the) most trusted ministers the Ameer possesses', whose authority derived from his relational proximity to Sher Ali Khan.[72] And most tellingly, the arbitration's opinion was delivered in Tehran rather than Kabul or a neutral venue.

The comparative frailty of the Afghan state was further reflected by the demands made by the center on regional power-holders. The Afghan commissioner was satisfied with Sistani allegiance to Sher Ali Khan, even while a leading *sardār* of Lash Jowain questioned the British arbiter on British support for Sistani independence.[73] The aim of the center was to co-opt regional power-holders into a political universe where Kabul was *primus inter pares*. This political order still used the idiom of segmentary allegiance, not territorial sovereignty. The British recognized and reinforced this with their emphasis on the genealogy of Sistani rule to justify their opinion favoring the Afghans.[74] And yet this universe, like its Persian counterpart, was in the midst of a profound transformation.

As with the Persians, the Afghans' willingness to partake in the Sistan arbitration was based on realization of the opportunities such arbitration presented. The British offered the Afghan center the opportunity to accomplish something it could not do alone, asserting and confirming its claims over a region which had been more or less independent since the disintegration of the Durrani Empire.[75] While this largely mirrored Persian claims, Afghan weakness meant that any such claims would be qualitatively different. The Persian commissioner engaged in a process of negotiation between the center and periphery, where the center had a slight, but widening advantage over the out-lands. As the Persian state progressively came to resemble Westphalian forms, the center increasingly won out over the periphery. In the Afghan case, the weakness of the center reversed the equation. The Sistani periphery held the advantage over a center at pains to win its political allegiance and rhetorical acquiescence. Thus the demands, in terms of formal submission, placed on Sistan by the Afghan monarch were less cumbersome than those put forward by the Persian shah.

'Ancient Rights and Present Possession'

As arbiters, the British determined the standard of judgment to serve as the basis of their award. In contrast to prevailing Western ideas of a 'scientific frontier' based on geographical exactness, the British decided early on that their criteria would be 'ancient rights and present possession.'[76] Although the British enunciated this standard, they did little to clarify it, failing to engage with its obvious contradictions and handicaps. What qualified as either 'possession' or 'ancient rights' remained obscure, as did Afghanistan's ability to lay claim to the lat-ter, when it was itself a state of relatively recent vintage.[77] However, the British focus on 'ancient rights' was in keeping with the ethos of government marking the post-Mutiny ethnographic state ruling the Indian empire.

Yet for all the focus on the supposed history of rights and control, its textual and topographical expression remained paramount for the British, an intellectual inheritance from the 'Sanskritization' efforts of Sir William Jones in the late eighteenth century. Thus a map of the disputed region was one of the most important intended outcomes of the mission. The British had an established history of textually express-ing both history and identity in cartographic form in the region. Lt John Macartney's map, produced during the Elphinstone mission to the Kingdom of Kabul in 1808–09, was central to British understand-ings of the relationship between people and territory.[78] By assigning people to a specifically topographical space in the cartographic repre-sentation of political order, the British territorialized people more powerfully and profoundly than through any other medium. For the officials of British India, mapping was an examination and disciplining of space and knowledge, and thus a mechanism of control.[79] By map-ping the Afghans, Elphinstone and Macartney established the hegemony of colonial knowledge over the area for future generations of colonial administrators.[80] The Goldsmid mission's task of cartographically expressing the political limits, and thus the identities, of the Persian and Afghan states marked the continuation of this same tradition. The Persians' dispatch of their own survey officer signaled an attempt to challenge the hegemony of the British colonial knowledge, and engage in the struggle for the cartographic depiction of control.

Although the arbitration served as a medium for the realization of new state forms through territorial delineation, marking a fundamental transformation of political order from tributary to territorial, the Persians and the Afghans used decidedly different 'dialects' to conceptualize this new political order. These shaped the arguments that their commissioners presented to the British arbiters in support of their respective claims. While both employed history to justify their assertions, they used it, or rather its language, very differently.

Persian arguments were produced by a political culture that had assimilated European norms to a greater extent, owing in part to their longer interaction with Europeans. The Persians had established regular contact with early modern European states from the early seventeenth century, whereas the first formal European mission to an Afghan court was Elphinstone's in 1809. The Persian statement, which read like a contemporary European legal brief, presented a bifurcated argument, asserting Persia's 'ancient rights' in Sistan and their textual acknowledgment by other powers.[81] The Persians justified their 'ancient rights' with references in the *Shahnameh* to Sistan as the hero Rustam's homeland, and Goldsmid acknowledged the role of such claims in the formation of Persian national identity.[82] Further, they offered a variety of documents 'demonstrating' the recognition of those rights by both the Afghans and the British, including Safavid *sanad*s, correspondence from the Barakzai *sardār*s of Qandahar, and a letter from Lord John Russell, then Prime Minister.[83] Relying on these documents, Persia argued that conquest by another power could not denude it of sovereignty. Simply put, force could not overturn text, or in their own words, 'temporary dispossession does not invalidate a natural and *universally acknowledged* [emphasis added] right....'[84] References to natural law and universality evidenced the adoption of European, Enlightenment-inspired political discourse. The Persians' emulation of European precepts of law, and the transition to a political universe largely defined by 'texts' and Westphalian norms, was eased considerably by their long-established textual traditions.

The Afghans, in contrast, presented a much more traditional case, resting in the main on actual control and personal allegiance. Their petition, three to four times as long as Persia's, was filled with aureate language, resembling a Persian court chronicle more than a legal brief. Rather than invoking written documents, the Afghan petition listed tribal genealogies, constructed and remembered orally. Afghan control was traced through the allegiance of individual *sardārs* in tributary relations with the Afghan Amir. In contrast to the Persian reliance on the *Shahnameh*, the Afghans claimed that the feats documented by their genealogical records were remembered in the popular songs of Sistan.[85] This argument resonated well with British understandings of 'traditional' Afghan political authority.[86] Whereas the Persian submission is virtually unmarked, the Afghan statement is heavily marked with explanatory references to historical events and editorial comments by British officials. Goldsmid's genealogy of Sistani leadership, published with his arbitral opinion, was simply another incarnation of this conceptual ordering of social and political authority.[87] The act of recording denuded the system of its flexibility, at least for the British. The British could discount new genealogical memories, created by the Afghans to explain the present political order, through reference to their own printed records.[88] History, always written for the present, became the hostage of a textual past.

Although Persians and Afghans sought to assert a fundamentally modern claim for their states, namely sovereignty over defined territory, they did so by appealing to vastly different traditions of legitimacy. By emphasizing their oral histories and 'traditions', the Afghans retained flexibility in delineating the limits of their political universe, which the Persians lost by writing those limits down. The Persians, however, enjoyed a stability in that political universe which the Afghans lacked. Text created stability by limiting opportunity for derivation. It enabled standardization, which reinforced central control. Speech allowed for flexibility, thereby undermining stability. Both were ways of creating memory and history, but different kinds of memory. In this case, text served as the language of European political order, speech as the language of the indigenous Afghan political universe. Yet both were built upon, and reflected, social structures that supported the different concepts of knowledge represented by text and speech.[89] The Persians' long-established textual tradition rested on educated literati, who formed the backbone of an urban government bureaucracy, whereas the Afghans lacked an equivalent class.[90] The Afghans remained, in many ways, a profoundly 'tribal' society. Consequently, the adoption of European norms of statehood proved considerably easier for the Persians.

In the event, the Afghans proved more successful, despite relying on more 'traditional' conceptions of political community. In fact this was why they were more successful, as their 'tradition' fully fitted British expectations and understandings. The Afghans could afford not to be as conversant as the Persians in the language of European political norms, precisely because Europeans had little interest in establishing those norms, or their power, in any penetrative manner in the Afghan kingdom. Instead, the British sought to bolster 'traditional' political authority in this peripheral buffer state, to ensure stability on the frontier.[91] In contrast, the Persians' Europeanization of their political space remained incomplete, and thus unstable. The British 'knew' Afghan political society, and perceived it to be fractious. Knowledge of its weaknesses made it amenable to British influence. The Persians, less influenced by Britain, were also less known. This could be dangerous, as it either invited Russian ambitions or allowed indigenous Persian power to grow. The British focus on and comfort with 'tradition' on the Frontier are telling, for over time they translated into policies which sought to codify local traditions and thus British understandings of this space. The Frontier thus became marked and defined as a space of static tradition, purposely excluded from the modernizing impulses and influences of the colonial, or even local states.

Conclusion

By ruling in favor of the Afghans, the British further spurred the Persian empire down the path of European statehood. Persia's poor performance in the arbitration created a desire among its elite to become more fluent in the language of European diplomacy and statehood. The Persians also redoubled their efforts at technical education, so that their survey officers would no longer be reliant on European maps.[92]

As for the Afghans, although they succeeded in part because of British familiarity with their political order, the British award quickened the erosion of that order. Goldsmid, while repudiating Persian claims in his arbitral opinion, agreed with the Afghan commissioner that the transfer of allegiances by rebellious Afghan *sardār*s was 'not held to

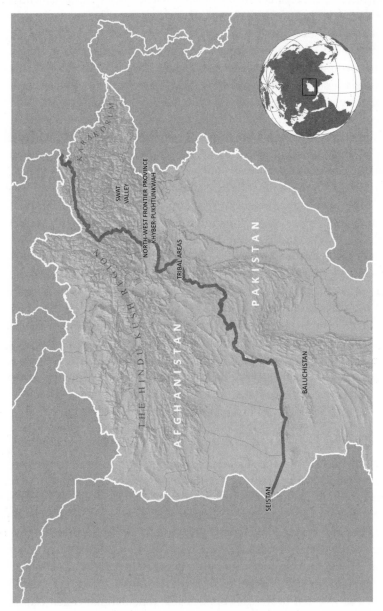

Afghanistan/Pakistan Frontier © Naula Cowan, George Washington University

affect the question of sovereign rights of the country.'[93] He further stated that 'the allegiance of Sistan was of a feudal nature which could not be transferred to suit the personal convenience of a temporary ruler.'[94] State sovereignty was inalienable, divorced from the vagaries of individual allegiance, even if sovereign claims could lapse through their non-assertion, as with Persian claims of 'ancient rights'.[95] While such relationships were central to authority in a political universe of suzerainty, sovereign control of land was divorced from relational allegiance. In these two lines, Goldsmid did for the Afghan center what it was unable to do for itself. He validated its claims of its sovereignty, not only *vis-à-vis* the Persians, but also, what was more important, in relation to its subjects.

The demarcation of the Perso-Afghan frontier was a process fundamental to the transformation of these states. For indigenous political communities, it marked a transition from a political universe based on indigenous and Islamic norms of order to one increasingly defined by European norms of statehood. Political authority in these emergent states moved away from the person of the shah or amir, where it once resided, to the abstraction of the state, where it was coming to rest. The religious legitimation provided by the *ulama* became of secondary importance as rulers attempted to secularize the political space the state sought to monopolize. With this move, political control and power likewise migrated from relational bonds with the ruler, the hallmark of a segmentary political order, to a grounding in physical space. Political identity was territorialized, often coercively by state authorities backed by imperial powers. The Perso-Afghan boundary arbitration was precisely this process put into action.

Indigenous actors sought to achieve through the offices of the British arbitrator what they could not manage alone: the assertion and recognition of their control over recalcitrant peripheries. By involving the British, they necessarily invoked the normative order British imperialism represented. Sovereignty and statehood thus colonized the spaces of the indigenous imagination, transforming the languages and landscapes of these political communities. But that colonization did not proceed evenly or uncontested. Local holders of authority and political actors used the language of sovereignty to advance their own claims to power, the content of which was quite different from that which Weber envisaged. Though the forms of Western political discourse may have been assumed, their substance was not. Instead, using those forms, local actors subverted their meaning, investing and inventing new significance in old vessels. Although the Goldsmid arbitration represents the assumption of contemporary European ideas of territoriality and political legitimacy by indigenous political authorities, it also underlines the incompleteness of that assumption.

Despite the fact the assumption of such Westphalian norms would be centrally important to the demarcation of the frontier as a practical and conceptual reality, rendering new lines of fragmentation in both the imaginations and the maps of local and imperial authorities, it remains hotly contested by the Frontier's inhabitants. Goldsmid's mission, while ostensibly demarcating the unitary division of the respective centers over their outlands, in actuality fragmented that division, at least in the Afghan case. It thus illustrates the heterogeneity of the Frontier and the potential of that heterogeneity for both unity and division, a potential that is simultaneously latent and contextually realized. The arbitration offered indigenous actors, local and otherwise, a new language of politics. Yet the underlying assumptions and values of those politics, namely Western, Westphalian ideas of political sovereignty, were at least partly lost in translation.

2

MANAGING 'HEARTS AND MINDS'

SANDEMAN IN BALUCHISTAN

The efforts of indigenous polities to gain fluency in the idiom of European forms of political community during the 1870s had their counterpart in the colonial state's attempts to understand the peoples it governed. Nowhere were these efforts more pronounced than along the Baluch Frontier, neighboring Sistan, where colonial administrators sought to govern local tribesmen through their own 'tradition'. Thus as native kingdoms came to grips with the idea of territoriality as central to political power, the colonial state tried to control indigenous peoples and politics through 'tradition'. Indeed, Frederik Goldsmid's ruling for the Afghans was largely justified in terms of 'ancient rights' and 'tradition'. Just as the Persian and Afghan kingdoms struggled to reconcile new concepts of community with older ones, so too did the colonial state attempt to marry modern ideas of governance with 'native' forms of governmentality. This chapter marks not only a physical shift along the Frontier, but also a shift in gaze away from indigenous to imperial polities, examining the efforts of the British Raj to rule the tribesmen of the Baluch Frontier. What is striking about this episode is the way the experience of encounter profoundly affected all involved, shaping both the tribesmen and the colonial state. This chapter relates to the overall themes of the book by offering yet another fragment of experience, one that not only shaped the Frontier's past, but continues to contour its present.

Baluchistan's Beginnings

In January 1876, what had been a long-running and increasingly ran-corous bureaucratic feud about how to manage the Raj's frontier in Upper Sind finally came to an end. The Government of India, which had demonstrated patient forbearance towards the different opinions held by officers of its various provincial governments, conclusively took a side. But rather than endorsing the senior official on the spot, himself a decorated soldier who had proven both his own personal courage as well as the potential efficacy of his preferred policy, the Viceroy Lord Northbrook opted for the young upstart.[1] Colonel Sir William Merewether, a veteran with nearly twenty-five years' experience on the Frontier and Commissioner of Sind, found himself passed over by Captain Robert G. Sandeman, a subordinate whom he had contemptuously referred to a as a mere 'boy' and an officer he had repeatedly and quite publicly dressed down for over-reaching himself.[2] Merewether took his defeat in his stride and went on to finish his colonial service with distinction, earning a CB (Companion, Order of the Bath), a place in the *Oxford Dictionary of National Biography*, and a memorial tower erected in Karachi.[3] But it was Sandeman whose star had risen, and it was he who would introduce, in short order, a revolution in government which set the tone for the remainder of the British Empire's governance of much of northwestern India, and indeed the wider world.

The system of governance which Calcutta endorsed in the winter of 1876, and which Sandeman put in place along the Baluch Frontier in the years following, was at one and the same time a system of conservation and a system of revolution which partially invented, partially codified, and partially altered tribal 'custom' and 'tradition'. By exploring the rise of the Sandeman system, as it came to be known, and its employment along the Frontier, it becomes clear that the British Indian government became both protector and arbiter of tradition. In doing so it largely defined the content of tribal custom and thus the communal character of the tribes themselves. Yet it did not necessarily understand its actions as innovations. Instead, British administrators by and large saw themselves as returning to the political equilibrium of a previous epoch that had been upset by the ambitions of tribal chiefs and the slothful, malicious government of local potentates.

While often referred to as 'indirect rule', governing local communities through 'tradition' was in fact extremely invasive of indigenous society. It was, after all, the colonial state that defined what was and was not appropriate and acceptable 'tradition'. Under Sandeman's tutelage, the British fashioned a tribal universe along the Baluch Frontier in accordance with their own understandings and administrative requirements, and then largely withdrew themselves from direct involvement in that universe. By doing so, they irrevocably changed the indigenous peoples with whom they interacted. Just as important, yet harder to discern, British actions on the Frontier fundamentally reshaped the nature of the colonial state. Through the exercise of multiple modalities of governance along the Frontier, as well as the ethos underlying these practices, the colonial state fashioned a kind of frontier governmentality. Frontier governmentality asserted the state's suzerainty through the administration of difference, deployed to keep people outside the colonial sphere. This was at odds with the supposedly universal standardizations at the heart of the modern Westphalian model of statehood, of which the colonial state is too often thought to be an adolescent form. Consequently, rather than being some sort of forgotten backwater where Calcutta and later Delhi simply held the line against wild tribesmen and dangerous Russians, the Frontier was in many ways where the colonial state defined itself.

Sandeman's success in the winter of 1876 raises a number of questions about colonial governance of the Frontier, about the nature of that frontier and about the colonial state. Why did the Government of India, a body known in the wake of the Mutiny for its conservative practice, opt for the junior officer who championed a system of governance almost totally at odds with accepted orthodoxy, and indeed the Government's own previous policies? What does this decision say about the practices of colonial governance and its effect on the inhabitants of the Frontier? And most important, what does this tell us about the colonial state itself? The answers to these questions are subtly complex. This chapter can only offer some initial thoughts and tentative hypothesis which will, it is hoped, spark further consideration. It explores the answers to these questions and their implications, arguing that what happened on this largely ignored and unknown frontier holds important lessons about the nature of modern imperialism, as well as its continuing legacy throughout much of the world.

In order to understand the implications of Calcutta's endorsement of Sandeman's little experiment, it is first necessary to outline not only the Sandeman system, but also the administrative competitors it ultimately replaced. As Sandeman himself freely admitted, his system drew upon the skills developed by a previous generation of Frontier administrators, but deployed them with different methods.[4] Such a discussion necessarily requires an examination of the main characters involved in this drama, not least Sandeman and his seeming nemesis Merewether. This is followed by an analytical discussion of the Sandeman system, examining in particular the use of the so-called *jirga* system. The use of the *jirga* firmly tied the Sandeman system to institutions of governance ubiquitous along the rest of British India's northwest frontier, although deployed in markedly different social milieus. The chapter ends by meditating on the effects of the Sandeman system on the tribesmen it was employed to govern.

Systems of Frontier Management

The history of the Frontier and its management is a complicated one.[5] The frontier the British inherited from the Sikhs at the end of the Second Sikh War in 1849 was ill-defined and poorly suited the defensive requirements of the Raj. It did not border a recognized foreign power, but rather separated the Raj from the 'wild' tribes living in the hills that continued into Afghan lands. The Frontier ran for over a thousand miles and was inhabited by a hodge-podge of peoples whose distribution was highly uneven. At best, '[i]t was simply accepted as a provisional hedge ... [that] kept the most troublesome of our always unsettled neighbours outside.'[6] Those 'unsettled neighbours' included Pathan, Baluch and Brahui tribesmen who lived in the hills, but who often had lands or at least relations on the British side of the Frontier. Adding to complications was the arcane administrative structure the British put in place. They divided the Frontier between the Punjab government, controlling roughly its northern two-thirds and the authorities of Sind, responsible for the southern third and themselves under the control of Bombay.[7] These two bureaucratic bodies developed their own systems of tribal management in keeping with the exigencies and experiences of their respective frontiers.

It was the section of frontier straddling the administrative divide between Sind and the Punjab that proved to be the site of so much rancor between Sandeman and Merewether. The district of Dera Ghazi Khan was the southernmost frontier district of the Punjab province. Ecologically, it sat between the arid mountains common to the districts to its north and the desert tracts marking the Baluch Frontier of Sind, south and westwards.[8] While the district itself supported a settled, agricultural population, beyond the Frontier the harsh climate encouraged nomadic pastoralism, as well as some transhumance amongst the tribes. These different ecologies created different frontier practices with the neighboring 'independent' tribes. Separated by a desert track from the Baluch tribes, it cost the Sind authorities little to leave them relatively alone; whereas the mountains of the north afforded shelter and hiding to the raiding Pathans common along the Punjab Frontier. This meeting spot of different 'ethnic' types, Baluch and Pathan, as well as different ecological worlds—deserts and arid mountain tracts—presented a rare combination where the standard practices of frontier governance were found wanting. It was thus the perfect place for Sandeman to incubate and hatch his new form of frontier governmentality.

The spat between Sandeman and Merewether 'was not a mere squabble between officials of adjoining provinces, but raised important questions of Imperial frontier policy.'[9] Indeed, Calcutta's endorsement of Sandeman transformed him into the chief architect of the system of frontier governance which bore his name and served as a foundation of British imperial power up until South Asia's independence in 1947.[10] His system is presently being used by the US-led NATO forces in Afghanistan, though it is doubtful they know its provenance.[11] Sandeman worked with the local tribes, integrating them into a system of imperial management and making them, in turn, the executors of their own oppression. In contrast, the system championed by Merewether and previously favored by both the Bombay and central governments on this Frontier was one of imperial disengagement. The tribes were to be left to themselves beyond the British Frontier. Any incursions they made over that Frontier were to be met with swift and violent reprisal. These two theses of tribal management had a long history on the Frontier and respectively represented the 'forward policy' and the 'closed border policy'.[12]

The systems advocated by Sandeman and Merewether are summarized best in a report from 1910, which states:

(a) The Sandeman policy ... consists of an active participation in the life and interests of the people beyond our administrative border, but with the least possible dislocation of the tribal systems.

(b) The close[d] border system whereby the tribes beyond the administrative frontier were left to work out their own salvation subject to the limitation that

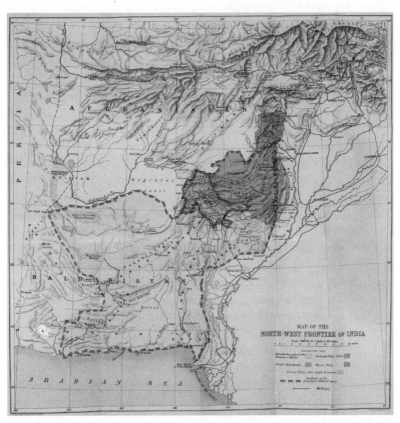

Reproduced by kind permission of the Syndics of Cambridge University Library

offences against the inhabitants of areas within our administrative border are punished by reprisals across the border, and that subsidies are paid to the tribes to keep the peace, particularly on main trade routes passing through or bordering on their territory.[13]

Sandeman's system, in his own words, was 'an attempt to deal with the hearts and minds of the people and not only with their fears'.[14] In contrast, the closed border system was one of 'uncompromising militarism' marked by the '"non-intervention-cum expeditions" system common to both Sind and the Punjab'.[15]

The closed border policy, essentially designed to keep the unwieldy tribes of the Frontier out of British territory, had been employed along both the Punjab and Sind frontiers since the 1840s. British officers and colonial subjects alike, including settled tribesmen living in British territory, were prohibited from venturing beyond the Frontier. Tribesmen inhabiting the hills were in the main denied access to British territories, including their markets and in many cases the tribes' lands on the settled plains. If the hill tribes crossed the British Frontier and proceeded to raid its inhabitants, the British responded with a blockade of the belligerent tribe. If this did not engender their submission, a military expedition was dispatched. In the fifty years between 1849 and the end of the century, the British dispatched sixty-two such expeditions to punish recalcitrant and misbehaving tribes.[16] Such expeditions used collective punishment as a means of governing the tribes, premised on the idea the tribes would police themselves in order to avoid such indiscriminate destruction.[17]

Central to the closed border system was the belief that 'coercion is discriminating mercy, which the instructions of government inculcate.'[18] Administrators and policy-makers alike held that frontier tribesmen needed to learn to fear the British Raj in order to be peaceably governed by it. William Merewether was a key proponent of the use of force against the tribes, writing:

[i]t is a great mistake to suppose that these wild tribes can be kept in order by simple arrangements and negotiations. They regard them as signs of weakness, and only become more bold and insolent each time that their lawless acts do not meet with the punishment they deserve. Soft measures will never answer. They must be made to feel the strength of the paramount power, and then anything may be done with them.[19]

Merewether's advocacy of force was based on his own experiences along the Sind Frontier where he made his name as a young officer through bloody expeditions against the Baluch and Brahui tribesmen during the early days of British authority in the area.[20]

Both problems and critics of the closed border system were many. First, it was extremely expensive. Military operations were costly and frontier warfare was often both protracted and ineffective. With no belligerents to engage directly, a number of expeditions simply burned deserted villages and crops, following a scorched earth policy to force the tribes' submission. Second, collective punishment of the tribesmen reinforced group solidarity and animosity towards the British. The system ignored the grievances of the tribes and viewed them as little more than objects of punishment. But frontier raiding was often the consequence of the hill tribes being denied access to their agricultural lands in the settled districts. Finally, the prohibition of travel by British officers beyond the Frontier essentially rendered the Raj blind with regard to information and intelligence of the inhabitants of the hills. It was subject to a self-imposed information drought.[21]

The closed border system had long been a favorite on the Punjab Frontier, where Sandeman cut his teeth. In the 1870s, however, the Punjab Government moved from simple modifications of the system to a full-scale overhaul, culminating in a new approach to frontier governance which envisaged and exercised a more intimate relationship with the tribesmen living beyond British jurisdiction.[22] Much of the thinking that underlay this shift was personified by Sandeman himself. As Deputy Commissioner of Dera Ghazi Khan in the late 1860s, he put into practice a system based on detailed knowledge of the tribes beyond the Frontier and personal interaction with them. While Sandeman's initial efforts encountered official agnosticism, their success eventually attracted the notice of his superiors, as well as the attentions of the Government of India.[23] Sandeman's actions ultimately proved, in the words of his assistant R.I. Bruce, the '*coup de grace*' to the closed border system.[24]

The Sandeman system consisted of three central elements which proved to be common features of later imperial systems of indirect rule. The first was that all tribes had a natural leader with whom the British could ally themselves and subsequently support. The key was identifying those individuals and gaining their trust. To gain such knowledge and trust, British officers needed to venture beyond the Frontier regularly. Sandeman led by example, establishing his summer residence for Dera Ghazi Khan at Sibi, in the Marri hills, beyond the

British Frontier. The second was a system of tribal levies which recruited tribesmen into the employ of the colonial state—protecting trade along various caravan routes such as the Bolan Pass, providing security for the *dak* (mail), and accompanying British officers on their official tours. These levies provided the manpower for local militias who served as the bulwark of order along the Frontier.[25] The third element of the Sandeman system was the use of 'traditional' institutions of tribal governance, most importantly the *jirga* (council) which effectively formed governing assemblies and tribal courts.

Each of these elements was designed to bind the interests of the tribesmen to those of the imperial state while at the same time being as minimally intrusive as possible.[26] To support the tribal leaders, known as *tumandar*s or *sardar*s, and to arouse their loyalty, Sandeman offered titles and honors in the form of *khil'at*s and *sanad*s, as well as political power and economic patronage. The tribal levies, carefully calibrated to achieve balance between the different tribes, were composed of men approved by local *tumandar*s, thus reinforcing their authority and influence. The levies were deployed only in their own territories, ensuring their depth of local knowledge and connections and thus their ability to influence local events. Finally, the *tumandar*s were offered a direct hand in local administration and self-government as members of the tribal *jirga*s. Only individuals endorsed by the colonial state could be members of the *jirga*s.[27] To ensure the acceptance of these offers initially by the *tumandar*s and subsequently by the tribesmen, they were often backed, quite literally, by a large military escort which accompanied Sandeman on his tours.[28]

Sandeman's system was essentially about the tribesmen policing themselves, with the tribal levies serving in the central role of a system of tribal responsibility.[29] Its success crucially rested on the tribesmen's willing participation, which in turn depended on their interests being served by it. He accomplished this, in part at least, through a clear communication strategy. One of his contemporaries insisted that:

'Sandeman's success…consisted in his making himself always accessible to the tribesmen, going to their villages, (or if nomadic their tribes or valleys) and listening patiently to every thing that they had to say on both sides and threshing the disputes out and then trying to settle them…. To be 'accessible' means a great deal.'[30]

Sandeman's accessibility facilitated the convergence of interests between the tribesmen and the colonial state.

Sandeman developed his system while Deputy Commissioner of Dera Ghazi Khan, a Punjab district bordering the Upper Sind Frontier where he was charged with administration of the district as well as relations with the trans-border Marri and Bugti Baluch tribes. These tribes, inhabiting areas beyond British territories, were ostensibly subjects of the Khan of Kalat, a local potentate the British had been in a treaty relationship with since 1854.[31] Because they were subjects of the Khan, relations with them were supposed to proceed through the Commissioner of Sind who was charged with relations with Kalat. When Sandeman approached the Political Superintendent of the Upper Sind Frontier, Colonel Robert Phayre, to rein in the Marri and Bugti raids that regularly erupted across the Frontier, Phayre informed him the Khan had no real authority over them.[32] The Khan's power was, in reality, a legal fiction and had been since shortly after the conclusion of the 1854 treaty when Kalat fell into a state of civil war.

Recognizing that the reality on the ground had outpaced bureaucratic practice, Sandeman took the initiative. He crossed the Frontier in order to deal with the Marri and Bugti tribes directly, rather than through the Khan of Kalat and by default the Sind authorities, who had no control over them. He quickly established a working relationship with the tribes and put an end to their raids on the Punjab Frontier. But Sandeman's direct dealings with the Marri and Bugti tribes were at odds with the policy followed by the Commissioner of Sind, William Merewether. Merewether viewed the Khan of Kalat as sovereign over the tribes and consequently advocated a policy of strict non-intervention with regard to relations between the Khan and his subjects. In contrast Sandeman, whose views were shared by Phayre, argued that the Khan's lack of authority meant he was no more than the head of the Brahui tribal confederacy, of which the Marris and Bugtis Baluch were not part.[33] Accordingly, the British should deal with the tribes directly when circumstances warranted, as well as offering their good offices to intervene in any conflict between the Khan and his *tumandars*.[34] Sandeman's and Merewether's different notions of authority reflected the competing ideologies and claims of the Baluch and Brahui elite, with the Khan insisting that 'traditional' social structure was feudal while his *tumandars* claimed it to be a decentralized confederacy.[35] Interestingly, the Khan and his *tumandars* enunciated their claims in a language familiar to the British, namely that of feudalism—similar to how the Persian and Afghan courts did with regard to the Goldsmid arbitration over Sistan.

The Government of India initially tried to allow the closed border and Sandeman systems to coexist in an uneasy tension, with one followed on the Upper Sind Frontier while the other was followed on the Dera Ghazi Khan Frontier. Calcutta was willing to countenance these different styles of frontier management partly because of the different topographies and settlement patterns prevalent on the respective frontiers.[36] But Dera Ghazi Khan presented a problematic case. As a Punjab official, Sandeman by and large followed the dictates of Lahore's policy. However, his district's border with Sind meant that that policy did not always complement those of the Sind government. Consequently, the tribes beyond the Frontier were able to play Sind and Punjab officials off against each other as their respective policies did not meld together into a coherent whole.[37]

This system of 'dual management', with no single officer responsible for relations with the same tribe on different provincial borders, was the source of much bureaucratic hand-wringing and frustration. In the words of one frontier officer, '[d]ual management only tends to fill sheets of foolscap and make confusion.'[38] On more than one occasion correspondence attempted to rectify the situation, with the respective governments appealing to Calcutta to endorse one or the other approach exclusively. A conference held at Mithankot on the banks of the River Indus on 3 February 1871 attended by Sir Henry Davies, Lieutenant-Governor of the Punjab, William Merewether, Commissioner of Sind, and Sandeman, as well as a number of officers concerned with the governance of their common frontier, was supposed to solve this interminable issue.[39] The conference, while denouncing the ills of dual management, in effect allowed it to continue. Sandeman was to pursue Lahore's policies in his district, while he was subordinated to Merewether with regard to the governance of tribes beyond the Frontier.

The Mithankot compromise quickly proved unworkable, forcing the issue to be revisited in 1876 to Sandeman's ultimate benefit. In justifying its decision to back Sandeman over Merewether's strenuous objections, the Government of India noted that:

The attempt to work two different systems by two different sets of officers, acting independently of each other, failed. The attempts to work a compromise between two systems by means of a combination of officers partizans of either,—seniors wedded to one,—subordinates to the other,—also failed, as might have been expected. No alternative remained but to place matters in the hands of one set of officers or the other,—to entrust their management to the Punjab exclusively or to Sind exclusively. The Govt. of India, rightly or wrongly, decided in favour of the Punjab, and the disconnection of the Sind officials from Khelat affairs followed as a matter of course.[40]

Yet even after the Government of India definitively sided with Sandeman, the significance of his victory remained ambiguous and the limits of his newly-won powers remained ill-defined.[41]

Sandeman's success was marked by the elevation of the Baluch Frontier to an Agency with direct responsibility to the central government, rather than through Bombay or Lahore. Sandeman himself was named the first Agent of the Governor-General in Baluchistan, charged with British relations with the court of the Khan of Kalat, as well as the administration of the districts constituting British Baluchistan and relations with the tribes inhabiting the areas falling under the Agent's jurisdiction. He served in this capacity until his death in 1892, and was assisted in these duties by three Assistants, as well as a large native staff.[42] During the remainder of his career, Sandeman oversaw the implementation of his system of tribal management, as well as the annexation of the districts of Sibi and Pishin, the campaign in Zhob, and the settlement of the Anglo-Afghan boundary.

Sandeman's Success

Sandeman's success had far-reaching ramifications which continue to be felt today. Apart from bestowing the now famous epithet 'hearts and minds' to posterity, his system became a central tenet of frontier governance for the remainder of British rule in South Asia and beyond.[43] While the argument between Sandeman and Mereweather may be narrowly construed as a bureaucratic spat over different systems of indirect rule, the stakes were in fact considerably higher. The system of 'indirect rule' Sandeman championed radically altered the social topography of the 'tribes' subjected to it, while at the same time exerting a profound, yet subtle effect on the colonial state itself. Thus it was not simply a matter of opting for a template of indirect rule which would later be replicated throughout the Indian, or indeed the larger British empire. Rather, Sandeman's system was a constituent element of a developing ethos and practice of frontier governmentality which came to define not only the limits of colonial authority, but also the nature of the colonial state.

At its most basic and essential level, the aim of frontier governance was to establish 'order' along British India's periphery. What exactly that meant depended greatly on one's perspective. According to many contemporaries and scholars, this was more than an exercise in 'good governance'; it was part of the canon of imperial security. The Frontier was to be a reliable barrier between the heartland of British India and an expansive Russian Empire. The maintenance of order there was thus a paramount concern of the Raj.[44] Disorder on the Frontier would simply invite disaster, in the form of Russian expansionism. There was no more forceful contemporary proponent of this point of view than Lord Lytton, the Viceroy who invaded Afghanistan to ensure the Frontier's security. He wrote to Sandeman that

[i]n my opinion, the main defect of the frontier policy of the Govt of India has hitherto been its treatment of frontier affairs without adequate reference to their interconnection as parts of one imperial whole. One indissoluble catena of very complex interests. Potentates such as the Khan of Khelat, or the Ameer of Cabul, are mere dummies, or counters, which could be of no importance to us, were it not for the costly stakes we put upon them in the great game for empire which we are now playing with Russia.[45]

Frontier governance was thus considered a central component of the so-called 'Great Game' of Anglo-Russian rivalry, and Sandeman's efforts were really about great power politics.[46]

The overriding focus of much scholarship on the calculations of imperial politics obscures as much as it reveals when it comes to the Frontier. While fears of Russian expansionism played a part in shaping imperial attitudes, these calculations were of secondary importance. What was of greater moment in fashioning frontier governance, under both the Sandemanian as well as closed border systems, was the nature of the Frontier itself. In contrast to both the Mughal and modern frontiers demarcating the limits of South Asian political entities, the northwest frontier of British India was not a space defined by penetrative state power, but rather by its absence. Both the predecessors and the successors of the British envisaged the border as defining the state where it was, and is, most visible and assertive of its prerogatives in the form of its military presence. As a state-centric space, the border has been historically an area of centrifugal tendencies where new state forms coalesced to break away from former centers.[47] For the British, however, the border represented no such thing. Despite the pretence that the border marked a clear distinction between spaces of order (that is, British territory) inhabited by settled British subjects, and spaces of disorder (that is, *yaghestan*) inhabited by tribesmen of the hills, the truth of the matter was rather more complicated.

The nature of the British Frontier was one not of sharp demarcation, but rather of gradual recession. The colonial state abandoned its pretence to power in spatial degrees, moving from assertions of sovereignty within the settled districts, to assertions of paramountcy in the tribal areas and agencies, to assertions of influence over Afghanistan.[48] This gradual ebbing of imperial authority as one moved further away from the settled districts had a perverse effect on the delineation of the Frontier. While the colonial state invested significant resources—diplomatic, political, military and economic—in the survey and delineation of a 'scientific border' with Afghanistan, its internal frontier, separating the settled (read civilized) districts from the hills (read wild), remained by and large a subject of local knowledge. The location of this latter frontier was never officially elucidated.[49] The hybrid character of the Frontier, composed of an outer 'scientific border' with Afghanistan and an inner 'zone', reflects a colonial state which straddled between the norms and forms of modern Westphalian statehood, with clearly delineated borders, and its own understandings of previous forms of political authority on the South Asian subcontinent. Moreover, it reveals an essential confusion of the colonial state; it was unsure of the meaning of the Frontier, as well as unable to assert its sovereignty over a demarcated border.

At its most basic, the colonial state has been conceptualized as simply a bastardized reproduction of the forms of politics of the metropole. In this guise, it was a vessel of European 'modernity' implanting its norms and values throughout the imperial realm.[50] Amongst the most important of these were the political forms it championed, in particular the 'modern' Westphalian state—a bureaucratized and centralized entity with a defined territory and population and a monopoly over legitimate forms of violence. With regard to the state at least, colonialism is thus seen as a story of state construction and centralization, marking the embedding of the modern state in the extra-European world. Some historians acknowledge the influence of local forms of politics on the colonial state, producing forms of hybridity and syncretism that transformed the embedding into more of a grafting of the modern state.[51] Yet even this misconstrues the profundity of difference between the colonial state of British India and Weber's 'ideal type' of statehood. Both the form and the content of the modern state were subject to enormous and often violent contestation in Europe, much less on the colonial periphery.[52] It is only with the flattening view of hindsight that the triumph of the Westphalian form of statehood appears both smooth and inevitable. The colonial state was at one and the same time fundamentally a European creature of modernity and a 'pre-modern' South Asian polity.[53] Nowhere was this more forcefully demonstrated than on the Frontier.

While many insist that British arguments over the form of frontier governance reflect the pragmatism of British administration, they reveal something more important. Debates about how to best govern the frontier present a different typology of power, a frontier governmentality that forcefully shaped the colonial state itself. The British did not have a preconceived notion of the proper form of governance of the frontier; nor, more profoundly, did they have a modernizing agenda that they sought to deploy here.[54] True, administrators talked about 'civilizing' the tribesmen through the slow penetration of imperial authority over time.[55] And many of the practices seen in the late nineteenth century here were premised on contemporary ideas of political economy as well as assumptions about human economic rationality.[56] However, these lacked consistent forethought in either conception or application that would warrant their characterization as part of an imperial project of 'modernity' on the frontier. Instead, the British adapted what they understood to be local and historical practice to their needs and institutions on an *ad hoc* basis. The back and forth between the closed border system, in its numerous guises, and the Sandeman system in its equally prolific number of incarnations attests to this.

What we see in the adoption of local practice is the shaping of another type of 'modernity'—an imperial modernity not contoured by Weber's ideal types, but rather by the colonial state's conceptualization of the frontier and categorization of its inhabitants. This was a traditionalizing modernity which did not seek to integrate, civilize and modernize the frontier's unruly tribesmen as imperial subjects like their Indian counterparts.[57] Rather, it sought to contain, conserve and traditionalize them separate from the colonial sphere. Hence it drew deeply upon the well of colonial memory, replicating the theses of government formerly championed by the likes of Munro, Malcolm and Elphinstone but subsequently displaced by the 'derivative discourse' of Indian nationalism. This frontier governmentality in turn shaped the imperial state, bureaucratizing practices of difference, endorsing the encapsulation of tradition, and codifying a border regime fundamentally at odds with the model of a Westphalian state.[58] It ran parallel with the clearly modernizing politics of constitutional reform, municipal boards and the divisive representative politics of communalism, excluding the frontier and its inhabitants from the unified, if highly fragmented space of colonial society. This powerfully ingrained a move towards the institutionalization of difference within the imperial bureaucracy, which served as a counterweight to the equally powerful moves towards universalism.

What distinguishes this frontier governmentality from other norms and practices of modern imperialism that some scholars have come to identify as 'colonial governmentality'?[59] Indeed, were Sandeman's efforts simply an aspect of the multi-faceted 'ethnographic state' which was so central to colonial governmentality in British India?[60] While the ethnographic state sought to document and enforce difference— through the census, through the all-India ethnographic surveys and through the codification of customary law—frontier governmentality, although mimicking some of these elements in form, lacked comparable penetration of indigenous society and thus substance. There was no equivalent work on the customary law of the Frontier—despite its repeated invocation by frontier administrators and its centrality in the Frontier Crimes Regulation (1872/1887/1901)—to that of the C.L. Tupper's multi-volume work on the customary law of the Punjab.[61] Frontier governmentality was not simply different in degree, but also in aim. Whereas the ethnographic state sought to assert imperial sovereignty effectively through the enforcement of difference, a kind of divide and rule strategy, frontier governmentality sought to assert its suzerainty through the encapsulation of frontier tribes. In the former, people were transformed into colonial subjects largely through the exercise of punitive measures; in the latter, tribesmen were at best imperial vassals defined largely by their exclusion from the colonial space. Thus the ethnographic state was about control through division while frontier governmentality was about order through exclusion.

While the ethnographic state instituted a regime of difference through the categorizing of colonial subjects, and subsequent treatment in discrete groupings, these groups were almost wholly encapsulated, or contained by the colonial state. They were, in the words of one scholar, subjected to the 'closeting of subject populations in a series of separate containers'.[62] One example of this containment in colonial India was the criminalized tribes, subject to regulation after the Criminalized Tribes Act of 1871.[63] Members of the criminalized tribes had few places to escape the control of the colonial state. Indeed, their movement was what the colonial state sought to regulate through their criminalization. To do this successfully, the state had to contain, or encapsulate these peoples within its own sovereign space—territory where it exercised ultimate authority. While this was possible on the Punjab plains, it was impossible on the northwest Frontier. The tribesmen here were not encapsulated as much as partitioned off from the colonial state and society. But this resulted from more than simply a practical lack of control. It meant that while on the Indian plains the British sought to civilize peoples like the Criminal Tribes through the sovereign regulation of normative codes of behavior and criminality, on the Frontier they made no such pretence.[64] Thus the frontiersmen were governed by their own 'traditions', rather than by the norms of the colonial state.

Sandeman's actions throw into relief a larger debate about the nature of indirect rule and its effect on colonial subjects, as well as colonial powers themselves. Sandeman authored his system at a time when other colonial authorities were grasping the 'problem' of frontier management. In South Africa, the High Commissioner Sir Bartle Frere, a former governor of Bombay who himself had served in Sind in the 1850s, deployed many of the strategies he developed in India in a disastrous, though ultimately successful war against the Zulu kingdom.[65] Likewise, in the United States, Native Americans were being encapsulated through the reservation system, a process marked by significant violence through to the end of the nineteenth century.[66] French authorities in Indochina, the Maghreb and Syria adopted similar approaches.[67] And elsewhere in the British Empire, other colonial administrations such as northern Nigeria under the governance of Sir Frederick Lugard later copied the elements of India's Frontier administration.[68] Within India itself, the debates that Sandeman's efforts both fostered and engaged had important implications not only for the northeast and Burmese frontiers, but also for the internal frontiers delineating the princely states from British India.[69]

The ambiguity of the Frontier's meaning and location complicated the colonial state's relations with the inhabitants of this nebulous grey zone. Were the tribesmen of the hills independent chiefs, as Merewether argued, or were they British subjects, as Sandeman insisted?[70] The answer to that question was significant as it would largely determine how the colonial state related with those people. If they were subjects, their raiding activities on the Frontier were nothing more than simple criminality which should be dealt with as a question of law and order.[71] If, however, they were 'independent chiefs', this was more than a matter of public order, but rather one of political relations. The position of these people remained both anomalous and undefined to the end of the nineteenth century, with Parliament itself reflecting this confusion. Lord Lansdowne, former Viceroy of India and then Secretary of War argued to his fellow Peers that:

To talk of tribal independence was a little misleading. There could be no complete independence in the case of people who had not the power of transferring their allegiance in any direction they pleased. That power was not given to the frontier tribes, and it was better, therefore, not to speak of them as independent. That condition of qualified independence was very common all through the Borders of India. The small frontier tribes were not strong enough to stand alone. They knew they must lean on some stronger Power, and in the case of the tribes...they should lean on us and not on any other Power.[72]

Debates about the tribesmen's independence necessarily had implications for the nature of the Raj's own sovereign claims. Thus the meaning and gradation of sovereignty within the colonial sphere remained ambiguous throughout the nineteenth century.[73]

The tribesmen were independent, but that independence was not on a par with the true independence of foreign sovereigns.[74] Rather, the tribesmen occupied an older political space increasingly squeezed by the modernization of the colonial state. They were vassals to the imperial state, which acted as their suzerain overlord. Whereas previously vassals in a suzerain political universe could owe allegiance to more than one suzerain, the Raj viewed such political pliability as dangerous.[75] Lytton recognized this reality in relations with the Khan of Kalat and Baluch *tumandar*s, noting that the norms of international relations required that only sovereigns relate with one another, but acknowledging that ignoring the power of the *tumandar*s would be foolhardy.[76] This semi-independence placed the tribesmen at the same time within the imperial orbit, but outside the colonial one. They were subject to the dictates of the former, but could not avail themselves to the protections of the latter. The tribesmen thus found themselves bound in a shrinking political universe of vassalage, and denied access to the modern political universe of colonial subjecthood.

The contours of colonial subjecthood were being crafted as the late nineteenth century wore on.[77] In the main, subjects were understood to owe their allegiance (and taxes) to the Queen, and in return guaranteed the good governance and impartial justice of the colonial state. Yet the frontier tribesmen were left out of this arrangement, denied access to colonial courts and British governance, while at the same time expected to act in accordance with the interests of the imperial state. Extending the benefits of colonial subjecthood to the tribesmen was a central plank of Sandeman's efforts to win their 'hearts and minds'. One contemporary characterized Sandeman's attitude as one that not only recognized the value of tribal cooperation, but more profoundly recognized that the tribesmen had rights which the colonial state should uphold.[78] Foremost amongst these rights were the right to fair government, the right to individualized punishment for wrongdoing, the right to respect for local culture and customs, and the right to fair compensation for services rendered to the colonial state. While not rising to the status of 'citizen', the tribesmen should at least be able to count themselves as British subjects, entitled to all the protections and obligations such a status entailed.

A corollary to colonial subjecthood was economic development. Governance of the Frontier required the colonial state to establish a physical presence in the area. Sandeman, while 'respecting' the independence of the tribes, saw access to the Frontier as paramount for the Raj. He was thus a keen advocate of both road and railway construction in what became the Baluchistan Agency—but only in the areas of British Baluchistan. Thus the Sibi and Quetta railways were key construction projects he oversaw, along with the creation of 1,500 miles of road in the region.[79] However, beyond establishment of a transport infrastructure designed first and foremost to facilitate the movement of British Indian troops, the economic development of the tribesmen remained a low priority, even for Sandeman. While the tribal levies recompensed tribesmen for their services by taking them into government employ, there was little else in the way of development.[80] No effort was made to establish the kind of irrigation works seen elsewhere in Sind or the Punjab, nor did the colonial state invest in any schemes save paying the tribal levies. Service in the tribal militias ultimately transformed the tribesmen into wage laborers, introducing colonial capitalism into the area by commodifying labor.[81] This in turn tied the tribesmen more firmly into the colonial economic system with minimal cost to the colonial state.

Many colonial officials, including Sandeman himself, insisted that the colonial state could do little as long as the tribesmen remained recalcitrant and suspicious of state-sponsored development efforts. But this obscures the fact that it was not in the interests of the colonial state to facilitate the Frontier's economic development. Such an undertaking would be expensive. More important, it could also undermine the tribesmen's rugged independence, which not only secured them from the colonial state but also inured them against the stirrings of nationalism emerging in British Indian society.[82] Indeed, development in the settled areas allowed for the flourishing of anti-colonial nationalism during the inter-war period in the form of the Khudai Khidmatgars of the North-West Frontier Province (NWFP). By ensuring the tribesmen's economic dependence on the settled areas under British control, the colonial state maintained a powerful check over the political independence at minimal cost.

While Sandeman's efforts may be depicted as part of the modernizing project of colonialism, designed to bring the tribesmen into a political relationship with the colonial state based on a kind of compelled social contract, this was not simply a move from 'status to contract'.[83] Sandeman's attitudes, though on the surface politically liberal, were, somewhat paradoxically, deeply Philistine. They drew upon the most conservative strains of imperial discourse. The rights Sandeman wanted recognized were essentially rights of difference. According to him, the tribesmen had a right to their customs and traditions, as well as a right to be governed by those customs and traditions. The idea of differential rights accorded with the classic colonial thesis of governance—the enforcement of difference amongst subject populations through legal pluralisms.[84] This stood in stark contrast to what was then becoming the norm amongst citizen populations in the imperial metropole, the enforcement of universal rights and obligations. Sandeman's advocacy was not about integrating the tribesmen into British Indian society, but isolating and encapsulating them from it, in the guise of 'protecting' them. The tribesmen were to be corralled into a political order largely shaped by the colonial state, but nonetheless separate from it.

One of the initial skeptics regarding Sandeman's experiment who noted the potential effects of Sandeman's traditionalization of Baluch society was Lord Lytton, a man not known for his intellectual acumen. Lytton's observations on, and potential objections to Sandeman's course of action are worth quoting at length:

You must bear this in mind (I cannot too strongly impress upon you) that Khelat is—socially—at this moment in much the same condition as that of France in the 13th century. The country is passing (under the inevitably turbulent conditions of such a process) from the tribal into the feudal system; and this last must again have to be absorbed into the increasing personal power of the crown; (that is to say, the sovereignty of the Khan must increase, and the power of the sardārs diminish if the country is to follow the natural salutary course of historic development, and eventually consolidate itself into an orderly social organism.) It is to the interest of the British Govt to accelerate this process by all legitimate means. It is not [emphasis original] in our interest to retard it, by artificially promoting or prolonging what you call the 'old customs of the country', or 'the ancient rights of the sirdars'....[85]

What Lytton noted was that state construction and centralization required the subjugation of alternate sources of political power to the sovereign authority of the state.[86] This was essential to the establishment of a modern 'Westphalian' state. Yet Sandeman's own actions prejudiced this by dividing the tribes and thus preventing the construction of any sort of centralized state power. Instead, through the exercise of Sandeman's own particular brand of frontier governmentality, the tribesmen were excluded from the 'modernity' of the colonial sphere and instead encapsulated in their own colonially sanctioned 'tradition'.

Jirgas *and Tribal Tradition*

Sandeman sought to establish a system of governance on the Baluch Frontier founded—in the wording of contemporary correspondence—upon 'tribal usage'.[87] The pillar of that system, and of Sandeman's particular type of frontier governmentality, was the *jirga*, sometimes referred to as 'council of elders'. *Jirga*s had both a political and a judicial character. Politically, the *jirga*—served as a forum of tribal consultation; judicially, it functioned as a tribal court. In their judicial capacity, codified by the Frontier Crimes Regulation of 1887, *jirga*s tried transgressors without the legal and evidentiary niceties of a colonial court.[88] This lax evidentiary standard was supposedly offset by the fact that such judicial *jirga*s were, in the main, limited to imposing a fine.[89] While the *jirga*s' decisions and punishments were ostensibly based on tribal custom and usage, the Deputy Commissioner retained the power to overturn *jirgas'* decisions, meaning that colonial administrators were the ultimate arbiters of tribal tradition.[90] Thus the colonial state's use of *jirgas* as a 'traditional' institute of governance fundamentally altered them, and in so doing the tribes that utilized them.[91]

Jirgas were commonly used by many Pashtun tribes, especially those inhabiting the Frontier around Peshawar where Sandeman first cut his teeth.[92] But the Pashtuns did not conceive of *jirgas* as a regular governing institution of the tribe. This transformation awaited the later innovations of the British imperial state. The Pashtun practice of the *jirga* reflected, in the eyes of colonial ethnographers, a tribal structure lacking hierarchy and thus clear leadership. *Jirgas* were conceived as discursive spaces where members had an equal voice; issues were supposedly settled by consensus. The egalitarian ethos supposedly represented by the *jirga* lay at the heart of imperial administrators' complaints of the Pashtuns' 'republican spirit', which made them difficult to govern.

Sandeman applied this *jirga* system to the Baluch tribes he initially encountered in Dera Ghazi Khan and later ruled over in Baluchistan itself. The Baluch had a more hierarchical tribal structure than their Pathan neighbors, making them, in the minds of British administrators, easier to govern.[93] In contrast to the Pashtun amongst whom use of the *jirga* was widespread, it was virtually unknown amongst the Baluch prior to Sandeman's introduction of it. According to Rai Bahadur Hittu Ram, Sandeman's chief native assistant:

'[p]reviously it had not been customary to hold jirgas in the Dera Ghazi Khan district, nor did the people there know what a Jirga was. The procedure had long been in vogue in Peshawar, but it was introduced into Baluchistan by Sir Robert Sandeman and it afforded much assistance in the administration of the country.'[94]

In order to construct a system of government which 'preserved' tribal tradition, through the use of idioms and institutions familiar to the tribes over whom he ruled, Sandeman introduced a key innovation to tradition—a largely alien institution which had been developed in a wholly different tribal context to meet a wholly different set of tribal concerns and circumstances. Clearly, this was the invention of tradition by the colonial state at its finest.

Sandeman's use of the *jirga* as an institution of tribal governance was central to his success on the Dera Ghazi Khan Frontier, as well as his success with the Khan of Kalat. Indeed, the key event of his second trip to the court of the Khan of Kalat in the spring and summer of 1876 was the adjudication of the grievances between the Khan of Kalat and his Brahui *sardar*s by a tribal *jirga*, leading to the conclusion of the Mustang Agreement. Sandeman characterized the decisions of this *jirga* as a reassertion of the *sardar*s' 'ancient rights' enshrined by the constitution of Nasir Khan I and Nasir Khan II, former rulers of the khanate, echoing the language Goldsmid used to justify his arbitral award. British contemporaries characterized that unwritten constitution as the 'Magna Carta of Baluchistan', and Sandeman's efforts as the restoration of ancient rights and duties.[95] British efforts to historicize the *jirga* and place it in comparison with their own historical experience continued the traditions of the philosophical histories which were favored in the Scottish Enlightenment and placed 'natives' on the hierarchy of civilizations, rather than distinguishing them on the basis of race.[96] The *jirga*, under Sandeman's watchful eye, asserted itself as not only the judge of traditional rights, and in this case wrongs, but of tradition itself, in the form of past precedent.[97] Sandeman subsequently held two *jirga*s a year, at his summer and winter residences in Sibi and Quetta respectively, which he called 'shah-i durbars', in a supposed reference to the *shah-i jirga* (kingly council) held by Nasir Khan I on his accession to power.[98] The need to historicize innovation, clothing it in the guise of 'tradition', was thus central to Sandeman's efforts from the outset.

While Sandeman may have 'invented' a 'tradition' in the form of the *sarkari jirga*s he employed on the Baluch Frontier, it was obviously one that met the consent, whether forced or freely given, of the Baluch *sardar*s. As is clear from the records, the *jirga*s often offered an improved settlement which would not necessarily be afforded parties had they faced, or had access, to colonial courts. Further, by including the *sardar*s as members of the *jirga*s, Sandeman gave them a vested interest in their operation, especially in light of the fact that the *jirga*s often kept some of the fines they imposed for redistribution within the tribe. This give and take between Sandeman and the Baluch *sardar*s marked an intensity—and, one might argue, equality—in negotiation not seen on the Indian plains. Further, the *jirga*s provide a perfect example of the frontier governmentality to which I referred earlier. Unlike most 'traditional' judicial institutions, or indeed most types of 'customary law' that these employed, the *jirga*s had jurisdiction over

71

civil and criminal law, applying the norms of 'tribal custom' to both. Thus the colonial state did not make the type of sovereign claim it did virtually everywhere else on the Indian subcontinent—namely a monopolization of legitimate forms of violence in the form of criminal law. Here the weakness of the colonial state meant it could enforce neither the norms nor the law of criminality which provided one of the few universals of colonial order.

Conclusion

The Sandeman system which triumphed in the winter of 1876 would go on to shape the face of colonial administration along the Frontier until the British withdrawal in 1947, even if it was not always the favored bureaucratic policy. The tribal levies Sandeman systematically pioneered were employed as far away as Gilgit, at the other end of the British Indian Frontier, as well as all the spaces in between. Sandeman's introduction of *jirga*s as an institution of tribal governance was formalized with the issuance of the Frontier Crimes Regulation for Baluchistan in 1890, nearly fifteen years after their first use. By introducing and institutionalizing the *jirga*, as well as the tribal levy system amongst the Baluch, Sandeman irrevocably altered Baluch society in the name of its preservation. Policing by tradition thus first required its invention, as well as its subsequent arbitration and maintenance of tradition by colonial authorities.

Sandeman's system had a profound, if less obvious effect on the colonial state as well. The forms of frontier governmentality that it employed sat in tension with the modernizing aspects of the imperial project. Despite Lord Salibury's claim that the '[f]rontier wars are but the surf that marks the edge and advance of the wave of civilisation',[99] Sandemanization proved a lasting defense against both the violence and the civilization of the colonial state for those tribesmen subjected to it. The frontier governmentality Sandeman's system reflected excluded the tribesmen from the colonial sphere through the *cordon sanitaire* of 'tradition'. But it also worked powerfully to shape the colonial state, making enforcement of difference, encapsulation through tradition, and the ambiguity of the political form and meaning of the frontier—the limits of the state itself—essential aspects of British colonialism.

When Pakistan assumed control over the areas inhabited by both Baluch and Pashtun tribesmen, it initially left the architecture of tribal governance in place. Indeed it remains in place in the Federally Admin-istered Tribal Areas today. Consequently, the tribesmen of the Frontier, in both Baluchistan and Khyber-Pakhtunkhwa, remain subjects rather than citizens. They are outside the discourse of citizenship, their 'tradi-tions' and 'customs' still preserved by the continued use of the Frontier Crimes Regulation in the tribal agencies which are now supposed to be a hotbed of a 'resurgent Taliban'. The administrative isolation that facilitated British governance of the region has led to its underdevelop-ment and exclusion from the national body politic. The tribesmen of the region remain precisely that—tribesmen defined by an epoch of colonial governance rather than citizens shaped by an era of nation-state construction.[100] When the Pakistani state has attempted to inte-grate through the application of universal law, as in the settled areas of Baluchistan, that integration has been marked by the sanguinary mili-tarism of a state in crisis, which continues with sporadic outbursts of violence to the present. State construction is, after all, a bloody busi-ness. The full implications of 'Sandemanization' are thus being seen, and lived, on the Frontier today.

Sandeman's little experiment in government has ultimately defined much of the frontier subjected to it. Its emphasis on local custom and tradition has worked to fragment frontier society in the name of its preservation. Thus at least a part of the Frontier's heterogeneity is state regulated, if not state enforced. Just as important, the assumptions underlying Sandeman's system—namely those of static frontier cul-tures, the need for their containment, and the expense of their govern-ance and integration—remain hallmarks of many of the policies pursued today. Consequently, any understanding of the Frontier's past and present requires an understanding of Sandeman, and more broadly of the frontier governmentality he helped author.

3

SITANA AND SWAT

PATTERNS OF REVOLT ALONG THE FRONTIER

Whereas the previous two chapters have examined ideas of territoriality and tradition, this chapter turns its attention to one aspect that features most prominently in any discussion of the Frontier—religion. It examines a community of resistance located in and around the Swat valley which used religious rhetoric in opposition to the British Raj, declaring a *jihad* against the infidel *sarkar*. Swat is the first and only Pashtun-majority area to be looked at, but interestingly the community was composed largely of plainsmen from Bengal, the then United Provinces and the Punjab rather than Pashtun tribesmen. This chapter thus once again throws into relief the complex heterogeneity which has historically constituted the Frontier and which stands in stark contrast to many of the simplistic tropes regularly employed to discuss this area today. Finally, the chapter argues the critical importance of the religious discourse emanating from the Frontier in shaping both official and unofficial views about Islam during the British Raj. In doing so, it underlines the centrality of the 'periphery' in defining the 'center', thereby challenging the notion that this area is somehow less integrated in or important to the world it is part of.

The Pakistani army's recent operations in the Swat Valley propelled, for a fleeting moment, this remote and picturesque landscape, often referred to as the 'Switzerland of Pakistan', to the center of world attention. The army's violent reconquest of Swat pitted government forces against a tribal *lashkar* (army) of 'Taliban' militants estimated to number 3,000.[1] This *lashkar*, under the command of Maulana Fazlullah, had previously driven the army out of Swat after a 'reign of terror' of targeted assassinations and executions of local police, supposed informers, and other officials deemed enemies of their cause.[2] Foreign observers have characterized these events as heralding a new front of the War on Terror, where the Taliban and their creed of 'Islamo-fascism' supplanted the power of civilized authorities in the valley. Pakistan's offensive to retake the valley followed heavy pressure from its Western allies, especially the US which views the deteriorating security situation in the country with dismay.

Much of the analysis of current events in Swat, and indeed along the Frontier as a whole, is divorced from any real understanding of the historical context shaping the region. General assertions about the 'wild', 'violent' and 'tribal' past of the Frontier ruled by 'custom' and 'tradition' abound, with little effort expended to critically consider such characterizations. The current bout of Islamic militancy is thus seen as unsurprising on this 'savage frontier' which has long been marked by religious fanaticism. Indeed, the Swat valley is no stranger to religious militancy or violence. The Tehrik-i Taliban-i Pakistan (TTP) led by Maulana Fazlullah originated from the Tehrik-i-Nafaz-i-Shariat-i-Mohammadi (TNSM) of the 1990s, which similarly challenged central state authority through violence clothed in religious rhetoric. But to simplistically link current violence to past 'fanaticism' is to fundamentally misconstrue and fail to understand both. There is a deeper history of violent resistance throughout the region speaking a religious idiom, but it is one with a sophisticated pedigree and lasting consequence for the wider world.

One of the most interesting episodes of that deeper history is the longstanding presence of a colony of 'Hindustani Fanatics' who traced their origins to the *jihad* of Sayyid Ahmad of Rai Bareilly in the early nineteenth century. From the inception of their rule along the Frontier in 1849 until their withdrawal from the subcontinent in 1947, the British watched this colony. These 'Fanatics' and the Frontier they inhabited were central in defining the attitudes and actions of the colonial state towards its Muslim subjects. Further, their legacy, or rather the legacy of the attitudes they helped shape, continues to possess an insidious power over contemporary understandings of violence and religion on the Frontier today. Echoes of nineteenth-century British administrators' fears of 'seditious Wahabis' may be heard in today's denunciations of 'Islamo-fascists' with roots in an unbridled embrace of Saudi-backed Wahabism.[3] The 'Fanatics' are thus central to the construction of epistomologies of the Frontier, as well as of Muslims both past and present.

This chapter offers a brief history of the colony of 'Hindustani Fanatics' focusing on the period between 1849 and 1947 in order to examine its effect both on the locality in which the colony was situated, and more broadly on the colonial state and the public sphere. The 'Hindustani Fanatics' were supposed to be at the center of the 'Wahabi' conspiracy put on public display in a series of trials in the 1860s and 70s, and immortalized by W.W. Hunter's polemical tract *The Indian Musalmans*. During the twentieth century, they were implicated in the seditious activities of Indian nationalists, as well as treasonous connections with the Germans during both world wars and the Bolsheviks in the interval. Yet their treatment by the colonial state, given these dangerous linkages, is profoundly perplexing.

Different officials' confused and often contradictory attitudes to, and actions taken towards, the 'Fanatics' reflect the heterogeneity of British attitudes towards the 'Muslim question'. Thus they fundamentally challenge and subvert the long-held consensus of British mistrust of a seditious Muslim populace in the wake of the revolt of 1857–58. Further, they reveal a colonial state and society marked by a cacophony of voices that shaped a more nuanced and seemingly comfortable relationship between British authorities and their Muslim subjects. The lack of sensitivity to the nuance of the colonial past has in part made possible the totalizing discourse of terrorism which marks the region in the post-colonial present. These themes are explored by examining the century-long tenure of the 'Hindustani Fanatic' colony on the Swat frontier and analyzing the colony's legacy both for the colonial state and for the frontier society in which it was embedded.

Setting the Scene: Swat in Context

The Swat valley is a large valley roughly 100 miles northwest of Islamabad, and approximately fifty miles northeast of Peshawar. Swat, with neighboring Chitral, Dir and Bajaur, is a rugged and mountainous realm, especially in its more remote reaches. Its population includes Yusufzai Pashtun who migrated to the valley sometime in the sixteenth century.[4] Though politically powerful, they do not constitute a majority of the valley's populace. Colonial and post-colonial ethnographers have often depicted the Yusufzai's 'tribal structure' as the central organizing principle of Swati society.[5] But tribes are not the only entities providing social structure. The valley has an important history of religious leadership, particularly by the Akhund of Swat, Abdul Ghuffar (1794–1877). Difficult access has made Swat, as well as surrounding areas, largely autonomous if not independent in the past, though the valley maintained some sort of nominal tributary relationship with the imperial powers ruling South Asia. During the epoch of British rule over the subcontinent, Swat remained largely outside the formal orbit of political control until early years of the twentieth century. In 1915, Swat was established as a princely state, a status it maintained until fully integrated into Pakistan in 1969, along with Chitral and Dir.

Swat's physical remoteness, and its political autonomy cum independence, often made it a center of resistance to centralizing political authorities of the north Indian plain. This resistance was not undertaken only by local tribesmen, but also by foreigners who found refuge along the periphery of Swat's remote mountain vastness.[6] In the nineteenth century, initially Sikh and subsequently British dominion over parts of South Asia were violently contested by a core of foreign religious resisters, mainly from Bengal and the United Provinces (modern-day Uttar Pradesh), and later from the Punjab, who at times made common cause with neighboring tribesmen. These rebels, whom the British termed 'Hindustani Fanatics', became a fixture of the Frontier for over one hundred years, both preceding and apparently outlasting British rule.

The 'Hindustani Fanatics', or *mujahidin* as they called themselves, arrived on the Frontier in the late 1820s, led by Sayyid Ahmed of Rai Bareilly who famously waged a *jihad* against Sikh suzerainty along the Frontier.[7] Following his death as a martyr in 1831 at the battle of Balakot, Sayyid Ahmed's surviving followers retreated into the mountains of Swat and established a colony near a village called Sitana on the Indus River in Buner country. Connections with like-minded supporters in north India, centered in the main around Patna, provided subscriptions and recruits, mainly poor Muslim villagers from rural Bengal and Bihar.[8] The 'Fanatics' made peace with the local tribesmen through a combination of political maneuvering and the maintenance of a low profile. They contested Sikh rule by periodic raiding and kidnapping, mainly of Hindu *bania* merchants, indicating a possible class element of their movement.[9]

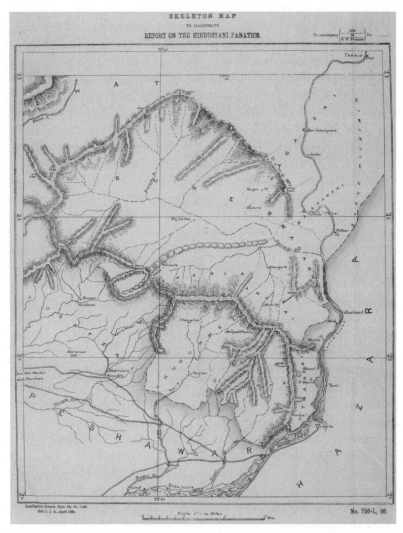

Reproduced by kind permission of the Syndics of Cambridge University Library

The British were well aware of the presence of the 'Hindustanis' and their previous activities along the Frontier. Initially contemporary opinion, official and unofficial, viewed Sayyid Ahmed and his followers rather benignly. Writing in the *Journal of the Asiatic Society of Bengal* in 1832, J.R. Colvin characterized Sayyid Ahmed and his writings, most importantly the *Siraj-al Mustaqim*, as 'Orthodox Sufism'.[10] Despite Colvin's assessment, over the course of the next forty years British understandings of Sayyid Ahmed and his Frontier followers underwent a profound transformation. The 'Hindustani Fanatics' became largely vilified in the eyes of later colonial administrators and were seen as decidedly anti-British.[11] Sayyid Ahmed's studies in Delhi under Shah Abdul Aziz, son of Shah Wali Ullah, and his participation in the *hajj* in the early 1820s were believed to be central in shaping his views and actions, and were considered evidence of his adherence to 'Wahabism' by later British commentators.[12] His followers were likewise stigmatized by the 'Wahabi' label, one deployed not only by the colonial state, but also by other Muslims.[13]

Yet while this vilification of the 'Wahabis' in general, and the 'Fanatics' in particular, has long been understood as widespread, if not hegemonic within colonial opinion, this was not the case.[14] Indeed, the inhabitants of the Frontier colonies were not always referred to as either 'Wahabis' or, a more consistently used term, 'Hindustani Fanatics'. Nor, more importantly, did these epithets always carry the pejorative malice or meaning they seemingly intend. This is not to ignore that British labelings rested upon power inequalities which enabled the British to 'name' the 'Fanatics' as such, a term the Hindustanis themselves neither chose nor recognized. But British labellings were far from monolithic. Indeed, the Hindustanis were referred to as anything from simple 'enthusiasts'[15] to militant 'crescentaders'[16] to 'mujahidin' and even 'talibs'.[17]

The British adopted the term 'Fanatics' in the late 1840s, shortly after they assumed control of the Frontier.[18] However, the evocative meaning of this term changed over time. Originally, it was not imbued with the negative connotations it garnered after the Mutiny, but rather was a contemporary one employed to refer to and characterize religious excess.[19] This was, after all, a period coinciding with the ending of the religious awakening sweeping early Victorian Britain, which many Company officers were personally affected by. There was clearly a moment in the 1860s and 1870s when 'Fanatics' carried negative implications, but this appears to have more an aberration than the norm. By the 1880s, other terms, including 'mujahidin', a term used by the colonists themselves and adopted by the British by 1890, began to appear in the colonial archives.[20] The continued use of the term 'Fanatic' to describe the Frontier colonists, common up to the British withdrawal in 1947, endowed it with a bureaucratic inertia that was more important than any sort of consideration to demonize or vilify the Hindustanis. Even during this period of disrepute, one is struck by how often British officials appeared largely unconcerned by the 'Fanatics' or their message.

Far from maintaining a negative general opinion of the subcontinent's Muslim adherents, prior to the Mutiny much of Anglo-Indian opinion was particular, based on local experience and local knowledge.[21] This particularity of experience meant that terms carried different meanings in different contexts. The presence of 'Wahabis' and 'fanatics' was widespread according to the colonial archives in the pre-Mutiny period, but the 'Wahabis' of Oman which the Bombay Presidency dealt with were a considerably different creature from the 'Wahabis' of Hyderabad in south India, themselves different the Frontier 'Wahabis' who are the focus here. The commonality of experience, understanding and vilification marking later British narratives of the 'fanatics' and 'Wahabis' had to await an all-India crisis that could unify these disparate rumblings.

That crisis was the revolt of 1857, which changed British attitudes towards Islam in general, and towards the Muslims of north central India and Bengal in particular. According to Hunter, and subsequent historians, the British viewed India's Muslims suspiciously, as 'seditious masses' perpetually on the point of rebellion. The 'Hindustani Fanatics' were linked to the Saddiqpur family in Patna, who themselves were linked to the Farazai movement in east Bengal, and, less clearly, to the uprising of Titu Mir in west Bengal in the 1830s.[22] These groups, though acknowledged by many officials to be distinct from one another, were lumped together under the label 'Wahabi'. 'Wahabi' became the ultimate byword for violent religious bigotry and a clear danger to the Crown, as revealed by the trials of 1865–71. It was most chillingly demonstrated through the murder of J.P. Norman, Chief Justice of the Calcutta High Court, in September 1871, as well as the assassination of Lord Mayo, the Viceroy, in the Andamans in February 1872.

By labeling the colonists as 'Wahabis', the British were trying to intellectually catalogue the movement originally founded by Sayyid Ahmed—establishing their genesis from extra-Indian movements of Islamic revival and renewal.[23] This was not simply the British attempting to vilify the colonists and their movement from the outset. The British initially showed scant concern not only for the colonists on the Frontier, but for their own subjects whom they labeled as 'Wahabis' centered in and around Patna. Rather, it appears the British were attempting to locate them within an Islamic intellectual universe.[24]

No single work has been more influential in the (mis)labeling of the 'Hindustani Fanatics' and 'Wahabis' than W.W. Hunters's polemic *The Indian Musalmans*, published in 1871. Hunter linked the Frontier 'Fanatics' to a larger Muslim conspiracy he believed sat at the heart of the Mutiny of 1857. His work came out at the height of the 'Wahabi scare' which centered on a series of trials in 1865–71, which convicted a number of 'Wahabis' for sedition, sentencing them to transportation to the Andaman Islands. Hunter's work added fuel to the fire, inflaming anti-Muslim sensibilities amongst British Indian society and in the process transforming into the demi-official voice of imperial opinion.

Following Hunter, it has become an accepted totem that the British 'official mind' and Anglo-Indian society were fearful of Muslim sedition, and predicated their actions and attitudes on such an assessment. Indeed, many contemporary observers characterized the 'Wahabi' prosecutions as the dismantling of a vast conspiracy whose threat to the Raj was on par with that of 1857. In framing the issue as a 'conspiracy', one marked by secrecy and fanaticism, little understood by those uninitiated in its ways, these observers harked back to other colonial experiences of the occult, namely *thuggee*.[25] As with *thuggee*, much of the 'Wahabi' conspiracy was based on the multiple understandings, and misunderstandings, which marked the Raj's 'official mind'. However, unlike the state's reaction there—creating an institutional investigative division which essentialized, catalogued and standardized knowledge into a colonially constructed conspiracy— institutional approaches towards the 'Wahabis' remained balkanized and disjointed. Investigations were the responsibility of local authorities, which at least initially communicated poorly with one another. The state did not invest in the construction of an anti-colonial conspiracy as it did in the case of the *thug*s.[26]

The colonial state's lack of a clearly coordinated institutional response was telling. Hunter's linkages and insinuations of an insidious and disturbing conspiracy was neither endorsed by nor echoed in official circles. As early as 1852, Lord Dalhousie dismissed the alarm local authorities voiced about the 'Fanatics' and their 'Wahabi' supporters, writing that '[t]he result of the impressions I have received has not been to create any anxiety on my mind'.[27] William Taylor's actions in Patna during the Mutiny were disowned both by the Lieutenant-Governor of Bengal, Frederick James Halliday, and by the Governor-General, Lord Canning. The idea that some sort of apocryphal Muslim conspiracy lay at the heart of the Mutiny was discounted with L. Bowring's report in 1859.[28] And while the appellate bench of the Lahore High Court upheld Herbert Edwardes' convictions of the Umballa conspirators from the first of the 'Wahabi' trials, it threw considerable doubt on his legal logic and reduced the sentences.[29]

Even when the British were busy prosecuting a number of their supporters, they treated the 'Fanatics' who returned to British Indian territories with marked leniency. Mayo ordered that any wanting to return to their homes in British territories be welcomed, instructing Punjab authorities, 'If true that the Hindoostanees from Sittana [sic] are taking refuge in British territory and giving themselves up, receive them, and send them to their homes through the Police, giving them something for their expenses, and taking care that they are properly treated'.[30]

He also endorsed the release of most of those arrested as 'Fanatic' supporters in the Punjab and Bengal.[31] And Col. F.R. Pollock, the man charged with watching and if possible extirpating the colony of 'Fanatics' during the 'Wahabi' trials of the 1860s and 1870s, viewed the rank and file recruits, as well as their supporters in India, as no worse than misled but honest religious adherents, comparing the latter to subscribers of the Moravian mission.[32] Such sentiments indicate that the British thought little of the danger posed directly by the 'Fanatics' themselves.[33]

The notion that there was a widely held fear of 'Wahabi' efforts to topple the colonial state does not stand serious scrutiny. When one peels back the rhetoric of Hunter, William Muir[34] and even A.C. Lyall,[35] officialdom, especially its more senior members, appears to have been largely unconcerned. None of the defendants in any of the 'Wahabi' trials were executed, despite their convictions for waging war against the Queen.[36] By the 1880s, all the convicted 'Wahabi' activists found themselves 'rehabilitated' by the colonial state—released from exile by a general amnesty issued by Lord Ripon and returned to the scene of their earlier conspiracies. One wonders if Hunter's polemic would have achieved the definitive stature it did had it not been for the assassination of Lord Mayo. Hunter's work was both heavily criticized and hotly contested by a number of people, not least of whom was Sir Sayyid Ahmed Khan. Many of these rebuttals, written by middle class Indian Muslim loyalists, were printed by either Government or Anglo-Indian presses, unlike Hunter's own work which was produced by a private publisher in London.[37]

The colonial record simply does not reflect a widely held perception that either the 'Wahabis' or the 'Fanatics' posed a pressing threat to the colonial regime. One repeatedly finds senior officials skeptical, if not wholly dismissive of the alarm and enthusiasm shown by their subordinates. These junior officers competed for their superiors' attentions, and patronage, in the marketplace of imperial crises. It would therefore serve any subaltern well to promptly inform central authorities of danger averted by their timely and forceful action. But many of the senior officials involved were familiar with imperial conspiracies, especially Lord Mayo who was Secretary of State for Ireland during the failed Fenian revolt of 1867.[38] They were thus not easily excited when their subordinates screamed of conspiracy and bloody murder. The top remained largely unconvinced.

The cacophony of voices marking contemporary debates and correspondence has been seemingly lost on subsequent generations whose understandings of the period are largely mediated through Hunter's writings. Calcutta's skepticism has been consistently overlooked or ignored by subsequent scholarship. At the time, there was no flattening and homogenization of the 'official mind', but rather a continual contestation, skepticism and even schizophrenia within an imperial bureaucracy manned by individuals holding starkly divergent views conditioned by different experiences and backgrounds.[39] What this reveals about the colonial state is important. Far from being a uniform informational order subject and beholden to contemporary caricatures of anti-colonial conspiracies and dangerous natives, in this instance at least a picture of a more intellectually vibrant universe emerges.

The reasons why later colonial officials and historians followed Hunter's lead and homogenized the 'official mind' are necessarily multiple. Amongst the most important, however, was the need for a singular view upon which to base the construction of colonial epistomologies about the Raj's Muslim subjects. Later British policies were based on the inherent difference and dangerousness of India's Muslims. Colonial administrators were not the only ones with an interest in constructing neat ethnographic and historical narratives of separateness. The vision of potentially seditious Muslim masses, though rejected by Indian Muslim leaders like Sir Sayyid Ahmed Khan, was nonetheless skillfully deployed by them to gain advantage from the Raj. The politics of Muslim separatism rested on the distinctiveness of India's Islamic *umma* from the 'Hindu' majority, and the recognition of this by the British. Sayyid Ahmed of Rai Bareilly, his followers and their progeny were depicted as religious 'fanatics' rather than peasant rebels, cultural refugees or economic migrants in search of opportunity beyond the British frontier. They served as a rhetorical foil enabling both colonial officialdom and Muslim loyalists to neatly contain dissent within clearly delineated bounds. This enabled the powers that be to minimize the importance and breadth of that dissent, constructing it as a wild aberration from the accepted colonial norm rather than a serious challenge to its multiple problems.

The 'Fanatics' and the Colonial State

The relationship between the colonial state and the 'Hindustani Fanatics' was unevenly marked by periods of ambivalence and quietude punctuated by occasional episodes of antipathy and violence. The British first 'discovered' the 'Fanatics' machinations against the Raj in 1852 when evidence a channel of secret and seditious communication between Sitana and their supporters in Patna implicated a *munshi* (native secretary) of the Fourth Native Infantry regiment in Rawalpindi.[40] In January 1853, the Company dispatched an expedition to chastise the 'Fanatics', who, it was reported, dispersed on the appearance of British forces.[41] During the 1857 Mutiny, a belligerent offshoot established nearby at Mangal Thana provided refuge to the surviving mutineers of the 55th Native Infantry (Rawalpindi) and became an 'asylum for bad characters'.[42] The British again sent an expedition to deal with the 'Fanatics', storming the heights of Mangal Thana where they found a citadel built of large stone and fine timber to house a permanent and sizeable garrison. Amongst the dead the British reportedly found down-country Indians from Rampur and Bengal.[43] Chastened, the survivors fled to a village called Mulka, which they furnished to accommodate upwards of 3,000 men.[44]

By the summer of 1863, the 'Fanatics' had resettled both Sitana and Mangal Thana. Such a direct challenge to British authority and prestige could not be countenanced. In October, the Raj launched what later became known as the Ambela campaign. Despite plans for a quick and surgical strike, the Raj found itself bogged down in a brutal frontier war with the tribesmen through whose territory they attempted to pass.[45] After two months, the commitment of over 9,000 troops, and nearly 900 casualties, the British were able to outlast the fractious tribal alliance they faced. A negotiated settlement led to the destruction of Sitana and Malka by local tribesmen under British supervision, achieving the expedition's ostensible objective.[46] Success, however, came at a high price. The Ambela campaign proved one of the costliest and bloodiest little frontier wars the Raj mounted in the nineteenth century.[47]

The Ambela campaign marked an important and ultimately short-lived rupture in British attitudes towards the 'Hindustani Fanatics' on the Frontier. However, its effects on attitudes towards their Muslim subjects in the subcontinent would be of greater consequence. In practical terms, it led to the break-up of the colony, which struggled to re-establish itself in tribal territory for the next twenty years. Indeed, the Raj did not violently engage the 'Fanatics' on such a scale ever again, and the 'Fanatics' desisted from embroiling themselves against British arms until 1888.[48] Yet Ambela became a catalyst for a colonial crackdown on the 'Fanatics' 'Wahabi' supporters in British territories, leading to the famed 'Wahabi' trials of 1865–71.

Just as important, Ambela led to a rupture in relations between the 'Fanatics' and their tribal hosts. The violence of the British expedition turned the local tribesmen against them, forcing them to live 'an uncomfortable and harassed existence'.[49] The Akhund of Swat, long a critic of the 'Fanatics' whom he denounced as 'Wahabis', forced their expulsion and in their retreat decimated their numbers.[50] Their treatment at the hands of both the Akhund and the various tribes of independent territory raises the question of the 'Fanatics' position amongst the peoples of the Frontier. The 'Fanatics' longevity there, over a century, has led some to point towards the tribesmen's ethos of hospitality.[51] At the same time, colonial sources insisted the tribesmen's patience was lubricated by the 'Fanatics' cash payments, making them a source of income in a poor area.[52] Either way, 'their existence so long among bold and impatient races is almost unaccountable', presenting something of an enigma.[53]

The 'Fanatics' presence amongst the tribesmen along the Frontier was no accident. Sayyid Ahmed's *jihad* against the Sikhs was located outside British territories at least in part because of the injunction that Muslims needed to follows the laws of their rulers, even if the lands they inhabited were part of the *dar-al harb*.[54] Once there, Sayyid Ahmed and his followers embedded themselves in local society and social systems in such a way as to ensure their long-term survival in what was potentially an extremely hostile environment. Early on, they formed a key alliance with a family of powerful local Sayyids on whose lands they were eventually given refuge at Sitana.[55] Often physically occupying borderlands on the extremities of tribal areas, the 'Fanatics' also occupied the social interstices demarcating different tribal groups. The 'Fanatics' played an important role as intermediaries in Pashtun society, something facilitated both by their religious legitimacy and charisma, as well as by their status outside local tribes' genealogies.[56] Yet they were successful at mobilizing the tribes only when the latter felt pressured by the penetrating influences of a centralizing colonial state, as during the Ambela campaign.

The 'Fanatics' were able to serve as religious intermediaries in tribal territory at least partly because they had a shared vocabulary with which they could relate to the Frontier tribesmen. As adherents of Sayyid Ahmed, the 'Fanatics' were part of a brotherhood resembling Sufi orders, the *tariqa-i Muhammadiya*, where loyalty was based on shared discipleship to a common *pir*. Such language of obedience and belonging resonated with the tribesmen's own genealogically defined system of social obligation, even if it did not directly overlap. But the ability of Sayyid Ahmed to root himself and his movement in tribal territory required more than simply the shared forms of Sufi religious practice. Rather, Sayyid Ahmed himself must have been familiar with the social norms and political language of the Frontier's Pashtun inhabitants. He had long operated in the Rohilla lands of the UP, and also had served in the army of the Nawab of Tonk, himself a Pashtun from Buner near Swat, where many Rohilla Pathans were employed.[57] He thus inhabited a Pashtun cultural milieu, which would have made him both familiar with and experienced in the language of belonging and alliance used by the Pashtun along the Frontier.[58] This would account for the ease with which he established himself amongst the Yusufzai of the Swat valley in the late 1820s. Sayyid Ahmed's subsequent martyrdom, his brotherhood of the *tariqa-i Muhammadiya* and the cultivation of a hagiographic memory of him, amongst both locals and the wider Muslim community of South Asia, provided his follows with much needed sanctity which would be an adequate substitute for their lack of genealogical connection with the Pashtun.

The importance and persistence of the forms of Sufi religious observance to the survival of the 'Fanatic' colony and Sayyid Ahmed's movement as a whole were little noticed by colonial authorities, despite J.R. Colvin's early observation of its centrality. Throughout its history, the Frontier colony and its adherents employed explicit Sufi imagery which likely resonated amongst the tribesmen. One such image, repeating itself time and again, was the iconography of the cave. Following his death in 1831, rumors spread that Sayyid Ahmed had not been killed but rather had retreated from the world only to reappear at the right time. The British reported that when newly arrived recruits from Bengal insisted on seeing some evidence of the Sayyid being alive, they were pointed to a figure at the mouth of a cave in the distance in the dwindling light.[59] Further, 'Asmas', the final location of the 'Fanatics' colony after 1900, is believed to have been a corruption of the Pashto word for 'cave'.[60] The continued use of Sufi rhetoric and imagery thus gave the Hindustanis traction in a tribal world, which the unbridled textualism of the 'Wahabis' would not have been afforded.

Post-Wahabi Trials

Even at the height of the 'Wahabi' scare, British officials largely affected indifference to the survivors of the Ambela campaign who remained in tribal territory. By 1883 they had regrouped at a place called Palosi, where they built a 'mud fort on the banks of the Indus'. The colony included nearly 600 fighting men, divided into seven companies referred to as 'jumiats' of about sixty to one hundred men each; five of these consisted of Bengalis, one of Punjabis and one of men from Delhi and the UP. Each man was armed with a musket or rifle, mostly Enfields, and the colony was reported to have arms for 2,000 men. At the time they were attempting to make percussion caps, but had not perfected the process. They had two Bengali gunsmiths who were charged with the maintenance of ordnance.[61] Despite the 'Wahabi' trials, the colony apparently continued to receive cash remittances from India unhindered,[62] and it was even rumored that they had obtained percussion caps for their muskets from Jullundur in the Punjab.[63] But the 'Fanatics' unity of purpose was shattered by disagreement over their relative inactivity *vis-à-vis* the British. Some abandoned the colony in protest of the failure to fight the British.[64] This disunity would continue to plague the Frontier 'Fanatics' for the remainder of British rule.

The late nineteenth century marks an interesting period for the 'Fanatic' colony and its relations with both the British and the surrounding tribesmen. In 1885, the leader of the colony, Maulvi Abdullah, wrote to British authorities directly, claiming that messengers carrying remittances worth Rs. 8,000 from British India had been stopped and interfered with by British subjects. In this extraordinary correspondence, Abdullah threatened the Government with unspecified reprisals if no reply was received within nine days.[65] Nothing was sent, with apparently no ill consequence. If the 'Fanatics' by and large refrained from directly confronting the British, the British in turn refrained from antagonizing the 'Fanatics'. They continued to allow relatively free passage to the colony, even of native men of standing with connections to princely states.[66] It was also at this time the 'Fanatics' made their first overtures to the Amir of Afghanistan, who denounced their labeling as 'Wahabis'.[67]

For the remainder of the nineteenth century, and into the early years of the twentieth, the 'Fanatics' refrained from openly antagonizing the British, although these years proved some of the most tumultuous for the Raj along the Frontier. The 'Fanatics' remained on the sidelines during the Bunerwal troubles of 1885, their participation in the 1897 Frontier revolt proved nothing noteworthy,[68] and during the 1908 disturbances they made only a 'half-hearted attempt to stir up trouble'.[69] The tribesmen's willingness to compromise with the British was reported to have made the Hindustanis wary of directly joining in tribal uprisings.[70] They did, however, use the hostilities as an opportunity to increase their fund-raising in north India, a tactic they repeated time and again.[71] But their lack of anti-British activities, save violent rhetoric, undermined their reputation as religious warriors and made their life along the Frontier rather uncomfortable.[72]

Their relative silence did not mean, however, that the 'Fanatics' were inactive. New recruits regularly arrived, with 120 from Bengal, the North-West Provinces and the Punjab appearing between April and July 1895 alone. The British described these men as 'all men of no position, being of the faqir and "talib-ilm" class' who arrived in twos and threes, passing themselves off as religious wanderers in British territories. They joined a colony estimated to number 580 inhabitants, 300 of whom were fighting men organized into one company of one hundred and four companies of fifty men each. These included twenty-four *sowar*s, fourteen gunners and twenty drivers. However, the arrival of new recruits was offset by the attrition of those who dispersed to their homes in British India, thought to be somewhere in the range of twenty to thirty per year.[73]

Despite their numbers, officials continued to adhere to the line adopted in the wake of the Ambela campaign, namely to treat the 'Fanatics' as people of no consequence. The Commissioner of Peshawar wrote in 1899:

The least notice taking of these people the better. Even if they ask for permission to come to India, I would treat them openly as of no account, and simply say that they might come or go as they please provided they behave themselves, and live out of the Punjab. I would, however, watch them as a precaution, and if they were found intriguing mischievously deport them again.[74]

With the death of their long-serving leader Maulvi Abdulla in 1903, it was thought the 'Fanatic' colony might break up. Instead, fifty more recruits arrived from Bengal in that year alone.[75] But their tenure remained insecure and they eventually relocated to a place called 'Smast' on the Barandu River, twelve miles from their old redoubt at Sitana. Smast, or 'Asmas' as it was also referred to, ended up being their final settlement, which they occupied continuously until the end days of the Raj in 1947.

The activities of the *mujahidin* again attracted British attentions during the First World War, when they appeared to be at the heart of trouble brewing on the Frontier. They allied themselves with a local religious notable, the Haji Sahib of Turangzai, who fomented anti-colonial intrigues along the Frontier after he fled Peshawar in 1915.[76] Further, the colonial authorities believed the colony to be in contact with the Afghan government, as well as Indian nationalists. Yet the British continued to consider the 'Fanatics' as not a danger, an assessment shared by their supporters in British India who dispatched 'several persons of substance... from Bengal, the Punjab, and other places in India, and have accused them [the 'Fanatics'] of deriving an income for many years from the enemies of the British Government, without making any return in the way of hostile action'.[77]

George Roos-Keppel, the Chief Commissioner of the North-West Frontier Province, offered a concise picture of both the 'Fanatics' and

British attitudes towards them in a letter he authored to the Foreign Secretary to the Government of India in October 1915. In it, he wrote:

I have been keeping an eye on the Hindustani fanatics and so far have found nothing to show that they are particularly active or dangerous. There are about four or five hundred of them in Chamla, living under a communistic system but ruled by their Amir, as the chief fanatic is called, the majority of them are the descendents of the Mujai-ud-din of mutiny days but from time to time since individuals mostly from the neighbourhoods of Lucknow and Moradabad have joined them and have also settled down and married there. In the course of the last fifteen years a good many of them have been to see me and I have had long talks with them and have come to the conclusion that their fanaticism is the trade by which they live and that they are not at all anxious to be committed to any warlike acts. At the same time in order to get their 'shukarana' they are bound to show some hostility towards us. A deputation goes every year to the Amir and receives presents from him but the deputation has several times been warned that Mujai-ud-din will get no more money from Cabul unless they do something to deserve it. They also get contributions form various parts of India. I am told that quite recently a Hindustani visited the fanatics and asked to see their Amir who, however, distrusted the visitor and declined to see him. The man went away without giving his name; he was escorted to the Indus by one of the fanatics and on leaving gave him a sealed parcel for the Amir, which, when opened, was found to contain Rs. 2,000/-.[78]

In the same letter, however, the 'Fanatics' were implicated in the disappearance of fifteen students from the Lahore Medical College who apparently fled to Asmas in the hope of joining an anti-British *jihad*.[79]

Notwithstanding Roos-Keppel's reference to 'our old friends of Mutiny times', and his assessment that they were 'professional fanatics... [who] have loudly beaten the drum of Islam but simultaneously sent messengers to assure me that they had no intention of doing anything more serious',[80] the 'Fanatics' activities became increasingly belligerent. They participated in disturbances along the Frontier during the war and actively agitated against the British war effort. At one point, posters appeared in the villages of Mardan 'with a manifesto from the Amir of Hindustani Fanatics that the day of liberty has dawned, Russians and English having been defeated by the Turks and Germans'.[81] The colony was later implicated in what became known as the 'Silk Letter case', which centered around clandestine communications between Indian nationalists and the Afghan government.[82] The 'Fanatics' renewed activity, after years of relative silence, aroused British attentions and led them to step up efforts at both surveillance and suppression.

Typical of that surveillance was a loyal Pathan recruited as an 'approver' and referred to in the records simply as 'G.B'. He originally gained access to the colony by claiming a desire to follow the Lahore students.[83] He proved a wellspring of information, providing a detailed picture of the colony and its politics and activities. According to G.B., the colony's population was approximately 600 strong, of whom 400 were fighting men. These men did no other work but military drill according to the English style, the manual for which had been translated into Arabic. The colony was completely dependent on remittances from India, as well as the Amir of Afghanistan who annually sent Rs. 2,000. Remittances must have been significant as G.B. estimated the monthly outlay of the colony at Rs. 15,000, which included the daily entertainment of nearly 100 guests by Niamatullah. If these numbers were true, the colony must have been a significant economic engine for the area.

G.B. disagreed with earlier assessments of the 'Fanatics' armed strength, stating they maintained only 120 Martini-Henry rifles, five eleven-shot rifles and nine seven-shot ones, as well as twelve pistols. This hardly presented a pressing threat to the eight battalions of the Indian army stationed along the Frontier. With regard to recruitment, '[t]he Amir's men travel throughout Hindustan and wherever they find anyone quarrelling with his family, or discontented at home, they bring him up to the Amir, telling him many lies to deceive him'. G.B. reported the *mujahidin* to be 'void of spirit' and largely unpopular with the local tribesmen with whom they were at feud for calling them 'kafirs'. Finally, he noted the presence of a press, run by a former head clerk of a Sikh state, probably Futehpur, which the colony used to produce propaganda sheets.[84] G.B.'s report depicted a healthy and active colony, whose members even included a father and son who were a *subedar* and *jemadar* respectively in the British Indian army. It should be noted that the rich picture provided by G.B.'s reports cost the Raj little. Yet while the cost of surveillance was nugatory, the cost of cataloguing, archiving and using that surveillance for over 100 years as the British did was not.

In 1916, Amir Niamatullah addressed the Chief Commissioner of the North-West Frontier Province seeking to establish peace with the Government to ensure the colony would no longer be subject to harassment. His letters were prompted by the arrest of couriers bringing collections for the colony from British India worth over Rs. 8,000.[85]

Niamatullah insisted that the colony had been at peace with the Government for years, but that if the Government continued to hassle it by interfering with the free movement of its peaceful members, the *mujahidin* would be forced to raid British territories.[86] After some negotiation, conducted on behalf of the *mujahidin* by Maulvi Barakat Ali, a former Extra Assistant Commissioner and Sub-judge in the Lyallpur District, Punjab and Maulvi Muhammad Ali (BA Cantab), former head of the Habibia College Kabul, a settlement was reached.[87] In return for the *mujahidin* assuming responsibility for all members of the colony and ensuring they did not behave in a hostile fashion against the Raj, the British allowed them free intercourse with the Indian plains and would release those arrested, restoring their property to them.[88]

Niamatullah's overtures to the Chief Commissioner were in keeping with a somewhat perplexing relationship with the Raj, full of violent language which failed to inspire violent action. Yet this disjuncture between words and actions was intentional. The Hindustanis' 'fanaticism' was a practiced technique of opposition that gave them a space within colonial society and political discourse. A pain they might have been to many administrators, but they were not beyond the pale. Instead, the 'Fanatics' technique of opposition meant that they became a fixture of the British Indian scene. Colonial authorities not only found the *mujahidin*'s lack of violent opposition enough to justify their inaction, but more importantly used their continued existence on the Frontier as a foil against which administrators could direct or channel more serious challenges to imperial authority. Thus, according to Hunter, the Frontier 'Fanatics' lay at the heart of a conspiracy underlying the Mutiny of 1857, rather than the Raj's moment of danger lying in an unaddressed accumulation of local grievances violently suppressed. Relations between the 'Fanatics' and the Raj, odd as they may appear, served both parties well during their century-long intercourse.

The seeming *entente cordiale* arrived at between Niamatullah and Roos-Keppel had its skeptics in both British and *mujahidin* ranks. C.R. Cleveland of the Criminal Intelligence Office wrote to the Foreign Secretary with his department's reservations of Roos-Keppel's secret peace. He noted,

Sir George appears to contemplate a future in which the fanatics will be at secret peace with us, while their supports in India will imagine that they are hostile and will continue to vent their jehad feelings by sending subscriptions, emissaries and disciples secretly to the Fanatics. We are satisfied that on the part of the Indian jehadis their relations with the fanatics have been tinged all through with a feeling of guilt and sedition, and we are extremely reluctant that similar conditions should prevail in the future. It is very unhealthy and probably dangerous for a number of person in India to continue to feel that they are secretly aiding and abetting the enemies of Government and we are most anxious to remove the outward appearance and inner consciousness of guilty practices from the whole community of Ahl-i-Hadis and Muhammadis. Concealed and secret peace with the Amir of the fanatics will fail apparently to change the practice of the Indian jehadis from political guilt to harmless religion.[89]

Concern for the 'Fanatics' psychological well-being aside, there were clearly some who understood their continued presence on the Frontier as a beacon of resistance to their religious brethren on the Indian plains.

Within the *mujahidin* camp the agreement led to a rift. Many of the schismatics fled to Chamarkand, an offshoot of the main colony at Asmas, in order to remain implacably hostile towards the British.[90] The Chamarkand colonists lived around the tomb of Mulla Hadda, an important local religious figure, which meant they could not be attacked without agitating the tribesmen.[91] Chamarkand became the center of anti-British activities, in clear contravention of the wishes of the Amir-i Mujahidin Niamatullah.[92] But Niamatullah was murdered in 1921 for his rapprochement with Roos-Keppel, clearing the path for reconciliation between the recently divorced colonies.[93]

At this time the *mujahidin* appear to have entered their final phase of hostile activism against the British. The colonies, in particular the more militant one at Chamarkand, were connected with both Indian nationalists and Bolshevik agents. The British believed they provided a conduit for weapons to the Bengali 'terrorists' and the Akali Sikhs.[94] Charmarkand was thought to receive Rs. 1000 per month from the Central Khalifat Committee and played a central role as a conduit between Indian 'revolutionaries', Kabul and the Soviets.[95] By 1925, the British had evidence of Maulvi Bashir, the leader of the Chamarkand colony, meeting the Soviet minister to Kabul, Mr. Stark,[96] and that the *mujahidin* received a substantial subsidy from the Bolsheviks.[97]

Although the British recognized that the Chamarkand *mujahidin* in and of themselves presented little danger,[98] their potential as a key link between dissatisfied Indian nationalists, intriguing Russian agents, and an untrustworthy Afghan government was unsettling. An intelligence assessment from 1925 noted,

The Chamarkand colony is extremely dangerous in some ways, but it has not itself the influence to further the general scheme which the Bolsheviks have at heart, and for the purpose of spreading Bolshevism among the masses in British India the colony can achieve very little of itself. The danger lies in its use as a link, or agency, between the Russians and the Extremist leaders of British India, and it is certain that it is chiefly of this purpose that it is being financed by the Russians.[99]

Consequently, the British sought to sow dissension between *mujahidin* colonists at Asmas and those at Chamarkand, using the former to curb the excesses of the latter.[100] Although it was a potential 'wasps nest', an undisclosed 'series of long, patient, and thoughtful steps' had rendered Chamarkand 'quiet and harmless' as far as the Raj was concerned.[101] Indeed, the British saw it as a potential 'emergency safety-valve' for the 'diehards' of the parent colony.[102]

The members of this 'unholy alliance' each had their own reasons to act collectively against the British. The Afghans proved consistently fickle in their support. As early as the 1880s the *mujahidin* were attempting to solicit Afghan support in the form of annual allowances. According to British records, the Afghans conditioned their support on explicit activities to benefit Kabul. Such activities included fomenting disquiet and unrest amongst the tribes of Bajaur and independent territory aimed at destabilizing British paramountcy in the area. The *mujahidin* found themselves increasingly dependent on Afghan subsidies as subscriptions from British India evaporated.[103] Kabul offered its largesse in the late 1920s, particularly to Maulvi Bashir who, it was reported, was promised Rs. 10,000 by the Amir at one point and given Rs. 24,000 by Abdul Azizi Khan, Minister of the Interior, at another.[104] In return for their investment, Afghan authorities appear to have exercised a modicum of control over the *mujahidin*, going so far as to warn them not to act in support of anti-British tribal activities without orders from the Afghan foreign ministry.[105] However, the *mujahidin*'s incessant infighting meant they were seen as a poor investment by Kabul, which suspended its annual subsidies in December 1934.[106]

During more than a decade of activism from about 1922 to 1934, the *mujahidin* undertook activities aimed at undermining British rule. They attempted to establish 'anti-British' schools along the Frontier, successfully setting up two with Russian money channeled through Chamarkand.[107] Recruits and subscriptions continued to trickle to the *mujahidin* from British India, but the colonies became increasingly reliant on Afghan subsidies. They published a newspaper, *Al-Mujahid*, originally in Persian but later in Pashto as well,[108] in which they wrote articles decrying British atrocities,[109] supporting the actions of the Afghan government,[110] and informing the readership of events in the wider world.[111] The British considered the paper did a 'good deal of harm' and banned it from their territories.[112] They even declared Chamarkand a 'revolutionary organisation'.[113] Yet despite British fears of the Bolshevik menace employing a motley collection of religious fanatics to spread its seed in South Asia, as well as concerns regarding Afghan intrigues along the Frontier, little came of the *mujahidin*'s efforts. Indeed, the colonies and their 'Fanatical' inhabitants made little impression on the Raj. They continued to be handicapped by perpetual infighting and participated minimally in uprisings against the British along the Frontier, such as the revolt led by the Faqir of Ipi in 1937.

During the final years of the British Raj, the funding sources and recruitment patterns of the *mujahidin* underwent some important changes. Whereas the 'Fanatics' previously had been largely reliant on subscriptions from British India, by the 1920s the *mujahidin* had become essentially beholden to subsidies provided by the Afghan Government. As these became more irregular and eventually dried up in the 1930s, the *mujahidin* turned to collections from their locality, accepting subscriptions from Chitral and local tribesmen.[114] Just as their sources of funding changed, so too did the composition of the *mujahidin* recruits. Bengalis, referred to as 'Hindustanis', became less prominent in the movement, while Punjabis and even Pathans took on an increasingly visible profile.[115] An offshoot colony in Waziristan even included some Shias, a striking fact given the *mujahidin*'s sectarian rhetoric.[116] What this demonstrates, is that over time rhetoric and its objectives changed, assuming the language of resistance which was becoming widespread both in South Asia and the contemporary wider world. If we understand the 'Fanatic' *mujahidin* as first and foremost resisters against alien rule who used religious rhetoric to explain their cause to themselves and the world at larger, we can better understand their later alliances with Indian nationalists and even Bolsheviks who offered a new idiom of resistance for a new time.

The British continued to watch the *mujahidin* until their withdrawal from the subcontinent in 1947. During the Second World War, the *mujahidin* remained largely quiet, although in 1942 they were mentioned on 'Azad Hind' radio from Berlin as a contact point for all anti-

British activists who wanted to get in touch with the Axis powers.[117] In terms of their relationship with the rapidly developing politics of Indian nationalism, they seemed largely indifferent. At one point, however, the *mujahidin* assumed an anti-Congress stance, warning through their newspaper *Al-Mujahid* that a purely Hindu Congress sought to establish Hindu dominance in India.[118] They also spread pro-Muslim League propaganda in Bajaur in the run-up to partition in 1947.[119] The last entry regarding the *mujahidin* in British records appears in the weekly intelligence summary from Peshawar for the week ending 21 June 1947.[120] As for their post-independence fortunes, these have yet to be explored. However, local tribesmen of Bajaur are reputed to remember Chamarkand as '*Da Mujahidino kali* (village of the Mujahidin)'.[121]

Legacies

The Frontier 'Fanatics' apparently outlasted British power in the subcontinent, making their uninterrupted presence in the area over a century in length. This in itself is a rather amazing feat. Outsiders to the tribal societies which they found themselves embedded in and often at odds with, the 'Fanatics' nonetheless carried on a precarious existence and established a home on the Frontier lasting multiple generations. They were in regular contact with sympathetic supporters in north India whose spiritual and material support proved key to their survival. They successfully recruited local tribesmen into rebellion against the Raj, most spectacularly during the Ambela campaign of 1863. The 'Fanatics' survival on the Frontier is itself a unique story. But their longevity was no mere idiosyncratic episode. Rather, it had important and long-lasting consequences for the Frontier, the British Raj, and South Asian society more widely.

The 'Hindustanis' in large part survived and indeed thrived as a community in the independent tribal areas because of their ability to embed themselves within local social systems through a common idiom of belonging, as well as their apparent utility and value to local tribes as sources of capital—economic, religious and political. Additionally, the regular arrival and departure of recruits from British territories seem to have continuously renewed the colonies' population. At least some of these recruits brought their families, and many of the reports regarding the health of the 'Fanatic' colonies refer to the presence of women and children. The changing ethnic composition of the community also affected its ability to survive, with Pathan tribesmen increasingly playing a role after the First World War. Yet there is little evidence to indicate that the colonies formed anything more than a symbiotic relationship with their local hosts. There is no indication that *mujahidin* intermarried with local tribes and Pashtun social mores mitigated against such a possibility. The colonists thus formed an integral, but unincorporated part of local society on the Frontier.

What, if anything, does the *mujahidin*'s century of activism on the Frontier tell us about the nature of revolt and religiously inspired violence in the region? In a way, they represent an archetype of revolt from which one can derive a pattern. We see a charismatic religious leader with a call to reform, misunderstood by external powers, but one with deep linkages and resonances in local religious rhetoric, understandings and sensibilities (that is, Sufism). The leader's reliance on a religious brotherhood renders his relations understandable within local social systems. In addition there are possible claims of belonging and relation that go deeper than simply religious affinity, as in the case of Sayyid Ahmed of Rai Bareilly. These connections enable the leader, who has a core following of foreign adherents themselves totally alien to the tribal universe and thus guests, to broker wider alliances when circumstances permit. Those circumstances are largely defined by the intrusions of a centralizing authority which is perceived by local tribesmen as threatening their independence and autonomy. They are anti-statist. The language cementing these alliances is religious in character, with Islam providing the tribesmen with a broader lexicon allowing them to relate to the wider, non-tribal and non-Muslim world.

The 'Fanatics' choice of a religious idiom for confrontation is unsurprising. Most revolts against colonial authority in the nineteenth century contained some sort of religious idiom to explain and justify their revolt, both to adherents and ostensibly to those they revolted against. The Mutiny was the example *par excellence*, filled as it was with millenarian overtures and innuendos. What is particularly interesting in the 'Fanatics' case is not their use of religion as an idiom of resistance, but the adaptations they made to that idiom over time in order to meet changing circumstances and maintain their relevance. Thus the 'Wahabis' of the mid-nineteenth century found themselves aligned with Sikh nationalists and Soviet Bolsheviks in the 1920s. By 1947, they were actively spreading Muslim League propaganda in the tribal areas. As important as the idiom of expression was the rhetorical value of violence to the 'Fanatics'. For adherents of a *'jihadi'* culture eager to bring about the downfall of the infidel *sarkar*, the 'Fanatics' reticence about engaging in violence is noteworthy. Instead, as a community they came to an incredibly durable understanding with the colonial state which, for the most part, saw them as innocent of anything more than rhetorical violence. Even those who disagreed with this stance, and spilled blood within the *mujahidin* community as part of that disagreement, refrained from attacking the colonial state. The 'Fanatics' thus fashioned a legacy of rhetorical opposition to the state, which arguably has been taken up by other members of South Asia's Islamic *umma*.

An equally important aspect of the 'Fanatics' legacy is how they defined public colonial discourse about Islam for the rest of the nineteenth century, and well into the twentieth. They were central to the construction of a colonial epistemology of otherness, namely India's Muslims. According to the likes of Hunter, the 'Fanatics' were the embodiment of the 'conspiracy' considered fundamental to the Mutiny of 1857, but never proved. Yet as the multiple, often contradictory attitudes held by various members of the colonial establishment towards the 'Fanatics' clearly demonstrate, there was no universal fear of sedition and distrust of Muslims. The colonial state nonetheless invested out of all proportion to their supposed significance in containing and policing the 'Fanatics' and their message. At no time was it thought these 'Fanatics' imperiled British authority. But that did not stop a century of surveillance, at times quite intensive, of this remote colony. The way the British shaped their prosecution of the 'Fanatics' and their 'Wahabi' supporters largely shaped the topography on which debates about public religious identities, particularly Muslim ones, later unfolded. This is a case of the 'periphery' defining the 'center'. The Frontier not only demarcated the limits of British authority, but also the nature of the colonial sphere.

The case of the 'Fanatics' serves to underline some important elements of the nature of the Frontier that have appeared time and again. First, their outsize importance in debates within the colonial state and public sphere, mirroring more generally the near-obsessive concern shown about the North-West Frontier, forces a reassessment of the relationship between center and periphery. This reassessment has its parallel in the need for a reassessment of the rural/urban dialectic that marks much of the current anthropological literature discussed in later chapters. Second, the fact the 'Fanatics' in the main came from places other than the Frontier, yet accommodated themselves within it, demonstrates the heterogeneity that has historically constituted this space. But third, the 'Fanatics' relative isolation and usual inability to graft their cause onto the grievances of local tribesmen evinces the fragmented nature of experience on the Frontier. At one and the same time they were an extremely secluded community of believers, but one that could relate to the Frontier world they were part of through circumstance and common idiom. It is this tension—of difference and similarity—which has historically been, and still remains, central to the construction of the Frontier.

4

THE PAST BECOMES PRESENT

The Frontier's past provides fertile ground for understanding its present. The last three chapters have demonstrated the centrality of the Frontier to the development of political authority in South Asia during the colonial period. They have also indicated that the experiences of political authorities, as well as local peoples, over the past two centuries have been extremely varied along the length of the Frontier. Those political authorities, though often acting in response to a set of unique local circumstances, have nonetheless conceptualized and framed their actions as addressing the entire Frontier. This discontinuity between local action and wholistic conception has created an underlying tension which remains a central problematic of the Frontier. To what extent is this, historically and ethnographically, a common space in any meaningful sense? Over time, external authorities' sensitivity towards, and responses to, local circumstance have lessened as modern states have striven for greater uniformity and bureaucratic centralization. But does the fact that external actors conceptualize and act towards this space as a unified whole make it such? And does such a framing of state policy artificially disguise the often contradictory tensions that have consistently marked state actions? Further, how has this conceptual uniformity affected local peoples, who have found themselves faced with constructions of their homes that have little to do with local lived realities? Indeed, how important and penetrative are those constructions in shaping local realities?

The preceding chapters examined three discrete episodes which threw up different fragments that have come to shape today's Frontier. The efforts of the Persian and Afghan courts to establish their credentials, even if only in an aspirational sense, as 'modern states' led to the realization of their authority over a specific geographic space. Their power was territorialized, and their limits demarcated, through the delineation of a border. Conversely, the colonial state, under the leadership of Robert Sandeman, eschewed the modernization of its frontier governance as too costly, and instead opted to control local Baluch tribesmen through their own 'tradition'. Yet that 'tradition' was a colonially-mandated innovation, if not creation *de novo*. More importantly, it embodied a government of difference which froze the tribesmen out of the 'modern' colonial space. Sandeman's actions make it clear that the dichotomy between 'tradition' and 'modern' is a false one; rather, they are mutually constitutive of one another. His frontier experiment is just one of the multiple types of 'modernity' that the colonial project produced.[1] Finally, the story of the Frontier 'Fanatics' clearly demonstrates not only the physical, but also the intellectual and conceptual links between this mountainous periphery and the imperial center located in the north Indian plains. Those links facilitated movement of ideas in both directions, and in so doing enabled the Frontier to shape the center as much as be shaped by it. The 'Fanatics' also highlight the importance of a religious idiom in molding the relational landscape between the Frontier and the plains, as well as the heterogeneity of this space. Together, these three episodes have illustrated our themes of the Frontier's simultaneous heterogeneity and coherence, while at the same time critically engaging some of the key issues affecting the Frontier and our understandings of it today.

While the focus thus far has been on distinct historical episodes, the following chapters move forward in time to the present. They also move northwest along the Frontier, focusing on the everyday lived experiences of the Frontier's inhabitants hailing from the regions of Chitral and Badakhshan, a mountainous region that traverses Tajikistan and Afghanistan. The first two chapters focus in particular on the connected nature of life in one village, Rowshan, in Chitral—a large and relatively prosperous village with a population of about 8,000 largely Khowar-speaking Isma'ili and Sunni Muslims. The final chapter casts its spatial net wider, following the mobile lives of people that Marsden came to know in Chitral across a wide variety of contexts in their home countries of Afghanistan and Tajikistan.

Thematically, the first ethnographic chapter focuses on local practices of travel within Chitral, and how the youth of Chitral learn about the spaces they inhabit and invest them with meaning. In much the same way that the chapter on the Frontier 'Fanatics' challenges the dialectic of 'center-periphery', this chapter deconstructs that of 'urban-rural', demonstrating the clearly 'cosmopolitan' spaces that Chitralis construct and occupy. The second ethnographic chapter is focused on the experience of 'refugees', labor migrants and sojourners, Afghans as well as people from southern Tajikistan who fled to Chitral during the years of upheaval in the 1990s in their own countries. The story here is about the multiple, overlapping processes of dislocation and relocation, as well as imagination and re-imagination of the Frontier by both the 'refugees' and their hosts. Like the historical chapters, this one reveals the multiple understandings and misunderstandings between peoples, as well as attempts by states to control these flows of people. Finally, the third ethnographic chapter explores the experience of 'return' that many of these refugees have had in going back to their 'homes' in Afghanistan.

Together, these three chapters underline how local practices of mobility shape the Frontier as it is lived and daily enacted. These ethnographic chapters complement the historical ones, building on and expanding their themes while at the same time focusing on the experiences of the Frontier's populace. They interrogate how some of the realities of the Frontier shaped by the past are understood and navigated by those who live there today. In doing so, the chapters conceptualize and analyze the Frontier as a deeply heterogeneous space, yet one whose fragments continue to compose, and be continuously reconstituted into a meaningful whole.

History to Hospitality

The chapters that follow trace Frontier Muslims as they move within and between the diverse spaces comprising their region. They note in particular the ways in which Frontier people reflect on the world they move through and alter and adjust their behavior as they do. The ethnographic material is informed and structured around two interconnected themes. The first is interested in the composition of local or intimate geographies of the Frontier, the texture this space takes for those who inhabit it, and the active steps they pursue in order to come to know their region of the world. These 'intimate geographies' are marked with the impression of human agency and active attempts to reflect upon local circumstances and the various worlds within which these are interconnected. As such, they further nuance the discussion presented in earlier chapters about the power of colonial states to displace indigenous forms of spatial imagination and colonize people's geographic imaginations.[2]

The second theme is concerned with a range of practices that make movement across this space possible, as well as central to understanding the selfhood and identities of frontier people. These chapters focus, thus, on a diverse range of local practices of mobility important in the region—from flight to self-exile to travel for leisure, as well as for trade. In addition, such practices of mobility are premised upon another custom long considered central to the moral character of Frontier Muslims: the provision of hospitality. Practices of travel and hospitality are interlinked in innumerable, often very paradoxical ways. Frontier travelers depend on the provision of hospitality in the worlds through which they move. Conversely, a reputation for being a good host depends on the willingness of people to travel beyond their own homes or villages.

Practices of mobility, customs of hospitality, and the underlying norms of behavior that shape them have historically been the subject of exogensis information orders, in particular colonial knowledge. These knowledges have, in the main, constructed static models of ethics and behavior characterizing the societies along the Frontier as bound by timeless 'tradition'. Nowhere is this more visible than in the codification of particular cultural practices and values as 'tribal codes', such as the 'Pukhtunwali', the so-called 'moral code' of the Pukhtuns. Likewise, practices such as hospitality are widely cited as offering unique insights into understanding how and why Frontier Muslims behave as they do. Today's understandings of the Frontier rely heavily on colonially inscribed visions of Frontier society, depicting many of its elements as 'ancient', if not downright primordial. Yet they often betray little or no recognition of the extent to which colonial states played a key role in the codification of local 'customs', *à la* Sandeman.

The provision of hospitality to Osama Bin Laden by the Taliban after the September 11th attacks on America, or rumors that Bin Laden was the beneficiary of a strict code of hospitality in Chitral's villages, are vivid examples of the extent to which the moral and political universes of frontier people are interpreted in relationship to enduring local customs.[3] The rhetorical emphasis on local practices of hospitality as constituting some binding moral code create the impression that

Frontier Muslims are locked in a static and unchanging world that is defined above all else by a strict and rigidly traditional code of honor or morality.[4] Such modes of thinking fail to address the ways in which Muslims along the Frontier tack back and forth between the ideal concepts of hospitality they might hold and voice in public, and the forms of hospitality that actually become operative in everyday life.[5] Understandings of Frontier society, just like Frontier society itself, are historically constructed and conditioned. Failure to recognize this, opting instead for a simplistic picture of some 'tradition'-bound society governed by primeval social strictures alien to the modern mind, can only have negative consequences for both the people of the Frontier and the foreign interlocutors present there.

Chitral: Unique Case or Microcosmic Whole?

The following three chapters deal with the insights that can be derived from the heterogeneity of the Frontier as experienced and reflected upon by its people through a consideration of forms of mobility that have, at various times in the recent and most distant past, converged upon Chitral. Today Chitral is an administrative district in Pakistan's North-West Frontier Province, which ethnically is predominantly Pukhtun. Until the winter of 2009, its only land connection to the rest of Pakistan was a road that closed in winter and took fifteen or so hours to traverse. The Pakistan state has recently finished an all-weather tunnel to Chitral which will ease access to its administrative headquarters, Chitral Town, and surrounding towns, as well as potentially open new trading routes through Afghanistan and on to the Muslim-majority republics of Central Asia. These potential routes are now a source of much discussion in Chitral and the wider region, as the populations of particular valleys advocate their suitability as the location for an all-weather road to Central Asia. Rumors also circulate about attempts by powerful business elites and merchants to block the opening of work on these roads, having recognized how they stand to lose their profits to Chitralis and northern Afghans because of them.

Chitral is populated largely by Khowar-speaking Sunni and Shi'a Isma'ili Muslims, who distinguish themselves linguistically and ethnically from the predominantly Pukhtun populations to the south and southwest of their region's high mountain valleys. In this way, Chitral is similar to other areas examined in previous chapters. Unlike other administrative districts in Malakand, Chitral has not been a site of major anti-Pakistan state Taliban insurgency activity over the past five years. Yet Chitralis have suffered as a result of this conflict. The main Chitral-Peshawar road runs through districts, such as Dir, deeply affected by the conflict. Chitrali men have died fighting the Taliban with the Pakistan Army and the Frontier Corps. In response, Taliban fighters have targeted and killed Chitralis whom they have actively sought out and found traveling through regions under their control.

It would be tempting to see Chitral, a largely non-Pukhtun region within the Frontier, as non-representative of wider Frontier life—a sort of ethnic enclave submerged in what is otherwise a world of predominantly Pukhtun modes of being Muslim. Alternatively, Chitral and its people could be interpreted as having been mapped by the colonial state and its post-colonial successors into the wrong type of political or cultural grid, better compared with other non-Pukhtun spaces along the Frontier. This study challenges these perspectives. Chitrali peoples' understandings and experiences of Frontier life are interesting because they offer a high mountain perspective on the world below. Chitralis are at one and the same time central to and separate from the Frontier. Their visions and understandings of Frontier life point to the contradictions inherent in their ambiguous experiences of this world. Yet the entire Frontier is made up of communities, regions and peoples—referred to in this book as fragments—that seem otherwise to not quite fit. Until now, these fragments have too often been viewed and treated from the outside as exceptions and minorities. They are curious islands of difference which pose intractable problems to nation-states and provincial governments seeking to create totalizing and unifying identity narratives. Most recently, when Pakistan's Frontier Province was renamed by its legislators as Khyber-Pakhtunkhwa in April 2010, Chitralis writing in print and electronic media complained that their distinctive identity had been denied by the region's majority politics.[6]

Like the following chapters, the preceding historical chapters focused on non-Pashtun peoples and places. Yet the Frontier is too often considered uniformly synonymous with 'the Pashtun'. This is a consequence of academic traditions which focus on certain peoples within the space that is today Afghanistan, but also, more profoundly, it is a living legacy of the colonial past.[7] The ethnographic assumptions first authored by British scholar-administrators in the nineteenth century remain deeply embedded in understandings of the region today. Those scholar-administrators dealt predominantly, though not exclusively, with the Pashtuns, and even conditioned their understandings of non-Pashtun peoples on their Pashtun experiences.[8] Yet neither in the past nor today has the Frontier been an exclusively, or even predominantly, Pashtun space. Excluding regions such as Chitral from the Frontier on the grounds that their incorporation into this political space was rooted in misconceived colonial or nation-state mapping projects, suggests that there is an 'authentic' Frontier just waiting to be found and properly defined and bounded. In contrast, we juxtapose the ways in which states, empires, communities and individuals have all, albeit in very different ways, sought to map and comprehend the Frontier.

Neat lines of ethnographic separateness collapse when one looks at the Frontier's lived experience, past and present. Far too little is known about the terms upon which diverse Frontier people partake in encounters with one another. Isma'ili Chitrali students studying in Peshawar, for example, interact and form lasting friendships with young Pushtun men from parts of Pakistan's tribal areas known for the intense anti-Shi'a dispositions of their inhabitants. Likewise, the 'Hindustani Fanatics', supposedly an earlier incarnation of similar sectarian feeling, maintained a colony amongst the Shi'a in Tirah. Dari and Tajiki-speaking men lived in Chitral during the civil wars that tore apart life in their home countries during the 1990s, whilst some Chitralis, though not Pashtun, are firmly enmeshed in Taliban-like forms and networks of Islam. In the pages that follow we meet many such people, and explore relations that cut across boundaries of ethnicity and sect. Equally in the past, some inhabitants of the Frontier became encapsulated by their own 'tradition', and thus cut off from the colonial sphere while others served the colonial state in tribal militias or even the army. The everyday reality of the Frontier is best understood neither in terms of the inexorable expansion of Talibanizing and radicalizing processes nor in terms of rigid ethnic distinctions between Pukhtuns and non-Pukhtuns, tribal, settled and one-time courtly Muslims. In this world of constant flux, rather, people refer to the specificity of their own lives and identities very often in relationship to the neighboring valley, village, or home as much as through references to categories, codified through colonial intervention, of persons, spaces and ideologies, such as the Taliban, Pukhtuns, Tajiks.

Our emphasis on the situated and constructed nature of people's identifications is not to say they lack concepts or awareness of the political importance of these externally codified categories. Chitralis talk about the negative influence of Pukhtun values on their lifestyles and, indeed, the immoral behavior of Tajik laborers in their villages. Very many have also experienced being stopped by state officials in Karachi, a city to which many Chitralis travel for work in the winter months, on the basis of 'looking like a Pathan' or a 'Khan Sahib'—the pejorative term that Urdu-speaking city dwellers use to refer to Pukhtuns, or those who are deemed to look like them. During the 1990s, moreover, Chitralis also complained that Karachi dwellers referred to them as 'Badakhshis', people from the Badakhshan region of Tajikistan and Afghanistan, thousands of whom lived in the city during Tajikistan's civil war, and the Taliban siege of northern Afghanistan. 'They [Urdu-speaking Karachi people] don't even know Chitral exists', one Chitrali man working in Karachi at a chemist said, 'and they think that we Chitralis are Badakhshanis, shouting at us in Urdu, "where there is a Badakhshi, there is always trouble".' More recently, especially since the conflict between the 'Swat Taliban' and the Pakistan Army in the Malakand Agency, Chitralis also increasingly fear being stopped by the Taliban on their journeys between their home villages and Peshawar because Chitralis were involved as soldiers in violent conflict with insurgents.

Yet in the messy world of everyday practice the relevance of such categories can often also be quickly deformed. Chitralis might say in conversations with one another that Pukhtuns are wild and animalistic, yet later argue that Chitralis are bad friends in comparison to the faith and loyalty of Pukhtuns. Young Chitrali men studying at university in Peshawar, for example, escape the suffocating network of Chitrali friendships that form in its hostels, and instead befriend their class-fellows from tribal areas such as Waziristan, saying these 'tribal people' (*qabaili roye*) are more honest, honorable and sensitive than their own villagers. Everyday realities, colonial-derived stereotypes and local modes of valorizing and engaging with difference through personal encounters result in the production of strands of Frontier life that are rarely explored in anthropological or historical work, despite their omnipresence. Amongst the most important of these strands are peoples' capacities to create and sustain relationships across boundaries of ethnic, ideological and religious difference, often assumed by outsiders to be unbridgeable. Such relationships point towards people's capacity to switch between different modes of behavior, comportment and ways of being Muslims as they move between the Frontier's different spaces, and traverse its many internal and external borders. They also point more generally to frontiers as spaces central to the production of unique forms of social solidarity and cooperation.

Such experiences of change and flexibility are historically well grounded, and facilitated by a common set of shared normative values, political principles, and relational forms. These included a Turco-Persianate ecumene which was the basis of a common court culture. Also, strains of nationalism in both Afghanistan and Pakistan, formal ideologies, such as communism, socialism and Islamism, and processes of globalization, including the formation and expansion of free markets and the near-constant movement of people, represent just a few expressions of such commonalities. At no time are these on better display than when people are on the move. They often seek to establish connections through shared experience, or lacking that, common expectations, practices and values. It is to the practices of mobility that we now turn, examining how meaning is reinvented and reinvested as part of the every day lived experiences of those who inhabit this heterogeneous space.

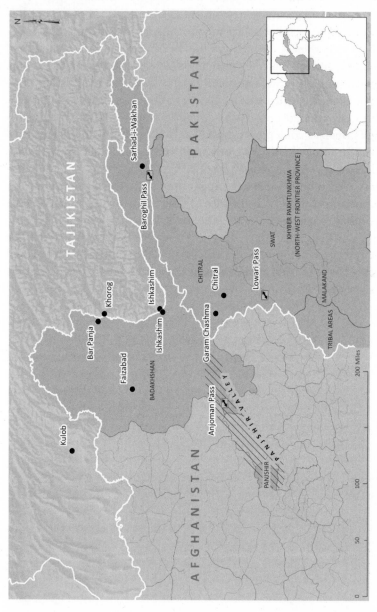

Northwest Afghanistan/Pakistan Frontier © Naula Cowan, George Washington University

5

A TOUR NOT SO GRAND

MOBILE MUSLIMS IN NORTHERN PAKISTAN

Mobility is extremely important for cultivating diverse modes of sociality and moral, aesthetic and intellectual sensibilities amongst Khowar-
speaking Chitralis. More will be said in the following two chapters
about the extent to which such Chitrali sensibilities are also invested
with wider forms of transregional significance; here the focus is on
intensely local practices of mobility. For many Chitrali Muslims, Chitral is more than just a remote, marginal or 'minority' Khowar-speaking ethnic enclave swamped in a Pukhtun-dominated Frontier. Neither
is it simply a colonially imposed administrative district. Chitralis are
interested in the nature of their region's own social heterogeneity. This
heterogeneity is something they actively nurture and sustain because it
provides them with the possibility of visualizing and experiencing their
region as offering them diverse potentials and possibilities for everyday
life. Chitralis openly talk about and reflect on the many different types
of spaces that they see as composing their region. They associate these
spaces with the enactment and inculcation of different yet interconnected modes of sociality and selfhood and ways of being Muslim, or
relating to Islam. Whilst many Chitrali Muslims are concerned about
the growing influence of what they refer to as Pukhtun forms of Islam
and sociality in their region, they also take active steps to cultivate very
different reference points. They see these reference points as being dis-
tinctively Chitrali, yet they also often reflect more on the complexity of
local understandings of 'fully realized humanity' than about ethnicity

or religion *per se*. Muslims in the region understand their world in relationship to a multiplicity of sometimes discrete and at other times negotiable and interactive modes of morality, sociality, cultural influence, political dynamics, and religious ideologies and concepts.

It is especially useful to think about Chitralis' attempts to understand and emphasize their region's plurality in relation to a form of travel important in the region that is often referred to by Chitralis using the English term 'tour'. The term is used to describe short trips that involve a one-night stay in the house of a friend in a nearby village. Tours, however, may also be more expedition-like journeys (*safar*) that see local travelers walking over high mountain passes and staying in the guest houses of strangers in the villages through which they past. At first glance tours appear to be a mundane form of local travel, yet they offer important insights into Chitrali perceptions of their region and its place in the wider world. These tours reveal how mobility informs the social construction and continual reconstruction of the Frontier. They also show how even apparently 'local' patterns of mobility play a critical role in the making of cosmopolitan subjectivities and self-understandings that are about more than Frontier culture. These subjectivities are often premised on people subverting rather than embodying the values, norms, moral codes and ideologies—in short, 'traditions'—that colonial authorities and national governments as well as Frontier politicians have employed to define the Frontier. Such subjectivities point to the ways in which very different strands of Frontier Muslim life exist side-by-side. This coexistence requires the region's Muslims to thoughtfully navigate and alter their behavior as they move within and between them. It has also led to 'consciousness of social diversity and a largely assumed knowledge of social differences', although on a geographical scale much smaller and apparently more 'ethnicized' than the Indian Ocean.[1]

Russian Olive Trees, Pakistani Army Generals and Village Youngsters

Chitral is made up of verdant villages sited on alluvial fans located within high mountain valleys flanked by snow-capped peaks and fast flowing rivers. The beauty of Chitral's landscape is the focus of much present-day Khowar poetic composition, which describes the feeling of 'freedom' (*azadi*) to be had from traveling through the region in spring—a season when many Chitralis follow the sweet scent of Russian Olive tree blossom up valley as the summer months progress. Yet Chitralis also say that they are 'mice-like' 'prisoners of the mountains' who live in the 'darkest corner' of the world. They make inter-regional distinctions between 'open' (*kulao*) and 'narrow' (*trang*) village life. Life in narrow villages, as well as small towns with busy bazaars, is said to cause people to feel 'heart explosion' (*hardi phat*) and put them in constant danger of mental 'collapse'. To offset these dangers, groups of young Chitrali men visit villages that are known for being old-fashioned and distinctive places full of 'wonders and marvels' (*aja'ibo ghara'ib*), or that have earned a reputation for the beauty, hospitality and 'life-loving' (*zindadil*) dispositions of their inhabitants. Having been a participant in many such tours I have come to recognize the degree to which tour-going is an important practice through which Chitralis purposefully seek to encounter, perceive and understand their region's valleys and villages and invest them as well as themselves with significance.[2] The presence of 'an idea of purposeful movement' associated with practices and activities other than religious pilgrimage, migrant labor or participation in armed militancy in the thinking of sedentary village Muslims in northern Pakistan raises important questions concerning the types of creative energy that people bring to the creation of intimate and local geographies.[3] Far from being the passive objects either of colonial cartographies of the Frontier or more recently of the expansion of radical Islamic landscapes of *jihad*, Chitralis play an important role in investing their lives and the spaces within which they live with multiple forms of significance.[4]

In addition to acquiring and sharing knowledge about their region, Chitralis also say that tours offer complex opportunities for the region's people to hone their capacity to enact and cultivate diverse modes of sociality and moral, aesthetic and intellectual sensibilities. This is why tours deserve to be treated as a kind of ethical practice that seeks to instill in people particular forms of moral virtue. In particular, touring is associated with a complex performative nexus of forms of wit, humor, irony and mockery, all connected to a broader idea widely held by Chitralis that both as humans and as Muslims they should strive to display and cultivate a curiosity in the overlapping worlds they inhabit. Both the tours and the spaces through which tour-goers travel are associated with troubles endured, hilarious jokes and audacious displays of wit. As a school-leaver and undergraduate visitor to

Chitral, for example, I was frequently whisked off in the darkness of night on the eve of annual wheat harvests on week-long excursions to distant valleys by boys my age. My friends only returned when they knew that the 'noisy threshers' had left their homes, and the 'polluting wheat-chaff' had long since left its diarrhea-inducing dust on the village's ripened apricots.

The groups of young men with whom I traveled were mostly studying in higher education colleges, and told me that they yearned to break free from the 'era of speed' that had come to characterize life in their 'developed' and 'city-like' village. In particular, they talked about the ways in which the expansion of their village's bazaar over the last twenty years had led its people to become *bazaaris* who no longer took pride in being hospitable but instead spent their lives 'running' after 'pieces of work' in the bazaar and its government offices. To escape all this *tensien*, they often decided to travel to 'remote' and 'backward' villages where bazaars are minuscule, guests are respected, and home-produced foods continue to be cultivated and prepared. Sometimes they stay with their Chitrali relatives, but they often say that being the guest in 'relative-houses' is painfully 'boring'. Instead, they invest great energy into choosing a house where they are likely to be treated as guests and not relatives.

In Chitral's dispersed yet intimate and interconnected villages being offered hospitality as a friend (*dost*), kin (*rishtadar*), or work mate (*korumo malgiri*) is a relatively simple task; being honored as a respectable 'outsider' and achieving the desired aim of experiencing a break from everyday village reality require more sustained displays of trickery and creative performance. Thus, my young village friends pursued a range of strategies to assume the honored status as 'guest' (*mehrman*) in a stranger's house for the evening. The enactment of identities very different from those performed during the course of everyday village life was a favorite strategy to adopt. They presented themselves as the sons of important local government officials and visiting religious preachers from elsewhere in Pakistan and as far away as Canada. These strategies were, however, rarely entirely persuasive. Names, bodily comportment and slips in performative standards frequently alerted hosts' attention to the family, village and religious backgrounds of my companions. Thus tours are not only a central way in which Chitralis purposefully create the intimate and local geographies of the Afghan Frontier that are the principal focus of this book, they also point to the ways in which such geographies are implicated in the emergence of alternative stands of social and political life that exist beside these.

Mobility: Old and New

A considerable body of anthropological work on travel focuses on the insights that ethnographic explorations of mobility afford into understanding the effects of globalizing modernity, ranging from the emergence of exclusive forms of transnational identities to cosmopolitan 'openness'.[5] As Enseng Ho has noted, however, there is a tendency for this writing to be 'obsessed with speed' to the extent that it fails to consider the ways in which older 'experiences of mobility' involved 'tactile, visual, auditory, affective, aesthetic, textual, and mystical'.[6] Travel, indeed, has long been an important dimension of Muslim life.[7] Historians have documented the importance of travelogues for understanding 'pre-modern' forms of Muslim subjectivity, notably in the Indian subcontinent.[8] They have also documented the role played by concepts of travel in Indian political thought. Javeed Majeed's study of the twentieth-century Islamic thinker Alama Iqbal argues that Iqbal 'defined himself against ethnographic representations of the "native" in which Indians were represented as being incapable of individual growth through travel', instead emphasizing a 'restless self' constantly reconstituted during a metaphysical inner journey.[9] This work emphasizes travel's role in the production of unfinished conceptions of self, which challenged the fixity of Indians as depicted in colonial accounts as well as bounded ideas of the modern nation.[10] Likewise, Ho's study of mobile Yemeni Seyyids and their role in the creation of an Indian Ocean Islamic ecumene shows that these men integrated into diverse societies across the Indian Ocean. What distinguishes Ho's work, however, is his emphasis on the way in which these people's experiences of their wider world contributed to rather than attenuating their sense of 'resolute localism'.[11]

In the light of this expanding body of anthropological and historical work on the relationship between mobility and identity, this chapter has two major aims. First, it explores the ways in which local practices of mobility are important to everyday life in Chitral because they are seen to cultivate in young village minds a sense of curiosity about their region and the diverse influences found therein. In so doing, it challenges the notion that the most important forms of mobility today are global and the harbingers of transnational 'cosmopolitanism'. Second, exploring the ways in which Muslims perceive and interact with their worlds also furnishes broader insights into the complexity of collective and personal forms of Muslim self-understanding. Mahmood has documented the ways in which 'piety-minded' Muslims in Cairo fashion themselves as good Muslims through the habituation of norms formulated according to the Islamic tradition and in response to Egyptian expressions of secular modernity.[12] Through analyses of ethnographic material that points to 'submission to certain forms of "external authority" as being 'a condition for the self to achieve its potentiality'[13] she challenges the cross-cultural relevance of 'Western modes of subjectivity that associate agency exclusively with an inner ego, constituted as thought and desire as independent of the body, nature, society and other extrinsic conditions'.[14] In a similar vein, Henkel focuses on the ways in which piety-minded Muslims in Istanbul seek to overcome local manifestations of modernity's 'heterogeneous lifeworlds' in order to live coherent Muslim lives, by visiting felicitous Muslim spaces and 'designating certain elements' of the city as 'significant and others as unimportant'.[15] Recent anthropological works, however, have paid less attention to the ways in which rural Muslims act within, perceive, and invest with relevance their worlds. As a result, the assumption that village Muslim life is static, bucolic and of little relevance for anthropological debates concerning wider trends currently affecting life in the Muslim world remains largely uncontested. It would be tempting, indeed, to assume that Muslims living in a remote and rural region of Pakistan travel primarily to visit kin, look for work, or make pilgrimages.[16] Yet they also travel for leisure, and so this chapter builds on the challenge the historical sections of this book pose to simplistic understandings of the center/periphery by addressing critically the equally problematic urban/rural dichotomy. It documents the practices through which Chitralis invest their region, its places and its landscapes with complex forms of personal and collective significance,[17] emphasizing the wider political significance of these forms of 'place making' within a landscape already deeply 'enshrined'[18] with contested forms of power and memory.[19]

All the Chitralis I know are aware of the importance of traveling to places that are 'felicitous Muslim' spaces for being Muslim.[20] Many of them undertake the pilgrimage to Mecca, embark on more local 'religious journeys', and debate amongst themselves the relevance of these for being virtuous Muslims.[21] Tours themselves are, indeed, inspired by a complex combination of both sacred and non-sacred motivations.[22] Visiting sacred sites, acquiring knowledge about Chitral and its people, escaping the moralizing constraints of daily village life, evading social claims placed upon them by their fellow villagers, and 'relaxing' are amongst the most important motivations for tours. At one level, these diverse motivations for touring illuminate the ways in which Chitrali Muslims experience their region thorough a complex bundle of thoughts and desires, which reflect a wider range of concerns than their knowledge of Islamic doctrinal standards. More significantly, many Chitralis associate movement outside the confines of their villages with a nexus of performance, curiosity in difference, the display of wit and what they refer to as a fleeting sensation of freedom (*azadi*) from the constraints (*pabandi*) of daily village life. Chitralis, in short, enjoy embarking on tours because such events furnish the possibility of experiencing 'unforeseeable configurations'.[23] More than simply offering a monetary release from Chitrali village life, tours furnish Chitralis with possibilities to both recognize and point beyond the 'inescapability' of the conditions that shape their everyday lives; understanding such events in their full complexity requires a consideration of the moments of 'self-reflection, self-interrogation [and] openness to the unforseeable' which they stimulate.[24]

An important fact is that when Chitralis seek to cultivate an appreciation for the heterogeneity of their region and its people, or think out loud about questions of sameness and difference, they do so in a region of Pakistan that is profoundly 'Islamized'. At first glance, Chitral's landscape suggests the hegemony of political Islamists who have sought to fashion Muslim life in the region according to reform-minded Islamic doctrinal precepts. Over the past twenty years there has been a notable increase in the construction of large mosques with domes and towering minarets—architectural styles that reflect Middle Eastern funding.[25] Chitral, moreover, is home to Sunni and Shi'a Isma'ili Khowar-speaking Muslims.[26] Today, the shimmering tin roofs of Sunni mosques and Isma'ili places of worship face off across Chitral's mixed Sunni-Isma'ili villages, graphically illustrating the importance of emergent 'sectarian geographies' to everyday Chitrali Muslim life.[27] Yet in the context of this world of prescribed faith many Sunni and Shi'a Isma'ili Chitralis do not simply, or without regard to their particular circumstances, interpret heterogeneity—old or new—as an obstacle to living a coherent Muslim life or as a threat to their society's truly Muslim nature.[28] The appreciation of Chitral's diversity, rather, adds another dimension to local understandings of their region's uniqueness and wider significance. By tracking how Chitralis circulate through their region and noting their performances during the course of these journeys, the remainder of this chapter illuminates the ongoing importance of dimensions of rural Muslim life long noted by anthropologists. Wit, irony and humor are important intellectual resources that Chitralis actively deploy to evaluate and understand the changing conditions and diverse historical influences currently shaping their daily lives.

Travel in the Indo-Persian Realm

Travel in Chitral today has been stimulated by modern developments—metalled roads, jeeps and minibuses are all important for Chitrali modes of everyday travel. At the same time, Chitralis often seek to mark out actively the difference between fast and purposeful journeys and slow and leisurely tours. Thus, Chitralis are often proud to tell stories about how they hired their village's fastest and most reckless of jeep drivers to take them to houses where they were required to offer prayers of condolence for the death of a recent relative. In doing so, they arrived at the house of sadness before members of other lineage groups (*qawm*) did. In contrast, when people prepare for their tours to far off villages and valleys, they often decide to travel by foot or even on horseback rather than by jeep or minibus. Tours thus become inscribed with different types of personal significance and pleasure.

The types of local travel explored here exist alongside other forms of mobility more familiar to the literature on globalization. Many Chitralis live and work in the hyper-modern cities of the Persian Gulf; even more are employed as laborers in Pakistan's cities. Each year, moreover, many of the region's men embark alone or in small groups for cities such as Peshawar elsewhere in Pakistan. Yet those not involved in such types of mobility do not think about themselves as unfortunate people left at home by more prosperous labor migrants. Instead, they travel widely in their own region. Indeed, they often contrast their ability to travel with the camp-bound existences of Chitrali living in the Gulf.[29] And they discuss the ability to travel as something that animated contentious political debates in their region's past and continues to do so amongst different categories of Chitralis today.[30]

The ethnography presented below explores the ongoing legacy of older courtly-derived forms of status and hierarchy and a rich 'high culture'—defined by its diverse and vibrant poetic and musical tradition—influencing modern Chitrali practices of travel. This ethnography points to the ways in which Indo-Persian culture influences Chitrali life and the modes through which the region's people imagine and experience space. Historical studies have increasingly emphasized the shared literary and cultural traditions that were important in a range of socially and politically diverse 'Persianate' settings.[31] These works are descriptions of journeys made to 'exotic' places, such as holy Islamic cities, but also to more 'familiar' settings within northern India. Such travel accounts were not simply frivolous literary excursions for Mughal India's scribes—travel writing was a vehicle used by court officials in order to demonstrate their 'command over the art of description' and 'allusion and comparison'.[32] The Persianate world was not a homogeneous, static, or territorially bounded cultural entity. It was defined, rather, by ongoing cultural interchange between India and Iran and with Turkic-speaking regions of Central Asia.[33] These complex processes of cultural exchange and transmission also helped create important 'hierarchies of culture'[34] within and across a Persianate realm that incorporated both Indian urban centers, notably Delhi and Lucknow in India and Bukhara in present-day Uzbekistan and rural regions of Central Asia.[35]

The cultivation of skills for the acquisition and sharing of knowledge about both familiar and more 'wondrous' (aja'ib) places forms an important dimension of Chitrali experiences of travel in their region today. In particular, reciting stories about Chitral's past is a recurrent feature of the discussions that Chitralis have with one another as they travel through their region. Chitralis often richly inject even their most mundane journeys from their villages to Chitral's district headquarters with meaning by reciting stories about the significance of particular places for their region's history, as well as understanding the current character of Chitrali people. On the main road between Rowshan and Chitral Town, which is plied by up to thirty minibuses per day, there is a small area of flat land in a small village through which the road passes. Whilst speeding in minibuses through this village, my friends often tell me and their traveling companions a story about an early British visitor to the region. This 'Britisher' was said to have been riding on horseback through the village when he came across a gathering of thin and shoddily dressed Chitralis. 'What are you doing?' he is said to have asked: 'We are the prisoners of the Mehtar', the people replied, 'our jailer is in a house having a lunch and a cup of tea'.[36] After much laughter, the significance of this story is expressed in terms of the inherent inability of Chitralis to actively seek out 'freedom' (*azadi*): 'We', my friends say, 'don't know how to be free—is it surprising that we remain prisoners of the mountains?'[37] Chitral, thus, is perceived as being a bounded region with important geographical limits, and many Chitralis contrast their ability to move with the immobility of their forefathers, yet they also talk about the ongoing influence of past experiences of confinement on their thinking and behavior today.

The constraints imposed upon mobility by Chitral's Mehtar (hereditary ruler) are often talked about in even more explicit ways. In the 'era of the Mehtar', Chitralis often say, a man who left the boundaries of Chitral was never allowed to return, whilst no man's land or family was safe from the ruling family's ceaseless greed to occupy Chitral's most beautiful places and marry its prettiest girls. Reflecting on the Mehtar's rule is something Chitralis often do as they travel by places associated with their region's courtly past. The excitement of 'embodied memories', reflective processes and movement form an important nexus that powerfully shape the articulation of viewpoints about the region's past.[38]

Many of Chitral's old forts continue to be inhabited by the descendants of Chitral's one-time princely family. These (today crumbling) forts are often located in scenic spots overlooking fast flowing rivers or in wooded mountain gorges. In the summer of 1998, I traveled with some Chitrali friends to a valley where the Mehtar had built a summer house in which he stayed whilst hunting ibex in the mountains. The two men with whom I traveled were from middle-ranking village families, in their mid-twenties, unemployed, and studying privately for BA degrees in the social sciences. Both were descended from Seyyid families claiming descent from the Prophet, and they often told me how the Chitral's Mehtars had feared their 'grandfather' (*bap*) so greatly that they had forced him into exile in a neighboring province of Afghanistan, Badakhshan (whose geographies are the focus of the final chapter of this book). Having nowhere to stay in the village, my friends decided that we should visit the Mehtar's summer palace and ask the princes if we could pass the night in their home. In order to persuade these young princes (at the time studying in expensive private schools in

Karachi and Lahore) that we deserved being accorded hospitality, my friends pretend to be *tahsildars* (local government officials), telling me that I should act out the part of a British Embassy official. The tactic worked. The young princes chatted with us, and later presented us with a prized meal of ibex meat curry. Yet rather than giving us a room in their guesthouse, they arranged for us to sleep on carpets beneath a Chinese Plane tree—the 'long roots' of which symbolize status power and authority—in its garden. This caused great irritation to my Seyyid friends, who told me during the night that the land on which we were sleeping had once belonged to their forefathers before it was usurped by the avaricious Mehtar of the time. Visits to the old seats of courtly authority and fleeting interactions with the region's princes stimulate Chitralis to cunningly repudiate the continuing importance of the old courtly order to life in the region today. At the same time, those mocking the old social order often legitimate what they seek to challenge by talking about their own pasts and genealogies. Thus, whilst few Chitralis may fully escape the 'immanence of the conditions' shaping their daily lives, the forms of wit and irony that are enacted during tours do give rise to 'undetermined moments of self-reflection, self-interrogation, [and] openness to the unforseeable'.[39]

Concerns over the types of vision associated with high land vividly illustrate the extent to which Chitral's landscape is 'enshrined' with both older and newer modes of power and competing conceptions of social order.[40] Visiting, buying land or building houses on 'high places' with views over villages, houses and hamlets is a source of great contestation in Chitral's villages. One man from Rowshan, for example, who hailed from a one-time lordly family, told an elderly man—purported to be a one-time 'serf' (*chermuzh*) yet recently elected as a local government councilor—that he should not allow his recent political success go to his head. 'Whenever I want', said the lord (*lal*) to his neighbor, 'I can look down from my veranda and gaze at your daughters'. The local councilor's reply mocked the lord's attack and sought to demonstrate that his thinking was locked in a bygone era. 'That may be the case', he responded, 'but then you should remember that all I have to do is stare up my chimney and see your wife'. Chitral's landscape is experienced as being 'enshrined' with older forms of status distinction, exclusion, extraction and violence, thus filling it with cross-cutting sentiments of 'anger, sorrow and jubilation'.[41] The 'embodied memories' stimulated by movement through Chitral's landscape produce modes of social critique that contest but also re-inscribe, for example, the importance of the old courtly order for present day Chitrali identity.

Memories of courtly power, colonial expansion, and newer conflicts over the validity of older forms of social distinction for modern life are 'anchored' within connected places,[42] constituting a distinct 'landscape of powers',[43] embedded with overlapping tensions that Chitralis experience, reflect upon and discuss during their travels. This overlaying of places with different forms of historical significance ensures that the memories of 'later generations do not displace earlier ones but perdure alongside them', thereby 'allowing each period to serve as a commentary on the others'.[44] Rather than conceptualizing Chitral's heterogeneity as a problem to living a coherent Muslim life, for many Chitrali villagers negotiating the complexities of conducting life 'with respect to distinctive epochs' that stimulate 're-occurring' senses of both modernity and tradition involves complex reflective processes.[45] Through such processes, Chitralis simultaneously challenge and reaffirm both older and newer influences on their lives. This illustrates, once more, the continually transforming nature of Frontier space, and the processes of active human agency that contribute towards this.

Divine Love and Sexual Flirtation

The 'multiply layered significances'[46] of Chitral's landscape are not, however, confined to the differential ways in which it has become embedded with older values, conflicts and embodied memories of violence. The landscape is also filled actively with different forms of moral and sacred significance by Chitralis; these afford complex opportunities for them to think and act in overlapping spaces according to different moral registers.

As in much Persianate Sufic composition, metaphors of travel are widely deployed by Chitrali poets in order to evoke the experience of ecstatic forms of love, or *'ishq*. The experience of ecstatic love is a key theme in the Persianate Sufi canon. It is often connected also to ways in which the poet's self is fashioned as he makes a complex inner spiritual journey.[47] In much Khowar-language poetry, for example, 'lovers' describe being left to wander alone in barren plains (*biyaban*) whilst searching in a maddened state for their 'beloved'.[48] These poems often invoke mountain pastures and passes, which transfer abstract religious concepts onto Chitral's own landscapes. 'Lovers' are depicted in these poems as world-renouncing Sufi mendicants walking for time immemorial over high mountain passes, with only a begging bowl (*kishti*) strung around the neck and a reed instrument (*surnai*) in the mouth. Performed by musical groups in village houses, these poems invest both travel and the landscape with the powerful imprint of Sufi concepts. This resonates with the efforts of the 'Hindustani Fanatics' who also deployed Sufi imagery, yet with very different political implications and a contrasting ethical subjectivity in mind.

There is usually a set pattern to the activities undertaken by Chitralis when staying in a friend's house for the evening. After tea and fruit at home, the host suggests taking a stroll (*chaker*) to a beautiful place in the village—usually a high riverbank or water channel. These places are often the host's *nishini*—the place where a man sits in the evening alone or with friends, contemplates expansive views (*nazria*) of his village, listens to the radio, composes poetry, or relaxes and smokes a cigarette, occasionally 'filled' with hashish.

Farid is a well known Chitrali singer, who lives in the region's district headquarters, Markaz, where he works as a medical technician, yet tries to visit his home village as often as possible. I visited him there in May 2001 with two other Rowshan men. He took us to the water channel on the mountain overlooking his house where, he told us, he had learned to sing as a 'boy' (*daq*). In his early teenage years, his father and other village elders (*lilotan*) had told Farid not to sing—it would distract him from his studies, lead him to make friends with 'bad' hashish-smoking village boys, and might also mean that respectable men refused to give their daughters in marriage to him. The *nishini* was out of earshot of the village, however, and had expansive views of the valley below. Distant although not detached from villages, *nishini*s, like sacred places elsewhere, offer the potential for the momentary experience of abstract 'emptiness'.[49]

The landscape this high water channel overlooks is richly invested with sacred and poetic histories. On the opposite side of the valley from Farid's *nishini* is the village and small dusty shrine of Chitral's most famous Sufi poet, Baba Seyar. Most Chitralis know Baba Seyar's love poetry, written after he fell in love with a married woman from a village near his own. So besotted with this woman was he that on meeting her whilst crossing the bridge that linked their two villages, he jumped into the fast flowing river below so as to avoid both immorally crossing her path and rudely turning his back. Farid often recites Baba Sayar's poems from his *nishini*. These poems compare the distinctive 'red land' of Sayar's beloved's village to her 'ruby red lips'.

At the same time, high land is not only associated with abstract religious concepts, but also with the presence of living spirits or fairies. The presence of spirits in Chitral's high mountain pastures adds both a degree of danger but also a further element of excitement to tours. The centrality of amulet-making to Chitrali modes of religious thinking and experience has been documented elsewhere.[50] The making of amulets is a morally complex practice because it involves men trained in the Islamic sciences using the words of God to help the region's Muslims in their everyday lives. In high mountain villages, however, Chitrali men and women are also said to be at an increased risk of being possessed by spirits (*pari*) who inhabit a world in the mountain peaks above. Such spirits enter the bodies of men and women, and especially dangerous places are narrow ravines which the *pari* can easily and quickly descend into from their homes in the mountain tops above. Some people, *pari-khan*s, however seek out the spirits actively and encourage them to enter into their bodies in order to be able to use them for worldly activities.[51] Tour-goers often combine their trips to high mountain valleys with visits to such people, whom they ask to help them in matters of love and also other things, such as passing examinations. Tour-goers distinguish themselves from jeep drivers, who are said to travel purely to seek out *pari-khan*s, to whom they pay vast amounts of money to say prayers that will allow them to realize their love relationships with the many girls who 'cross their paths'. In contrast, tour-goers combine their visits to the possessed with other activities, such as visiting friends or seeing beautiful villages, and they might even say they visit the *pari-khan*s in order to 'research' or even test the activities of such people than to use them. Moreover, some of Chitral's best-known possessed people live in valleys that are known for being home to reform-minded and even pro-Taliban mullahs. Shortages of land and water in such places are said to have led to many of these people attending religious seminaries in 'down Pakistan' and embracing strict ways of being Muslim. For Chitralis of Isma'ili background, indeed, traveling through predominantly Sunni populated valleys in order to visit a *pari-khan* who is equally popular among Sunnis and Isma'ilis alike adds what is talked about as being an important element of danger or even risk to the tour. Once again, then, different types of landscape animated on the one hand by belief in the spirit world, and on the other by doctrinal forms of Islam whose adherents often claim that such practices as the 'cooking of prayers' (*du'a pacheik*) or use of spiritual techniques to use the power of the *pari*, are un-Islamic, exist side-by-side one another in Chitral's valleys.

While on the one hand filled with 'anger, sorry and jubilation',[52] Chitral's landscape is also injected with abstract religious concepts that posit the possibility of experiencing moral, selfless and devotional-like feelings of love to one's beloved, human or divine. Whilst not being pilgrimages in any simple sense, journeys to the *nishini* of a friend or to a *pari-khan* play an active role in investing Chitral's landscape with personal yet abstract forms of significance.

Such sacred spaces—be they the homes of *pari-khan*s, ravines that the spirits are known to inhabit, or a man's *nishini*—embody the possibility of experiencing things beyond the everyday because of their connectedness to the quotidian world.[53] *Nishini*s do not merely transcend the everyday, but are invested with the possibility of experiencing more bodily forms of action and emotion as well. High land is a source of considerable moral and emotional contestation in Chitral. A man's *nishini* does not simply exist in a geographical realm beyond this one. Often sited on high land *nishini*s are exactly the type of place where village boys may be able to view the houses, bodies and brightly colored clothing of their beloved ones below. Their potential to offer penetrating views of the landscape and the bodies to be found within it does not escape the attention of village elders—fathers scream at young men sitting on hillocks and elevated water channels, accusing them of loitering solely in order to 'look at' the village girls. Visitors to villages too are aware of these dangers, and always ask their friends if other villagers will object to them sitting on high places.

Village girls too are actively involved in these disputes; they become angry with young men whom they accuse of looking at them with 'immoral eyes'. On one occasion a young man in his late teens took me to a 'high place' where he told me we would have expansive views of the valley below. As we sat atop the crest, a young woman approached from below with a flock of sheep, and I soon realized that my young host's interest in the 'view' had a distinctly carnal dimension. The young woman was also aware—shouting at the boy to go away, and asking him why he brought his guests to this place exactly at the time she returned with her sheep.

Sites of personal significance are often richly injected with sacred dimensions. Yet they also signify the possibility of enacting categories of thought, emotions and sociality, which should ideally be abstract, moral and non-worldly, but also, on the limits of the village, have the potential of assuming more direct and bodily forms. Abstract and Sufi-derived conceptions of non-worldly love sit uncomfortably alongside feelings of lust, desire and love that are widely considered as being illicit and posing a threat to the order of everyday village life. This all takes place, moreover, in a setting where politically influential mullahs have sought to 'Islamize' Chitrali society both top-down and bottom-up, and where it is widely held that reform-minded forms of Islam and those influenced by Pukhtun cultural values hostile to Sufi-influenced ways of being Muslim are currently all-powerful.[54]

Very few Chitrali Muslims simply designate some spaces as being 'significant' and 'Muslim' and others as being 'unimportant'.[55] Anthropological work on sacred spaces is helpful in understanding this complexity because of the emphasis it places on the ways in which 'fragmented quotidian existence' and the potential experience of abstract 'emptiness' are two related, rather than opposing, 'poles of experience'.[56]

The Morality of Mobility

Negotiating this multiply-configured historical, moral and sacred landscape is a complex process, which is often of intense personal significance, yet also fraught with conflict, tensions and moral ambiguities. These processes of negotiation are not something that Chitralis do unthinkingly or automatically. Rather, as youngsters they are trained to learn the correct emotional and moral dispositions that are attached to particular places. During tours, young Chitrali men hone their capacity to enact contrasting modes of performance in relation to their region's heterogeneously constituted landscape. At the same time, tours ensure that young villagers' minds are injected with curiosity about their region, and thus are central to the production of complex structures of emotional and intellectual attachment to Chitral as an interconnected regional locality.

Chitralis discuss both the negative and positive dimensions of travel as a recurrent feature of village life. At one level, villagers often question one another's morality by making assertions about the motives and destinations of their journeys. Young men in particular told me that they were 'compelled' to listen repeatedly to the complaints of their parents (*naan-taat*) who accused them of being 'loafers' (*baghola*) and 'wanderers' (*kosak*) traveling in order to avoid doing hard agricultural work at home. The terms *baghola* and *kosak* imply very serious forms of immoral behavior. *Baghola* refers to a young man who 'walks' freely, is known to drink alcohol, smoke hashish, not study, and 'lead on' or even have illicit sexual relations with village girls. The term *kosak* is used to talk about young women who frequently move unaccompanied beyond the confines of their home, visit neighbors and or even make trips to other villages to visit their friends and relatives. Such forms of mobility in excess are assumed to be an important indicator that a woman is sexually *free* (an English term often used in Khowar) or lax.

At another level, villagers emphasize the role played by travel in contributing to the healthy and moral development of young village minds. Travel ensures that the wider 'village environment' fosters 'high thoughts' and not 'low' and 'immoral' conversations, notably backstabbing and gossiping. Villagers often contrast the 'impoverished thoughts' of men whose lives are confined to their homes and the village with the 'life loving' attitudes of elderly men who, despite their advancing age, frequently leave their villages in order to travel across the region. Men, and paradoxically, women who 'sit in their homes' and 'make work' of becoming old risk 'going mad'. In particular, the noises (*hawaza*) associated with the repetitive experience of village life are said to pose a very serious threat to a person's mental and physical health. Family arguments, children crying, fights with villagers over the supply of irrigation water, and repeatedly listening to village gossip, it is said, make 'the brain crazy' (*kak aspah*).[57] In contrast, village 'lovers of life' (*zindadil insanan*) who travel widely earn both 'value' and 'position' in society. They become known personalities (*shaksiyat*) in villages across the region, and spend time sitting in the peaceful guest houses and gardens of their friends rather than amongst their screaming children at home.[58] Villagers today, thus, are deeply concerned about the negative effects of unseating forms of thought and emotion on the behavior of village people and the collective morality of the village as a whole. These are dangers they often connect to the pressures of life in the 'era of speed' in which they say are currently living, and they talk widely about the need to do things to promote balance (*barra bari*) in their daily lives; traveling is one of the most important ways in which they seek to do this. Living a mobile Muslim life, in short, simultaneously enriches and impoverishes the properly moral nature of Chitrali society. Yet mobility is held as being central to a person's appropriate ethical and intellectual development, which is activated in youth, but should ideally be carried through adulthood into elderly life.

In the light of these complex attitudes towards travel, Rowshan villagers invest great efforts in ensuring that morally appropriate forms of travel are an important dimension of everyday village life. Village children (*tsetsek*) are taught the benefits of travel to their everyday lives from a very young age. When I travel, for example, from Rowshan to a nearby village, the elder brother and sisters in the house in which I stay often encourage me to take one of the children with me. They tell me that they are anxious that the children are excessively shy and bored; one of the best ways of ensuring that children grow into 'social' adults is by taking them on *tour*s. Travel, they say, affords children the opportunity to sit with 'different types of people'. Alongside being educated in schools that encourage 'critical thinking', attending musical programs, and spending time in the company of jokers and story tellers, travel is a practice through which Chitrali Muslims invest the minds of village youngsters with a curiosity about their region, and the capacity to understand the joys and virtues of living creative intellectual lives.

As village children mature, however, their traveling often becomes a focus of family conflict. Parents worry that their once 'rose-like' children are now growing into excessively polite (*sharif*) or dumb (*ghot*) automatons, who will be 'useless' (*abbas*) individuals, unable 'to do anything', and thus in constant danger of being tricked and deceived by less scrupulous villagers when they grow older. At the same time, however, parents must also ensure that their children become 'active' young adults and not immoral loafers who prowl the region's villages in search of pretty girls, drink alcohol and smoke hashish and pose a constant threat to the reputation of the family, the hamlet, and the wider 'sectarian community' to which they adhere.

Village youth develop a wide range of strategies to travel frequently and widely despite the contradictory messages emerging from their parents who encourage them to be social but also emphasize the moral dangers of excessive time spent outside the home. Occasionally, they leave the houses in the darkness of night to avoid being asked by their parents the detested question 'where are you going and why'? On a day-to-day basis they walk along hidden village paths mostly used by women in order to ensure that they are not seen loitering in the bazaar and reported to their parents by its suspicious shopkeepers (*dukan-daran*). Twice a year or so, young village male youths (*nau juan*) embark on tours to other villages, telling their parents that they are going to visit their relatives. During the course of these tours, usually in groups of two or three friends, young men, instead, often avoid staying with their relatives, and present themselves to the strangers in whose houses they stay in a distinctly performative mode.

Rowshan's male youth mainly embark on tours to nearby villages and valleys. Yet far from being a homogeneous ethnic or linguistic space in any simple sense, Chitral is characterized by a great deal of internal heterogeneity and is seen by Chitralis as offering numerous possibilities for experiencing difference. This runs contrary to the externally generated expectations of sameness which mark understandings of the region and the larger Frontier, especially those that label it one-dimensionally as an 'Islamist frontier'.[59] There are three major valleys near Rowshan, all of which are known for being very different and inhabited by Chitralis who exhibit contrasting qualities. The villages to the south of Rowshan are said to be home to carefree people who live relaxed and luxurious (*ayashi*) lives—the outdoor performances of music and dance in these villages are said to be especially 'hot' and 'enjoyable', and Rowshan's youths often travel to attend such events together. In contrast, the valley running parallel to Rowshan's is said to be home to 'hardened' Muslims, who are also a touch mean. Yet they live in beautiful villages that make visiting the valley worthwhile. Finally, five hours' drive to the north of Rowshan is a valley known for being traditional and old-fashioned. Its people are said to be simpletons whose lives have been barely touched by the modernizing changes affecting life in places such as Rowshan. Purdah in this valley's villages, for example, is said to be less strict, making chances of glimpsing an unveiled girl with rosy red cheeks a real possibility.

Tour-goers often decide not to wait for a jeep on the side of the dusty road, but, instead, walk to the village they intend to visit. Walking is considered safer than traveling in an overcrowded jeep. More important, it makes chatting and meeting people during the course of the journey easier. Chitralis actively seek to invest tours with slowness, thereby distinguishing them from other types of travel that see travelers sitting in jeeps and minibuses in order to quickly accomplish a piece of work or visit their relatives. Tour-goers often walk until they see a house that appears plush enough to suggest that its owner can provide a decent meal. A freshly slaughtered chicken and plates of home-grown rice are what my friends mostly hanker for. The ability to extract a rich evening meal, indeed, is a talent greatly valued in Chitral, and young Chitrali villagers deploy a wide range of strategies in order to fill their stomachs as best they can.

These strategies of extraction can often be distinctly self-edifying for tour-goers who take pleasure in demonstrating their precocious wit and cunning at the expense of less educated hapless villagers. Yet they also have a particular history in the region's past, and this points towards the ways in which new forms of recreational travel interact with older forms of mobility and self-understanding associated with Chitral's courtly past. In order to persuade the strangers with whom they are staying to feed them, my friends sometimes claim that they are government or NGO officials. The hosts themselves are often aware of the tactics being deployed by their guests, and will occasionally let them know of the event's status as a 'game' by sending revealing winks of the eye across the guest room. Nevertheless, very occasionally, hosts lose their temper and threaten to throw 'the liars' (changatu) out of their houses. As elsewhere in South Asia, the tours of princes and latterly colonial as well as post-colonial officials around their realm was one important strategy through which authority was enacted in Chitral.[60] The Mehtar often traveled around the region with his courtly retinue, and during such tours it was the duty of particular noble status groups who were exempt from the paying of land tax to provide him with cooked food (ashimat).[61] Today, fierce contests erupt regarding whose privilege it is to invite the visiting Chief Examiner to dinner at their home. Yet people from lower status backgrounds mock the ways in which the elders of the ashimat families are proud to remind villagers that they had once cooked food for the Mehtar.

The tours that Chitrali men and boys make are not always short three-day affairs that involve visiting relatives, friends or strangers in nearby valleys; sometimes they travel much further. Thus, I have been with groups of men to visit a remote village in the far south of Chitral (approximately an eight-hour jeep drive from Rowshan) which is home to a community of Tajik-speaking people brought to Chitral 'many years ago' in order to make matchlock rifles for the Mehtar. I have also made numerous trips to three valleys that are home to Chitral's non-Muslim Kalasha community, with both Sunni and Shi'a Isma'ili Chitral friends.[62] Strikingly, these valleys, rather than being seen as posing a one-dimensional threat to the truly Muslim nature of Chitrali society, are frequently visited by groups of Chitrali men who form friendships with Kalasha people, and take the opportunity to drink the wine and home-brew spirits they distil in their homes. At the same time, when Chitralis visit these familiarly exotic places, they also seek to acquire knowledge about the places they are visiting. They ask questions about the history of the people with whom they stay, the types of agriculture they practice, the food they eat, and the languages they speak, and share the information they have gathered with friends, relatives and neighbors when they return to their homes.[63]

There is an important ethnographic dimension to Chitrali tours that goes beyond merely encountering exotic others within their realm. Chitralis recognize the ways in which 'heterogeneous people, things, processes are "thrown" together' in ways that challenge 'the completeness of the "cultural formations" to which one might be tempted to think they belong'.[64] Furthermore, the emphasis they place on the pleasures of searching out and transmitting knowledge about Chitral indicates the dangers of assuming that any automatic or pre-existing 'community of knowledge' exists in Chitrali modes of self-understanding.[65] Rather, Chitralis both recognize and are interested in the ways in which their region and its inhabitants bear the imprint of complex historical processes. This diversity is considered important, moreover, because it renders Chitral a region worth ceaseless exploration. Chitralis' critical reflections on their own past underline the important intersection between past and present that continuously shapes this region.

Many of the tours on which I have embarked have been with groups of young men in their early and mid twenties. These groups were often made up of both Sunnis and Shi'a Isma'ilis. In the context of village life, some tour-goers were known to hold hardened sectarian ideas—one of my Sunni companions, for example, even went through a period of refusing to eat meat killed by Isma'ilis on the grounds that it was unlawful or *haram*. Yet during tours, these mixed Sunni-Isma'ili groups stayed in the houses of families belonging to religious communities other than their own, and shared food with one another.[66] Many scholars have explored the ways in which as Muslims engage in transnational mobility, especially to 'the West', they become 'disembedded from national contexts and resettled in interstitial spaces' and 'develop an increased capacity to recognise, account for and debate difference within their religion'.[67] It is not only long-distance labor migrants or elite cosmopolitans who develop such capacities for recognizing, debating and—momentarily at least—overcoming difference. Chitrali tours are an everyday social practice that are often purposefully deployed by people in order to—albeit temporarily—distance themselves from the concerns of sectarian difference and status distinction that permeate everyday village life.

Hence, when traveling, my friends pretended to be English tourists, Canadian Ismai'lis preachers, and Punjabi visitors from 'down Pakistan', constructing themselves not as Frontier Muslims encapsulated by tradition, but as syncretic, strategizing, cosmopolitan actors within a global context. The shared experience of high-intensity performances that called upon people to enact identities very different from those associated with everyday village life was an especially powerful and memorable dimension of these tours. Their performances were often not particularly convincing. On one tour we made to a very remote Chitrali valley, my traveling companions told our countless hosts that their group was made up of two English-speaking Canadian Isma'ili preachers, one Chitrali man who was employed as their translator— and I was told to act out the part of the son of a Pakistan Army General. I had to spend several minutes persuading my friends that our strategy would perhaps be more successful if I told our hosts the truth—that I was a visiting student from Cambridge University. One morning, however, our supposedly Canadian Isma'ili missionary colleague woke up and after having eaten his breakfast, asked his host in fluent Khowar if he would give his permission for them to leave. In one fell swoop the night's performance had been rendered an embarrassing farce. One of the group's quick-thinking members, acting out the role of the missionaries' translator, made a stab at saving the situating: 'Well done, well done your Khowar is coming on very well', he said to his friend, before confidently turning to the host and saying, 'See how quickly he's learned Khowar; how fast their minds work—we'll never learn English in a hundred years'.

Village youths talk about these 'secret' tours as proof of their capacity to outwit their parents and evade doing hard agricultural work at home. At the same time, they also demonstrate the uneducated simplicity (*sadahagi*) of villagers living in more 'backward' (*pasmanedah*) villages than their own. Nevertheless, parents appear to tolerate and even encourage such forms of behavior as indicators that their children are witty (*namakeen*), independent-minded 'lovers of life'. The tales of extravagant youthful tours become an important way in which villagers remember their own childhood and applaud the cunning (*chalaki*) of their fellow villagers. Tours are often recorded for memory on video cassettes that are shown repeatedly in the houses of villagers; these cassettes stand as testimony to the ways in which young village men endured hardships during their journeys, and as proof of their ability to have fun and outwit and make fools of the people they met.

In his work on rural Lebanon, Michael Gilsenan has documented the ways in which 'the youth' are constantly tested by one another and other 'young men' in their rhetorical and performative ability, by engaging in 'contests of mockery'. Artfully engaging in these contests allowed youths to stake their claim to being considered as young men. Embarking on physically testing tours, during which young men also demonstrate their capacity to trick, outwit and deceive fellow Chitralis, is one such important way that Chitral's youth (*nau juan*) stake their claims to manhood (*moshigari*). At the same time, however, touring is about more than contests of mockery and trickery alone. Tours are an important way in which young Chitralis forge complex 'structures'[68] of emotional attachment to their locality. They are also a social and ethical practice that cultivates young village minds with curiosity about their wider world whilst also developing locally valued skills for the acquisition and sharing of knowledge.

During the course of their tours within and across their region, Chitralis encounter spaces of modernity and tradition, Muslim and non-Muslim, Chitrali and other, as well as freedom and constraint. These heterogeneous spaces and the very different performative roles that are enacted within them are not conceptualized as being a one-dimensional threat to Chitrali Muslim life. They are held by many Chitralis to be important in different yet connected ways for maintaining the mental and moral health of Chitralis and their wider society. Appreciating and handling this complexity are understood by Chitralis as requiring the art of moving between different spaces and shifting their performances in relation to changing indexes of behavior as they do. Such attitudes stand in stark contrast to the homogenizing colonial narratives for the Frontier authored by the likes of Robert Sandeman, as seen in Chapter 2.

Conclusion

This chapter has explored the ways in which tour-going is central to the ways through which Chitralis map, configure and conceptually order Chitral as a regional totality. Chitral is not defined in any simple sense as some homogeneous ethnic, religious or linguistic identity, but rather in terms of being a socially heterogeneous place that offers the potential for being Chitrali Muslim according to very different performative registers. In stark contrast to the colonial discourse of static homogeneity that deployed the language of 'tradition' to encapsulate the mobility, social possibilities and creativity of frontier people, Chitralis subvert such claims made by past and present state authorities through the continual reinscription of both themselves and the landscape through which they travel. The values of this world are not those of deference to tradition, but rather an open willingness and capacity to tease, subvert and contest 'tradition'.

The ethnography explored here has sought to contribute to debates in anthropology concerning the relationship between Islam, modernity and politics and the understanding of the Frontier. It has focused on local practices of mobility that build on a longstanding culture of Persianate travel whilst also reflecting newer anxieties about mental and emotional balance that villagers express as being a product of the 'era of speed' in which they say they are now living. Far from being a dead space of immobile villagers who live on a world periphery and inhabit sub-proletarian habituses, mobility is central to the ways in which young Chitrali men are trained in locally valued modes of understanding and perceiving their world.[69] Through tours young Chitrali Muslims hone their capacity to be witty, funny, clever and strategic adults capable of evading the multiple claims that will forever be placed upon them by fellow village people; and behaving in ways that are appropriate to particular places and social contexts.

Many Chitralis see tours as playing an important role in ensuring that village life does not become intellectually stagnant or morally corrupt. This is notable because Chitral is a mountainous region of Pakistan's North-West Frontier where unemployment, migration to Pakistan's cities as well as the Gulf, and support for Islamist political parties are all important features of daily life. It is tempting to imagine that radical and deeply sectarian forms of Muslim self-understanding would be a focus for enthusiastic support amongst village youth living in such a setting. What the ethnographic material explored in this chapter suggests, however, is that the coherence of reform-minded forms of Islam is deeply contested by Muslims living in this politically volatile setting. Tour-going is an important practice that many Chitralis seek to nurture, sustain and map onto the lives' spaces of Chitral other, very different strands of Muslim life. Prominent amongst these are the forms of work that they invest in cultivating complex emotional and intellectual attachment to their region and a curiosity regarding its social, cultural and religious heterogeneity. Scholars and policy-makers who label the entirety of the Frontier as homogeneously 'Islamist' or even 'Pukhtun-Islamist' have concealed these alternative strands of daily life and the forms of work from which they emerge. In doing so, they have exacerbated the tendency to treat the Frontier's history within a narrow, teleological and 'ethnicized' framework. They have also foreclosed the possibility of those active in policy-making circles envisioning alternative futures for the Frontier in which Islam is treated as one of several sources of values important to the political decision-making of the region's people, as opposed to being the only one.

A number of recent studies have highlighted the role played by Muslim religious habits, practices and modes of expression in the shaping the ethical dispositions of piety-minded Muslims living in cities such as Cairo, Istanbul and Beirut.[70] What this chapter has emphasized, however, is the ways in which Chitrali touring cultivates a modality of understanding and perceiving the wider world founded not on the active cultivation of embodied ethical dispositions but on the appreciation of a mindful, if often skeptical, curiosity about the region's heterogeneity. As Chitralis move through their region they continually invest it with different types of significance and meaning. They talk about contrasting emotional and moral qualities and memories as adhering to different types of spaces and places. The cruelty of the region's courtly past, the significance of its rich tradition of Persianate Sufic poetry, and opportunities for romance and sexual flirtation are constantly evoked. These different spaces sit uncomfortably alongside one another but are connected by people who move within and between them. This contributes to Chitrali people reflecting on the nature of the conditions shaping their everyday lives, rather than simply being shaped by them. In spite of the pressures placed upon Chitrali Muslims to conform to Islamic doctrinal standards, during the course of their tours Chitralis expect one another to question, reflect upon and interrogate the conditions of their everyday lives.

The cultivation of such modes of critically perceiving the world stands in contrast not only to anthropological depictions of Islamic ethical selfhood amongst piety-minded Muslims in urban settings, but also to the emphasis that young men in Karachi place on 'somatic' forms of masculinity within which personal dignity is achieved above all else through displays of 'physical strength and courage'.[71] Drawing monolithic distinctions between 'rural' and 'urban' Islam is an old anthropological practice that has been rightly discredited in recent years.[72] Nevertheless, considered comparisons of contrasting yet interactive forms of Muslim self-understanding as they are enacted in cities, small towns and villages illuminate much about the complexity of the Muslim world today. Above all, they go a long way to challenging the relevance of simplistic rural/urban and center/periphery dichotomies for understanding the complex religious and political dimensions of geopolitical spaces such as the Frontier. Instead, they show how far the expectation that people should question and think critically about the conditions of their everyday life need not necessarily be seen always, primarily, in terms of the grafting of liberal secular standards onto unsuspecting non-liberal subjects; it can also be related to lived practices—such as tours—that people embark upon to become thinking and self-reflective human subjects.

Having explored the ways in which Muslims living in Chitral invest their region and its villages and valleys with wider personal, political and collective significance, creating local geographies of the Frontier in the process, the next chapter documents the ways in which local practices of mobility are also central to the mapping of Chitral within a broader and transregional arena, as well as the forms of shared yet plural identities that develop in this space.

6

MUSLIM COSMOPOLITANS?

TRANSNATIONAL VILLAGE LIFE ON THE FRONTIERS
OF SOUTH AND CENTRAL ASIA

Building on the theme developed in the last chapter, namely local practices of mobility, this chapter explores the richness and complexity of
interactions and encounters between Chitrali people and travelers to
the region. It argues that transregional forms of Muslim identity
encompass people who enact their identities in relation to a wide range
of ethnic and linguistic markers, as well as to varying forms of the
Islamic doctrinal tradition. Such identity formations do not merely
extend spatially across different nation states; they also involve the
forging of connections between Frontier Muslims who have experienced the differential effects of both Russian and British imperialism.
Given the expanding body of work on the Frontier as a place where
population movements have played a role in the emergence of abstract
and often militant forms of 'global Islam', it is tempting to imagine
that a Tajik Muslim from post-Soviet Tajikistan living in a Chitrali
village might seek to smooth over the complexity of his or her experiences of difference by embracing an abstract form of global Islam.[1] Or,
indeed, that such Muslims travel to Chitral with the sole aim of becoming an active member of a violent Islamist movement. In contrast, this
chapter documents the sophisticated ways in which older collective
memories of migration are redeployed by the region's Muslims to
understand and interpret movement across what are today the region's
international boundaries. It also emphasizes, however, the healthy dose

of contingency that also helps to make the particularity of the situations and locations in which mobile people act out their identities. Older experiences of mobility, in short, influence present-day engagements with globalizing processes, but not in any simplistic or deterministic way. The chapter thus examines the uses of a constructed past to shape the present, a theme similar to that presented in the historical chapters, yet different in that the present chapter focuses on the attitudes and actions of local inhabitants.

Ethnographically, the chapter's focus is on relations between Chitrali Sunni and Shi'a Isma'ili Muslims, and non-Chitrali outsiders from elsewhere in Pakistan, as well as Tajikistan and Afghanistan, who live in the region's villages and towns. In order to explore these relations as fully as possible, it locates them first within the broader connective world of this part of the Frontier—exploring the historic, social and cultural connections between Chitral and neighbouring parts of Afghanistan and Tajikistan. Second it documents both the ways in which these continue to shape village life in the region today and the transformations they have also undergone.

Chitral's long border has been exceptionally porous, especially since the start of violent conflict in Afghanistan in 1970s. Since 1979, Chitral has been home to thousands of permanent and semi-permanent Afghan refugees (*muhajiran*). In addition, the region saw an influx of significant numbers of men from Tajikistan who fled their country after the collapse of the Soviet Union in 1991, when a civil war raged between rival factions seeking power in Dushanbe. It was my interest in these connections, and the worlds from which the many Tajiks and Afghans I had come to know in Chitral came, that led me to travel to Tajikistan and Afghanistan in 2005 in order to meet men who had once been 'refugees' in Chitral yet who, between 2001 and 2003, had mostly returned to their 'homelands' (*watanan*).[2]

The wider and more theoretical concern here is with what Vinay Gidwani and K. Sivaramakrisnan call 'invisible histories of movement' between remote villages in an expansive extranational mountain realm.[3] This realm, however, lies at the 'fringes of the intellectual frameworks known as "area studies"', and its people have experienced the divisive effects of the geopolitics of the Cold War.[4] As a result, few scholars consider either the connections between Muslims inhabiting the peripheries of South and Central Asia or the ways in which these illuminate the nature of Muslim thought and self-understanding in these settings and beyond. As is often noted in the case of other 'borderlands', it would be tempting to think of Chitrali Muslims as, above all else, living on the margins of the Pakistan nation-state and on the periphery of South Asia. In contrast, this chapter 'jumps scale' by considering the wider regional and analytical significance of relationships between Chitrali Muslims and their neighbors in Tajikistan and Afghanistan.[5] It thus echoes a larger claim made previously in this book, that the Frontier is no mere periphery, but rather a definitional space constitutive of the multiple 'centers' it is appended to. Moreover, the Frontier is representative of other such spaces both similarly situated and similarly influential. A consideration of these transregional ways of being Muslim points towards the significance of 'identifications, hybrid identities, diasporic existences, minorities, and marginal communities' that remain overlooked in much work on Islam within and beyond South Asia's Muslim societies.[6]

There is a growing body of work giving the impression that the most salient extranational forms of 'Muslim identity' on the Pakistan-Afghanistan Frontier, and in other comparable contexts, are abstract, religious ones created through the processes of globalizing modernity and tied to the displacement of older local identity registers.[7] Yet these studies overlook the role played by transregional dynamics in the shaping of ways of being Muslim and both personal and collective forms of self-understanding in the context of such frontiers.[8] 'Global Islam', indeed, is now a sort of gate keeping concept for the study of Islam in South Asia, and more particularly Pakistan, which means that ways of being Muslim that are neither local and vernacular nor fluid and limitlessly global are rarely the focus of sustained investigation. Such a dialectical approach has its limits. To transcend these, it is important to emphasize the multidimensionality of everyday Muslim identifications in a transregional setting that traverses Central and South Asia, and so the chapter contributes to, rather than challenging older debates about the importance of bounded distinctions to Muslim life.[9]

Cosmopolitan Islam

The concern with transregional forms of mobility and the forms of personal and collective Muslim self-understanding they stimulate connects the findings presented here to anthropological work that theorizes with greater nuance than work on 'global Islam' types of identity 'imaginings' that are wider in scope than national, sub-national, or ethnic ones.[10] Much of this work addresses the opportunities and problems posed by terms such as 'globalization', 'cosmopolitanism' and 'transnationalism' for analyzing 'folk understandings of the global, and the practices with which they are intertwined'.[11] Cosmopolitanism and 'open-ended subjectivities' that enhance 'potentialities for engagement with "otherness"' remained until recently associated predominantly with global cities and elites or places claimed by international trade and the global traffic in meaning, rather than working-class labor migrants.[12] As a result of these debates there is now a wider recognition of the ways in which open-ended subjectivities may emerge from rural-rural migrations or amongst working-class migrants to cities, as much as, if not more than, from transnational movement by mobile elites between global cities.[13]

Scholars have, however, also challenged work that treats cosmopolitanism simplistically as the 'celebration of cultural sophistication'—that is, 'tolerance'. Cosmopolitanism, rather, is understood as a discursive devise through which 'a specific and exclusive local identity' is 'objectified and valorised'.[14] It is also often recognized as being more of an economic vehicle than a form of ideal 'tolerance'—speaking more languages allows traders to sell more things.[15] Most useful about these debates concerning cosmopolitan self-understandings is their recognition of the ways in which even exclusive forms of identity arise from wider links, a process that Engseng Ho refers to as 'resolute localism'.[16] Exclusive forms of self-understanding are not only the product of interactions between openness and closedness. They are also often purposefully injected with a sense of cosmopolitanism.

A highly particular set of cosmopolitanism practices is enacted by Muslims living in the cross-section of the Frontier explored in this chapter and the one that follows. By documenting the ways in which village Muslims negotiate diverse registers of allegiance and identity during the course of their daily lives, the chapter draws attention to the complexities of Muslim life in a territorially porous and internally diverse region. These practices lead to the production of exclusive interests and identities. Yet they also call on the region's people to switch between very different indexes of being Muslim. Undoubtedly such complex self-negotiations have always been a feature of the Frontier, but one that has been largely unrecognized by past scholarship and government policy. Indeed, the sophisticated emotional agency such practices point towards runs contrary to the totalizing and homogenizing social models which are used to describe the Frontier's present and past, and on which so much current policy is predicated. Focusing on the importance of a complex form of cosmopolitanism to life in the Frontier also offers an important corrective to the overwhelming tendency to treat the identity of frontier people solely in the terms of 'tribe', 'ethnicity' and 'Islam'.

It is striking to note how much of anthropology's recent engagement with cosmopolitanism—both as ideology and practice—has emerged from ethnographic work exploring the historical dynamism of the connective nature of Muslim life: in short, Islam's status as a 'networked civilization'.[17] Many studies focus on avowedly religious yet dispersed forms of translocal diasporic networks, such as those embodied in Sufi brotherhoods[18] or global movements of Islamic reform and purification.[19] Others theorize about the ways in which the circulation of long-distance traders, pilgrims, and holy men of religious authority all contribute to a shared sense of Muslim community and the making of transcultural Islamic spaces or ecumenes.[20] There is also a growing recognition now of the complex tensions that exist between Islam's status as a 'networked civilization' and the emphasis that modern forms of nationalism place on the integrity of national boundaries, as well as the ways in which Muslims living in particular transregional contexts seek to resolve or live out these tensions in their daily lives.[21] Much of this work focuses on 'coastal Muslims' living in the expansive Indian Ocean region and argues that transregional ways of being Muslim in such littoral spaces have been long overshadowed by works that explore Muslim life in the so-called heartland of Islamic textual learning in northern India.[22] In Chitral, too, connective ties of kin, trade, and religious knowledge are all central to the making of transregional forms of Muslim collective identity that challenge conventional core–periphery models of the sacred geography of Asian Islam.[23]

Yet there are also dimensions of life in this region that make the ability of the region's people to negotiate this heterogeneous space in cosmopolitan-like ways notable and different from other regional contexts. Over the past thirty years life along the Frontier has come to be defined by refugee flows generated by violence, the fragmentation of the Afghan state, and the breakup of the Soviet Union all of which pose unique threats to such historically embedded modes of Islamic cosmopolitanism. Pakistan's North-West Frontier Province, today known as

Khyber-Pakhtunkhwa, has been profoundly affected by political instability, military conflict, and displacement over the past three decades.
Most anthropological work on 'refugees' in Pakistan focuses on 'displaced persons' living in 'camps'.[24] 'Uprooted' Afghans living between
camps and the Frontier's reformist Deobandi *madrasa*s are, indeed,
recognized as having played a critical role in the emergence of de-ter-
ritorialized forms of 'Muslim identity', the so-called radicalization of
Frontier Muslim identities, and the displacement of older identity registers.[25] It is against this background of representations of the Frontier
that the roles of Afghan and Tajik refugees in the remaking of local
forms of Islamic cosmopolitanism are explored ethnographically
below.[26] The sophistication of such forms of action documented here
is only surprising, however, if we uncritically accept the colonial image
of a static Frontier society, an image in part designed to facilitate exogenous control of the region and its peoples by limiting their movement,
and thus opportunity for change.[27]

Sulton's Story

Sulton came to Chitral from the southern Badakhshan region of
Tajikistan in December 1999, two years after the cessation of full-scale
military conflict there but during a period of great economic hardship
and political uncertainty. His mother tongue is an Iranian-Pamiri language, Shughni, but he also speaks Tajiki Farsi, Russian, and now
Khowar and Dari (Afghan Farsi). On his arrival in Chitral, a member
of the family with whom I stay found him on a cold winter's night
outside one of the village's places of Isma'ili worship. Like the Khowar-
speaking Chitrali family in whose house we both lived, Sulton is a
Shi'a Isma'ili Muslim. During his first months in Chitral, Sulton frequently told the family, themselves descendants of influential *pir*s (spiritual authorities), that it was his search for Isma'ili religious knowledge
that had motivated him to embark on his journey to Chitral. Isma'ilis
in Tajikistan, he said, had little knowledge about Isma'ili doctrine, as
a result of the anti-religious policies of the Soviet Union, and he wanted
to return home with a certificate of Isma'ili education.

Sulton's stay in Chitral would not result in him acquiring any
abstract sense of affiliation with a shared Isma'ili communal identity,
however. Sulton spent most of his days collecting water, threshing
wheat, chopping wood, and even planting roses. Yet his stay in the vil-

lage was eventful. He was known as 'hot headed' by the villagers. On one occasion, for instance, he gave a village boy, Aftab, who had a reputation for being something of a loafer—a result of his public attempts to meet girls and his fondness for shamelessly smoking hashish in the village lanes—a sound beating over a disagreement concerning the division of the village's scant water supplies. Sulton also fell out with the Isma'ili family with whom he stayed. He accused them of putting him to work but teaching him nothing about religion. One evening, he fought with the family's younger brother, saying, 'I have come to Pakistan to go back with something and not to be treated like your slave'. He left the home, now pursued also by the village police, who were threatening to charge him with assault, and never returned.

On 8 September 2001, I met Sulton again, this time on the polo ground at the region's administrative headquarters, Markaz. Sulton had radically transformed his personal appearance. When first in Chitral, like most other men from Tajikistan, he had worn Western-style trousers and had been clean-shaven. Now, he appeared bearded and dressed in *shalwar kamiz*. He also pointed in the direction of the group of men who had accompanied him to the ground, bearded and donning black turbans; he told me they were Afghan Taliban based in the city of Jalalabad. He had been working for them as a driver since leaving Chitral the previous year.

If Sulton had not embraced any abstract commitment to Isma'ili religious knowledge or community during his stay in Chitral, neither had he been unthinkingly Talibanized by his experiences in Afghanistan. Sitting underneath the cool shade of the famous Chinese Plane tree where Chitrali polo players rest their horses at half time, Sulton whispered to me that he had not become a Sunni, nor had he renounced his Isma'ili faith. Rather, in the company of his newly found Taliban companions, he merely pretended to be a Sunni. 'They don't know I'm an Isma'ili, don't tell them', he told me. The dissimulation (*taqiya*) of adherence to Isma'ili doctrine and practice is a marked feature of historical and present-day of Isma'ili experience. What is distinctive about Sulton's case, however, is that it involved an Isma'ili from Tajikistan joining the Taliban, a Sunni and predominantly ethnically Pashtun movement, widely known for its deeply hostile and violent attitudes towards Shi'a Muslims. Pretending to be a hard-line Sunni in such an ambience is not a simple task, especially for a post-Soviet Isma'ili. Sunni and Shi'a Isma'ilis pray in very different ways, and Sulton told me that he stood at the back of gatherings and imitated his Taliban bosses as best he could. I noticed these men leaning on their plush new Toyota Hilux, gazing at Sulton and myself chatting, and decided that this was not the place to linger. Instead, I returned to the polo ground and watched the equally captivating spectacle of the game between the Chitral Police and the Chitral Scouts descending into a physical brawl involving players and their uniformed supporters alike, an event that would lead to curfew being imposed in the town the following day.

After September 11, I lost touch with Sulton but often wondered what had happened to him. In March 2002, I was informed that Sulton had returned to Chitral. He was now said to be working in the house of a man from a one-time noble (*adamzada*) background, known as a lord (*lal*) across the region, and who owned, by Chitrali standards, a substantial amount of land in a relatively remote village to the north of the region. This *lal* was a Sunni, although he was also known throughout Chitral for expressing near blasphemous statements. He also had a well-earned reputation for being Chitral's most prolific hashish producer, and it was now rumored that he was diversifying his smuggling activities into apricot schnapps—in production of which my former Talib friend, Sulton, was said to be investing his talents, to great effect.

The next time I met Sulton was with the aforementioned lord on a snowy afternoon in December 2005. We arranged to meet at dusk on the polo ground, where Sulton told me that he felt he was now the proverbial 'prisoner of the mountains' (*zomo qaidi*). If he returned to Tajikistan, he would almost certainly be arrested by Tajikistan's security forces, who were suspicious of all people who had fled to Pakistan or Afghanistan during the civil war, and even more suspicious of those who had yet to return. If he traveled to 'down Pakistan' (*aff Pakistan*) to meet officials at Tajikistan's embassy, he feared that he would picked up by the Pakistan police, perhaps sent to Guantánamo Bay, or even deported to Tajikistan, where he risked standing accused of leaving his country without authorization during the civil war and being harshly treated by its police and intelligence agencies. Sulton then pulled out a bottle of apricot schnapps that he had hidden down his trouser leg and presented it to me as a gift before bidding farewell.[28]

Sulton's story highlights the very different ways in which states are directly involved in the production and regulation of transregional mobility. It illustrates how what Chapter 2 explored as 'encapsulation by tradition' is something that Frontier people themselves recognize and experience as central to the ways in which states and transnational organizations active along the Frontier seek to govern, control and limit their daily pathways and existences. Sulton's mobility is pervaded by a sense of surveillance by the nation-states through which he travels, and this is often manifested in a fear of their intelligence agencies. Moreover, Sulton also recognizes the ways in which very different forms of transnational policing and surveillance—those arising from the United States and the so-called 'War on Terror'—add a further layer of complexity to the consequences of his transregional mobility. In spite of such limits, however, more neutral places, notably Chitral, continue to afford him complex opportunities for repeating cycles of arrival, departure and return. At the same time, Sulton illustrates the importance of the types of everyday strategy that anthropologists have long recognized as being characteristic of life in borderlands. He is not merely a nameless refugee, passively buffeted by distant international events, but is rather able to embark on complex courses of action in response to rapidly changing geopolitical circumstances.

Sulton's trickster-like ability to artfully instrumentalize the relationships he builds with Chitrali Isma'ilis, Sunni smugglers, and the Pukhtun Taliban is an important reminder of the social and moral multidimensionality that borderland life may inject into even the most apparently bounded forms of collective identity. Thus, Sulton persuasively switches between different registers of Muslim subjectivity as he moves through the region, backgrounding and foregrounding the significance of these to his being as his moves along. Enseng Ho has described the history of the Yemeni Hadrami diaspora in relationship to a 'landscape of places that closed or opened' to different categories of people in relationship to 'internal divisions' and 'external rivalries'.[29] Sulton's Chitral odyssey illustrates exactly the type of work deployed by people who move through such shifting moral landscapes, which are divided by colonially imposed boundaries and invested with shifting forms of global political significance. A wily frontier strategist and a sophisticated, calculating mountain cosmopolitan, Sulton affords us a unique glimpse into the making and working of actual cosmopolitanism on the Pakistan-Afghan Frontier, reminding us again of the need to understand the creativity of Frontier actors rather than understanding their agency in terms of the narrowness of tradition.

Politics, Culture and Islam on the Fringes of the Persianate World

Sulton's capacity to move with skill and grace across his world did not take place in some vacuum-like place of the 'in-between', bereft of pre-existing ties and markers of common histories, cultures, and societies. Few appreciate the degree to which northern Pakistan, northeast Afghanistan, and southern Tajikistan—a region known today primarily for the ongoing search for Al Qaeda militants, the 'War on Terror' and heroin cultivation—form an interconnected region of the Muslim world that is remarkably diverse in relation to its size and sparsely populated terrain.[30] To better understand this region, it is necessary to chart the ways in which these societies and places are historically connected. Doing so brings attention to the importance of older networks for understanding the shape and nature of life in the region today, networks rarely considered important in accounts that treat the Pukhtun 'tribes' as the only transnational actors of any significance in this space. Chitralis' relations with their neighbors illuminate other types of social and imaginative work that are invested by Chitralis and others in understanding, responding to and sometimes subverting the tendency for their region to be mapped and imagined by states and elites as being part of a predominantly Pukhtun space.

I was aware throughout my fieldwork in Chitral that many Chitrali Muslims have a strong sense of identification with a broad transnational region that is similar in important ways to what historians of precolonial India describe as a 'Persianate' realm. The previous chapter explored how Persianate forms of high culture in the form of music and shared literary traditions shape the thinking and practices of Chitralis.[31] This chapter and the one that follows seek to relate such forms of cultural transmission to the shared forms of Persianate political economy in which they are also located. For Persianate societies also shared similar types of political authority defined by a marked focus on kingship, distinctions between commoners and aristocrats, and a courtly, literate, bureaucratic tradition.[32]

Throughout much of the nineteenth century, each of these regions was once a quasi-monarchical state, or princely kingdom incorporated into a central Asian khanate.[33] To the north, for example, the fiefdoms of what today is Badakhshan in present-day Tajikistan were, until the expansion of the Soviet Union, embedded within tributary relationships with the court of the Emirate of Bukhara.[34] In a similar way, the kingdom of Afghan Badakhshan was enmeshed in a shifting and often tense relationship with the centralizing Afghan state.[35] Likewise, the territorial boundaries of the Chitral princely kingdom, which was part of both tributary and conflictual relations with the states of Badakhshan and Kashmir, constantly shifted in relation to the factional succession disputes within the region's 'ruling family'.[36]

The ruling families of many of these realms enjoyed a very high degree of shared kinship with one another, and the ongoing implications of this interconnectivity for the political cultures of both northern Afghanistan and Pakistan will be explored in the next chapter. At the same time, it was also a region of intense instability provoked by ongoing factional struggles within and between the region's 'states', where the flight and exile of rulers and princely contenders to courtly power was a widely deployed political strategy.[37] These migrations were not only made up of rulers and their followers, but also included villagers fleeing the predatory designs of their lords. They encompassed the carriers of Persianate linguistic and cultural practices, such as poets from the court of Kabul who 'wrote the history of Chitral in Persian poetry', composed praise poetry in honor of its Mehtar, or ruler, and taught the court's children Persian.[38]

This political interconnectivity was further enhanced by flows of people between these polities before and shortly after the expansion of Russian and British colonial power in the region.[39] Population movement included traders and pilgrims en route to Mecca from Chinese Turkestan.[40] Complex systems of patronage that incorporated quasi-aristocratic gentry elites and folk described as 'serfs' (*chirmuzh*) and 'servants' (*khidmatgaran*) in Khowar and tenants (*dehqan*) in Dari were central to the region's political economy. Such people often moved with the region's interrelated lordly elite whom they served or sought to escape their influence by relocating to distant locales.[41] Moreover, the transfer of 'slaves' between these mountain realms, is another shared dimension of past experience for the region's people, the legacy of which continues to be a sensitive topic of debate today.[42]

In what ways have the cultural forms of this courtly Persianate culture been re-formed within the context of South Asia's modern nation-states?[43] Many scholars have argued that the divisive effects of colonialism and nationalism obscured the range of ties that once connected this diverse Indo-Persian realm.[44] Others suggest that pre-modern Persianate traditions have been stripped of their vitality and rendered an apolitical part of South and Central Asia's 'national cultures'. These questions have coalesced into debates about continuity versus change in the historiography of South Asia that increasingly recognize 'the significance of diverse remnants of the precolonial past for cultural life in modern times: not only through their deliberate reinvention in nationalist and religious revivalism but also through more diffuse forms of moral inheritance'.[45] We now explore these issues anthropologically by asking what, if any, are the forms that Persianate society and culture continue to take in a world of 'global Islam' and boundary-oriented nation states?

Persianate Modes of Being Muslim

Despite now being fully integrated within the Pakistan nation-state and the Khyber-Pukhtunkhwa Province, many Chitrali Muslims continue to speak and read Farsi. There is a very strong tradition in Chitral of the performance of Khowar love songs, which are deeply influenced by Persianate *ghazal* poetry. In recent years, moreover, many Chitralis have told me that the region's poets are using more and more complex Farsi words and phrases in their writing. Much social science literature on Pakistan focuses on the 'Punjabization' of Pakistan's cultural and political life.[46] Yet Chitralis talk about processes that could be described as the 'Farsization' of their popular culture. Chitralis who speak Farsi, moreover, are not confined to elderly and noble men educated during the final days of the Chitral court. Younger men from a wide range of backgrounds have also learned Dari, most notably from Chitral's Afghan refugees.[47] At the same time, the region's *ulama*, or *dashmanan*, continue to talk about the ability to read religious texts, especially Rumi and Hafiz, in Farsi as a sign of great erudition and a source of unique spiritual insight, despite their own education in reform-minded Urdu and Pashto-medium *madrasa*s that teach the Islamic sciences through the use of Arabic texts.

Almost all Chitralis, moreover, say that Farsi is the 'sweetest' language of all and proudly comment that Khowar is more closely related to Farsi than the North-West Frontier Province's *de facto* language of politics and religion, Pashto. What Chitralis themselves talk about as the expanding significance of Farsi in their region's popular culture has taken place alongside Chitral's political incorporation into the North-West Frontier's political culture over the past thirty years. As noted above, during this period Pakistan's so-called Islamist political parties, whose leadership is predominantly Pukhtun,[48] have become a central feature of political life in Chitral and sought to contest regionally distinctive ways of being Muslim there.[49] Chitralis, thus, invest much imaginative work into mapping their region as a space richly influenced and informed by high forms of Persian culture and language. At one level, this imaginative work forms a complex local response to the interplay between Islamist and Pukhtun ethnic politics that has come to shape both many of the political debates in the Frontier in recent years and the ways in which it has been represented and understood by local and foreign states. At another level, the degree to which both forms of Islamic thought and identity associated with Pukhtun Islamists and other conceptions of being Muslim that valorize the ongoing influence of high Persianate culture interact with one another shows that the local geographies of Frontier Muslims are rarely best understood in terms of one or other reference point, be it a religious, regional or ethnic one. A more productive way of exploring this complexity is in terms of a multiplicity and plurality of reference points, seeking to understand how these are invested with different types of significance at particular spatial and temporal junctures. Such an exploration throws into relief the heterogeneity that simultaneously fragments and connects the Frontier.

The problems of talking about interconnections between ethnicity, religion and region are clearly evoked in a careful consideration of the cultural and religious plurality that inform the contours of being Muslim in Chitral. Playing an active role in making and being a part of this extranational cultural space does not simply eclipse the power of more vernacular-like forms of self-understanding rooted in adherence to the diverse and cross-cutting registers of locality, language, and doctrine. For all Rowshan villagers, 'being Chitrali' and speaking Khowar are critical reference points that distinguish them from other ethno-linguistic groups in Pakistan and beyond, most especially Pashto-speaking 'Pukhtuns'. Furthermore, the invisible histories of movement did not take place between a Khowar-speaking Chitral realm, on the one hand, and a generalized Persian-speaking realm on the other. Diverse registers of linguistic difference and attachment to locality were and remain an active feature of life in the region. Major languages spoken, in addition to the notionally 'national' languages of Urdu, Dari and Tajiki, include a range of Indo-Iranian languages that are, although to widely differing degrees, closely related. These include Khowar, Shughnani, Kalasha, Wakhi, Rowshani and Yidgah.[50]

Islam, likewise, does not define a religious continuum in this wider region in any simple sense. Two types of Islamic doctrinal traditions are represented in the region: Sunni and Shi'a Isma'ili. Isma'ilis are taught to believe the Aga Khan is the 'living Imam', the closest direct descendant of Muhammad and therefore a man of unique spiritual insight and power—he is also referred to as the 'talking Qur'an', or *qur'an-e natiq*.[51] The village people with whom I work are all Khowar-speaking Muslims, yet they categorize themselves as being either Shi'a Isma'ili or Sunni. There have been moments of violent conflict between the followers of these deeply divergent Islamic 'doctrinal clusters', both during the colonial period, notably in 1924, and in more recent years in 1982, 1999, and 2001.[52]

Islam, thus, divides as much as it unites the region's Muslims. At the same time, however, it is not simply the case that within their 'sects' Isma'ilis and Sunnis stand unified. The Isma'ili Islamic tradition is an important and shared source of faith, self-understanding, and experience in all of these settings; yet there are also important debates taking place amongst the region's Isma'ilis concerning what distinguishes them not simply from Sunnis, but also from other Isma'ilis, both those who live in villages on the other side of the Tajikistan-Afghanistan-Pakistan borders, but also those in other global regions where Isma'ilis also live. Isma'ilis in the region talk a great deal about their collective memories and experiences of 'cruelty' (*zulm*) in the Sunni-majority courtly and latterly nation-states within which they live. In recent years, Isma'ilis in Afghanistan have faced violent attacks by the Sunni *mujahidin*,[53] which led many of them to flee to Chitral, especially between 1992 and 2001.[54] In Chitral, too, powerful Sunni religious authorities trained in Pakistan's religious seminaries campaigned throughout the 1990s for the Pakistan state to declare Isma'ilis non-Muslim infidels (*kafiran*).[55] In 1999, it was widely rumored among Chitrali Muslims that the Aga Khan was considering evacuating all of Chitral's Isma'ilis to Canada in the event of a major upsurge in violent sectarian conflict in the region. Shared experiences and the imagination of flight, thus, are marked features of the collective memory of Shi'a Isma'ilis across all of these diversely constituted realms.

Neither the shared historical memory of Sunni cruelty nor the more recent interactions between Afghan and Chitrali Isma'ilis have resulted in the creation of an elevated sense of Isma'ilis' internal sameness.[56] Isma'ili religious self-understandings are always relationally defined—

formed by the complex intermeshing of centripetal as well as centrifugal processes that, we argue, are an important dimension of the making of many different dimensions of Frontier life. Interactions among Afghan, Chitrali, and Tajik Isma'ilis, emerging from the porosity of the region's boundaries over the past decade, have contributed to a growing emphasis on Isma'ilis' internal sameness. This sense of sameness has been actively fostered by the organization of the Isma'ili religious leadership, whose central offices are based in Paris and London. These offices have actively sought to patronize new religious elites and authorities, whose claims to religious authority are based not on traditional claims of descent from the Prophet but on having received an education in the religious texts, as well as Isma'ilis' hermeneutical approaches to interpreting these. To this end, there are men and women from all the locales discussed in this part of the book who have attended courses of Isma'ili religious learning in Karachi, Kabul and Dushanbe, as well as in Paris, London and Toronto. Some are now based in Isma'ili institutions in these locations and visit their home regions on official missions to convey new religious and other messages from the center. New religious edicts have also been drafted and conveyed to Isma'ili Muslims in the region that seek to reform Isma'ili ritual practice there according to apparently worldwide Isma'ili standards.[57]

Yet these homogenizing processes have not inevitably weakened other types of attachment to locality, regional custom or, indeed, globally oriented identities other than those associated with global expressions of being Isma'ili. In short, no miniature Isma'ili arch within a broader and rapidly emerging Shi'a crescent which (according to political scientists such as Vali Nasr)[58] links politically resurgent Shi'a Muslims from Beirut to Lucknow has been forged. Rather, the region's Isma'ilis often talk about the cultural differences that distinguish them from one another, and the tension between sameness and difference that continues to inform their thinking and everyday lives. They engage in contested struggles concerning the extent to which a person's descent from the Prophet makes him or her closer to the Imam than ordinary believers. Yet they also claim that their 'traditions' are different from those of Isma'ili communities elsewhere in South Asia and beyond, notably Gujarati-speaking Khoja Isma'ili, who are often talked about as being especially influential in the offices and institutions of the Aga Khan. Indeed, Khoja Isma'ili forms of Isma'ili faith and practice are often criticized by Frontier dwellers, sometimes being said to be alien to the region.[59] What local reactions to these processes suggest is that abstract 'global' types of Islamic consciousness are not innate within communities, simply waiting to be realized. 'Competing interpretations of orthodoxy and legitimacy', rather, 'can be seen as rival forms of cosmopolitanism' all of which share the goal of 'uniting Muslims by insisting on universal standard and practices'.[60] Ultimately, however, such attempts to unite Muslims also give rise to different types of Muslim self-understanding that remain simultaneously present and do not efface one another. Islam, rather than standing loftily above the Frontier's fragments, is instead fully implicated in the ongoing remaking of these fragments.

From Cross-Border Smugglers to NGO Workers: Persianate Connectivity, New and Old

If modern refugee flows and institutionalized forms of 'transnational Islam' have not simply led to the displacement of registers of Muslim self-understanding rooted in complex forms of Persianate culture, then neither have the region's boundary conscious nation-states eradicated older forms of interregional connectivity or modes of imagining selfhood that are expansive and international if not necessarily 'Islamic'.

The influx of men into Chitral from the post-Soviet state of Tajikistan in the late 1990s, in addition to Sunni and Isma'ili Muslims from Afghanistan, adds another layer of complexity to the historic and cultural transregional connections described above.[61] Chitral became a unique and interactive space that connects the predominantly Muslim societies of postcolonial Pakistan, post-Soviet Tajikistan, and 'semi-colonial' Afghanistan.[62] People whose lives had been divided for nearly a century once again shared the intimate spaces of Chitrali villages.[63] Before exploring ethnographically the nature of the social interactions that took place between villagers and strangers in Rowshan, the chapter offers a broader introduction to the contexts from which these came to the village. What follows is based on six fieldwork visits to Tajikistan's Badakhshan Province in order to meet Pamiris, the term widely used to refer to the Isma'ilis who live in the high mountain villages of both Tajikistan and Afghanistan and who lived in Chitral between 1992 and 1999 as refugees.

During the course of these visits, I have been told by men how they had swum across the Pyanj River into Afghanistan, where they bar-

tered with Afghan Wakhi-speaking villagers for kerosene and alu-
minium dishes in return for precious Afghan supplies of oil and rice,
as well as tea from Chitral.[64] Villages on the Afghan side of the border
also told me how during the worst years of the war in Tajikistan they
had woken up to discover that the carpets in the guest rooms of their
houses had mysteriously disappeared, apparently removed in the
darkness of night by their neighbors on the other side of the border.
All of these trips by local actors were clandestine and officially illegal,
yet the state officials of Tajikistan allowed them to take place purportedly for 'humanitarian' reasons. Indeed, stories are told of how Tajiki
KGB officials whose duty it was to monitor such cross-border movement would find themselves in uncomfortable circumstances when—
disguised as Afghans—they bumped into the fellow villagers across
the border in houses in Afghanistan. Importantly, however, not all of
the holders of political power and authority in mujahidin-controlled
Afghanistan were willing to allow such flows of movement to take
place—Pamiri men have also told me how they were detained and
jailed by mujahidin commanders during their trips into Afghan territory on their way to Chitral.

In small groups, Pamiris traversed the Afghan Wakhan corridor and
the high passes of the Hindu Kush, eventually reaching Chitrali villages after a three-day walk. Chitral occupied an important place in
the geographical and imaginative horizons of all the Pamiris I spoke
to. Village elders remember their grandfathers walking to Chitral in
order to procure tea, sugar, and salt before their region's incorporation
into the Soviet Union. Others told me that their grandmothers were
Chitrali, and they could remember the names of the Chitrali villages
from where they had come and asked me if I had visited these places.
One man even remembered some of the Khowar words that he had
been taught by his grandmother as a child and asked me to tell him
what they meant. Thus, Tajik men did not simply enter Chitral as displaced persons; they arrived, rather, with previously existing reputations and holding historically informed expectations of the nature of
Chitrali life.[65]

Connections between all of these regions have changed rapidly in
relationship to unfolding geopolitical circumstances. After the Ameri-
can-led defeat of the Taliban government in Kabul in 2001–2, the
Chitral-Afghan border was effectively sealed whilst the Tajikistan-
Afghan border also became the focus of multi-million dollar border

strengthening projects.[66] Some movement of men involved in the sale of arms and heroin continued, but it was far more controlled and regulated by state authorities—notably the border police of both countries—than was the case during the period of 'the *jihad*'. The UNHCR and the government of Pakistan also actively pursued initiatives designed to encourage the return of Pakistan-based Afghan refugees to their country.[67] These changes were also reflected in the speeches of politicians in Chitral. The mullah who was Chitral's elected representative in Islamabad between 2002 and 2007 called upon the Government of Pakistan to expel Afghans from his region, claiming they had brought murder and drugs to it, a position that was especially popular with Chitrali traders whose businesses were in direct competition with Afghan shopkeepers.

These changes have had important consequences for the livelihoods and personal experiences of the region's mobile mountain Muslims. Since December 2001, few Farsi-speaking Afghan and Tajik peoples have been able to enter Chitral without either Afghan refugee cards or Pakistani visas and internationally valid passports. Some Afghan refugees with legal documentation stayed, but most left. It is noteworthy that many of those who did leave continue to hold Afghan refugee cards. Some of them continue to make frequent returns to Chitral in order to participate in education courses run by small-scale private tuition centers (especially English language and computer training), sell cheap second-hand cars from Afghanistan at higher Pakistan prices, and visit the Chitrali families with whom they lived during the previous thirty years.[68] Yet, as we will see in the next chapter, such forms of movement have also become more difficult. Others who remained in Chitral without proper documentation, like Sulton, now lived in a region of uncertainty, surrounded by heavily policed boundaries and thrust into the international spotlight after September 11.

The closure of the Afghan-Pakistan border had a profound impact on people's everyday lives. The region's interconnected Frontier economy underwent rapid change. Cross-border trade in meat and precious stones, especially lapis lazuli and polo horses from Afghanistan, and kerosene and wheat from Chitral abruptly ceased. Precious stones for eventual export to Sri Lanka, Dubai and Hong Kong were now taken to Peshawar via Kabul, rather than across Chitral's mountain passes. The roads that crossed these passes and the tea-houses dotted along them—packed a decade previously with donkey and mule trains—are now empty, tea-house owners having shifted their businesses to small towns on the Afghanistan-Tajikistan border such as Ishkashim.

Local attitudes to these important changes in the region's border regimes are complex and ambiguous. Afghan villagers in Badakhshan told me that because of new border controls they could no longer walk to Chitral to work, but they could not afford the expensive journey for work to Kabul either. Others, however, commented that they no longer needed to travel to Chitral. There was now work to be found in their own region as laborers on development projects, soldiers in the Afghan National Army and Border Police, and, for those who had had a formal education, as clerks, teachers and government officials.[69] They also remarked that now hard times had fallen upon villagers from Chitral's upper valleys, who were 'compelled' to come to Badakhshan in order to sell their livestock, as prices in Afghanistan were now higher than in northern Pakistan. Such complex attitudes are also invested with further ambiguity because the new sources of wealth and employment in Badakhshan are also widely said to come with important strings attached. During a visit to Ishkashim in Afghanistan in 2010 I watched with local villages how Afghan helicopters brought the bodies of two young men (soldiers in the Afghan National Army) who had been killed in Qandahar fighting against the insurgents. These deaths provoked debates amongst local politicians and members of the Afghan security apparatus concerning the relationship between this largely Isma'ili part of Badakhshan and Afghanistan and the wider world. Why, asked some local politicians, should their peaceful and largely Isma'ili-populated region suffer from a distant war in southern Afghanistan? Security officials retorted that Afghans should never think locally—such modes of thinking posed a threat to the nation, and also failed to recognize that Afghans were politically successfully when they acted with national rather than local issues in mind.[70]

Chitral was simultaneously affected by comparable global transformations, although with very different consequences. By July 2003, the only Afghans living permanently in Chitral were Sunnis who owned butchers' shops and bakeries. Many Chitrali shopkeepers complained that the bazaar felt 'empty' (*khali*). Chitral's small elite of traders had profited greatly from the sale and smuggling of food and fuel transiting to northern Afghanistan. Their activities as border traders had unleashed important socio-economic tensions and dynamics within Chitrali society at a variety of levels. Not only did those involved in cross-border smuggling often assert their wealth in the region in political ways, by standing for election for example, their activities also played an important role in changing local attitudes towards what constituted morally proper forms of economic life. It was, thus, often men from 'honorable' (*khandani*) or gentry families who traded with Afghans. While these trader-smugglers often successfully deployed their money in election campaigns, they were also said by many Chitralis to have made money from 'dishonorable' practices that reflected poorly on their aristocratic family pedigrees. 'My relatives were very angry', one man in his mid-forties and from a gentry family told me, 'because I made money selling paraffin and potatoes that I bought from Afghan traders. They used to say to me, "what type of a lord are you if you sell potatoes?"' The closure of such trading routes and the restriction of the possibilities they offered for personal and familial enrichment after September 11th 2001 meant that Chitral's smuggler-traders had to find new activities and sources of profit, something explored below.

Chitral's status as a place of profit and security for Afghans and others also changed. By 2007, many Panjshiris who had lived and traveled in Chitral increasingly said that they feared for their lives in the region. Supporters of the Taliban lived in Chitral, they said, and these people saw Panjshiris and other Dari-speaking Afghans as collaborators with the Americans against the Taliban insurgency. More important, whilst Chitral remained almost entirely free of the violent militancy that came to shape everyday life in districts of the North-West Frontier Province located only a two or three hours drive away, transport links to Chitral were greatly affected by these conflicts. Chitralis travelling on roads between Chitral and Peshawar through regions nearby to Swat were targeted and killed by the Pakistan Taliban, purportedly because of the major role that Chitralis played in government operations against the militants, especially as soldiers and policemen in the Frontier Corps, Pakistan Army and Chitral Scouts. Afghans also recognized that the profits to be made from Chitral's small markets were slight compared to those to be made from markets in Central Asia.[71]

Yet, even in the context of the imposition of apparently rigid boundaries, and the demise of sources of profit and security for those who sought to cross them, connections between these regions have an uncanny ability to reappear. The borders that divide the region's people open as they close. International development NGOs, especially the Aga Khan Development Network, have been active in Chitral since

1983.[72] They have been undergoing significant downsizing in Chitral since the beginning of the current millennium but are expanding their operations in the post-conflict settings of Tajikistan and Afghanistan. Their one-time Chitrali employees are often attracted by the prospect of handsome US dollar salaries to work in Afghanistan. Well-educated, brought up with Afghans and speaking fluent Dari, Chitrali men are especially attractive candidates for these posts, even more so as the escalating Taliban insurgency has made mobility for 'non-local' foreigners increasingly difficult. Several Chitralis now live and work in Kabul and in both Afghanistan's and Tajikistan's Badakhshan regions.[73] These often include men who used to trade with Afghans across the border with Badakhshan during the *jihad* and whose economic lives suffered from the closing of the Chitral-Afghanistan border. Notably, their relations going back to the era of the *jihad* and before, with men who were once *jihadi* commanders and cross-border traders yet are now local officials and elected political representatives, mean also that they can work in these jobs with great effectiveness.

Thus, if the free and unregulated movement of refugees, laborers and traders between Tajikistan, northern Afghanistan and Chitral that characterized life there between 1981 and 2001 is now of far more restricted significance, men and women working in NGOs are playing an important role in comparable processes of regional interconnection. Indeed, the NGOs for whom they work actively seek to promote 'regional integration'. In the summer of 2010, for example, one Chitrali Isma'ili man who works for the Aga Khan Foundation invited Chitral's most famous musical group (the Nobles) to perform at a celebration of 'Pamiri culture' that was organized by the Aga Khan Foundation in Khorog, the administrative headquarters of Tajikistan's Badakhshan Province. The celebration was part of a process of regional integration that was actively sought, encouraged and fostered by this regionally and internationally influential NGO.

Yet these NGO workers are critical to such processes of regional integration not simply because they carry out the policies of the organizations for which they work. They also derive and develop other forms of personal satisfaction from their employment in the region. These forms of satisfaction reflect the continually evolving nature of the transregional identity formations that are the focus of this chapter. They also provide insights into the actual processes through which wider, internationally-oriented, cosmopolitan subjectivities continue to emerge

157

in the region. One man from northern Pakistan, for example, Sohail, is a descendant of a family of Chitrali Seyyids, and now a contractor for NGOs working in Tajikistan. He told me how, during his seven years working as a program manager in the borderlands of Tajikistan and Afghanistan for the Aga Khan Foundation, he had realized that his 'identity' fluctuated between two poles. One of these was 'Persian' or *ajami* and reflected, he told me, the influence of Persian linguistic forms and cultural values (*ajam*) on his indigenous Chitrali culture. The other identity pole was rooted in the 'Arab' ethnic identity of his Seyyid ancestors. He had increasingly come to recognize the importance of this pole to his identity because of his rich interactions with Seyyid ancestors on both sides of the Tajikistan-Afghanistan border in Badakhshan.

A range of expansive identities are produced and created in this region. One of these involves an active commitment to Isma'ili collective identifications, and is partly made possible and energized by the patterns of mobility that organizations such as the Aga Khan Foundation make possible. Another treats these connected regions of Pakistan, Afghanistan and Tajikistan as a 'culture area' and promotes this, for example, through organizing shared musical events, which are also predominantly although not exclusively Ismai'li. In addition, however, men like Sohail also identity themselves as the inheritors of even more expansive identities that are shaped as much by ideas of 'Arab' and 'Persian' as 'Ismai'li' or 'Pamiri'. These ideas are, indeed, important and recognizable to Muslims across much if not all of South Asia, and in many connected contexts beyond. Faisal Devji argues that the categories 'Arab' and 'Persian' should not be seen as simply markers of 'ethnic identity'. They speak, rather, to the ethical concerns of South Asian Muslims, and their understandings of the moral constitutions of Muslims, registering different 'philosophical principles that could be identified by different names over more than one civilization', as for example between 'Arab' insistence on the 'letter of the law' and 'Persian' perfection of a 'contemplative life'.[74] These modern Chitrali reflections on such philosophical principles highlight the history of changing limits and opportunities in terms of mobility, employment and imagination that have been created by the border and the forms of political economy it produces. They also bring attention to the ways in which this world, while highly diverse, is also informed by Persianate forms of culture and Islam.

Insiders and Outsiders: Intelligence Officers, Red Army Soldiers, and Dushanbe Artists

Having explored the broad political and cultural context shaping the experiences and movements of Afghans, Tajiks and Chitralis across this expansive mountain frontier realm, the remainder of the chapter explores in the context of Rowshan the everyday negotiation of regional heterogeneity. It thus tacks away from people's abstract relations with culture and religion, to the ways in which these are manifested in people's social relations with one another.

What follows focuses on the forms taken by interactions between incomers and Rowshan people. Rowshan villagers refer to Afghans and Tajiks in their village as 'outside people' (*berieo roye*) and 'strangers' (*nagoni*). Many social scientists continue to depict refugees as rootless people, devoid of a particular national culture and, as a result, excluded from the national imaginaries of the countries in which they live. States and their publics consider them, in other words, an impure threat to what Liisa H. Malkki has termed the globally hegemonic 'national order of things'.[75] For Malkki, such folk have one of two options: they must either create 'nation-like' identities in order to forge for themselves a space in the 'national order of things', or subvert that order by emphasizing their 'liminality'. These arguments have been forcefully contested in recent years, most notably by Aihwa Ong, who suggests that Malkki fails to explore the 'complex, ambiguous and interweaving processes that transform refugees back into citizens', noting that 'particular states and their publics may be *for* and *against* refugee influx at different points of time'.[76]

Despite their use of the term 'outsider', Rowshan people deploy a wide range of categories to describe the men from Afghanistan and Tajikistan living in their village. These diverse ways of imagining and categorizing refugees have major implications for shaping the nature of the interactions that take place between villagers and outside people and, therefore, Rowshan villagers' cosmopolitan 'appreciation of ideas, things, and beings from many places'.[77]

Rowshan people's conceptualizations of 'outsiders' is characterized by a very high degree of complexity.[78] There are three major categories of 'outsiders' (*nagoni*) that are relationally referred to one another during everyday conversations between Rowshan villagers. First, there are Khowar-speaking people who have settled in Rowshan since migrating there from nearby villages. Second, there are the *alghani* or

159

Pashto-speaking Pukhtuns from both Afghanistan and Pakistan who live and work in the village, mostly as hawkers and shopkeepers. Third, there are those people whom Rowshan villagers describe as the 'doers of Farsi' (*farsi-korak*)—these are the Dari- and Tajik-speaking refugees and laborers from Tajikistan and Afghanistan who are the central focus of this chapter. Those of the *farsi-korak* who have come to Chitral from territories that are part of modern Afghanistan are referred to largely not as 'Afghans' but as 'Kabulis'. Chitralis use the term 'Kabuli' to refer not to people from the city of Kabul, as is now common in Afghanistan, but to the territory of Afghanistan. On returning to Chitral through the winter route by way of Afghanistan, Chitralis often say they have come home through Kabul. The continued usage of terms such as Kabul by Chitralis reflects the ways in which older understandings of space that are now shaped one-dimensionally by the 'national view of things' continued to inform the wider spatial geographies of the region's people. This usage also serves to underscore a point made in the introduction concerning the complexity of debates about naming spaces and peoples in the region, and the importance of using names in relationship to the particular contexts in which they are evoked.

These different types of 'outsiders' are placed within a moral hierarchy that is known and understood by most Rowshan villagers. Villagers perceive different categories of outsiders as capable of bringing strikingly contrasting forms of immorality to village life. Pukhtuns, largely from the tribal region of Bajaur, but also often hailing from Afghan nomadic or *kuchi* backgrounds, and involved in the sale of cloth, are widely perceived as being the most dangerous type of stranger. They are associated with many types of criminality, notably theft, child snatching, and drug smuggling.[79] By comparison with Pukhtuns, Rowshan villagers see Farsi-speaking 'Tajiks' as less morally corrupting. Some Farsi speakers live with their families in Rowshan, where they own very respectable businesses; many have lived in Chitral for up to thirty years and speak fluent Khowar. The ability of these 'refugees' to speak Khowar is something that villagers contrast to what they perceive as the inability of Pukhtuns to learn their civilized and sophisticated language.

Rowshan villagers, however, do not simply essentialize all 'Kabulis' or Dari-speaking refugees as 'doers of Farsi'; they also classify these folk on the basis of more finite distinctions. They categorize most 'doers of Farsi' as falling into one of two types. First, the term 'Tajik' (*tazhi*) is widely used to refer to Farsi-speaking people from the Badakhshan and Panjshir regions of Afghanistan. These people are often blamed for introducing 'murder' (*qatil*) into the region, although this discourse is more widely articulated in Chitral's urban district headquarters, Markaz, than in village settings such as Rowshan. Second, Rowshan villagers deploy very different stereotypes to talk about another category of outsiders who are, nevertheless, also said to be 'doers of Farsi'. 'Wakhiks' are Wakhi-speaking Isma'ili people who have long migrated to Chitral largely as seasonal laborers (*mazduran*) from the Wakhan corridor, a valley that is divided latitudinally between Tajikistan and Afghanistan.[80] Wakhi is a Pamiri Iranian language, but it is different in significant ways from other languages spoken in Chitral and Badakhshan. Wakhiks are said by Chitralis to be harmless simpletons (*nacharagan*) who have 'nothing in their head' (*kaka nikie*). They are the upcountry hicks (*sarhadi roye*) against whom Rowshan villagers often define themselves as cultured (*tazhibyi haftah*) city-dwellers (*shaharo roye*).[81] Chitralis also say, however, that Chitralis themselves have lost many positive human qualities during the course of their long struggle to become fully realized humans (*insanan*), yet that the simple honesty (*sadahgi*) of their forefathers remain visible in the straightforward thinking and behavior of their Wakhik neighbors.

My Chitral friends spoke with the 'doers of Farsi' in the village in Farsi, although amongst themselves the 'outsiders' talked in a very wide range of Pamiri Iranian languages, including Wakhi, Shughnani, Rushani and Ishkashemi. These incomers lived mainly in groups of as many as ten men in cramped rooms in the village's small bazaar that they rented from Rowshan people. Some of them lived alone or in pairs in village houses, where they also worked as agricultural laborers. Rowshan's bazaar, a largely deserted space after the evening prayers, was, between 1995 and 2002, filled until late into the night with the sound of Tajik and Afghan music played on the *ghaljak-i pamiri* (a three-stringed instrument with a tin can used as a resonator that is an important part of the musical traditions of Badakhshan).

These 'outsiders' did not, however, live lives confined to the small teahouses (*chai khana*) and rented rooms of Rowshan's dusty bazaar alone. Complex cultural and religious transactions also took place between Chitralis and 'outsiders'. Persianate cultural forms were not simply a pre-existing feature of Rowshan cultural life. As a result of the interactions between villagers and outsiders, they also continually leaked into daily village experience and were rendered into a shared focus of identification. The Afghan and Tajik guests (*menu*) were not treated simply as demeaning household servants, lowly immigrants in need of patronizing support, or amusing diversions from the monotony of daily village life. Rather, some Tajik men quickly earned a reputation for being cultured and creative, and many Rowshan villagers became close friends with the incoming 'doers of Farsi'. This was not as visible, however, in Chitralis' interactions with Pukhtun traders and hawkers (*alghani*). The *alghani* were rarely, if ever, invited as guests or friends into Chitrali homes. On a number of occasions, indeed, Pukhtun hawkers were forced to leave the village's hamlets after having been accused by Rowshan men of encouraging village women to waste their precious resources on useless trinkets.

Rowshan villagers chatted with Farsi-speaking men, introduced me to them as their friends, and even invited them into the intimate spaces of their family homes. They were also seen as a critical intellectual resource. They taught some villagers how to read Sufi books by Persian mystics such as Hafiz, Sa'di and Shiraz. A particular visible space where Persianate cultural forms could clearly be seen leaking into village life was Rowshan's bakery shop, opened by refugees from Afghanistan's Panjshir Valley in 1998. Each afternoon, the shop would be full of village boys who gathered to learn Dari and recite verses from Farsi poems. One young Rowshan man in his early twenties, Zulfikar, generated such a passion for the study of Farsi that he even chose to embark on a master's degree in Persian literature at Peshawar University. Notably, he was also able to persuade his parents of the worthiness of his subject by saying that he would easily find well-paid employment with a non-governmental organization working with Afghan refugees in Peshawar. Afghans also contributed more widely to the cultural life of Rowshan. Juma Khan, an Isma'ili man in his early twenties from Afghanistan's Wakhan corridor who lived in Chitral between 1995 and 1997, frequently relayed reports about Sunni *mujahidin* hostility towards Wakhik Isma'ilis to his Chitrali friends. At the same time, during collective 'Chitrali' evenings of music and dance, villagers often persuaded him to perform Afghan and Wakhi songs on his wooden flute.

Many men from Tajikistan earned reputations for being 'artists'. They were invited to paint the walls of Rowshan houses with mountain scenes, depictions of deer and peacocks, and portraits of the current Aga Khan.[82] These murals were a significant innovation to the decorative standards of Rowshan homes. Hitherto, many Rowshan Isma'ilis had not even dared to display photographs of the Aga Khan inside their guesthouses for fear of being vilified as 'idol worshippers' (*bud parast*) by Rowshan Sunnis, still less to paint full-scale portraits of him on their walls. Young Rowshan Sunni men, undergoing training in the Islamic sciences in Deobandi *madrasas*, often say that the 'kind angels of paradise' will never enter a house in which images of the human form are to be found. Wall paintings of the Aga Khan have the power to invoke even stronger emotions; they furnish evidence that Isma'ilis commit *shirk*, or associationism, by treating the Aga Khan as a kind of demi-god. Framed photographs of the Aga Khan are often found in Isma'ili households, yet many Isma'ilis remove these from their guest houses when they are expecting Sunni visitors known to hold uncompromising attitudes toward both images and Isma'ilis. This strategy of concealment, of course, is not applicable to wall paintings, which therefore embody the expression of Isma'ili forms of self-understanding in a shifting space located between the privacy of the home and the public arena of the bazaar.

Conversations about life in Tajikistan and Afghanistan were common between Sunni and Ismai'li Rowshan villagers and Farsi-speaking outsiders. In these, the assumptions held by many Rowshan villagers about the monolithic 'backwardness' (*pasmandhagi*) of Badakhshan and its people were frequently challenged by the graphic accounts given by Tajikistan's 'refugees' about life in their region. Sitting in small groups in village orchards, we were often told that Badakhshan, like upper Chitral, was mountainous, remote, and populated predominantly by Isma'ilis Muslims. Yet these regions of Afghan Badakhshan were also amongst the most important providers of government soldiers and officers to the Afghan Army during the pro-Soviet governments of the 1980s. Men who worked threshing and collecting the crops of Chitralis also told their 'employees' how they were trained in the field of intelligence work in Tashkent and Bishkek, and in military tactics in Moscow and St Petersburg. This emphasizes again the degree to which frontier people actively experience and think about their region not as a distant periphery but as an integral space connected to multiple centers.

Chitralis also learned from Tajik men that across the River Pyanj, a very different model of the Badakhshani village was in place. In contrast to the stereotypes widely held by Chitralis about 'backward' (*pasmandah*) Wakhiks, villagers in Tajikistan's Badakhshan Province enjoyed electricity and metalled roads that had been built by the Soviet government—such forms of 'modernity' had yet to penetrate Rowshan village life. My Chitrali friends also discovered that the men now working as laborers in their fields had been engaged in very different forms of employment before the Soviet Union's breakdown. Rowshan's Tajikis told dramatic stories about how they had been parachuted as spies and translators into Afghanistan by the Soviet army. Through such conversations, Rowshan villagers gained insights into and made comparisons between the complexity of the wider setting in which they lived and the diverse types of modernizing transformations its people had experienced over the past century. Through these interactions, Rowshan people increasingly saw themselves as existing within a transnational realm where vernacular identities existed alongside a more expansive set of Persianate values, as well as the sometimes unifying and at other times divisive bonds of religion.[83]

The Chief Minister is Coming: Please Move Inside!

Nation-states, international organizations, and older and newer imperial formations have played and continue to play very different roles in the simultaneous production and division of this transregional space. A study of interactions between 'refugees' and 'local villagers' in Chitral would be incomplete, therefore, without a consideration of the role of the state in the regulation and surveillance of this movement. Particularly useful for understanding the production of actually existing forms of cosmopolitan practices in this geopolitically sensitive setting is an acknowledgment that these are not merely the product of a contradiction between a remote locality and a distant state acting (or failing to act) on that locality. Rather, local 'faces' of the Pakistan state are often themselves producers of complex forms of transregional identity.

Despite Rowshan's relative remoteness, there are law courts, a police station, and a deputy superintendent of police in the village. As has widely been noted, the police are never a monolithic force instrumentally responsive to central command, but are always firmly situated within particular social contexts.[84] In Rowshan, they did not merely imagine refugees as dangerously destabilizing and polluting influences on the bounded certainties of village life. Rather, new interactions that took place between the state and the 'refugees' did so in a space richly invested with the imprint of shared forms of sociocultural values concerning the status of the refugees as guests, co-religionists, friends, laborers, and the possessors of shared histories. This played a critical role in shaping the interactions between the Chitrali faces of the Pakistan state and the refugees.

The legal status of 'outside people' was a source of confusion in the village. In December 1995, for instance, the Chief Minister of Pakistan's North-West Frontier Province was planning a visit to Rowshan. Such a high-level state visit to Chitral is relatively rare, and when such events do occur, they entail considerable levels of security and displays of protocol. A police escort accompanies the Chief Minister everywhere he goes. Many Rowshan people told me that they were worried that the police accompanying the Chief Minister would see the illegal Tajiks and deport them. Unlike Rowshan's several Afghan refugee families who held identity cards, the men from Tajikistan were not able to secure legal documentation within Chitral and were often too frightened to make the long journey to 'Pakistan' in order to do so.

The men from Tajikistan were aware of their legally precarious position in Rowshan, yet also often talked about their experiences of social solidarity in the village. As a matter of routine, they avoided going to the region's administrative headquarters because they feared being detained by the Chitral police there. One Wakhi-speaking man in his late forties whom I met in Tajikistan in October 2005 had worked and lived with a Seyyid family in Rowshan for five months. During this period, he had only been to Markaz once, and even on that occasion he had been too scared to walk around the bazaar, for fear of being caught by the police. Instead, he stayed put in the vehicle in which he traveled. There is also a police station (*thana*) in Rowshan, yet this man and others told me that they did not fear Rowshan's police. Indeed, he told a gathering of neighbors in his village in Tajikistan's Wakhan corridor that on the day he had left Rowshan for Tajikistan, not only had a village policeman helped him find a vehicle that was going to the northern Afghan border, but he had told the driver that his passenger was simple, poor, and going home with gifts for his family—under no circumstances, therefore, should he be asked for a fare.

Collaborations between Chitral's police, villagers and the incoming Tajiks sometimes took a bigger and more significant form. One day before the Chief Minister's visit in December 1995, for example, Rowshan's deputy superintendent of police, at the time a bearded Sunni man from Markaz who could usually be seen in the early evening fingering his prayer beads and sauntering towards the mosque, drove his police vehicle around the village and publicly announced on a loudspeaker that any people from Tajikistan staying in the village who did not hold identity cards should not go to the bazaar but instead stay with Rowshan families the following day. If not, they risked being deported to their homes and also getting Chitral's police into great trouble. Rowshan people frequently invoke the great sacrifices (*qurbani*) they have made for their Tajik brothers (*brargini*) and guests. 'Chitrali hospitality' thus led to an open-ended individual subjectivity that promoted interactions with Farsi-speaking outsiders, and also allowed Chitralis to draw boundaries around more exclusive forms of cultural 'intimacy'.[85]

The collaborations that took place between Rowshan's police force, villagers and refugees clearly challenge, any simple notion that refugees and citizens are inevitably related to one another as in Ong's words, 'irreconcilable opposites'.[86] Refugees interact not with faceless states that exist outside local contexts but with institutions that are 'deeply imbued' with 'socio-cultural values' and embedded within particular historicosocial spaces.[87] The 'state' is multiply constituted, and its faces engage 'refugees' through different matrixes that include but are not defined by the logics of national inclusion alone. The historical chapters of this book have discussed the multiple faces of the state, and the ways these manifest themselves in different contexts. Anthropologically this section has also documented different and intensely local 'faces of the state',[88] and explored how these are clearly imbued with sociocultural values that both provide the basis for cosmopolitan appreciation and engagement with people from very different backgrounds and also construct boundaries around more vernacular forms of shared selfhood and community.

We Are Not Wakhik! Transnational Muslim Identifications

Far from provoking the emergence of de-cultural and avowedly religious forms of Muslim identity, it is clear that Rowshan's refugees facilitated a range of older and newer forms of cultural interchange and contributed to Chitral's status as a transregional setting in which the everyday practice of coexistence with Afghan and Tajik incomers is one important cosmopolitan dynamic. When Chitralis shared their homes, engaged in conversations, and sought out these men as their friends, they were interacting with people who, for example, had experiences of work and education in the Soviet world. It would be misleading to think, however, that the cosmopolitan appreciation for diversity that is a visible feature of Rowshan village life only informs the lived nature of relationships between villagers and incomers, and therefore is generated by an external impulse or even global force that has instrumentally forged a break in the local subjectivity of Chitrali people. Rather, many Chitralis are aware of their families' own transregional pasts.[89] Older and newer forms of transregional mobility play an important role in the personal and family narratives of Chitralis today. By examining this one can explore the way people's older experiences of mobility in a culturally complex transregional space shape their current experiences, understandings, and strategies of negotiation with what today are transnational flows.[90]

Rowshan villagers recognized that the flows of Afghan and Tajik people into their village were a product of the collapse of the Soviet Union and the the collapse of the government of Dr Najibullah in Afghanistan. Yet these movements of people were also talked about in terms of their relation to older patterns of migration in the region. Rowshan Chitralis often tell me that most of their region's people are the descendants of both Farsi- and Wakhi-speaking 'Afghans'. They also have an in-depth historical awareness about these migrations. One woman, now in her early seventies, told me that her father, along with his wife and two children, had fled the Wakhan corridor in order to avoid being forced to join the Afghan army. Historians have indeed documented the social dislocations caused by the attempts of successive Afghan emirs and leaders—notably Abdur Rahman Khan—to weaken the authority of Badakhshan nobility and extend the authority of the Afghan state in the region.[91] This woman's parents and many other Wakhiks settled in Chitral and were gradually incorporated into the region's fluid and changing system of status hierarchy. Some of the Afghan incomers, especially those from more noble backgrounds, were presented with gifts of land (*mehrabani zamin*) by the Mehtar of Chitral, while others became the serfs (*chirmuzh*) and servants (*khanazad*) of Chitrali gentry families.[92]

The forms taken by Chitralis' narrations of their own transregional pasts vary greatly and have very different implications for local forms

167

of self-understanding. Folk from relatively high-status backgrounds claim descent from noble families that were once influential in the court of Badakhshan, until they fell out of favor with the realm's monarch, or *mir*. Muhsin, a Sunni Chitrali man in his mid-thirties, told me that his grandfather came to Chitral from Badakhshan after a dispute with the *mir* of Badakhshan. His grandfather was apparently welcomed to Chitral by the Mehtar of the time, who gave him land and even arranged for him to marry a local girl. As a child, Muhsin often traveled to Badakhshan in order to visit his relatives; during these visits, he learned to speak fluent Dari. In Chitral, however, Muhsin and all his brothers say they are Chitrali, speak Khowar, and have married Chitrali women, although they are still referred to as 'Kabuli' by some Chitralis in their home town. Nevertheless, they are now reactivating their familial ties in Afghanistan. Muhsin's brother, Sajjad, traveled to Kabul in 2004 with the aim of finding employment as a vehicle mechanic in the city's rapidly expanding non-governmental sector. In Kabul, he stayed with some of his Afghan relatives who were originally from Badakhshan but had moved to Kabul in the 1970s, and occupied positions in the state security services since then. Muhsin himself had worked as a tour guide for foreign journalists, whom he had taken across Afghan Badakhshan, and simultaneously had also built up an expansive network of connections with the region's *mujahidin* commanders.

The reactivation of ties with Afghanistan by Chitrali families was not, then, simply confined to Chitralis hosting Afghan 'refugees' in their houses. Many Chitralis have visited Afghanistan over the past two decades. Their travels play an active role in making and sustaining their place in what is a Persianate cultural zone.[93] Travel is a well-documented dimension of Indo-Persian literary culture.[94] Tales of journeys (*safar*) are also a frequent source of Chitrali conversation.[95] The mother of the Isma'ili Seyyid family with whom I stay, now in her early sixties, often tells me that her mother was from Badakhshan and spoke fluent Farsi, but only very rough (*shum*) Khowar. She was the daughter of a well-known and influential family of Badakhshani Isma'ili Seyyids who was given in marriage to Chitrali Sunni gentry family. This Seyyid family hails from a cluster of villages known as Zebak, and they are widely respected as *pir*s by many Isma'ilis throughout Chitral, Badakhshan, and southern Tajikistan, where they have vast networks of followers (*muridan*).

After the withdrawal of Soviet forces from Afghanistan in 1989, the eldest son in the household, Ameen, made an epic two-month horse-back journey to visit the house of his maternal grandmother, as well as to find a Badakhshani horse, renowned in Chitral for being excellent for high-altitude polo. Ameen continues to tell stories rich with vivid images about the authority of the *pir* of Zebak, who had, indeed, pre-sented him with gifts of horses, yaks and cows. Since the early 1920s, when Bombay-based Isma'ili 'community' leaders actively sought to strengthen their channels of communication with Chitrali Isma'ilis, the authority to transmit both the edicts or *farman*s of the Aga Khan and Isma'ili religious knowledge more generally has, in Chitral, become increasingly the preserve of the Isma'ili Tariqa Board. This is the inter-national Isma'ili body that coordinates, among other things, the reli-gious education of the world's Isma'ilis. In contrast, the spiritual authority of Afghanistan's *pir*s remained far less contested by global developments in the organization of the world's Isma'ilis until the US-led defeat of the Taliban in 2001–2, which made it possible for Isma'ili institutions to play a more significant role in the transmission of reli-gious knowledge to Isma'ilis within Afghanistan.

Ameen's accounts of Badakhshani religious life emphasize the differ-ences that he saw in the form of Ismai'li authority in Chitral and Badakhshan. They amount to a close and almost ethnographic descrip-tion of this familiarly exotic realm. Ameen also shared much informa-tion about the current nature of Isma'ili experience in Badakhshan with his fellow Rowshan people. He told his fellow Isma'ili village people that he had seen the Sunni *mujahidin* beating up Badakhshani Isma'ili villagers, thereby sharing with fellow villagers first-hand knowledge about the Afghan refugees currently staying in their houses and working in their fields.

The presence of Afghan refugees in Rowshan thus reactivated Chi-trali kinship connections with Afghanistan and memories of transre-gional family histories. This process of reactivation, however, was not always a sweetly reasonable one. The descendants of the 'servants' of Chitral's one-time gentry-like families have invested considerable energy in concealing their Wakhik family backgrounds. For such folk, the historical consciousness of Chitral's connections with the wider region can undermine their attempts to transform their position in Chitral's shifting system of status hierarchy.

Pachambeh Khan, a man from Zebak in his mid-thirties who fled Afghan Badakhshan complaining of the cruel treatment of Isma'ilis there by powerful Sunni *mujahidin* commanders, stayed with a Rowshan family who were the descendants of mid-twentieth-century Isma'ili migrants from Badakhshan. This family is poor by Rowshan standards. Fourteen people in total, they live in a small house, own very little land, and when Pachambeh Khan was staying with them none of the family members held paid employment. Pachambeh Khan was a well-incorporated feature of this family's life, however. The family's three daughters, all of marriageable age, did not observe *purdah* before him because they considered him as among their 'close' (*schoie; qarib*) relatives. They also cared for him when he fell ill—which was said to be because he had fallen in love with a beautiful Chitrali girl from a nearby hamlet. The intimate nature of this family's relationship with Pachambeh Khan the Zebaki was the cause of much discussion in Rowshan. This family's decision to host Pachambeh Khan 'proved', according to one man with whom I spoke (who at the time was in his mid-eighties and from a wealthy and one-time lordly family) that these folk were not real (*asil*) Rowshan people at all but Wakhiks (*wakhik*).

Talking about extra-Chitrali family backgrounds is a sensitive dimension of village conversation, which is important because of its role in local understandings of Afghan, Tajik and Wakhi 'others'. These are topics of conversation that are not only sensitive for the region's poor, one-time serfly families. We shall see in the next chapter how inheriting and benefiting from transnational ties of kin also have Janus-faced implications for powerful, lordly families in Afghan Badakhshan today. Equally important, however, are the ways in which such conversations feed into the construction of shared forms of Chitrali selfhood and the internal divisions, boundaries, tensions and ambiguities surrounding authenticity that are central to these. Having and admitting to a transregional past may confer prestige, knowledge of distant places and conditions, and access to unique forms of spiritual insight. Yet it may also be unwelcome proof of a family's low status in the past, their tenuous claims to the village's land and its water resources, and the possibility that the moral unit of the village is being threatened by the presence of insincere interlopers bent on concealing their hybrid pasts.

These dualistic understandings of transregionality, 'openness' and 'closedness'—what Ho refers to as 'dynamic signification' that marks the 'movements of individuals' and presides over 'the coming and goings of numerous persons across space, time and culture'—illustrates the extent to which some Chitralis contrast their cosmopolitanism with others who cannot participate in such forms of mobility or have not done so.[96] At the same time, it also points towards the ways in which Chitralis make finite distinctions between different forms of transregional mobility and the types of people who undertake them. While some types of mobility, when practised by men from lordly or religious families, are glamorous, personally enriching, and motivated by noble causes, others are practiced by the wrong people, for the wrong reasons, and in the wrong way. Villagers whose family members had once served as the laborers and domestic servants of the region's lordly families, a practice transformed though not eliminated by introduction of government land reform legislation in the 1970s, are especially open to such accusations of improper mobility.

The narration, therefore, of twentieth-century histories of movement from Wakhan to Chitral is a matter of extreme sensitivity in Rowshan today. Indeed, many people go to great lengths to deny that they are Wakhiks at all—one woman who had migrated with her father to Chitral as a young child frequently became angry with villagers if they said she was Wakhik. Since I first visited Chitral in 1995, I have often talked with Rowshan villagers about their extra-Chitrali origins, yet it is only in recent years that I have heard stories about my friends' 'Wakhik' grandparents. One man in particular, Lablabu Khan, has given me many insights into this domain of Chitral life and history. In his early forties, and from a village in a Chitrali village close to Afghanistan, Lablabu now lives in Rowshan, where he is a low-grade government employee. His wife's mother came to Chitral from the Wakhan when she was ten years old—her father, she told me, was fleeing conscription in the Afghan army. His mother-in-law worked in the household of one of the region's gentry-like families. Then, as now, her family lived on a small plot of land, which they had been 'given' by the lordly family for whom they worked. In recent years they, like many other such Chitrali families, have benefited from the opportunities for social mobility provided to Chitralis by rising literacy levels, employment in the local wing of the Pakistan army (the Chitral Scouts) and police, and labor migration to Pakistan's cities. Two of her sons, although not formally educated, became junior commissioned officers in the Chitral Scouts until they retired and built impressive houses on

171

land overlooking not only their ancestral home but also that of their one-time lords. Her other two sons work as medical technicians in Karachi's prestigious Aga Khan University.

Lablabu Khan often tells me that he considers talking about matters of status, family descent, and hierarchy to be a highly impolite feature of Chitrali conversation (*mashkulque*). Hearing conversations about such matters, he tells me, makes his brain 'cook' and go 'mad'. When staying in Rowshan in order to undertake his duties in the government department for which he works, he stays in small house built of mud bricks on land owned by his boss. He frequently complains that although his boss' family is kind and honorable, other people in the village ask him to do odd jobs without payment. These requests are a source of great irritation to Lablabu's eighteen-year-old daughter, who has benefitted from a post-college training-focused education, and, who frequently tells her father that he should refuse to work as a favor for anybody, and should consider all his equals and not his bosses nor his lords (*lalan*).

The relatives of the *pir* of Zebak often told Rowshan villagers and me proudly about their connections in Afghanistan. They presented themselves as people with historically significant pasts that connect them to different places and mean that they are familiar with 'conditions and personalities' beyond the immediate setting of Rowshan and Chitral.[97] Lablabu Khan, in contrast, urged me to write about and bring to the surface the cruel ways in which Chitralis talked about Wakhiks. In so doing, he highlighted his own recognition of the dynamic tension between 'openness and closedness' that is a prominent feature of the cosmopolitan discourses of Chitral's higher-status trans-regional families.[98] In contrast to Rowshan's Seyyid families, then, men such as Lablabu Khan consider the reactivation of memories about familial connections with Afghanistan and the Wakhan to be sensitive and even dangerous. They have the capacity to undo the active and often disappointed attempts made by such men to transform their families' place in Chitral's shifting system of status and descent.

Interactions between Chitralis and refugees invoked different types of transnational self-understanding that were weighted with importance for different reasons. Some villagers have openly sought to reactivate their ties with Afghanistan and sometimes even treated these as a critical economic resource. The presence of Afghan refugees from Badakhshan stimulated some Chitralis to travel to Afghanistan, not to fight in the country's *jihad* but to visit their relatives. The capacity to make such journeys, enjoy the hospitality and even command the respect of distant relatives, and display the gifts with which they were presented was a source of glamour for Rowshan villagers. Others, in contrast, have sought to suppress their connections with the wider Farsi-speaking world. Being labeled an Afghan by one's fellow Chitralis also has very negative implications for certain groups of people in Chitral today. Just as the practices of labelling by the state seen in the first chapters of the book were not innocuous exercises in categorization, but instead carried profoundly important implications for the treatment and markers of status, so also locally generated, ascribed and assumed labels carry important ramifications for the mobility and experiences of the region's people.

Memories of transnational mobility and experiences of social solidarity in this space continue to be activated by the refugees and migrant laborers who have now returned to their homes, or moved as migrants to new places once more. One of the themes addressed in the next chapter will be constructions that one-time Afghan traders and refugees make of their time in Chitral. One of the reasons why the lives of men from Tajikistan's Badakhshan region whom I knew when they worked in Chitral are not explored further below is that it is now easier to find these people working on construction sites in Moscow, Alma Atta and Ekaterinburg than farming in the Pamirs. I have, however, met some men from Tajikistan whom I had known in Chitral.

During my first visit to Chitral in 1995/96 the family with whom I stayed hosted two men from Tajikistan who, during the course of their journey to Chitral, were caught in a snowstorm on a mountain pass and severely affected by frostbite. My host family took the men from house to house in Rowshan and collected enough money to help them travel by plane to Karachi and the Aga Khan Hospital in that city. Some months later the men returned on crutches, having had their toes removed in surgery. Later that summer they went back, on foot, to Tajikistan. In February 2007, along with my co-author, and again in the summer of 2009, I met one of these men in his home village on the Tajik side of the Wakhan corridor. On both occasions he remembered the foreigner in Rowshan, telling me how on his return from Pakistan he had attended classes for amputees in a hospital in Tajikistan's northern city of Khujand and had learned to walk again there. His fellow traveler could also walk easily again, and was now living in Moscow where he worked as an 'artist'. Far from remembering his time in Chitral solely through the lenses of trauma, however, he said that his motivation for traveling to Pakistan had been to 'see the world' (*jahon bini*), not to work—he had been something of a 'ruffian' or 'hooligan' who enjoyed to travel and take risks since his childhood. In the room in which we were sitting, he pulled out from a box (*sanduq*) a small notebook that was clearly made in Pakistan. He opened it and revealed pages replete with photographs of him during his Pakistan journey, often also with the Wakhi and Chitrali families whose guest he had been. The photos depicted scenes both before and after his operation. The notebook was also full of drawings of flowers and diary entries, poems, and proverbs written in Cyrillic Tajiki, as well as the jottings of his Pakistani friends in Urdu. This man's material memories of his experiences of travel in Chitral and Pakistan in the form of a travel log recall the Persianate *safarnama* written by Indian scribes that were identified earlier as being a key dimension of Persianate culture. Indeed, he told me that he intended to publish a book about his travels. The ongoing importance of such forms of literary composition highlights too the ways in which experiences of mobility are shared and transmitted across generations. This man's daughter and niece sat with us on that day, and he contrasted their lives bound in the village and Dushanbe to his that had been enriched both by his travels during military service in the era of the Soviet Union, and to Pakistan and Afghanistan after its collapse. One of his reasons for writing the book, indeed, was to allow his children the possibility of experiencing his mobility, albeit vicariously and mediated by his text and their imaginations. The diary serves, then, as a powerful reminder of the multi-dimensional nature of Frontier mobility, of the ways in which experiences are often colored both by trauma and the experience of fragmentation, yet also, by vivid memories of lived expressions of solidarity between people who recognized themselves as being both different from and similar to one another. These forms of solidarity have their roots in the shared historical worlds, and cultural patterns of equivalence, that have been the focus of this chapter.

Conclusion

Over the past thirty years, Chitrali villagers have employed post-Soviet Tajik men in their fields, learned Dari from Afghans, and embarked on journeys to their ancestral villages in northeastern Afghanistan. All this movement between deeply connected yet also discontinuous settings has stimulated practices of cosmopolitanism that valorize people's ability to move with art and skill across their wider world. These cosmopolitan practices are neither the one-dimensional products of civil war nor the straightforward outcomes of global migration. They bear the imprint, rather, of older cultural influences, such as Persianate practices of travel. Both nation-states and foreign powers frequently interpret these patterns of mobility and the relations they forge between Muslims from apparently incompatible backgrounds as a dangerous source of instability. Yet local faces of the Pakistan state collaborate with the region's mobile Muslims, while some international non-governmental organizations have also sought to instrumentally generate transregional forms of connectivity. These two elements—mobility and the consequent cosmopolitanism—run in the face of colonial conceptions and efforts to categorize Frontier society as simultaneously simple and static.

In short, the intimate relations and ever-changing life histories and experiences of people in this region illuminate much about some of the most momentous events that have affected their lives in the past three decades, the impact of these on the relationships between these transregional societies, and people's ways of being Muslim. The multidimensional ways of being Muslim documented here should certainly not be seen in terms of their unbounded fluidity. Nor should one think that no Muslims in the region have embraced radical ways of acting within and against the world around them. Rather, people living in this expansive transregional setting frequently shift between very different indexes and ways of being Muslim during the course of their daily lives. In so doing, they forge intricate, intimate, and dynamic relations with other Muslims, not only from different places, ethnolinguistic groups, or confessional backgrounds, but also with very different life histories and personal experiences of this transregional space. It is important to note that most of the region's Muslims do not simply 'smooth over' their experience of this complexity by adhering to rule-bound forms or 'de-culturalized' forms of 'global' Islam.[99] Rather, these relations lead to the production of intertwining forms of complicity and critical engagement with the forces behind the momentous changes that the region's people have experienced over the last thirty years. The indexes of being Muslim that the region's people enact are cross-cut by competing forms of sectarian, social and ethnolinguistic distinction. They also bear the imprint of the differential effects of both

British and Soviet imperial expansion. As a result, as Muslims move between their region's different spaces, they identify with very different values, traditions and things—some of which stand in stark contrast to one another. Sulton, for example, joined the Taliban but did not refashion his Muslim self according to ultra-orthodox forms of doctrinal Islam. Instead, he tactically switched between different ways of being Muslim, and, in the course of doing so, identified with an ostensibly homogeneous Isma'ili community, the Sunni Taliban, and a local smuggler of apricot schnapps.

These shifting ways of being Muslim and the modes of identification they stimulate are thus always about more complex processes than the meanings that Muslims attach to their 'identities'. Rather, Muslims living in this transregional setting fashion personal ways of being Muslim that are richly informed by and facilitate projects of identification with a diverse range of intellectual, cultural and aesthetic influences and standards. These include local musical traditions that build on an expansive Persianate Sufic poetic heritage and Persianate styles of miniature painting that have interacted with Socialist art genres. The modes of identification that such ways of being Muslim stimulate, therefore, are richly nourished by complex processes of recognition, interaction and exchange.

The next chapter looks at the ways in which these same Afghan refugees in Chitral experienced their return to Afghanistan. Given the complexity of these experiences and the extent to which these men and their wider community identities have come to be shaped by their relationship to major political figures in Afghanistan, 'the political', as well as the domains of religion and ethnicity, is shown as being central to these men's understandings of the heterogeneous make-up of the Frontier and their capacity to move across and within it. This final chapter probes more deeply the shared symbolic and classificatory devices that allow frontier people both to engage in highly local, changeable and contextually-defined practices of personal and collective self-identification and, simultaneously, to navigate and understand the changing world in which they live.

7

GEOGRAPHIES OF PROFIT AND SECURITY

'RETURN' TO AFGHANISTAN AND BEYOND

As the preceding chapters have demonstrated, frontier Muslims shape, understand, invest with significance and reflect upon the diverse contexts that they experience on a daily basis. Chapter 5 focused on the diverse forms of religious sensibility that Chitrali Muslim inculcate and enact in differing temporal and spatial contexts. The last chapter moved away from sacred and secular landscapes, examining how people's identities are constructed in relationship to changing hierarchies of status, sect and ethnicity. Frontier identity formations are thus neither local nor global, neither regional nor national, but rather transregional. More importantly, the transregional dimension of Frontier identity formations does not merely reflect the extension of a spatial scale of cultural sameness. Instead, it illuminates a suite of forms of personal and collective work that Frontier Muslims embark upon to make, activate and suppress connections with their fellow frontier people. This focus on the world constructed by local inhabitants stands in stark contrast to that conceived for them by external state authorities, which the first part of the book dealt with. The juxtaposition of these locally and state constructed visions is not meant to demonstrate that one version is 'correct' and the other 'incorrect', but rather to foreground the multiple constructed realities both inhabiting and shaping the Frontier past and present.

This chapter adds a further layer of complexity to our attempts to understand the workings of the Frontier as a heterogeneous yet coherent context. After having presented explorations of Chitralis' mobility within their valleys, and the complex interactions between Chitralis and incomers, 'the field' in this chapter is neither Chitral nor a wider space that encompasses it. Its focus, rather, is on social networks that encompass a range of different types of borders that demarcate the multiple types of space, polity and culture with which this book is concerned. What these social networks share in common is that they have all collided in Chitral at varying stages of their development. We shall see how the actors who make up these networks have progressively expanded their own circuits of movement, thereby both simultaneously bringing 'together people and things that otherwise might remain disconnected' and altering the value, meanings and significance of those people and things, as well as the places in which they are located.[1] The perspective found in Chitral is replicated in other localities along the Frontier, themselves conditioned by local contexts.[2]

Many of these networks were introduced in the last chapter. They incorporate Badakhshani and Panjshiri refugee and labor movements in and out of Chitral. Analyzing them from different spatial positions, this chapter documents their shape and nature not only from Chitral, but from other locations where they come together, especially in northern Afghanistan. Ethnographically, the chapter adds to our ongoing interest in the Frontier's heterogeneity through a consideration of the ways in which mobile people of the Frontier enact their identities in relation not only to Islam and cultural difference, but also to varying and contested images that depict the Frontier for one reason or another as a space of global political significance.

The material in this chapter is based on research conducted with people in Afghanistan immersed in the process of adapting to life there after many years living in Chitral. Over the past thirty years the importance of Afghanistan to the imagination and self-understandings of Muslims living in a wide variety of social and political circumstances has been noted by several commentators. Faisal Devji has shown how Afghanistan's and the Frontier's landscapes have come to encapsulate certain global forms of Muslim thought and identity, notably those enshrined in 'the global *jihad*'. The Frontier's landscapes are deployed in complex and creative ways by 'the *jihad*'s' media-savvy proponents. Films and photographs of men such as Osama Bin Laden hiding in caves and gorges signal, according to Devji, the success of these men and their followers in escaping from the world of immoral capitalism and cultural globalization, contemporary trends they seek to oppose and resist. Likewise, the chapter on the 'Frontier Fanatics' also demonstrated how the Frontier was envisaged as a singular space of religious refuge and revolt against foreign, godless rulers by South Asian Muslims, and more powerfully by the British as well. Anthropological treatments of Afghan refugees living in Iran have also sought to show how young Afghan men and women seek to live up to images of their country as a unique space of *jihad* whilst also cultivating other dimensions of their identities and worlds, such as a mastery of Persian poetry.[3] What, however, of the men and women who live out their daily lives in Afghanistan? How do they conceptualize and experience everyday life within a space that occupies such an important dimension of the moral and ethical geographies of contemporary global Islam, and has done for years?

This chapter seeks to locate a consideration of people's meaning-making endeavors across this space within the context of the region's changing political economy. During the course of fieldwork with men returning to Afghanistan who have lived much of their lives in Chitral, I have become aware of the ways in which this region's changing political economy is leading its peoples to readjust the lens through which they view, evaluate and experience particular places and categories of people. These changes are particularly visible when considering the relationship between those from and beyond Afghanistan. Soviet-era images of Afghans as barbaric, poor and uneducated are often expressed by diverse categories of people in Tajikistan, for example. Yet the relevance of these stereotypes is being challenged as the texture of interactions between Afghans and Tajikis changes. Afghan traders are a prominent feature of Central Asia's markets. They bring cash, capital, companies and products to the bazaars of Dushanbe, Tashkent and Alma Ata, as well as smaller cities that are also often located close to international trade routes—Shimkent, Turkmenabat, and Khujand—across Central Asia. As a result of their trading activities, Afghans are now frequently coded by Central Asians as wealthy wife-takers and merchants rather than being barbaric and poor. Outside the Afghan embassy in Dushanbe, for example, a Tajiki man and I chatted with an unveiled Tajiki woman as we waited for our visas. She was dressed in Tajiki 'national dress' (*atlas*) and told us that she had married an Afghan and now lived between Dushanbe and Kabul. 'You must have to wear different clothes there and cover your face', said the man. 'Not at all', she replied, 'Kabul is as advanced as Dushanbe today'.[4]

Another important fact is that such changes in local understandings of how the region's different geopolitical spaces and people interact with, relate to, and are positioned against one another are also talked about by people as having critical implications for the future of their region. 'There'll never be war like before', one Panjshiri man in his mid-forties told me. 'Before we went to Pakistan, where there was nothing. Now Afghans can go to Tajikistan and find freedom (*azadi*) and luxury (*ayashi*) there. Who is going to fight like before? In those days our eyes were closed, now they are open'. Indeed, the young men whose lives are explored in this chapter, and with whom I have driven around northern Afghanistan as they talked about their plans to get hold of million dollar development projects as contractors, are the same characters explored in the previous chapters as jeep drivers and small scale butchers in Chitral. What these perspectives show is the malleability of, and interrelationships between, both identity and ambition in this ever-changing space.

The changing nature of the Frontier's relationship with the rest of the world, thus, is something actively thought about by its peoples, and considered by them to have had deeply ambiguous effects on their lives. This chapter explores these ambiguities and the ways in which they shape the modes through which people traverse an expansive and complex surface, and the form of the networks they create through an ethnography of life on the move with people traveling to work, live, trade, visit relatives, and sometimes just to relax. These journeys in friends' battered up Corollas have taken me to the cities of Kabul, Mazar-e Sharif and Kunduz, the small Afghanistan-Tajikistan border towns and districts of Ishkashim and Shughnan, as well as the ancestral villages of my informants in Badakhshan and Panjshir. They also involve places outside Afghanistan itself, notably Peshawar, Dushanbe and London. My aim is to ask: 'What is it like to move about in a space whose contours have already been mapped within the matrices of morality?'[5] There has been a tendency to overlook such an anthropological line of questioning and focus instead on the ways space is mapped by nation-states or invading militaries according to ethnic or tribal compositions. However, a look at more inchoate alternative geographies of experience of the Frontier held by its inhabitants reveals forces for regional coherence that the top-down approach of many studies neglects.[6] Consequently, this chapter implicitly highlights and explores the limits of the preceding historical inquiry. It therefore throws into relief one instance where our collaborative impulses crash against the rocks of disciplinary limits. But it also underlines how our interdisciplinary approach proves a richer collage than one firmly rooted in a single intellectual paradigm.

Afghanistan on the Move

The perception that Afghanistan's 'opening' has led to major changes in its people's political sensibilities connects with much recent anthropological and historical work on Afghanistan that has focused on the centrality of migration and mobility for social and economic life within and beyond the country. Historians have illustrated the ways in which migratory movements and diasporic-like forms of community self-understanding are central to Afghan collective identity formations. Nile Green, notably, has argued that the tendency of many historians to treat Indo-Afghan social and political formations within the rubric of 'Indian' rather than 'Afghan' history has led them to overlook the extent to which it was in this Indo-Afghan diasporic context that 'many features of the Afghans' sense of their historical identity crystalized in terms of a sense of the defining limits between self and the world that was stamped on the present through the heavy imprint of the past'.[7] Green argues that 'the historical consciousness of the Afghans ... took shape in connection with the experience of migration into India and the encounter there with forms of social, religious and political organisation that differed from their own, including larger scale formations—cosmopolitan and imperial—that shook the social foundations of these diffuse bands of tribesmen'.[8] Historically established diasporas of Afghans outside the geographical limits of the country play a critically important role in reformulating collective identities within it.

Anthropological work on Afghanistan has also come to place migration and mobility at the center of people's understandings of themselves. Migration, dispersal and diasporic community life are not a one-dimensional product of conflict, but are rather, as Monsutti so clearly demonstrates, pivotal for Afghanistan's future development.[9] Monsutti's sensitive study of the mobile lives of Shi'a Hazara Afghans in the Pakistani Frontier city of Quetta, their home villages in Jughuri, Hazarajat, Iranian cities including Tehran and Mashad, and coal mining communities in south western Pakistan documents the fundamentally 'networked' nature of Hazara personal and collective life.[10] Hazaras deploy complex choice-making processes when making decisions about where to live and work. For this community, family and community life involves people traveling and moving in multiple directions, which allows them to benefit from different economic resources, profit margins, and transforming circumstances. It also allows them to think and act in strategically diverse ways in relationship to changing political conditions, such as distributing their loyalties across different political parties. The networks, in short, that criss-cross Afghanistan's cultural, religious and international boundaries lie at the heart of the lifeways of Afghan and neighboring peoples.[11]

It is also important to ask how Afghanistan's relationship with the wider world has shaped the forms of moral values, as well as modes of normative thinking and debating practised by its peoples. As noted in the introduction, excellent studies exist of the different moral and cultural values that make up 'Afghan culture' and the antagonistic ways in which these relate to one another.[12] Yet how are people's conceptions of virtuous living, ethics and appropriate behavior shaped by their region's diverse interactions with the world outside? In the first part of the book we considered such interactions from the perspective of high politics and anti-colonial revolts. This issue is now addressed in relationship to people's experience of boundary-crossing mobility.

These issues are now being addressed by scholars in two distinct bodies of scholarship. First, an expanding body of work addresses the centrality of Africa's relationship to the rest of the world for understanding of key cultural, political and moral dynamics there. Bayart, for example, uses the term 'strategies of extraversion' to highlight the ways in which various actors in Africa 'mobilised resources from their (possibly unequal) relationship with the external environment'.[13] Sub-Saharan Africa's interaction with the rest of the world is not so much a 'relationship', he argues, as an 'organic linkage', or a 'consubstantive' interaction between inside and outside. His study focuses predominantly on the ways in which 'sovereignty in Africa is exercised through the creation and management of dependence'.[14] Yet he also touches upon the myriad ways in which sub-Saharan Africa's 'baroque relationship' with the outside world is mediated materially rather than at any abstract level. Consumption practices, for example, and especially those to do with fashion and clothing, 'instantiate an individual's self reflexivity and also his or her relationship with others, and in the first place with political authorities foreign or home grown'.[15] We saw earlier how imperial connections facilitated common practices, such as Sandeman's tribal governance, in regions as diverse as the Frontier and Nigeria. Just as colonial administrators felt Sandeman's tactics could have traction in geographically distant but socio-culturally similar spaces, so too does Bayart's analysis find footing in the Afghan context.

Second, anthropological and historical work on 'diasporas' emphasizes how studies of apparently scattered and dispersed trading communities are of interest not simply for the insights they offer into the ways in which mobile actors connect geographically divided parts of the world economy. Studies of globe-trotting Hadrami traders and Tibetan merchants[16] add further 'shades and textures' to our understanding of spaces, such as this and other transregional frontiers. Such spaces are larger in scale than regional communities and nations—the traditional focus of much anthropological work.[17] Nevertheless, despite differences in scale they also form inter-connected wholes, historic regions, that also endure through time. This chapter takes up Ho's call for more nuanced attempts to describe translocal spaces in their own terms, arguing that the Frontier is not just a politically created 'borderland' but an interconnected region. It also shows the role played by its mobile peoples in its continual making, and expands this body of literature, which has focused on oceans, to an inland littoral sharing many of the same features.

As the last chapter demonstrated, frontier people can move across their diverse region in artful and even cosmopolitan ways. At the same time, this does not mean they are accustomed to travel and movement to such an extent that they consider the differences they encounter during the course of their journeys to be unworthy of thought, reflection and moral judgment. Rather, they value and recognize 'the multiple points of contact that are articulated with the experiences of other peoples', and they do so by registering and talking about similarity and difference, perceiving particular places as being unique, and also thinking about the nature of life between such nodes.[18] They also theorize the ways in which prolonged stays in one place have important effects on the thinking and feeling of individuals.[19] It is their modes of doing so, and the effects of these on their collective identifications, that animate what follows.

Ethnography of Life on the Move

I am often asked what it is like to conduct fieldwork in Afghanistan.[20] Most of the fieldwork on which this chapter is based has been undertaken with people who identify themselves both as Farsi-speaking 'people of the north' and as either Panjshiris or Badakhshanis (often also referred to as Badakhshis).[21] These people also identify themselves in relationship to particular valleys and administrative districts of Badakhshan (for example, Jurm, Zebak, and Ishkashim), and villages in Panjshir (most of the Panjshiris who lived and worked in Chitral and whose life trajectories I explore below hail from the villages of Dasht-i Rewat and Safid Shir in the upper reaches of the Panjshir valley). I came to know these people during my periods of fieldwork in Chitral, where many of them were born. In Afghanistan, I mostly stay with my friends in their houses, although in Kabul I have also stayed in hotels, as my friends have been newly building their houses. I also spend a lot of time traveling with them in the north of the country, as they travel for work, although my ability to do this in my last three trips to the country (September 2009; January 2010; July-September 2010), have been curtailed because of the growing dangers faced by road travellers in the north of Afghanistan, especially between Kunduz and Kabul but also during periods of political sensitivity within Badakhshan. They have also taken me to their home villages and houses in Badakhshan and Panjshir. Few of the people with whom I work live permanently in these places, visiting them only for a few days at a time, and relatively infrequently at that.

The ethnography is based on my experiences of living and traveling with these men, and the conversations that I have had with them in both Khowar and Dari.[22] Not only were many of them born in Chitral, but their own 'elders' have also lived most of their adult lives outside their valley, often in Kabul or other Afghan towns, especially Kunduz, to which they migrated in the 1960s, eventually opening shops selling spare parts for cars and trucks and later also mechanic workshops. Today, these men's offspring own petrol pumps in the same towns. If few of the people I know have been born or raised in either Panjshir or Badakhshan, then hailing from these provinces, belonging to a particular village and side-valley, and being part of a kinship group or *qawm* are important and intersecting dimensions of all of these peoples' personal and collective identities.[23] This combination of living highly mobile lives and continuing to forge attachment to particular places forms interrelated and not opposing dimensions of their worlds—places derive their significance from their connectedness to the world beyond.[24]

In addition to following men I had known in Chitral back to Afghanistan, I have had meetings with returning refugees that have often been mediated by others who live outside Afghanistan. When I first traveled to Kabul, for example, I called my Chitral-based Panjshiri friends in Rowshan who gave me the names and mobile telephone numbers of their friends and relatives living in Kabul, some of whom I knew and others of whom I was introduced to. Having met these men, I was taken to their homes in Kabul and in other Afghan cities. In this way, my network expanded beyond those I had known in Chitral, including many who had lived there but whom I had not known, and still more who had never lived in Chitral. In addition to working with these people in Afghanistan, I have also met them on their business trips to Dushanbe in Tajikistan and also met others who now live in London.

In contrast to Chitral, where I came to know a group of people very well over the course of several years, my fieldwork in Afghanistan has involved getting to know people and their families in a much more fragmented way and over many shorter visits. This is partly because of the highly mobile nature of their lives, but also because of practicalities of fieldwork in Afghanistan. The people whose lives I was interested in exploring for a book concerned with the Frontier's geographies were those who were constantly moving. This, however, also made it difficult for me to focus on one place—a node in their many networks. Moreover, even the act of tracking them down has often been difficult. Contact numbers come and go as SIM cards are changed and lost, for example, and even when able to contact people they have often moved to a place that is impossible for me to visit, such as southern Afghanistan.

In the face of all of this flux and rapid change, I have had to develop the type of flexible tactics and strategies that are always important in anthropological work, yet perhaps highly developed in this type of context.[25] These strategies have required me to be mobile, seek out characters in a range of locations, and be willing to change the goal of particular fieldwork visits at very short notice. I have found this way of doing fieldwork difficult, tiring, frustrating, time consuming, and sometimes not as fruitful as I had hoped. This is not least because, as the previous two chapters have demonstrated, my fieldwork in Chitral revolved around focusing on a particular place and the social relations that informed it. I initially sought to undertake single locality fieldwork as I began the research on which this chapter is based, yet found such a form of fieldwork to be impossible, for reasons I now explore.

I met Ahmed and his father, for example, when they came to visit their Panjshiri relatives in Rowshan, Chitral for three months in 2000. They came partly to flee the Taliban, and partly because Ahmed's father was sick and needed hospital treatment—Rowshan has an excellent hospital built by the Aga Khan Health Programme.[26] Their relatives owned the bakery in Rowshan discussed in the last chapter and we were friends. Ahmed asked me if I would teach him English and I did so—on and off—for some time. Ahmed then returned to Kunduz, where his family had settled some forty years previously, first establishing a mechanical workshop and then jointly owning a petrol pump with a Pashtun. When I visited Afghanistan in December 2006, with my co-author, one of the Rowshan baker's relatives took me to see Ahmed in Kunduz. I then made four further visits to see him and his friends and family in Kunduz between 2006 and April 2009,[27] spending time with Ahmed as he finished his schooling; joined his father's business; left that business and worked with his brother at the family's petrol pump; went to Tajikistan to try to open a shop selling religious books printed in Pakistan with another of his brothers; returned to Afghanistan having found life in Dushanbe hard and dull, and joined ISAF forces in Kunduz as a translator—a position he eventually left. Kunduz, thus, became my main fieldwork 'site'. During a visit to Afghanistan in September 2009, however, I was unable to visit Ahmed and his family. I was told by my friends in the city that Kunduz's importance as a center of insurgency now made it too dangerous for me to visit as I had before. 'It is not that Kunduz that you visited last year', one of my friends told me.[28] Instead, then, I spent time with Ahmed's brother who was working as a cement trader in Dushanbe at the time. On my most recent visit to Afghanistan in July-September 2010 I was once more unable to meet Ahmed because, according to his closest friend, he had joined the Taliban. During this visit, I returned to Badakhshan, which was regarded as being safer, and spent time in villages there with men who I had known as refugees in Chitral.

The ethnography on which this chapter is based, then, is not 'multi-sited' in the sense that the term was first conceived and used by Marcus.[29] It is better described as an ethnography of life on the move, something that incorporates the investigation of social networks and routes as well as the actual experience of movement. As a result, it does not seek authoritative insights into the particularity of the linguistic and cultural constructions that shape the lives of those whom it is about. Its central aim, instead, is to contribute to this book's attempt to understand the Frontier as a heterogeneous yet coherent space that is connected by its own people's lives and patterns of movement, even if this coherent space is constituted by many different types of places and involves varying people arriving from vastly different directions to connect these settings. With this aim in mind, the burden of my fieldwork has also not been about the location or number of locales that I should compare with one another, but, rather, the grounds upon which I make choices to 'talk to particular people, visit specific spaces, and witness specific events *within the field*', in this case, the Frontier.[30]

Beyond Jihad: *Northern Afghan Geographies of Trade*

Afghanistan specialists have documented the significance of northeastern Afghanistan, particularly the Panjshir and Badakhshan, to modern Afghan history, especially to the anti-Soviet *jihad* and the post-Taliban state-building strategies of Hamid Karzai and his allies.[31] Another reason why northern Afghanistan's Dari-speaking communities have been a focus for recent scholarly research is their once pivotal importance to Afghanistan's opium economy: opium has been grown, refined, consumed in Badakhshan. An important route for the smuggling of narcotics out of Afghanistan and into Tajikistan, the Central Asian states and beyond also traverses the province.[32] Less is known about the everyday lives of ordinary people from these regions of the north. The role played by Islam and ethnicity in these people's identities and moral universes is often taken for granted, especially concerning those who were once connected or affiliated to the anti-Taliban Northern Alliance. Panjshiri identity, especially, is often treated as being fashioned almost solely in relation to the changing place of powerful Panjshiri power-brokers in Afghanistan's central government. Stereotypes, important within and beyond Afghanistan, depict Panjshiris as aggressively seeking political influence in government ministries. One man in Mazar-e Sharif, for example, said to me: 'Even young Panjshiris cannot move beyond the *jihad* and want to behave like *mujahidin*. They even hold their mobile telephones as if they were walkie-talkies, speak to people on them as though they were issuing military orders, and turn them onto loudspeaker mode so everybody can hear them'.

This chapter cannot document the self-identifications of Panjshiris and Badakhshis in all their complexity—a book topic in itself—or, indeed, give an-depth discussion of their changing political and economic fortunes in post-Taliban Afghanistan, concerns that have been addressed by political scientists.[33] Yet it does seek to provide anthropological insight into the ways in which Panjshiri and Badakhshi men, including traders, *mujahidin* commanders turned elected representatives, and also young men adapting to life in Afghanistan having returned there from Chitral, Pakistan, construct their identities and worlds. They do so in relation not only to the anti-Soviet *jihad* and Islam, but also to their complex and highly varied life experiences, and the varied yet connected landscapes in which their lives are played out.

As we have seen in the previous chapters, many of the one-time Chitral-based Afghans are traders. The bakery and butchers shops of Rowshan's Panjshiris featured in the last chapter because they were an important site of debate and cultural interchange between Chitrali villagers and the Afghan newcomers. These were, however, not simply 'small family businesses', the basis of basic 'peddlers' or isolated outposts of Panjshiri activity. They existed, rather, within a much broader nexus of networks that were 'constituted spatially, across villages, bazaars, even global regions, and temporally, through lineage to ancestors'.[34] A consideration of these networks reveals more than the complexity of the region's economy: the Frontier's trading geography also furnishes insights into the perceptions Panjshiris hold about the worlds they traverse on a daily basis.[35] In contrast to the many and important trading tribes and peddler communities whose social structures have been documented by anthropologists and historians, the case study I present of Panjshiri trading networks concerns rural traders who make their money from exchange-wary villagers and small town dwellers. Successful trading communities are most often studied in the context of urban environments. Yet it is in rural areas that traders face some of their most difficult challenges—often being resented by locals who see trade as immoral profiteering and traders as obsequious and lacking honor.[36] Panjshiri traders, however, straddle both rural and urban environments. Their activities and the effects of these on specific locales, as well as their complex understandings of themselves as rural dwellers with sophisticated urban backgrounds, challenge the rigid distinction so often drawn between 'rural' and 'urban' people.

Panjshiris in Chitral were active in the pursuit of business and trade and went to great lengths to diversify their sources of income. Those I knew best, the Pansjhiris in Rowshan, at first owned a butchers shop (a temporary construction made of wooden planks and covered with wire to keep out the flies) in the village bazaar. In later years, the family opened a 'bakery' shop (a large building they rented from a Chitrali landlord in the village bazaar, replete with large wooden containers for rice and dhall), which was widely said by Rowshan villagers to be the best and most economical of shops in their village. The Panjshiri business success story, indeed, was a much talked of feature of the 'village economy' among Rowshan villagers. Importantly, the family lives of all the people I explore here do not involve ties of kin to Chitral.[37]

These shops were connected to networks of Panjshiri travelers, traders and sojourners both within and beyond Chitral. There was constant influx of the relatives and fellow 'village people' of these men into Chitral from Afghanistan. Sometimes these people were seeking seasonal labor, sometimes fleeing the Taliban. Still more were bringing loads of lapis lazuli for sale in Peshawar, while also buying foodstuffs and spare parts to take back to their stores in Afghanistan. During the years of Taliban government in Afghanistan, the Rowshan-based butchers often walked to areas in northern Afghanistan controlled by the Northern Alliance to bring livestock back to Chitral. They sold cows, sheep and yaks in their butchery shops and also exported them to the markets of 'down Pakistan'. In particular, they went each summer on one or two occasions to the Afghan Pamirs—a journey that would take them a month or more. They also owned animals in the high Pamirs, which were cared for them by farmers from local communities, a practice that Shahrani and others have shown to be often connected to the sale of opium to highland dwellers and the entrapment of these communities into debt relations with traders.

The choice of the butchery trade by Panjshiris, however, is also illuminating for this book's concern with Frontier practices of mobility for other reasons. In a pasture-scarce region like Chitral, being a successful butcher requires the capacity to cross international, regional and cultural boundaries, not just to understand the complex configurations of cost and value in these different contexts. These men were not, thus, mere butchers or traders in meat but merchants who bridged diverse political and cultural worlds.[38]

In the communities where they travel and purchase livestock Panjshiris do, indeed, inhabit roles other than that of 'butcher' (*qasab*).

They are often literate, and thus officiate as scribes at religious events, such as marriages. This is especially the case in remote regions of Afghanistan. In July 2010, for example, I was invited to witness a wedding in a remote village in Badakhshan by a Panjshiri butcher, Rahim, who owned a small butcher's shop in Ishkashim. Rahim was responsible for drawing up the contract (*maktub*) concerning the responsibilities of the groom to his father-in-law to be. The young man was to live in the house of his wife's father, a type of marriage referred to locally as *khana-i khusur*, literally son-in-law of the house, and often referred to by anthropologists as bride service. It is a marriage type that requires agreements to be made over the nature of labor to be provided by the groom to the father-in-law in return for marrying his daughter and living in his house. There are a variety of reasons why this type of marriage might be preferred, but in this case it was because the bride's father only had one son, said to be unwell and thus unfit to do hard labor.[39] Over the course of the afternoon, Rahim oversaw the drawing-up of a contract that stipulated the period of time for which the groom would work for his father-in-law as a shepherd (*chopan*): seven years. Those gathered also agreed that if the son-in-law were to break the contract, then he would pay to his father-in-law the equivalent of the monthly salary of a shepherd until the end of the seven-year period. It was Rahim the butcher's intervention that secured that the contract took this form. On a number of occasions Rahim considered that the parties' intentions for the contract were breaking the stipulations of *shari'a* law. At one point, the groom's father suggested that his son should work for the father-in-law for the rest of his life, but Rahim argued that this would result in the enslavement of the 'boy', which would be entirely unacceptable according to *shari'a* law. Rahim also pressed for a clause to be introduced to the contract concerning what would happen if the groom and his wife decided to leave the house within the stipulated period: unless such a clause was included, he remarked to those gathered, the contract resembled enslavement more than marriage. The circulation of Panjshiri butchers across the region, then, is bound up with more than the movement of meat and money alone. Such men are also critical to the transmission of Islamic knowledge and the performance of key life cycle rituals, as well as the complex and subtle forms of legal negotiation and reevaluation of local practices such as bride service that are a central feature of these.

Panjshiri shopkeepers, indeed, also introduced villagers in Chitral to new consumption patterns, often associated with 'modern' forms of sociality. They introduced sweet '*bakeries*' to Chitrali villagers, who, instead of making enormous pots of rice for their guests at 'times of happiness and sadness' increasingly distributed Panjshiri-made 'cream rolls' instead. This new trend was supported by some villagers who argued that it was a rational way of conducting life, especially the village's emerging middle class of NGO employees. Yet it was treated by others as a sign of meanness of the village's new rich and an abdication of their responsibility to 'the poor'. The cakes they sold quickly became central also to another ostensibly urban practice in Chitral's villages—the children's birthday party, or *salgira*, which was quickly rounded upon by Rowshan's Sunni religious leaders as being un-Islamic. Strikingly, then, whilst Panjshiris had moved to Chitral from the upper villages of their own valley, they became associated in Chitral with urban and modern forms of life, thus placing themselves also at the heart of conflicts and social tensions with which such processes are everywhere associated.

In addition to bakeries and butcher's shops, families from Badakhshan in Rowshan owned two or three 'hotels' or 'tea houses' (*chai khana*) with eating areas and dark, communal sleeping areas. In summer these were crammed with Pushtun hawkers, and peddlers from the Frontier's tribal areas involved in the collection and sale of scrap metal and skins from across the region's villages. During the day, Chitralis often ate plates of Afghan rice in these eateries, remarking that 'the Tajiks have taught us how to cook rice and sit in hotels'.[40] The Panjshiris and Badakhshis who owned these hotels said that when they had first arrived in Chitral they were only able to find salty tea and bread to eat, and that it was they who had taught Chitralis how to 'eat and drink'. One man told me, '[W]e went to Chitral expecting to find something different from that which we already knew, but discovered their situation was even worse than ours'.[41]

Panjshiri geographies of trade, thus, speak both to topographies of profit and loss and to processes of Islamization, modernization, development and urbanization. Yet the latter like the former did not arise solely from outside the region in the form of development programs led by states or development organizations, but also from within it. In these ways, Panjshiris came to be seen by Chitralis as, and represented themselves as being, the bringers of forms of urban culture and consumption to a once remote village. One Chitrali, indeed, told me that he feared that the extreme modernity of the Afghans was ruining his region's traditional culture once and for all. He had been shocked to hear during a recent trip through the Afghan province of Kunar on his way home from Peshawar that all music in the country was accompanied by electrical sounds, unlike that in Chitral which had remained true to its 'traditional' form. In remoter villages, as we have seen, people also interacted with Panjshiris as learned people able to write and read, as well as knowledgeable about the Qu'ran.

Markers of ethno-linguistic identity in the Frontier assume salience then, not only when they are performed in relationship to the domain of 'the political'. Their significance and meaning are also generated in relation to the particular types of economic activity to which they are connected—ethnicity's significance to everyday life always needs to be treated alongside a consideration of local political economies.[42] Another observation also emerges from this study of Panjshiris' own understandings of their ability to have an effect on the world: what is often referred to by anthropologists as 'agency' is a highly valued feature of their own modes of personal self-understanding and ways of evaluating self-worth.

These butchers, bakers and hotel owners in Rowshan were part of, or even an outpost of, a much wider set of Panjshiri business and kin networks in Chitral. There were two centrally important nodes. One of these was Chitral Town, the region's administrative headquarters, and home to the largest numbers of settled and transient Panjshiris. Most of these families lived in stone houses in what had originally been a designated refugee camp. Some rented shops in Chitral's large bazaar, where they owned businesses in money trading, gem stones, butcher's shops, shoe shops, and shops selling clothing worn mostly by Afghans such as waistcoats and combat-style trousers; these people used the profits of their businesses to rent town houses, and sometimes even bought their own. The second major node was a village located close to the Afghan border and on the key land route from Chitral to both Panjshir and Badakhshan during the years of the Taliban's government in Kabul, called Garam Chashma. This too was an important place for people across northern Afghanistan, many of whom traveled there to purchase goods for their shops or to receive arms distributed for the resistance against the Soviet Union. It was also a site that attracted Pakistani economic and political actors because of the availability of cheap wheat and petrol destined for Afghanistan yet re-smugglable back into Pakistan for sale at high profits. Automatic weapons were also smuggled into Pakistan for sale to the militant organizations that were established in the country from the 1980s onwards.[43]

Much strategizing and thinking, then, for Panjshiris living in Chitral was about the recognition and exploitation of changing business opportunities. Space was and continues to be conceived in terms of profit and loss. Eventually the business choices of Panjshiris as well as their access to Afghan markets and products (especially animals for slaughter) meant that in large villages such as Rowshan and Garam Chashma, and towns such as Chitral, Panjshiris were the owners of some of the most profitable businesses. These ties, connections and patterns of mobility created an alternative geography within Chitral, where nodes of Panjshiri business activity acted as important destinations for newcomers and business traders to the region.

For many Panjshiris, indeed, the experience of life in Chitral is remembered not merely in terms of being displaced persons or refugees, but also often in terms of the depth and complexity of their social worlds in the region. When I meet Panjshiris today in Afghanistan and elsewhere, such as London, and mention particular places in Chitral, they often remark to me that mentioning these names raises memories of the 'era of the *jihad*'. They talk about the distinctive types of sociality, friendships and camaraderie that characterized that era, or *zamana*, as we share names of Panjshiris and other Afghans we have known in Chitral. This is important because by doing so they are invoking an image of social solidarity within the Frontier, of a positive understanding of collective selfhood experienced there, rather than the one that is so often advanced—that of abject 'refugees' in need of, yet debased by the support they receive from, the 'international community'.

As the previous chapter demonstrated, after the removal from power of the Taliban government in Afghanistan in late 2001 the configurations of space, economy and sociality in the wider region quickly changed. Chitral shifted within approximately two years from being like a hub and way-station within expansive regional trade networks to being an apparently far more peripheral economic space.[44] We have addressed some of the effects of this change on Chitral in the previous chapter, and now follow the lives of Afghans who had lived in the region after it had come about.

Not all the Panjshiri families returned to Afghanistan. Rowshan's bakers and butchers stayed, for example, preferring to maintain their business interests in Chitral, rather than risk new investments in

193

Afghanistan. Some of them visited Afghanistan, for the first time since leaving as children, and saw their extended families there after many years. Marriages were also arranged across the border. The eldest brother of the Rowshan Panjshiris, for example, arranged the marriage of his sister with his father's brother's son, a Panjshiri resident in Kunduz. The Kunduz family traveled the long journey through Kabul and the province of Kunar to 'pick up' the girl from Chitral by jeep, before traveling back as a wedding party to Chitral. Kinship relations were maintained, then, between distantly placed families. At the same time, however, family reunification did not lead to the clustering of these people according to their ethnic or kin groups, as a reading of the Frontier's geography through the lenses of ethnicity would have us expect. Rather, the scattering of Panjshiris across the wider region was maintained as they continued to maintain homes and businesses in Chitral and Peshawar, Badakhshan and Panjshir, as well as all of Afghanistan's major cities. This scattering was critical in providing continued opportunities of trade and profit and for wider processes and acts of regional connection.

Many Chitral-based Panjshiris did move back to Afghanistan. The two Rowshan businesses were jointly owned between three brothers, each of whom ideally should have had his own business. Thus, the family put their profits together and bought for one of the brothers who had been working in the Rowshan bakery a shop in the town of Baharak in Afghanistan's Badakhshan Province; this is the same town where the husband of his sister, although resident in Kunduz, also runs a shop selling spare parts (*purzajat*). Panjshiris often say that their people have been important 'spare parts sellers' (*purza furoosh*) since the expansion of car ownership in Afghanistan in the pre-socialist revolution era (*qabil az inqilob*). Yet the ongoing association of Panjshiris by other Afghans with this particular business is also a source of anxiety and moral ambiguity for some from the valley. They argue that while many Panjshiris are now highly educated (*ba sawad*) and involved in a variety of professions (*qasp*) and trades in and beyond the country, they continue to be stigmatised by their co-nationals as lowly *purza furoosh*. Nevertheless, in Tajikistan, which has seen an influx of new cars and vehicles in recent years because of the value these hold in exchange for heroin, Afghans with knowledge of car parts and mechanics are a highly sought after resource. Many other Panjshiri-Chitralis built houses in Kabul and rented vehicles they had bought in Chitral to international organizations. Others, however, saw opportunities for profit not in Kabul and other Afghan cities but in small towns and villages with bazaars similar to Rowshan's. A one-time Chitral-based Panjshiri I know (Rahim) now works as a butcher in the Afghan-Tajikistan border town of Ishkashim. Many Panjshiris, especially from the valleys upper reaches, whose peoples have a detailed knowledge (*'ilm*) of the quality and prices of precious stones (*sang*), especially rubies (*yaqut*) and emeralds (*zamarud*), visit or own shops in Ishkashim because the town is an important arrival point for high quality rubies from Tajikistan's Badakhshan Province. These men procure rubies from men and women across the border in Tajikistan, whom they have established long-term relations with, and meet regularly at the official weekly border bazaar (*bazaar-i mushtarak*) held between Afghan and Tajik territory.[45]

Panjshiris who had been based in Chitral have also embarked on trading activities beyond Afghanistan. Several Panjshiris, who also speak Chitrali, now live and trade in the town of Khorog in Tajikistan's Badakhshan Province. In Khorog, they import second-hand Western clothing from Karachi which they would not be able to sell in Afghanistan, where Indian and Pakistani fashions are more popular and socially acceptable. They are, however, able to sell skirts and dresses to Pamiri women in Khorog, where most women and girls tend to wear 'Western' rather than 'Tajiki' clothing. At the same time, they also buy and then smuggle into Afghanistan expensive rubies, or *yakut* that Pamiri women bring to them from their home villages. These networks of Panjshiri clothing and ruby dealers themselves extend in myriad directions criss-crossing the Frontier, extending to the high altitude and predominantly ethnically Kyrgyz city of Murghob, close to Tajikistan's borders with Kyrgyzstan and China. From there, the rubies are delivered to their relatives and other big gem stone traders in Kabul's precious stone market, and the shops of relatives in Peshawar's old city. In this way these Panjshiri traders bring into contact through movement, trade and the circulation of both luxury (precious stones) and more basic (second hand clothes) objects and commodities these Panjshiri traders being into contact different parts of a vast and mountainous space that is divided by several international borders. Their networks, indeed, stretch beyond the Frontier, most especially to the Jaipur in India, and also to Hong Kong—both key nodes in the world's lapis lazuli and precious stone trades.[46] Chapter 5 explored how important institutions such as the Aga Khan Foundation are directing and shaping the nature of processes of 'regional integration'. Yet Panjshiri traders, far from being merely smugglers (*qochoqbar; qochoqchi*), also play a very powerful role in bringing together people, places and things that might otherwise have remained disconnected, and they often do so in a way that transgresses boundaries of religion and ethnicity rather than reinforcing them. This is in addition to the roles that also play as the learned and educated figures for rural communities.

It is very important, however, not to create a picture of the Frontier as a space of free and unfettered movement for all, or, indeed, a space where if a trader has wealth then he can move with ease.[47] Rather, markers of ethnicity shape peoples' experiences of and ability to move across this multiple border zone. Panjshiri traders in Khorog and other places in Tajikistan often claim that they face few problems with the police and security authorities in the country, saying they are able to obtain visas and live with ease there. By contrast, men of Pukhtun background often say that they are targeted by Tajikistan's authorities. Indeed, Dari-speaking traders have also confirmed to me that if they have few problems living in Tajikistan, the same cannot be said for Pukhtuns. One Pukhtun cloth trader—a *kuchi*, or nomad, whose family is from Loghar, eastern Afghanistan, yet who has lived in the Mohmand tribal region of Pakistan's North-West Frontier since the mid-1980s, and whom I first came to know as a shoe trader in Rowshan in the mid 1990s—told me in the Afghan-Tajikistan border town of Ishkashim how he had lived for three months in the town of Khorog. He had opened a shop selling cloth there but had constantly been hassled by the police:

'Oh Pashtun', the police used to tell me, 'you have got your own place to go—Qandahar, why don't you go there, and join the Taliban?'. I used to say I don't want to do that—just because I am Pashtun does not mean that I am a Talib. 'Then we know why you have come here you dirty Afghan—to get the Tajiki girls—is that what you want to do? Is that why you have come?'

As the first half of the book highlighted, state-work at borders across the entirety of the Frontier often involves attempts to impose rigid identity categories on the malleable identity and livelihood practices of local people. And, as in other comparable frontier spaces inhabited by transborder people, a person's ability to move and profit from such worlds is constrained by a complex interaction of ethnic, religious, racial and national identity markers, as well as the forms of document (passports, visas, and national identity cards especially) that register and codify these.[48] Nevertheless, frontier people continue to develop strategies and forge forms of social relations that allow them to keep as wide a range of possible places in play with one another.

Geographies of Islam

Whilst living in Chitral, Panjshiri and Badakhshani families also engaged in things other than trade; geographies of the Frontier are not only informed by opportunities for profit. Many of the children of these families were not educated in government or private schools during their stays in Chitral, but many were. Yet when I was teaching at an English-medium school in Chitral, a great commotion was caused in the school when the son of the Panjshiri butcher was admitted as a fee-paying student. Several, indeed, went through to the highest levels of Pakistan's education system, securing Masters degrees in Agriculture from Peshawar University and going on to work for major international development corporations in Afghanistan. Some young men who studied at school in Chitral have now been sent by their fathers to study at university and college in India.

Many families also sent their children for education in Pakistan's *madrasas*, especially those in the Frontier, which are largely affiliated to the Deobandi 'school' or 'style' (*maslak*) of Islamic thinking. Sending their children to these *madrasas*, however, raises complex anxieties for many of them. Deobandi forms of Islam are now important across Afghanistan regardless of ethnic and linguistic differences. Afghan students have been taught the Islamic sciences even in the Deoband *madrasa* in India itself since its very inception.[49] Many of the trained Islamic scholars and jurists from these regions studied in Deobandi *madrasas* in South Asia from the 1920s onwards, and, after partition of 1947, in both India and Pakistan.[50] By the late 1990s, however, whilst there remained a very diverse range of different types of Deobandi *madrasas* in Pakistan—some focusing more on scholarly Islamic debates than others[51]—a perception had emerged within the region that the Frontier's *madrasas* were both predominantly Pukhtun and tied to Afghanistan's Taliban government.[52] For Panjshiri and Badakhshi refugee-trader families in Chitral, this raised major concerns about the suitability of such *madrasas* for their own children. Some Badakhshis have in the past supported and fought alongside the Taliban, and this continues to be the case today, although, until now, such support is localized in particular valleys in the region.[53]

Panjshiris and Badakhshis thus have had to develop complex strategies for surviving in the world of the Frontier's *madrasa*s, being keen to seek out Deobandi religious knowledge in Pakistan whilst also recognizing that these *madrasa*s are predominantly Pukhtun, and attended by some people at least who are hostile to Dari-speakers from northern Afghanistan. Young men have told me how they are apprehensive about how they will be treated by their fellow *madrasa* students—fearing they will call them both 'Russians' and the spies of America. One strategy to survive in the *madrasa* is to deploy the malleable approach to personal identity that we have explored in this book. Agha Jan, for example, a Panjshiri I knew in Chitral and have also met in Kabul, told me how when he was studying in a Peshawar *madrasa* he pretended to both students and teachers that he was Chitrali. He only spoke Chitrali and Urdu in the *madrasa* he attended, never speaking in Dari, fearing that if he did his students would accuse him of being a spy for the French or the Americans. Eventually it was a Badakhshi who supported the Taliban who told Agha Jan that he knew he was a Panjshiri, yet said nothing to other *madrasa* students or teachers, and Agha Jan finished his studies in the Islamic Sciences. Panjshiris who have returned to Afghanistan from Chitral continue to send their children to study in *madrasa*s in Peshawar. They say that they are very careful when choosing which *madrasa* they should send their children to, selecting those that are known for being open-minded (*rowshan-fikr*), home to teachers not interested in questions of ethnicity, and located in parts of the Frontier that are 'modern', such as Peshawar's central Sadar Bazaar.

How do these geographies of learning relate to those of trade discussed above? Traders are, as we have seen, often more than just traders—they often serve as impromptu religious officials in remote villages, for example. At the same time, in contrast to most of the Chitrali *madrasa* students I knew, who largely aspired to become teachers of Arabic or Islam in the region's schools, and clearly embodied their status as religious authorities by growing beards and donning turbans, many Panjshiri one-time *madrasa* students often re-enter the trading professions of their relatives. After his return to Afghanistan from the *madrasa* in Peshawar, Agha Jan neither kept a beard nor sought work in the 'religious market'. Instead, he took his father to hospital in India, and stayed on in the country as a refugee seeking a route to Canada, while also trading in goods between Delhi and Kabul. Thus, in the same way that Chitrali youth bring together the experience of more carnal and spiritual forms of love in the context of the *nishini*, the everyday worlds of young men from northern Afghanistan enfold together geographies of profit and of Islam in a way, suggested below, that also serves as a powerful critique of the attempts by Islamist organizations such as Al Qaeda to define the Frontier as a zone of retreat from capitalism.

Finally, and importantly, as the nature of the Taliban insurgency changes together with political conditions in the Afghan Frontier men trained and educated in *madrasa*s will also adopt new positions in relation to the insurgency, the nature of a political settlement, and the presence of foreign military forces in the country. One young man of Panjshiri background whom I have known since he moved in 2000 to Chitral—where I taught him English, a language that he later used to procure work as a translator with ISAF—was, by 2010, fighting with the Taliban. This man's story, like Sulton's in the previous chapter, illustrates that there is no simple link between ethnicity and particular forms of religious ideology. A Tajik may become a Talib just as an Isma'ili may too. Islam relates in complex, ambiguous and shifting ways to markers of ethnicity and language, relations that always also bear the mark of changing political circumstances.

Youth Return: Urban Life, Modernity and War

Having explored the moral and geographical landscapes of Panjshiri trading networks, this section turns to the lived experiences of return by refugees to Afghanistan, noting particularly how the move from Chitral to various locations within Afghanistan has been experienced by young people. It focuses on the changing geographies of work and economy in Afghanistan, especially those associated with a situation of chronic war and insecurity, and the way young men have reflected on their experience of 'return' to this context. These processes of reflection have been central to the modes through which these men have forged moral subjectivities that emphasize the importance of hard-nosed pragmatism to surviving in the Frontier. Thus they also critique openly and poke fun at attempts by Al Qaeda and others to frame this space as a moral refuge from capitalism and cultural globalization. Yet such pragmatically-oriented subjectivities are embraced and embellished by young men who also talk about the forms of moral self constructed by young Chitrali men, which revolve around an idea of detached curiosity.

'Return' from Chitral's villages to Afghanistan has been difficult for all of these young men—land prices in all Afghan cities are high, and many families I know say they are constantly faced with the threat of eviction by 'the state', which claims their settlements are illegal. Conflicts with the Kabul police have, indeed, ensued, shots have been fired, and men killed. Most are told they can stay put for now, but many have brought arms from their villages just in case. Many of the young men I know told me how their 'return' has, thus, also required them to alter their ambitions. Haroon, for example, who drove a jeep in Chitral, and now works with the Afghan National Army, told me that he had hoped his daughters would go to school and be educated. Having returned from Chitral, however, the state of the roads, attitudes of his neighbors, and general levels of danger led him to realize that educating them would be impossible.

Employment and money are also ceaseless sources of worry for the returnees with whom I have spent time. One relatively 'easy' option is to take work with NATO military forces, mostly as translators (*tarjuman*). A job that requires much more than the name suggests— 'translators' are often armed and sometimes actively involved in military action. It is 'easy' because many of these men learned English at schools in Pakistan, not because the choice to participate is made without continually reassessed moral reflection. Some men say they are even keen to find such work because they will do anything for good money, upon which, they tell me, 'the good life' depends. For others, the religious permissibility or otherwise of such work is paramount in their decision making processes. One young man, Ahmed, for example secured a job as a translator at a NATO base in northern Afghanistan; the day after commencing work he asked for religious edicts or *fatwa*s from his town's most respected religious authorities concerning the permissibility of his job, and they told him the work was *halal*, so long as he did not put his fellow Afghans' lives in danger. Only after securing four *fatwa*s did he eventually ask me, 'would you agree that four is enough?' Other young Panjshiri men just laughed when I told them of Ahmed's search for religious legitimacy.

The pressures of such work are great, casualties not infrequent. Criticism of fathers who allow, compel or encourage their sons to work for ISAF is an important feature of much daily conversation. One man, for instance, lost a son to a remote controlled bomb in the city of Jalalabad. When he 'sent' his younger son to work as a carpenter at a US base in Mazar-e Sharif, his relatives roundly declared him a fool. Nor does such work go without comment from friends and family, even if its Islamic legitimacy has been confirmed. It is shameful to have to ask fellow townspeople to step aside and be searched by ISAF forces. And these young men fear they will be the target of anti-government forces now or in the future.

Some have made significant money whilst serving the Americans, however, and it is to the world of 'business' that they have now turned. The Kabul-Kunduz road is lined with petrol stations jointly owned by Panjshiri men. Others have established construction companies, which build foreign financed projects in Afghanistan's provinces. Line drawings of a school for a province in the north sit alongside designs for prison surveillance towers for Qandahar in the offices of these men, where many prefer to spend their nights rather than return to their family homes on the city's outskirts. Trading too is big, and transnational. Cheap cement is freighted to northern Afghanistan from Pakistan, before being moved onto Tajikistan, with the help of Tajik businesses partners or *sharik* (partners) who are said, however, to be untrustworthy.

Money makes enemies, of course, especially so when the stakes are as high as a $500,000 prison watchtower project—relatives are accused of 'fleeing' with bags of cash, friends of hiding the profits of jointly owned petrol pumps, business partners of secretly dealing with traders from Tajikistan on whose cultivation for the 'trust of trade' much money has already been spent. The world, they say, has 'turned on its head'. And anyway, money or not, they are often referred to by longer-term Kabuli city dwellers as being, *'atrafi'*, provincial: rude, ill-mannered, backward, never worthy of that fashionably dressed Kabuli girl whose heart they thought they had caught. If the urban-rural boundary is often partial and fluid from the perspectives of these people themselves, then there are contexts in which an ideology of rural-urban distinction is imposed upon their identities.

Such forms of stigma emerge not only on the basis of being an *atrafi* in the city. Many also say that when they returned to Kabul even their fellow village people recognized that they had spent most of their lives in Pakistan. 'They call us *dhall khor* [lentil eaters]', said one man I know who was born and brought up in Chitral. 'They can tell that we have come back from Pakistan easily, by our haircuts, the way we speak, and also because we don't know Dari that well—we don't know all the complicated terms for the government ministries in particular, because we learned their Urdu equivalents in Pakistan. This gives us away (*malum mesha*) as having lived in Pakistan very quickly'. The fear of being 'given away' suggests here, as with the case of the 'Wakhis' in Chitral, the complex and tense relationship between trans-regional and national registers of identity difference. A heightened awareness of how one might be judged as someone 'from Pakistan' (*az Pakistan*) highlights how people think about the ways in which prolonged stays in a place negatively affect a person's identity.

Nevertheless, many of these young men continue to talk publicly about their attachment to Chitral. Many say that the only reason they returned was to respect the wishes of their parents who no longer wished to live as 'refugees' in Chitral, underscoring key generational differences in both the experience of life in Chitral and return to Pakistan. Young men continue to reaffirm their connections to Chitral, making telephone calls to their friends and sometimes to illicit lovers there. Their families also host Chitralis who visit Kabul in order to search for work as electricians and petrol pump attendants, or to travel to the shrine of Ali in Mazar in order to attend the celebrations marking the Spring Equinox or Nowruz. Many young men say that it is too dangerous for them to travel safely to Chitral because they are known there to work for security companies active alongside NATO, something that places them at risk from Taliban fighters both in Pakistan and on the road to Chitral through Kunar. Yet some do make return visits to Chitral's villages anyway, treating it as a sort of 'safe haven' to which they can escape if caught up in enmity relations in Afghanistan. Abdul, for example, who is in his mid-twenties and originally from a village in the upper reaches of the Panjshir, returned to Afghanistan from Chitral only to go back to Chitral after his enemies in a long running blood feud had threatened to take revenge and kill him now that all of the parties in the conflict were 'back home'. He stayed in Chitral for several months, driving a taxi that he had brought with him from Afghanistan, until his uncle came to a compromise or *sulh* with the enemies. Abdul then returned to Kabul and worked for a security company in the south of the country.

In the midst of this confusing world of violence, bereavement, aspiration, struggle and disillusionment, however, one of the most memorable dimensions of my fieldwork with these men was joining them in the mock performance of the many news and current events discussion-style television programs that are shown on Afghanistan's cable and satellite television channels. These exhilarating performative displays take place whenever the opportunity arises and are an important example of the complex forms of imaginative and creative work that these young men deploy to reflect on and understand the worlds in which they live. Long car journeys between the cities where my friends lead their highly mobile lives—Kabul, Mazar and Kunduz—and the houses of relatives, near and distant, are two favored arenas. These young men rejoice in acting out the roles of a tough talking TV presenter and his 'respected guests'. The mock programs see my friends play the part of presenter, Afghanistan's Interior minister, a *mujahidin* commander, the Iranian envoy, and an Afghan Communist. The presenter speaks Dari fast, and with an official accent, asking his guests for their opinions on contentious political questions.

These questions are indeed ones that I am often asked as a researcher in the country, and those that Afghans ask one another on a daily basis. Should ISAF forces stay in Afghanistan? Will war return to Afghanistan if the British and Americans leave? For what reason did the British and Americans come to Afghanistan in the first place? Are British soldiers financially supporting the Taliban and using contacts they cultivated with Pushtun people during the colonial period to do so? Are the *mujahidin* commanders a positive or negative dimension of the country's political landscape?

The guests in the mock programs never hold their words. 'There are three types of Taliban, not one', announces the faux commander, 'the Taliban of the British, of Pakistan and of Al Qaeda—all of them share one aim, however, to deny political recognition to the men who spent thirty years fighting for the freedom of Afghanistan, its people, its religion, and its culture: the mujahidin'. 'Afghans free' interrupts the Communist: 'if Afghans were free they too should be able to meet and have fun underneath the trees (*zir-e darakht*) like all others'. 'Nonsense', replies the man impersonating the minister, 'all this talk of Taliban and Al Qaeda is senseless. Afghanistan is today made-up of two types of Al Qaeda: the *al-guida* (the fucked) and the *al-fayeda* (the seekers of profit)'.

At first glance, such television news chat programs in Afghanistan are exactly the type of medium that a nexus of local actors, the Afghan state and foreign 'development' agencies has used to promote liberal modes of critical thinking. Indeed, many Afghans tell me that the Americans are *chalak* or cunning. Instead of forcing them to change their 'culture' as the Russians tried to do, they are gradually weakening it by showing Indian dramas with the aim of pushing the country's people to embrace Western forms of family life. Hence the pleasure these young men take in playing the part of informed contributors to Afghan political debate could be seen either as a way in which such modes of liberal subjectivity come to be actively inculcated or, alternatively, as a practice through which they are mocked and resisted.

Yet as much recent anthropological work on the ways in which people receive messages from the media demonstrates, the dynamics involved in such encounters are more complex. These dynamics range from active processes of discrimination to 'watching and listening without taking up the position of the text's addressees'.[54] As Abu Lughod has shown in her study of Egyptian television serials, they may also involve the selection of limited moral messages in media texts that otherwise appear to be divorced from people's everyday lives.[55] What is especially important about this case, moreover, is the ways in which these young men are already building on an existing repertoire of play acting and mimicry, as well as forums for the display of wit, that have long been an important dimension of performance and intellectual life in Afghanistan.[56]

This particular encounter points towards the importance of imitation for the ways these men receive and reflect upon such mediated messages. This, of course, was also the case in Chapter 5, in which young Chitrali men pretended to be Isma'ili missionaries from Canada and the sons of Pakistan Army officers.[57] Mimesis, Willerslev has recently argued, is a concrete practice that 'puts the imitator in contact with the world of other bodies, things, and people, and yet separates him from them by forcing him to reflexively turn in on himself'.[58] In societies where 'people are never solely themselves but always at the same time something else ... everyday activity is not just routine and unreflexive practice', but, instead, 'demands a kind of "deep reflexivity"'.[59] This deep reflexivity is certainly visible in the everyday lives of the young men described in this chapter, as it was to the Chitral youths whose tours we followed in Chapter 5. In both contexts young men derive pleasure from imitating, mocking and also learning from their country's most influential figures. Yet, importantly, they also deploy these performances to question the conditions of their daily lives. After the mock television program described above we drove around Kabul's bazaars identifying the *al-guida* and the *al-fayeda*. These processes of mimesis are important practices through which they both reflect on their daily lives and actively make claims on those in authority—warlords, state officials, foreign troops—to treat them not as unthinking people contained by cultural 'traditions' but as sophisticated and self-reflective humans.

Warlords: Mujahidin *in Transformation*

Chitral was not only a destination point for the traders, agricultural laborers, and jeep drivers detailed in the previous pages. It also became home to some of northern Afghanistan's most politically powerful men who considered it an important safe haven during the anti-Soviet *jihad*, and for this reason established their party offices and homes in Chitral Town. These included the former President Rabbani (d. 2011) who built a house in Chitral. In addition to powerful political leaders who lived in Chitral, many also 'sent' their brothers and children there during the *jihad*. Having explored, then, the shifting identities and life trajectories of young men with experience of moving across the Frontier, we now explore the trajectories of movement of the 'commanders'.[60] These provide a further Frontier fragment, and thus a perspective on how the region's shape has changed in relation to unfolding geopolitical events, and the nature of actors' experiences of this transformation.

The continuing power and importance of so-called 'warlords' in Afghan politics, society and state building have of course been the focus of much comment and debate over the past decade. It is important, however, not to think of such men as uni-dimensionally defined according to their ability to act in a coercive manner. Understanding their politics, rather, requires recognition too of their tactical strategies of self-transformation and presentation. In this world, shaped as much as it is by power relations with the wider world, both footloose smuggler/laborers like Sulton and the men of power and authority whose lives I now explore constantly demonstrate themselves as being adept at artful, strategizing, and even cosmopolitan-like behavior.

These are, indeed, dimensions of the lives of such men that are the focus of open discussion and debate within the country. There is much discussion in more public and intimate contexts, for example, about how the appearance of these commanders has changed—men I know often comment on how the '*jihadi*s' have trimmed their beards to make them virtually non-existent. Indeed, after the powerful governor (*wali*) of a major Afghan province suggested that he could return to the hills and fight should political processes not go in his favor, a politician known more for his wit and bravery than for wealth and power is purported to have asked: 'How could the governor do such, he has become so accustomed to spraying his neck with French perfume and wearing English ties'. The governor's comment recalls, of course, Bin Laden's depiction of Afghanistan's mountains as a holy and enduring refuge from capitalism. The question posed by the politician, moreover, also shows how far this book's central concern—the texture, meaning and significance of the Frontier's landscape and how this relates to people's everyday worlds—is the focus of open forms of moral contestation that are also invested with major political significance in the region today.

One of the themes that previous ethnographic chapters of this book identified regarding forms of 'equivalence' that shape the Frontier's landscapes concerned the ways in which forms of power, hierarchy and authority that speak to a 'Persianate' past and are continuously embedded in the physical landscape of Chitral, as it is visualized and experienced by Chitralis and other frontier people who travel there. Now explored are the ways in which these are also evident in Afghan Badakhshan. Far from being rendered into rubble by the past thirty years of war and conflict, Persianate geographies of power persist and remain of vital importance to the authority of the powerful and the nature of their relations with local people. 'Warlords' in Badakhshan, indeed, often come from 'lordly' backgrounds, not dissimilar to those I described in Chitral. Such men are often descended from high status families who trace their descent from the great seventeenth century South Asian reformer-scholar *pir*s—Shaikh Ahmad Sirhindi, for example—and were powerful figures in the small states or fiefdoms that made up Badakhshan. Some of these men's fathers also served as Badakhshan's representatives to Zahir Shah's parliament in the 1960s/70s—something that they often remind 'their' villagers of during election campaigns today, telling them, 'We have experience of dealing with people and we have contacts in Kabul with those who count'.[61] These commanders share, then, cultural ideas of power and authority comparable to those we saw as important for Chitral's lordly elites.

Such ideas of power are also 'embedded' in Badakhshan's landscape in similar ways as they are in Chitral's. The capacity of the Chitrali lord, for example, to be able to sit in the cooling shade of Chinese Plane trees and watch the goings-on of 'his' people from raised land is a critical feature of Badakhshan's landscape. Indeed, party leaders and activists of the People's Democratic Party of Afghanistan recognized this. They hacked down the Chinese Plane trees of local lords or *mirs* in Badakhshan when such 'feudals' left the region in order to relocate their families in Chitral and launch the anti-Soviet *jihad*. Today, the stumps of trees on the hilltop houses of the *mirs* that were destroyed by those they refer to as 'the Communists' are once again sprouting branches. Badakhshi MPs sit underneath these branches as they meet villagers and supporters on their yearly visits from Kabul. They also recite the names of powerful Afghans who, on visiting their village, chose not to sit in their comfortable and newly built guest house, but, instead, to recline underneath the Chinar (Chinese Plane) and enjoy its cool shade.

These men of power and influence, indeed, sometimes have known ties of kin with places beyond. As we saw in Chapter 5, such ties and connections are never politically neutral—this is something felt by the politically powerful and aspirant in this region of Afghanistan. In the same way that low-status families in Chitral sought to conceal their connections with Afghanistan's Wakhan corridor, so too are the connections between powerful men in Badakhshan to Chitral a subject of sensitive discussion now. On the one hand, such connections are proof of 'the *jihad*'s' key slogan—'Islam has no borders'. At the same time, however, this slogan, for many, has now turned sour: Pakistan and 'the West' are held responsible for supporting the Taliban and their rise to power. In this political context, and more broadly in settings where Islam's genealogies and the idea of the 'nation-state' interact with one another, ties with Chitral connect men of influence not merely to 'the outside' but also, now, in the context of the 'national order of things' to Pakistan. Villagers talk about the connection of these men and families with 'the outside' (*berun*) as symbolizing the injustices of their region's pasts: the powerful warrior lords might have brought superior forms of Islamic knowledge to the region but they are also accused of having captured its best land from the region's ordinary people.[62]

Islam's capacity to give shape to a wide space though its relationship to kinship ties and the transmission of religious authority along complex genealogies has been subtly yet recognizably reconfigured as it has come to exist alongside other ways of imagining space and boundaries, especially those connected with the nation.[63] During the *jihad*, however, ties with Chitral were not only treated as a stain on a man's potential for being 'truly local'. The region was, rather, considered by the commanders and the influential as one of the Frontier's most reliable 'safe havens'. These men—like the traders discussed earlier in this chapter—remember the *jihad* and their everyday lives in Chitral not in terms of their having been 'refugees' in 'Pakistan', but as a period of unity, the *'dawr-e mutahid'*, which some of them now claim to miss. As noted above, many of them enjoyed ties of marriage to Chitral's ruling families. These ties, indeed, helped their families settle in the region. Their well connected relatives also assisted them in their political and business activities—they soon became official representatives of all the refugees who had fled to Chitral from northern Afghanistan.[64]

Chitral's status as a safe haven for these figures has, however, shifted in the context of changing geopolitical circumstances. New geographies of security and danger have spawned. As Pakistan's growing complicity with the Taliban government emerged in the late 1990s, the shape of this space and the geographical distribution of people around it changed. Commanders moved their families out of Chitral to Dushanbe in Tajikistan—a city that was free of Soviet rule, and one where Northern Alliance men were held in much respect both because of the leading role played by Ahmad Shah Masoud in negotiating the end of the civil war and because of their 'Tajik' identity. Leaving Chitral, however, was complex and difficult for these men. Some of them left behind the graves of their fathers who died and were buried in Chitral. They complain that they have not been able to pray at the tombs of their fathers since leaving Chitral, but also hope each year that they will be able to travel to these religious sites on the occasion of one or other of the major Islamic festivals. Simultaneously, however, having left Chitral they also re-established ties with the communities of Badakhshan in Tajikistan discussed in the previous chapter. This was lucrative given the ease with which these connections could help speed Afghan opium across the border and on to markets in Moscow, Amsterdam and London.[65]

The sons, brothers and cousins of *jihadi*s also traveled along this route. En route to London these men stayed in the homes of relatives with very different ideological pasts. Amar, the son of a major *jihadi* commander, for example stayed in the home of a former Badakhshani People's Democratic Party of Afghanistan (PDPA) official in Moscow, in a 'safe house' in Bucharest where he learned some Romanian with a girlfriend, with a one-time Hizb-i Islami commander uncle in Germany, and with a relative in London whose Afghan air force plane Amar's brother had ordered to be shot down during the *jihad*—only to forgive the pilot and instruct his men to save him yet also make him fly for the *mujahidin* (who used captured Soviet aircraft and pilots). His journey and the forms of solidarity upon which it depended—forms of solidarity themselves enriched by complex and interwoven stories of past betrayal and forgiveness—underscore the degree to which the Frontier is made and re-made not only within the geographical space of Afghanistan and Pakistan but also in the lives of its people beyond. Some gained citizenship rights and 'leave to remain' in London, where they now work as drivers, chefs and shopkeepers, whilst also marrying their relatives—based not in Badakhshan but in Houston, Texas. These men travel to Kabul seeking lucrative contracts with the British military in Helmand or at the US base at Bagram. Or just to visit their brothers' during the course of their election campaigns—trips they use as an opportunity to take their young children to see their ancestral villages and have photos taken of themselves brandishing Kalashnikovs whilst riding on horses brought specially for them from the mountain pastures by their brothers' *dehqan*, or tenant/laborers.

The brothers of other commanders were deported; they left their jobs as CD packers in northern England to return to Kabul and join their brothers who in the meantime had become elected officials in the Afghan government. After their return, their marriages, delayed ten or more years after engagement, were finally conducted. They also travel to Dubai and New Delhi—global cities that have now taken Chitral's place as a regional safe haven and space of profit—in order to stake out property, collect rents, open businesses such as car parks and restaurants, and deliver their brothers' children from danger, especially in election years.

The commanders-cum-MPs also travel widely and often on official government business. Yet even official trips often incorporate the work of kinship and the re-making the webs of connections with which this and the past chapter have been concerned. Relatives whom they had helped to escape Afghanistan during the era of the *jihad* are visited. These relatives are found not only across the river that separates

Afghan Badakhshan from Tajikistan but also during the course of these men's travels to the US and Europe. They return from visits to Washington and Berlin with souvenir pictures of photo calls with Condoleezza Rice, and, more significantly, of yet more family members whom they were also able to meet. Some of these relatives trained in the 1970s in the great Islamic University of Al Azhar in Cairo now write books about Naqshbandi Sufism and Afghan history by day, while driving taxis between Freemont station and San Jose Holiday Inn at night. Their sons, however, were brought up in the US and have no knowledge of Pashto, speak Dari with a thick American accent, and ask the visiting anthropologist to explain to them the historical significance of their families.[66] Yet these young men also make trips to Afghanistan when they might test their hand at assuming a grandfather's position of *pir*, or man of spiritual power and authority, events they record and then later post on 'YouTube'.

International Cosmopolitans

We have been arguing throughout this book that the Frontier is a rich connective zone between different parts of the world whose people are highly informed about that world, and aware of their status as powerful actors in it. They and the world in which they live are shaped perhaps above all else by that connectivity. The book's ethnographic part is concluded with an exploration of the precise types of knowledge that the people we have come to know over the preceding pages have of the wider world, and the ways in which they transmit this amongst themselves.

Nearly a decade after the fall of the Taliban, Kabul is a city both of 'return' and of 'departure'. Not all those who have returned are refugees from neighboring Afghanistan, Iran and Central Asia. Neighborhood and kinship ties in Kabul are enriched and complicated too by the return of Afghans from places further afield: London, California and Germany in particular. Afghan families and men with experience of life in Virginia and Essen have returned to Kabul, where some have established successful construction businesses (often with an Iranian American partner to lend their documents greater credibility when perused by their main customers, the US military), and others have taken up teaching positions in the city's university. Such people, however, also live in fear of being kidnapped. One Panjshiri I met had been chased by kidnappers to the third storey of a house that was being built opposite his own; he jumped to escape, paralyzing his arm yet rescuing himself from his potential abductors. Now this man is thinking of a new place to move. The US no longer feels either like home or safe, but neither, increasingly, does Kabul. It was to Mumbai, Delhi, Pune, Cairo and Istanbul that he was thinking of moving when I last met him. These are all places, he says, where his children can learn to be Muslims, although 'educated and informed Muslims' rather than 'Afghan Muslims'. Moreover, as many of these people note, for families involved in businesses such as construction and logistics like themselves the decision to move to India, China or Istanbul is more sensible than going back to America or the UK—places, they say, which like the USSR before them are now clearly losing their place in the world. Indeed, if as we have seen Chitral is talked about in terms of the social solidarity of the *jihad* era, then life in London and Virginia is more likely to be remembered through memories of having to take low and demeaning jobs, of being the proverbial 'dog washer' (*sagshu*) of the Afghan diaspora—'dog washer' being an exceptionally pejorative term that connotes the willingness of Afghans living in non-Muslim lands to carry out the most demeaning of jobs for the sake of money. The making of decisions such as this one about future patterns of relocation will signal the emergence of new frontier geographies and positioning of Afghanistan's diasporas beyond the arena of Pakistan, the Gulf and Iran.

For the young men whom I knew in Chitral, however, and who may well have ties of kin to people who reached the West thirty or more years ago, these wealthy merchant returnees, are concerned to offer important economic possibilities, and, like the commanders, their lives are also a source of much moral discussion.' I have often met one-time American-based Afghan businessmen on the flight to Kabul, and having chatted to them, been invited to their homes and offices in the city. As I usually travel around Kabul with young men I had known in Chitral, I often take them to the houses of my newly found contacts—something that is accepted given concerns of safety and security in the city. Returnees from the West—who live in large, modern houses with soft Turkish carpets and powerful 4x4 vehicles—are lucrative contacts, and exactly the type of person I am asked to introduce to my friends. Such men offer the hope of employment or support for a fledgling company, but, perhaps, are more likely to offer to sponsor a man's education in an Afghan *madrasa*.

Not all of those who have recently returned from 'the West' live in such style, however. The stays of others were far shorter. Many Panjshiris have been refused refugee status in the countries to which they have traveled, or made to live in cramped quarters of refugee camps. Aga Jan, for example, a Kunduz-based Panjshiri in his mid-thirties, lived for several years in London, where he worked in a Pakistani owned Pizza Hut. His asylum case failed but he stayed on anyway, until he was eventually deported, a year or so before I met him in Kunduz. He showed me the documents relating to his case and the appeal he had made from Afghanistan, as well as his application for another UK visa. In between the legal documents were the photographs of his marriage party—to a woman he had married in Lahore, after they had met in Leicester. The UK authorities, however, denied him the right to live in Britain, questioning the legality of the marriage and stating that nothing stopped the couple from either living in Pakistan or Afghanistan. At present, however, Aga Jan is jobless in Kunduz, and has told his Pakistani wife that she should continue her life in Leicester without him. His brother, a cement trader who lives between Kunduz and Dushanbe—a city in which he also has a local wife—tells him to come to Tajikistan and start trading there.

The extent to which asylum claims are seen as being of great political relevance for Afghanistan is also clearly evoked in the ways in which some people look back at their decision to return home in a different light. Gul Agha—also a Panjshiri who lives between Kabul and Kunduz—spent five years in a refugee camp in Norway, having also lived or passed through Paris, Holland and Germany. Shortly after September 11th the friend he was with persuaded him that it was time to take the money being offered by the Norwegian government, and return home. How long could they stay playing snooker and receiving benefits, not even being allowed to work? Having returned to his family in Kabul, and driving a taxi daily between the cities of Kunduz and Kabul whilst listening to a cassette of Russian pop music he picked up during a three month stay in Moscow on his way to Oslo, Gul Agha not only teases his friend now for being weak and making him return home prematurely; he also threatens to immolate himself in front of the Norwegian embassy if it does not give him permission to return to Oslo. 'Are we not also human?' (*ma ham insan nistim*) .

Conclusion

This chapter has sought to elaborate upon and underscore two key themes of central importance for this book. First, the Frontier is a fractured space defined by its heterogeneity, yet it is also a region that maintains coherence through time. Frontier people are deeply aware of the plays of historical change and continuity that shape their lives. This allows them to navigate and engage with this space in the fluid ways that have been documented in all the three preceeding chapters. They have the capacity to read the many and multi-valent signposts that mark out particular categories of people and place as they encounter them across the Frontier. These signposts include the hill-top houses of lords, Chinese Plane trees, and the butcher's shop of a Panjshiri gem trader, for example.

Second, whilst this world is navigated by the use of recognizable categories of place and of people—ranging from lord to Seyyid, serf to footloose trader—it is also a space within which people constantly strive to emphasize dimensions of their humanity and citizenship that transcend these recognizable social categories and sometimes, too, that of 'Muslim' itself. In contrast to the visions of the Frontier as a sacred space free from the polluting influence of capitalism that are promoted by Bin Laden and others in Al Qaeda, the young men whose lives this chapter documented view the Frontier as much through lenses that deftly seek out spaces of profit, accumulation, affection and safety, and navigate away from areas of loss and danger, as according to considerations of moral purity. This focus on profit and security does not mean, however, that Frontier people do not have a highly developed understanding of their own or their region's moral and political significance to the wider world. Indeed, they cultivate such an understanding through engaging in complex practices of mimesis, debate and imitation. The political and citizenship claims frontier people make to the wider world are, moreover, often framed in relation to discourses of shared humanity, rather than just in terms of distinct cultural categories—for example 'Muslim', 'Afghan' or 'Tajik'. The failure to acknowledge the importance of this vocabulary and the deeply thought out conceptions of humanity on which it lies, reflects the distorted nature of the windows through which the outside world has tended to view and engage with the Frontier. In place of such acknowledgment, outsiders have emphasized the importance of understanding the 'cultural sensitivities and particularities' of 'Afghans' and 'Muslims'. As the first half of the book showed, these forms of categorization are derivative of earlier colonial understandings of 'tradition', and thus are a source of the ongoing problems the wider world has encountered in the Frontier.

EPILOGUE

In the preceding pages, we have presented a collage of images and experiences of the Frontier. Particular episodes, locations and peoples have been juxtaposed next to one another in order to construct a variegated image of a space which remains unfamiliar to many in the West, despite the depth of involvements of their governments there—politically and militarily—over the past two hundred years. Throughout, we have presented the precarious balance between centrifugal forces that threaten to fragment any meaningful idea of the Frontier and the centripetal forces which just as forcefully attempt to portray the Frontier as some sterile, stereotyped whole. The Frontier is a space with meaning as a whole. Yet, rather than the certain and bounded meaning of a fixed and unchanging culture, this meaning is constantly being fashioned, contested and re-fashioned. The Frontier remains highly heterogeneous space in which the experiences, peoples and practices of one valley or desert track differ drastically from those of their nearest neighbor. But this does not render it a space of disjuncture. The Frontier offers diverse opportunities of solidarity, at the same time it imposes limits that fragment.

As a heterogenous space, the Frontier is multiply conceived, defined and experienced. The preceding chapters have attempted to put that heterogeneity on display. The historical and ethnographic chapters of the book analyze discrete fragments constituting the Frontier. We have sought to illustrate how the past continues to shape the present here, both explicitly and implicitly. We have also sought to examine how different Frontier inhabitants and shapers of this space have conceptualized and acted within it. Whether it be the Qajar and Durrani courts, the frontier-administrators of the British Raj, the 'Fanatics' of Hindu-

stan, Osama Bin Laden, the youth of Chitral, Badakhshani power holders or Afghan 'refugees', all have had a significant effect on the
topography—conceptual and physical—of the Frontier.

What then are we to make of this space? How are we to understand
it, if at all? What relevance does it have to the world beyond the confines of the high mountain valleys of the Hindu Kush? And what are
the practical implications of the way of thinking about the Frontier we
have argued for here—for policy-makers, publics, as well as local communities? There are all multi-faceted questions which this work can
only begin to answer. We believe, however, the book raises important
possibilities with regard to each of these, possibilities we continue to
explore in our own research, hoping that other scholars will follow.

We hope this book offers a glimpse into the complexity of the region
and we urge policy makers to consider the Frontier's heterogeneity as
they shape their actions, current and future. We offer the historical
chapters as both a reminder and a warning: a reminder that others
have treaded the path Western capitals are now walking down; a warning that in pursuing similar policies, strategies and tactics as their predecessors, it is unrealistic for today's imperialists to expect a different
outcome. The anthropological chapters challenge the simplistic tropes
about static and primitive peoples. Together, they clearly demonstrate
that despite the best efforts by political authorities, even local ones, to
regulate this space and control the lives of its inhabitants, many of
those efforts have come to naught. The people of the region have
learned to bend and sway adeptly to the political winds without breaking. They have repeatedly demonstrated an uncanny ability to slip past
the barriers put in place by the multiple states and state-forms they
come into contact with, or, even more subversively, to turn these to
their own advantage. This does not mean that state control has not
had a profound effect on the region. On the contrary, the intrusions of
political authorities—colonial, national and neo-imperial—have been
arguably the most important factors shaping the Frontier. But it does
underline the fact that efforts at regulation have often led to perverse
and unintended consequences.

Many of the voices and experiences explored here run at odds with
those normally presented about the Frontier. Some might argue that
the picture of a sophisticated and cosmopolitan world we have advanced rests on our familiarity with its 'minorities'—those who inhabit
the margins of this world and are, therefore, especially skilled at subtly

navigating it. But we make a larger claim here. Our aim has been to offer a richer language to discuss the region's diversity and heterogeneity. The often assumed dichotomies of 'majority/minority', urban/rural, 'elite/subaltern', 'warlords/victims' are limited in the understandings they can provide of the Frontier. While such ways of representing heterogeneity might have purchase for some, for many this world is seen through an altogether more flexible and inchoate set of categories, reflecting the ups and downs of people's own experiences, and the constantly changing boundaries of the limits and opportunities they face. The inchoateness of these categories is visible in the deft responses of Frontier people to life in a world of such flux. It is also evident in the fluidity of their ambitions for the future, and their ability to profit from rapidly changing circumstances. Cross-border smugglers, thus, have deftly integrated themselves into international agencies as development specialists, while one-time taxi drivers in Chitral have assumed responsibility as security officials in Kabul. The least of the Frontier's problems, contrary to much that is written about it, is a lack of 'human capacity'.

There is a profound need for greater recognition of the complex and historically shifting ties that bind this region's peoples together, as opposed to the simplistic divisions between ethnic groups, 'classes' or confessional solidarities encoded into maps of it. This is precisely why we describe the diverse parts of the Frontier explored in this book as 'fragments' rather than as 'minorities', 'sects' or 'tribes'. We have documented a world, and its past, currently convulsing under the pressure of extreme forms of violence that divide its populations and communities. Yet we have also sought to give insights into the nature of everyday life in this world, which is colored as much by memories of social solidarity and companionship experienced during times of violent conflict as by the breakdown of these. And further, to emphasize that this is a world in which people make everyday efforts to stay attuned to constantly changing issues of global importance, constructing their thinking and moral universes in relationship to these issues rather than to a static and unchanging attachment to 'tradition'. Indeed, while the topic is beyond the scope of the current book, our investigation of the past's complex relationship to the present along the Frontier suggests that this space might also offer especially rich opportunities to understand how historically-informed imaginings of the future are also central to the forms of political and moral agency exerted by ordinary people.

The Frontier, we have suggested, is at one and the same time idiosyncratically different from any other, and yet archetypically representative of so many similarly situated 'peripheries' of the global political and economic order. It is exemplary of many locales produced by the processes of globalization that have taken root over the past two centuries. The conceptualization of the Frontier as an 'other' space, 'out there', which is acted upon by powerful centers is one that does not stand the force of critical scrutiny. Indeed, as the historical chapters demonstrate, this is a space that has often exerted a formative influence over imperial and national centers. Further, Frontier people are not some species of isolated rural dweller, or traditional tribesman, but rather are highly mobile citizen-subjects inhabiting a cosmopolitan world that they both critically conceive and creatively construct. Neither the Frontier nor its inhabitants are alone in being marginalized, while at the same time performing an almost subversively central role in globalization. Spaces such as the Sahara, Somalia, the Thai-Burmese border or indeed the South China Sea are similarly situated 'frontiers' which scholars are only now beginning to explore as places integral to the modern global order.

The Frontier is subject to continuous conceptualization and reconceptualization as part of a multiplicity of imaginaries thought of, performed and enacted by a diverse cast of players. It bears the imprint of those who have sought to construct it—politically, culturally and socially. The builders of the Frontier—from the British colonial officials to Chitrali NGO workers of this book—have not always realized their part in its construction. But it is too often the case that the moral imaginaries projected onto this space from afar—be they the morally purifying ones of global Islamists, of US politicians intent on 'saving' Afghan women from tribal and Islamic primitivism, or indeed, of activists who call upon people in the West to recognize the Taliban as an anti-imperial rather than archaic force in the modern world—have all too often had little if any purchase on, or indeed interest in, the worlds of those on the ground. Such imaginaries are made and remade through relationships of power inequality, and the results are constantly contested by both the 'losers' and the 'winners' of those relationships. Yet, as we have sought to show, the Afghan Frontier is at heart an organic, historic region that for those living there is ultimately a social reality, one, like all others, that is being constructed in perpetuity.

NOTES

INTRODUCTION

1. D.S. Richards, *The Savage Frontier: a History of the Anglo-Afghan Wars*, London: Macmillan, 1990.
2. Alessandro Monsutti, *War and Migration: Social Networks and Economic Strategies of the Hazaras of Afghanistan*, New York: Routledge, 2005; Robert Nichols, *A History of Pashtun Migration, 1775–2006*, Oxford: Oxford University Press, 2008.
3. James Scott, *The Art of not being Governed: an Anarchist History of Upland Southeast Asia*, New Haven: Yale University Press, 2009 . For a contrasting analysis that places hierarchy, aristocracy and 'state-like' political structures as central to the organization of even the most apparently egalitarian 'non-state' societies, *see* David Sneath, *The Headless State*, New York: Columbia University Press, 2007.
4. *See for instance* Fredrik Barth, *Balinese Worlds*, Chicago: University of Chicago Press, 1993.
5. *See* Gyan Pandey, *Routine Violence: Nations, Fragments, Histories*, Palo Alto: Stanford University Press, 2006 for a call for historians to contest 'the state's construction of history' through a consideration of life forms that the self-defined 'mainstream' labels as 'minority', p. 42. The present book seeks to extend the perspective developed by Pandey and others by placing the constructions of space and time made both by states and fragments, as well as by more and less powerful actors in region, alongside one another. Our approach thereby allows for a greater appreciation of the disjunction and overlaps of these constructions.
6. Andrew M. Roe, *Waging War in Waziristan: the British Struggle in the Land of Bin Laden, 1849–1947*, Lawrence, KS: University of Kansas Press, 2010.
7. Roberto J. Gonzalez, *American Counterinsurgency: Human Science and the Human Terrain*, Chicago: Prickly Paradigm Press, 2009. *Cf.* Montgomery McFate, 'Anthropology and Counterinsurgency: The Strange Story of their Curious Relationship', *Military Review*, March/April 2005.

8. Nicholas Dirks, *Castes of Mind: Colonialism and the Making of Modern India*, Princeton: Princeton University Press, 2001.

9. Nancy Lindisfarne, 'Culture Wars', *Anthropology Today*, 24, 2008. *Cf.* Talal Asad, *On Suicide Bombing*, New York: Columbia University Press, 2007.

10. For a discussion of past examples of this, *see* M. Jamil Hanifi, 'Editing the Past: Colonial Production of Hegemony through the "Loya Jerga" in Afghanistan', *Iranian Studies*, 37, 2004.

11. Roberto J. Gonzalez, 'Going Tribal: Notes on Pacification in the 21st Century', *Anthropology Today*, 25, 2009, p. 19.

12. Shah Mahmoud Hanifi, *Connecting Histories in Afghanistan: Market Relations and State Formation on a Colonial Frontier*, Palo Alto: Stanford University Press, 2011.

13. *See* Giustozzi and Orsini, 'Center-periphery Relations in Afghanistan: Badakhshan between Patrimonialism and Institution-building', Central Asian survey, 28 (1), 2009, pp. 1-16.

14. Shah Mahmoud Hanifi, 'Pashto Resistance to Print', Paper presented at Rethinking the Swat Pathan conference, School of Oriental and African Studies, London, 11–12 June 2010. *See also* Shah Mahmoud Hanifi, *Connecting Histories in Afghanistan*. Richard Tapper advances a similar argument regarding the relationship of Persian to Turkish and Persian to Turk: 'Local-level Constructions of "Turk" and "Persian"' in M. Djalili, A. Monsutti and A. Neubauer (eds), *Le Monde turco-iranien en question*, Geneva: Karthala, pp. 195–210.

15. G. Vom Bruck and B. Bodernhon, 'Introduction', *The Anthropology of Name and Naming*, Cambridge: Cambridge University Press, 2006.

16. Simpson and Kresse capture this point well in relationship to their discussion of how the Indian Ocean 'hosts a society based on the fact that it knows enough about itself to know that, really, it does not exist'. E. Simpson and K. Kresse, 'Introduction'. In *Struggling with History: Islam and Cosmopolitanism in the Western Indian Ocean*, edited by E. Simpson and K. Kresse, London: C. Hurst and Co., 2007, p. 26.

17. Frederik Barth, *Ethnic Groups and Boundaries: the Social Organization of Culture Difference*, London: George Allen and Unwin, 1969.

18. Frederick Cooper, *Colonialism in Question: Theory, Knowledge, History*, Berkeley: University of California Press, 2002.

19. B.D. Hopkins, *The Making of Modern Afghanistan*, Basingstoke: Palgrave Macmillan, 2008.

20. M. Marsden, *Living Islam: Muslim Religious Experience in Pakistan's North-West Frontier*, Cambridge: Cambridge University Press, 2005.

21. Joint trips were made to Afghanistan in December 2006 and Tajikistan in February 2007.

22. Susan Bayly, *Asian Voices in a Postcolonial Age: Vietnam, India and beyond*, Cambridge: Cambridge University Press, 2007.

23. Thongchai Winichakul, *Siam Mapped: a History of the Geo-body of a Nation*, Honolulu: University of Hawaii Press, 1994.

24. Janet L. Roitman, *Fiscal Disobedience: an Anthropology of Economic Regulation in Central Africa*, Princeton: Princeton University Press, 2005.
25. Michiel Baud and Willem van Schendal, 'Toward a Comparative History of Borderlands', *Journal of World History*, 8, 1997.
26. *See for instance* W.C. Chang, 'Venturing into "Barbarous" Regions: Transborder Trade among Migrant Yunnanese between Thailand and Burma, 1960s-1980s', *Journal of Asian Studies*, 68, 2009; Eric Tagliacozzo, *Secret Trades, Porous Borders: Smuggling and States along a Southeast Asian Frontier, 1865–1915*, New Haven: Yale University Press, 2005; C. Patterson Giersch, 'Across Zomia with Merchants, Monks, and Musk: Process Geographies, Trade Networks, and the Inner-East-Southeast Asian Borderlands', *Journal of Global History*, 5, 2010.
27. E. Simpson and K. Kresse, 'Introduction', pp. 20–3.
28. Ghislaine Lydon, *On Trans-Saharan Trails: Islamic Law, Trade Networks, and Cross-cultural Exchange in Nineteenth-century Western Africa*, Cambridge, New York: Cambridge University Press, 2009.
29. John Heathershaw, *Post-conflict Tajikistan: the Politics of Peacebuilding and the Emergence of Legitimate Order*, London: Routledge, 2009.
30. See for example Joshua T. White, *Pakistan's Islamist Frontier: Islamic Politics and U.S. Policy in Pakistan's North-West Frontier*, Arlington, VA: Center on Faith & International Affairs, 2008.
31. David Edwards, *Heroes of the Age: Moral Fault Lines on the Afghan Frontier*, Berkeley: University of California Press, 1996.
32. Faisal Devji, *Landscapes of Jihad: Militancy, Morality, Modernity*, London: C. Hurst and Company, 2005.
33. Mukulika Banerjee, *The Pathan Unarmed: Opposition and Memory in the North West Frontier*, Oxford: James Currey, 2000. *See also* Faisal Devji, *The Terrorist in Search of Humanity: Militant Islam and Global Politics*, New York: Columbia University Press, 2008.
34. Sana Haroon, *Frontier of Faith: Islam in the Indo-Afghan Borderland*, New York: Columbia University Press, 2007.
35. *See for example* Hugh Beattie, *Imperial Frontier: Tribe and State in Waziristan*, London: Curzon Press, 2002.
36. Recognition and serious consideration of the region's heterogeneity have long been central to anthropology dealing with the Frontier. *See for instance* Fredrik Barth, 'Swat Pathans Reconsidered', in F. Barth, *Features of Person and Society in Swat*, London: Routledge & Kegan Paul, 1981, pp. 121–81.

1. THE PROBLEM WITH BORDERS

1. A version of this chapter was originally published as B.D. Hopkins, 'The Bounds of Identity: the Goldsmid Mission and the Delineation of the Perso-Afghan Border in the Nineteenth Century', *Journal of Global History*, 2, 2007. It is reprinted here with kind permission from Cambridge Journals.

2. The term Persia is used here, rather than Iran, as the one with contemporary currency.

3. On the formation of Afghanistan's frontiers, see R. Gopalakrishnan, *The Geography and Politics of Afghanistan*, New Delhi: Concept Publishing Company, 1982, pp. 70–113. On the Durand Line, see Robert Nichols, *Settling the Frontier: Law, Land and Society in the Peshawar Valley, 1500–1900*, Oxford: Oxford University Press, 2001, pp. 133–57. For Persia, Firoozeh Firoozeh Kashani-Sabet, *Frontier Fictions: Shaping the Iranian Nation, 1804–1946*, Princeton: Princeton University Press, 1999.

4. M.E. Yapp, 'The Legend of the Great Game', *Proceedings of the British Academy*, 111, 2000.

5. Winichakul, *Siam Mapped*.

6. *See generally* Hopkins, *The Making of Modern Afghanistan*; Hanifi, *Connecting Histories in Afghanistan*.

7. Peter Christensen, 'The Qajar State' in C. Braae and K. Ferdinand (eds), *Contributions to Islamic Studies: Iran, Afghanistan and Pakistan*, Aarhus: Aarhus University Press, 1987.

8. Ibid.; Kashani-Sabet, *Frontier Fictions*.

9. Winichakul, *Siam Mapped*, p. 16.

10. Thongchai Winichakul, 'Maps and the Formation of the Geo-body of Siam' in S. Tonnesson and H. Antlov (eds), *Asian Forms of the Nation*, London: Curzon, 1996, pp. 69–70.

11. Indu Banga, 'Formation of the Sikh State, 1765–1845' in I. Banga (eds), *Five Punjabi Centuries: Polity, Economy, Society and Culture, c. 1500–1990*, New Delhi: Manohar, 1997, p. 92.

12. Winichakul, 'Maps and the Formation of the Geo-body of Siam', p. 83.

13. *See generally* Lauren A. Benton, *A Search for Sovereignty: Law and Geography in European Empires, 1400–1900*, Cambridge: Cambridge University Press, 2010; Lauren Benton, 'Colonial Law and Cultural Difference: Jurisdictional Politics and the Formation of the Colonial State', *Comparative Studies in Society and History*, 41, July 1999.

14. Richard Burghart, 'The Formation of the Concept of Nation-state in Nepal', *The Journal of Asian Studies*, 44, Nov. 1984, p. 121.

15. For colonial South Asia, *see* Matthew Edney, *Mapping an Empire: The Geographical Construction of British India, 1765–1843*, Chicago: University of Chicago Press, 1990.

16. Hopkins, *The Making of Modern Afghanistan*, pp. 84–90; Manoucher Parvin and Maurie Sommer, 'Dar al-Islam: The Evolution of Muslim Territoriality and its Implications for Conflict Resolution in the Middle East', *International Journal of Middle East Studies*, 11, Feb. 1980, p. 14.

17. For alternative ideas of territoriality and administration in Muslim societies in general, Ibn Khaldun, *The Muqaddimah: an Introduction to History*, New York: Pantheon Books, 1958; Ernest Gellner, *Muslim Society*, Cambridge: Cambridge University Press, 1981.

18. Burghart, 'The Formation of the Concept of Nation-state in Nepal', pp. 114–15; Graham Clarke, 'Blood, Territory and National Identity in Himalayan States' in S. Tonnesson and H. Antlov (eds), *Asian Forms of the Nation*, p. 217; J.C. Wilkinson, 'Traditional Concepts of Territory in Southeast Arabia', *The Geographical Journal*, 149, Nov. 1983, p. 308; Winichakul, 'Maps and the Formation of the Geo-body of Siam' in S. Tonnesson and H. Antlov (eds), pp. 76–7.

19. For robes of honour (*khil'at*), Stewart Gordon (ed), *Robes and Honour: the Medieval World of Investiture*, New York: Palgrave, 2001.

20. For local indigenous concepts of territoriality, Nigel J.R. Allan, 'Defining Place and People in Afghanistan', *Post-Soviet Geography and Economics*, 42, 8, 2001, pp. 545–60; David Edwards, *Heroes of the Age: Moral Fault Lines on the Afghan Frontier*, Berkeley: University of California Press, 1996, pp. 82–8; Kashani-Sabet, *Frontier Fictions*; Pirouz Mojtahed-Zadeh, *Small Players of the Great Game: the Settlement of Iran's Eastern Borderlands and the Creation of Afghanistan*, London: Routledge Curzon, 2004.

21. Michael Fisher, *A Clash of Cultures: Awaadh, the British and the Mughals*, New Delhi: Manohar, 1987, p. 123.

22. Robert D. Crews, *For Prophet and Tsar: Islam and Empire in Russia and Central Asia*, Cambridge, MA: Harvard University Press, 2006; Adeeb Khalid, *The Politics of Muslim Cultural Reform: Jadidism in Central Asia*, Berkeley: University of California Press, 1998; Paul Georg Geiss, *Pre-Tsarist and Tsarist Central Asia: Communal Commitment and Political Order in Change*, London: RoutledgeCurzon, 2003.

23. Burghart, 'The Formation'; Fisher, *A Clash of Cultures*; C.J. Hall, 'The Maharaja's Account Books: State and Society under the Sikhs, 1799–1849', PhD thesis, University of Illinois, 1981; Winichakul, 'Maps'.

24. The best synopsis of competition for Herat in this period is Abbas Amanat, 'Herat VI. The Herat Question', in Eshan Yashater (ed), *Encyclopaedia Iranica*, vol. XII, New York: Encyclopaedia Iranica Foundation, 2004.

25. M.E. Yapp, *Strategies of British India: Britain, Iran and Afghanistan 1798–1850*, Oxford: Clarendon Press, 1980, pp. 96–152.

26. The Bengal Government reject the request of Shah Shuja-ul-Mulk, the deposed king of Kabul, for military assistance to recover possession of his kingdom, December 1816-October 1820, *Board's Collections*, India Office Records (hereafter IOR) F/4/688/18899, London.

27. For example, Edward Ingram, *Britain's Persian Connection, 1798–1828*, Oxford: Clarendon Press, 1992.

28. Kashani-Sabet, *Frontier Fictions*.

29. Ellis to Viscount Palmerstone, 29 April 1836, *Political & Secret*, IOR L/PS/9/99, London; Richard Bonney, *Jihad: from Quran to bin Laden*, London: Palgrave Macmillan, 2004, p. 228.

30. *See generally* Kathryn Babayan, *Mystics, Monarchs and Messiahs: Cultural Landscapes in Early Modern Iran*, Cambridge, MA: Harvard University Press, 2002.

31. Senzil Nawid, 'The State, Clergy and British Policy in Afghanistan during the Nineteenth and Early Twentieth Centuries', *International Journal of Middle East Studies*, 29, 4, 1997, p. 587.

32. Parvin and Sommer, 'Dar al-Islam', p. 14, quoting Siyar Shaybani, *The Islamic Law of Nations*, Baltimore, MD: Johns Hopkins University Press, 1966, p. 56.

33. *See generally* Hamid Algar, 'Religious Forces in Eighteenth and Nineteenth Century Iran', in Peter Avery *et al.* (eds), *The Cambridge History of Iran, vol. 7: from Nadir Shah to the Islamic Republic*, Cambridge: Cambridge University Press, 1991, pp. 705–31; Barbara Metcalf, *Islamic Revival in British India: Deoband 1860–1900*, Princeton: Princeton University Press, 1982.

34. Hamid Algar, *Religion and State in Iran, 1785–1906*, Berkeley: University of California Press, p. 196; Nawid, 'The State'; Christine Noelle, 'The Anti-Wahabi Reaction in Nineteenth century Afghanistan', *The Muslim World*, 85, 1–2, 1995, pp. 23–48.

35. This is discussed in more detail in Chapter 3.

36. Hopkins, *The Making of Modern Afghanistan*, pp. 152–5.

37. Duke of Argyll to Goldsmid—Instructions, 9 August 1870, *Goldsmid Collections*, IOR MSS.Eur.F.134/21, London.

38. For a discussion *see* Valeria Fiorani Piacentini, 'Notes on the Definition of the Western Borders of British India', in B S. Amoretti and L. Rostango (eds), *Yad-nama: in memoria di Alessandro Bausani*, Rome: Bardi Editore, 1991.

39. F.J. Goldsmid, 'Introduction', in *Eastern Persia: an Account of the Journeys of the Persian Boundary Commission 1870–71–72. Vol. I: the Geography with Narratives by Majors St. John, Lovett, Euan Smith, and an Introduction by Major-General Sir Frederic John Goldsmid*, London: Macmillan, 1872.

40. M.E. Yapp, 'British Perceptions of the Russian Threat to India', *Modern Asian Studies*, 21, 4, 1987, pp. 647–65.

41. Dominic Lieven, *Empire: the Russian Empire and its Rivals from the Sixteenth Century to the Present*, London: Pimlico, 2003, pp. 201–87.

42. Hopkins, *The Making of Modern Afghanistan*, pp. 67–70.

43. To Duke of Argyll, 7 July 1870, *Goldsmid Papers*, IOR MSS.Eur.F.134/21, London.

44. Statement of arguments in support of Persia's sovereignty over Sistan, 8 July 1870, *Goldsmid Papers*, IOR MSS.Eur.F.134/21, London; Statement of Afghan Commissioner Saiad Nur Muhamad Shah, 1872, *Goldsmid Papers*, IOR MSS.Eur.F.134/21, London; 'Ketabcheh-e Tahdid-e Hadud; Sistan va Baluchistan', *Farhang-e Zamin*, 28, 1990, pp. 299–307.

45. Euan Smith, 'The Perso-Afghan Mission, 1871–72', in *Eastern Persia*, p. 337; Goldsmid to the Duke of Argyll, 30 April 1872, *Goldsmid Papers*, IOR MSS.Eur.F.134/4, London.

46. 'Report on the Province of Seistan with Reference to the Proposed Arbitration of HBM Government on the Question of Ancient Rights and Present Possession', 22 May 1872, *Goldsmid Papers*, IOR MSS.Eur.F.134/21, London; H.L. Wynne, 'The History of Seistan and Lash-Jowain', 6 July 1870, National Archives, Foreign Office (henceforth NA FO) 60/386, 41, London.

47. See Chapter 2.

48. Stewart Gordon, 'Legitimacy and Loyalty in Some Successor States of the Eighteenth Century', in J.F. Richards (ed), *Kingship and Authority in South Asia*, Cambridge: Cambridge University Press, 1998, pp. 328–30.

49. General Goldsmid's memo to Major Smith, n.d., *Goldsmid Papers*, IOR MSS.Eur.F.134/3, London.; Goldsmid to Ronald Thomson, 10 July 1872, *Goldsmid Papers*, IOR MSS.Eur.F134/3, London.

50. Memorandum of the Proceedings of the Final Meeting of the Sistan Mission held at the British Legation at Gulhak on the 19th August 1872, 20 August 1872, NA FO 60/392, London.

51. Euan Smith, 'The Perso-Afghan Mission, 1871–2', p. 265; see also Persian Commissioner to Goldsmid dated 8 February, Enclosure no. 17 in Goldsmid to Aitchinson, 11 March 1872, NA FO 60/392, London.

52. Smith, 'The Perso-Afghan Mission', p. 262.

53. Smith to Goldsmid, 7 February 1872, NA FO 60/392, London.

54. *See for instance* St. John to Goldsmid, 14 January 1872, *Goldsmid Papers*, IOR MSS.Eur.F.134/11, London. On the center's relationship with local lords and their influence on frontier politics, Mojtahed-Zadeh, *Small Players*; Piacentini, 'Notes'.

55. *See for example* A. Amanat, 'The Downfall of Mirza Taqi Khan Amire Kabir and the Problem of Ministerial Authority in Qajar Iran', *International Journal of Middle East Studies*, 23, 4, 1991, pp. 577–99.

56. For a description of that universe, Mojtahed-Zadeh, *Small Players*, pp. 1–6.

57. Smith, 'The Perso-Afghan Mission', pp. 266, 297.

58. Smith, 'The Perso-Afghan Mission', p. 337. Compare Mojtehad-Zadeh, *Small Players*, pp. 66–70, 122–49, 174–90.

59. *See for example* Translation of the Shah's autograph to the Sadr Azem, 21 October 1872, NA FO 60/393, London; Translation of a letter from the Sadr Azem, to the Heshmat-ul-Moolk, Ameer of Kain and Seistan, dated 1st Rejeeb 1289 (5th September 1872), 21 October 1872, NA FO 60/393, London.

60. Substance of letter from the Nazim-el Mulk to the British Legation, 23 August 1872, NA FO 60/392, London.

61. Mojtahed-Zadeh, *Small Players*, pp. 174–208.

62. Smith, 'The Perso-Afghan Mission', p. 289.

63. *See* Ranajit Guha, *A Rule of Property for Bengal: an Essay on the Idea of Permanent Settlement*, Paris: Mouton & Co., 1963. *See also* Robert Travers, *Ideology and Empire in Eighteenth Century India: the British in Bengal*, Cambridge: Cambridge University Press, 2007.

64. Pollack was given a field commission equivalent to Goldsmid's for the mission.

65. Frederic John Goldsmid, 'Introduction' in *Eastern Persia*, p. xxxi, n. 1, quoting Alison to Mayo, 23 October 1871.

66. Smith, 'The Perso-Afghan Mission', pp. 289–90.

67. Goldsmid, 'Introduction', p. xxxix.

68. *See for example* Goldsmid to the Duke of Argyll, 30 April 1872.

69. Goldsmid, 'Introduction', pp. lii–liii.

70. 'Ketabcheh', p. 295. The British thought little of his skills. Memorandum of a meeting held at the house of Sadr Azam at Niaviran in the evening of 7 August 1872, *Goldsmid Papers*, IOR MSS.Eur.F.134/13, London.

71. Goldsmid to the Duke of Argyll, 12 October 1870, NA FO 60/386, London.

72. Pollock to Goldsmid, 1 March 1872, *Goldsmid Papers*, IOR MSS. Eur.F.134/11, London.

73. Goldsmid to the Duke of Argyll, 12 October 1870, NA FO 60/386, London; Smith, 'The Perso-Afghan Mission', p. 326.

74. 'Appendix C: Genealogical Trees, with Notes, for the Sistan Chiefs of Kaiyani, Sarbandi, and Sharaki Families; also the Nharui and Sanjarani (Toki) Baluchis of Sistan' in *Eastern Persia*.

75. Goldsmid to Aitchinson, 17 March 1872, *Goldsmid Papers*, IOR MSS. Eur.F.134/21, London; 'The History of Seistan and Lash-Jowain'; Noelle, *State*, pp. 240–89.

76. See for instance Mayo *et al.* to the Duke of Argyll, 7 July 1870, NA FO 60/386, London; Yapp, 'British Perceptions', p. 663.

77. Goldsmid to Aitchinson, 17 March 1871, *Goldsmid Papers*, IOR MSS. Eur.F.132.21. *See also* Mayo to the Duke of Argyll, 2 September 1869, NA FO 60/385, London.

78. Hopkins, *The Making of Modern Afghanistan*, pp. 21–3. *See also* Punjab and the Countries Westward of the Indus, 1809, IOR X9972, London.

79. Edney, *Mapping*, pp. 25, 53.

80. The US is doing precisely the same today, both with its Human Terrain System and with efforts of mapping Afghanistan's 'ethnic and tribal topographies'.

81. Statement of arguments in support of Persia's sovereignty over Sistan, 8 July 1870, *Goldsmid Papers*, IOR MSS.Eur.F.134/21, London; Statement of Afghan Commissioner Saiad Nur Muhamad Shah, 1872, *Goldsmid Papers*, IOR MSS.Eur.F.134/21, London. *See also* 'Ketabcheh', pp. 299–307.

82. 'From the earliest date recorded in the histories of this country up to the present day, the pages of Persian history are full of the name of Sistan'. Memorandum of Mirza Saiad Khan to the British legation, 7 August

1872, *Goldsmid Papers*, IOR MSS.Eur.F.134/21, London; Frederic John Goldsmid, 'Appendix A: The Sistan Arbitration', in *Eastern Persia*, p. 399.

83. Goldsmid, 'Appendix A', pp. 397–8, 407.

84. Ibid., p. 397. *See also* Substance of letter from the Nazim-el Mulk to the British Legation.

85. IOR, GP, 'Statement', 1872.

86. Hopkins, *The Making of Modern Afghanistan*, pp. 11–33.

87. Goldsmid, 'Appendix C: Genealogical trees, with notes, for the Sistan chiefs of Kaiyani, Sarbandi, and Sharaki families; also the Nharui and Sanjarani (Toki) Baluchis of Sistan' in *Eastern Persia*.

88. Brinkley Messick, *The Calligraphic State: Textual Domination and History in a Muslim Society*, Berkeley: University of California Press, 1993, p. 252.

89. For a discussion, *see generally* Jack Goody, *The Interface between the Written and the Oral: Studies in Literacy, Family, Culture and the State*, Cambridge: Cambridge University Press, 1987; Messick, *The Calligraphic State*.

90. The Shi'i Qizilbash formerly served as private secretaries, constituting an early government bureaucracy. Burnes to Macnaghten, 14 October 1837, *Political & Secret*, IOR L/PS/5/129, London.

91. *See generally* Hopkins, *The Making of Modern Afghanistan*.

92. Kashani-Sabet, *Frontier Fictions*, pp. 33–4.

93. Goldsmid, 'Appendix A', p. 397.

94. *Ibid.*, pp. 404–5. The characterization of the frontier as a space of a 'feudal political order' is one much repeated throughout the colonial archives.

95. 'The History of Seistan and Lash-Jowain, 6 July 1870', NA FO 60/386, London.

2. MANAGING 'HEARTS AND MINDS': BALUCHISTAN AND SANDEMAN

1. Memorandum: Khelat Affairs.—Sir W. Merewether and Major Sandeman, April 1876, *Political & Secret*, IOR L/PS/7/8, London.

2. Rai Bahadur Hittu Ram, *Sandeman in Baluchistan*, Lahore: Superintendent of Government Printing, 1916, p. 6. For an example of Merewether's assessment of Sandeman, see Commissioner in Sind to Foreign Secretary, Calcutta, 14 January 1876, *Political & Secret*, IOR L/PS/7/7, London.

3. Philip Woodruff, *The Men who Ruled India: The Guardians*, London: Jonathan Cape, 1954, pp. 141–2.

4. Richard Isaac Bruce, *The Forward Policy and its Results: or Thirty-five Years Work amongst the Tribes on our North-Western Frontier of India*, London: Longmans, Green and Co., 1900.

5. For a summary, *see* James W. Spain, 'Political Problems of a Borderland' in A.T. Embree (ed), *Pakistan's Western Borderlands: the Transformation of a Political Order*, Durham: Carolina Academic Press, 1977.

6. T.H. Holdich, *Political Frontier and Boundary Making*, London: Macmillan and Co., 1916, pp. 272–3.

7. For a discussion of the effects of such divided authority, *see* I.F.S. Copland, 'The Baroda Crisis of 1873–77: A Study of Governmental Rivalry', *Modern Asian Studies*, 2, 1968.

8. For a description of both the ecology and the history of Baluchistan, including Sandeman's activities, *see* Brian Spooner, 'Baluchistan: Geography, History and Ethnography', *Encyclopedia Iranica Online*, http://www.iranica.com/articles/baluchistan-i.

9. Thomas Henry Thornton, *Colonel Sir Robert Sandeman: His Life and Work on our Indian Frontier*, London: John Murray, 1895, p. 40.

10. For a detailed discussion of the Sandeman system, *see* Christian Tripodi, 'Good for One but not the Other: The 'Sandeman System' of Pacification as Applied to Baluchistan and the North-West Frontier 1877–1947', *Journal of Military History*, 73, July 2009.

11. B.D. Hopkins, 'The Problem with "Hearts and Minds" in Afghanistan', *Middle East Report*, 255, Summer 2010.

12. For a brief description of these systems and their origins, *see* Spain, 'Political Problems of a Borderland', pp. 5–17. Thornton referred to these different approaches as the 'Lyttonite' and 'Lawrencite' systems respectively. Thornton, *Colonel Sir Robert Sandeman*, p. 41. The 'forward policy' is commonly known as the Sandeman system, also referred to by Thornton as 'Sandemanian system'. Thornton, *Colonel Sir Robert Sandeman*, p. 240.

13. 'Our Military Policy with the Tribes on the North-West Frontier of India', 1910, *Sir Douglas Haig Papers*, National Library of Scotland (henceforth NLS), Acc. 3155/H89K, Edinburgh.

14. Sandeman's letter of 19 April 1891 in Thornton, *Colonel Sir Robert Sandeman*, Title page.

15. Ibid., p. 40.

16. Lal Baha, *N.-W.F.P. Administration under British Rule, 1901–1919*, Islamabad: National Commission on Historical and Cultural Research, 1978, p. 5.

17. Although of questionable efficacy, the expeditions were popular amongst otherwise idle officers who saw them as an important testing and training ground for the Indian Army in times of peace. Further, the idea of collective punishment was prominently enshrined in the Frontier Crimes Regulation, first passed in 1872, and then again in 1887 and 1901. It was incorporated into the Baluchistan Code in 1891.

18. Burn to Lumsden, 30 Aug 1850, *Foreign Department, Secret Consultations*, National Archives of India (henceforth NAI), New Delhi.

19. Memorandum, 22 January 1875, *Political & Secret*, IOR L/PS/7/1, London.

20. In one incident in 1847/48, Merewether was reported to have annihilated a party of nearly 700 Baluch 'outlaws', killing half the Bugti Baluch warriors. F.J. Goldsmid and James Falkner, *Merewether, Sir William Lockyer (1825–1880)*, Oxford: Oxford University Press, 2004, http://

www.oxforddnb.com/view/article/18586; Fred Scholz, *Nomadism and Colonialism: a Hundred Years of Baluchistan, 1872–1972*, Oxford: Oxford University Press, 2002, p. 91.

21. Somewhat paradoxically, the Raj predicated its policy of punishment on a caricatured understanding of the 'uncivilized and wild tribesman' who only understood brute force, an understanding based on its own information order. *See* Hopkins, *The Making of Modern Afghanistan*, pp. 11–33.

    On the idea of 'information panics' which regularly seized the Raj, *see* C.A. Bayly, *Empire and Information*, New Delhi: Cambridge University Press, 2002.

22. Although proposed by Lord Lytton in 1877, the true overhaul of frontier governance came with Lord Curzon who, in 1899, created the North-West Frontier Province. Minute: Reorganisation of the frontier, 17 May 1877, *Political & Secret*, IOR L/PS/7/14, London.

23. Bruce contended that 'instead of the support of the authorities gaining him his successes, his successes gained for him the support of those in authority'. Bruce, *The Forward Policy and its results*, p. 63.

24. Bruce's pronouncement of the death of the closed border system ultimately proved premature. The Government of India would continually return to variants of both the closed border system and the Sandeman system for the remainder of its tenure in South Asia. Bruce, *The Forward Policy and its results*, pp. 26–7.

    Following his success in Dera Ghazi Khan and later in Baluchistan, officers were allowed across the Frontier and the first tribal agency in the Punjab, the Khyber Agency, was established in 1878, with four others following in the next twenty years. Baha, *N.-W.F.P. Administration under British Rule, 1901–1919*, pp. 6–8.

25. While levies had previously been employed along the Frontier, as part of the Baluch Rifles and the Sind Irregular Horse and in the Punjab Frontier Force, their use had been neither as systematic nor as politically targeted as it became under Sandeman. For a discussion of the levies used along the entirety of the Frontier, *see* Memorandum on the different systems adopted on the North-Western Frontier for the employment of local levies, 1888, *Bruce Papers*, IOR Mss.Eur.F163/7, London.

26. Sandeman himself insisted, 'If we knit the frontier tribes into our imperial system and make their interests our...and as long as we are able and ready to hold our own, we can certainly depend upon them being on our side'. Sandeman, 'Relations with Frontier Tribes' in Thornton, *Colonel Sir Robert Sandeman*, pp. 358–9.

27. The *jirga*s affiliated with state governance, and whose membership was regulated by Deputy Commissioners and other colonial officers, were known as '*sarkari jirga*'s. Quddus characterizes the authority assigned to members of the judicial *jirga*s under the FCR as elevating them to the status of 'demi-gods'. Syed Abdul Quddus, *The Tribal Baluchistan*, Lahore: Ferozsons Ltd., 1990, p. 86.

28. On his second mission to the Kalat in the summer of 1876, Sandeman's escort consisted of three companies of the Fourth Sikhs, two companies of Jacobs Rifles, 100 sabres of the Fourth Punjab Cavalry and two mountain guns. Bruce, *The Forward Policy and its Results*, p. 62.
29. Sandeman went so far as to advocate the dissolution of the Sind police force in 1882. Lower Sind Frontier Police, October 1883, *Foreign Department, A Political E*, NAI New Delhi. *See also* Erskine, Commissioner in Sind, to Sir J. Fergusson, Governor of Bombay, October 1883, *Foreign Department, A Political E*, NAI New Delhi.
30. Davidson to Bruce, 21 August 1901, *Bruce Collection*, IOR Mss.Eur. F163/1, London.
31. The treaty recognized the Khan's authority over the Baluch tribesmen, granted him an annual subsidy of Rs. 50,000, and stationed a British agent at his court. These were the terms of the treaty signed by Jacob and the Khan in 1854, and which were largely repeated in the treaty of 1876. For a history of British relations with Kalat and Baluchistan prior to Sandeman's assumption of control in 1876, *see* Thomas Anthony Heathcote, 1969, *British Policy and Baluchistan 1854–1876*, Ph.D thesis, University of London.
32. Phayre's analysis was shared by other experienced frontier officers. Bruce wrote 'I remember Sir Henry Green, who knew the Beluches well, laughing at the idea of the Beluch chiefs having any power for good over their tribes'. Bruce, *The Forward Policy and its Results*, pp. 18–19. Phayre supported Sandeman's efforts, a stance which won him the ire of both Mereweather and the Bombay government. He was removed from his position and posted as the Resident to Baroda. Copland, 'The Baroda Crisis of 1873–77, pp. 101–2.
33. Colonial ethnographers considered the Baluch and Brahuis separate races. *See for example* M. Longworth Dames, *The Baloch Race: a Historical and Ethnological Sketch*, London: The Royal Asiatic Society, 1904, pp. 15–16. They also considered Baluch identity to be that of a 'political and not an ethnic unit'. Denzil Charles Jelf Ibbetson, *Outlines of Panjab Ethnography: Being Extracts from the Panjab Census Report of 1881, Treating of Race, Language, and Caste*, Calcutta: Superintendent of Government Printing, 1883, p. 195.
34. Bruce, *The Forward Policy and its Results*, pp. 57–8.
35. Nina Swindler, 'Kalat: The Political Economy of a Tribal Chiefdom', *American Ethnologist*, 19, August 1992, p. 559.
36. Thornton, Punjab Secy., to Aitchinson, GoI Secy., January 1875, *Foreign Department, Political A*, NAI New Delhi.
37. A.W. Hughes, *The Country of Balochistan, its Geography, Topography, Ethnology and History*, London: George Bell & Sons, 1877, pp. 226, 231–34.
38. Bruce to Duke, 16 April 1889, *Bruce Collection*, IOR Mss.Eur.F163/1, London. Bruce went on to suggest that the only solution was '[t]o manipulate these fellows, one must be able to knock their heads together'.

39. For a synopsis of the conference, *see* Secretary to the Government of Punjab to Secretary to the Government of India, Foreign Department, May 1871, *Foreign Department, Political A*, NAI New Delhi.

40. Memorandum: Khelat Affairs.—Sir W. Merewether and Major Sandeman.

41. Sandeman argued with his successor in Dera Ghazi Khan over jurisdiction and control of the tribes. *See for instance* Thornburn, Deputy Commissioner, Dera Ghazi Khan, to The Commissioner and Superintendent, Derajat Division, August 1883, *Foreign Department, A Political E*, NAI New Delhi.

42. For the Agency's administrative structure, *see* Resolution—By the Government of India, Foreign Department, 1877, *Foreign Department, Political A*, NAI New Delhi. To see how quickly the Agency, and Sandeman's responsibilities grew, *see* Sandeman to Lord Ripon, 6 January 1883, *Ripon Papers*, British Library (henceforth BL), Mss.Add.43613, London.

43. While 'hearts and minds' is often mistakenly attributed to Lieutenant-General Gerald Templer of Malayan Emergency fame, there is a link between Sandeman's ideas of imperial governance and those of imperial retreat. Harold Briggs, author of the Briggs Plan which was the basis of British counter-insurgency efforts in Malaya, served in Baluchistan during the 1930s with C.E. Bruce, then Political Agent of Baluchistan and son of R.I. Bruce, Sandeman's first assistant. 'Lieutenant-Colonel C.E. Bruce', *The Times*, 26 January 1950; 'Lieutenant-General Sir Harold Briggs', *The Times*, 28 October 1952. *See* B.D. Hopkins, 'The Problem with "Hearts and Minds" in Afghanistan', *Middle East Report*, 255, Summer 2010.

44. *See generally* Ainslie T. Embree, 'Pakistan's Imperial Legacy' in A.T. Embree (ed), *Pakistan's Western Borderlands: the Transformation of a Political Order*, Durham, NC: Carolina Academic Press, 1977.

45. Lytton to Sandeman, 29 September 1876, *Bruce Collection*, IOR Mss.Eur. F163/1, London.

46. For a critique of the 'Great Game' *see* Hopkins, *The Making of Modern Afghanistan*, pp. 34–60.

47. On Mughal ideas of the frontier, *see* Jos Gommans, *Mughal Warfare: Indian Frontiers and High Roads to Empire, 1500–1700*, London: Routledge, 2002, pp. 1–10. Pakistan's continuing concern about calls for 'Pashtunistan' cannot be underestimated.

48. Embree refers to this as the 'three-fold frontier'. Embree, 'Pakistan's Imperial Legacy', pp. 25–8.

49. Compare this with the practices of the colonial state its northeastern frontier with the Nagas. Peter Robb, 'The Colonial State and Constructions of Indian Identity: an Example of the Northeast Frontier in the 1880s', *Modern Asian Studies*, 31, May 1997.

50. For a discussion of the multiple meanings of modernity, *see* Frederick Cooper, *Colonialism in Question: Theory, Knowledge, History*, Berkeley: University of California Press, 2002.

51. *See for example* C.A. Bayly, *Origins of Nationality in South Asia: Patriotism and Ethical Government in the Making of Modern India*, Delhi: Oxford University Press, 1998.

52. Cooper, *Colonialism in Question*, p. 23.

53. *See for instance* C.A. Bayly and Susan Bayly, 'Eighteenth Century State Forms and the Economy' in C. Dewey (ed), *Arrested Development in India: The Historical Dimension*, New Delhi: Manohar, 1988.

54. They did, however, have strong preconceptions about the inhabitants of the Frontier and their social constellations. The tribesmen of the Frontier were often compared to the Highland clans of Scotland, an intellectual tradition dating from Mountstuart Elphinstone's mission to the court at Peshawar. Hopkins, *The Making of Modern Afghanistan*, pp. 11–33.

55. *See for example* Memorandum, 29 Aug. 1851, *Foreign Department, Political Consultations*, NAI New Delhi; Commissioner of Sind to Governor of Bombay, 17 June 1870, *Political Department*, Maharasthra State Archives (henceforth MSA), Mumbai; Political Superintendent on the Frontier of Upper Sind, to the Commissioner in Sind, May 1871, *Foreign Department, Political A*, NAI New Delhi.

56. Matthew K. Lange, 'British Colonial Legacies and Political Development', *World Development*, 32, 2004; R.O. Christensen, 'Tribesmen, Government and Political Economy on the North-West Frontier' in C. Dewey (ed), *Arrested Development in India*, pp. 177–8; Beattie, *Imperial Frontier*, pp. 186–9.

57. *Compare* Robb, 'The Colonial State and Constructions of Indian Identity.

58. On the idea of encapsulation, *see* Nina Swidler, 'Brahui Political Organization and the National State' in A.T. Embree (ed), *Pakistan's Western Borderlands*, p. 111.

59. David Scott, 'Colonial Governmentality', *Social Text*, 1995.

60. Dirks, *Castes of Mind*, pp. 43–60.

61. C.L. Tupper, *Punjab Customary Law*, Calcutta: Office of the Superintendant of Government Printing, 1881.

62. Mahmood Mamdani, *Citizen and Subject: Contemporary Africa and the Legacy of Late Colonialism*, Princeton: Princeton University Press, 1996, p. 49.

63. *See generally* Andrew Major, 'State and Criminal Tribes in Colonial Punjab: Surveillance, Control and Reclamation of the "Dangerous Classes"', *Modern Asian Studies*, 33, July 1999; Anand Yang, 'Dangerous Castes and Tribes: the Criminal Tribes Act and the Magahiya Doms of Northeast India' in A. Yang (ed), *Crime and Criminality in British India*, Tucson: University of Arizona Press, 1985.

64. For a discussion of how British governmentality sought to regulate the Indian moral as well as political sphere, *see* Sandra Freitag, 'Collective Crime and Authority in North India' in A. Yang (ed), *Crime and Criminality in British India*.

65. Damian O'Connor, *The Zulu and the Raj: The Life of Sir Bartle Frere*, Knebworth: Able Publishing, 2002.

66. James Gump, 'The Subjugation of the Zulus and Sioux: a Comparative Study', *The Western Historical Quarterly*, 19, January 1988.

67. Tripodi, 'Good for One but not the Other', pp. 12–13. Personal communication, Professor Martin Thomas 27 May 2009.

68. Sir Frederick Lugard employed a similar system in Nigeria during his tenure as Governor-General (c. 1914–19). Frederick Lugard, *The Dual Mandate in British Tropical Africa*, 1922, reprint London: Frank Cass & Co. Ltd., 1965, pp. 193–230; Tripodi, 'Good for One but not the Other', pp. 11–12.

69. Robb, 'The Colonial State and Constructions of Indian Identity'.

70. On previous British attitudes towards the Frontier tribes, *see* Report Shewing the Relations of the British Government with the Tribes Independent and Dependant on the North West Frontier of the Punjab, from Annexation in 189 [sic] to the Close of 1855, 30 May 1856, *Foreign Department, Political Consultations*, NAI New Delhi.

71. Memo by Mereweather, January 1875, *Foreign Department, Political A*, NAI New Delhi.

72. Quoted in Bruce, *The Forward Policy and its Results*, p. 342.

73. Michael Fisher, *Indirect Rule in India: Residents and the Residency System*, New Delhi: Oxford University Press, 1998, pp. 445–8.

74. Lord Lugard, referring to tribes in Africa, wrote '[b]y the term "independent" in this connection is meant "independent of other native control."' Lugard, *The Dual Mandate in British Tropical Africa*, n. 1, p. 200.

75. See Chapter 1.

76. Memorandum on Khelat, March 1877, *Foreign Department, Political A*, NAI New Delhi.

77. For a discussion of citizenship and subjecthood in the African context, *see* Mamdani, *Citizen and Subject*.

78. '[O]ne weak point in all the old discussions was that few considered the welfare of the tribes, the honourable exceptions were the Sandeman school, who have always said that the tribes *have* rights. *Admittedly* the settled districts who pay the taxes have the prior rights and theirs *is* the first claim and they must be protected from the tribes. Once that protection is secured the rights of the tribesmen to a tolerable livelihood by other means than robbery under arms must be recognised'. Frontier Policy: a lecture delivered at the Staff College, Quetta, November 1930, *Jacob Papers*, IOR Mss.Eur.F75/13, London.

79. Tripodi, 'Good for One but not the Other', p. 22.

80. R.O. Christensen estimates that at the height of the tribal levy system and military recruitment of the tribesmen, the most heavily targeted tribes received up to a quarter of their income from these government payments. R.O. Christensen, 'Tribesmen, Government and Political Economy on the North-West Frontier' in C. Dewey (ed), *Arrested Development in India*, 1988, p. 180.

81. Compare this with Mamdani's assertion that the commodification of land was central in colonial construction and control of the free peasantry in Africa.

82. Alex Maroya, 'Rethinking the Nation-state from the Frontier', *Millenium: Journal of International Studies*, 32, 2003, p. 285.

83. Bernard S. Cohn, 'From Indian Status to British Contract', *The Journal of Economic History*, 21, 1961.

84. *See generally* Benton, 'Colonial Law and Cultural Difference'.

85. Lytton to Sandeman; *see also* Government of India to Secretary of State to India, March 1877, *Foreign Department, Political A*, NAI New Delhi. *Compare* Lytton's language here to that used by Goldsmid in his arbitration discussed in Chapter 1.

86. The comparison of non-European tribes with the European feudal past has long been acknowledged as problematic, if not simply wrong. Colin Newbury, *Patrons, Clients and Empire: Chieftancy and Over-rule in Asia, Africa and the Pacific*, Oxford: Oxford University Press, 2003, p. 8.

87. Sandeman may thus be fitted into the long tradition of indirect rule using tribal tradition and customary law. For a discussion of the scholarship on this in the case of colonial British Africa, *see* Thomas Spear, 'Neo-traditionalism and the Limits of Invention in British Colonial Africa', *Journal of African History*, 44, 2003.

88. 'The Punjab Frontier Crimes Regulation, 1887' in *The Baluchistan Code, Containing the Local Enactments in Force in British Baluchistan and the Local Enactments in Force in the Baluchistan Agency Territories, etc.*, Calcutta: Superintendent of Government Printing, 1890. While first passed in the Punjab in 1872, the Frontier Crimes Regulation was not extended to Baluchistan until it was modified and re-passed in 1887.

    For an example of that evidentiary standard, see the rules Sandeman recommended for the disposal of criminal cases in which the plaintiff and defendant were Baluch or Brahuis of the same tribe. Rules, March 1877, *Foreign Department, Political A*, NAI New Delhi. Part of the reason for the more relaxed evidentiary standards acceptable to the *jirga* proceedings was the belief held by many colonial officers that tribesmen perpetually lied under oath. *See generally* G.R. Elsmie, *Thirty-five Years in the Punjab*, Edinburgh: David Douglas, 1908. The belief that tribesmen perpetually lied under oath fit colonial authorities' broader claim that Europeans, unlike the natives, were 'culturally conditioned to observe the sanctity of court rules'. Benton, 'Colonial Law and Cultural Difference', p. 574.

89. In contrast, colonial courts could impose not only a fine, but also imprisonment, transportation, whipping or even death. Later versions of the Frontier Crimes Regulation gave tribal *jirga*s limited powers to impose fines, transportation and whipping.

90. FCR, Chapter I §3(1); Chapter III §13–14.

91. Shaheen Sardar Ali and Javaid Rehman, *Indigenous People and Ethnic Minorities of Pakistan Constitutional and Legal Perspectives*, Richmond, UK: Curzon Press, 2001, pp. 50–5.

92. *Jirga*s were similar to the *panchayat* system of village councils widespread throughout colonial India. However, the latter lacked the judicial powers of the former. Quddus, *The Tribal Baluchistan*, p. 86.

For a modern history of the *jirga*, *see* Ali Warduk, '*Jirga*: Power and Traditional Conflict Resolution in Afghanistan' in J. Strawson (ed), *Law after Ground Zero*, London: Glasshouse Press, 2002, pp. 191–8; Quddus, *The Tribal Baluchistan*, pp. 83–9.

Prior to his service in Dera Ghazi Khan, Sandeman served as an Assistant Commissioner in the Peshawar District with responsibility over the Otmanzai tribe, who inhabited the region towards the Swat valley. In this capacity, he participated in the Ambela campaign of 1863. Copy of a letter from Commissioner and Superintendent Peshawur Division to Secretary to Government Punjab, No. 165 Dated 10 September 1863, December 1863, *Foreign Department, Political A*, NAI New Delhi.

93. *See for instance* Ibbetson, *Outlines of Panjab Ethnography*, p. 193; Thornton, *Colonel Sir Robert Sandeman*, p. 28.

Officers with experience on the ground did not always share such generalizations. For example, R.I. Bruce, Sandeman's First Assistant, asserted that the pliability of the tribes had less to do with their innate character than with the support the *malik*s (chiefs) received from the Government. Bruce, 1st Asst. Agent to the Governor-General for Baluchistan, to Sandeman, November 1878, *Foreign Department, Secret*, NAI New Delhi *See also* Bruce, *The Forward Policy and its Results*, pp. 18–19.

For an interesting discussion of the implications of this, *see* A. Le G. Jacob, 'Waziristan', *Journal of the Royal Central Asian Society*, XIV, 1927, pp. 253–4.

For an analysis of the legacy of these stereotypes, *see* Paul Titus, 'Honor the Baloch, Buy the Pushtun: Stereotypes, Social Organization and History in Western Pakistan', *Modern Asian Studies*, 32, July 1998.

94. Ram, *Sandeman in Baluchistan*, pp. 3–4. Thornton discounts Hittu Ram's assessment, instead arguing that Sandeman simply 'revived' the institution. He further offered etymology of the word, comparing it with Greek and Latin practice in a clear attempt to historicize it in order to qualify it as tradition. Thornton, *Colonel Sir Robert Sandeman*, pp. 21–2. There is no mention of the practice amongst the Baluch in Ibbetson's census notes, even though he discusses it with reference to the Pathan. Ibbetson, *Outlines of Panjab Ethnography*, pp. 193, 195, 201.

Quddus writes that Nasir Khan I introduced *jirga*s as the basis of the Brahui tribal confederacy after Ahmad Shah Abdali granted him authority over the area; however, the practice subsequently fell into disuse until Sandeman's resurrection of it. If this is correct, Nasir Khan seemingly borrowed a Pashtun custom from the first Pashtun monarch of Afghanistan. Quddus, *The Tribal Baluchistan*, pp. 84–5.

95. Quoting from *The Pioneer*'s obituary of Sandeman, in Bruce, *The Forward Policy and its Results*, p. 226.

96. Hopkins, *The Making of Modern Afghanistan*, pp. 11–33.

97. *See for example* Translation of Appendix D: Statement of complaints made by Jalawan Sirdars against the Khelat Government and the decision arrived at regarding them by the Committee of Arbitrators, as below appointed, with sanction of the Khan of Khelat and approval of complainants, by Major Sandeman to arbitrate at Mustang in July 1876, March 1877, *Foreign Department, Political A*, NAI New Delhi. *See also* Translation of Appendix C: Statement of complaints made by Brahuis of the Sarawan faction against the Khelat Government, in regard to confiscation and attachment of lands, &c., formerly held by complainants, as brought before the Committee of Arbitrators approved by the Khan of Khelat and the complainants, in Camp, Mustang, in July 1876, March 1877, *Foreign Department, Political A*, NAI New Delhi.

98. These were supposed to be modelled on Nasir Khan I's *shahi jirga* ('king council'). Quddus, *The Tribal Baluchistan*, p. 85.

    Sandeman and his assistants R.I. Bruce and Rai Bahadur Ram included summaries of the *jirga*s judicial activities as part of their annual reports. *See for example* Sandeman to the Sect'y to the Govt of India, Foreign Department, 22 April 1891, *Crown Representative's Records*, IOR R/1/34/10, London; R.I. Bruce, 'Administration Report of the Baluchistan Agency for 1885–86' in *Selections from the Records of the Government of India*, Foreign Department, London: 1888.

99. Quoted in Titus, 'Honor the Baloch, Buy the Pushtun', p. 657.

100. 'Pakistan's Tribal Areas: Appeasing the Militants' in *Asia Report*, Islamabad/Brussels: International Crisis Group, 2006, pp. 5–9.

3. SITANA AND SWAT: PATTERNS OF REVOLT ALONG THE FRONTIER

1. *See for example* 'Pakistan-Taliban deal: Islamic law for peace in Swat Valley', *Christian Science Monitor*, 16 February 2009, seen at: http://www.csmonitor.com/2009/0216/p99s01-duts.html. Last accessed 3 March 2009.; 'Pakistan makes a Taliban truce, creating a haven', *New York Times*, 17 February 2009, seen at: http://www.nytimes.com/2009/02/17/world/asia/17pstan.html. Last accessed 3 March 2009.

2. *See for instance* 'Taleban's stranglehold brings fear to Swat', *BBC*, seen at: http://news.bbc.co.uk/1/hi/world/south_asia/7851790.stm. Last accessed 3 March 2009.

3. The worst example, which draws a direct line between the Frontier 'Fanatics' and today's terrorists, is Charles Allen, *God's Terrorists: The Wahabi Cult and the Hidden Roots of Modern Jihad*, London: Abacus, 2006.

4. 'Swat', *Encyclopeadia of Islam*, 2nd edn. Seen at: http://www.brillonline.nl/subscriber/uid=1368/entry?result_number=1&entry=islam_SIM-7229&search_text=swat#hit. Last accessed 4 March 2009.

5. *See for example* Fredrik Barth, *Political Leadership among Swat Pathans*, London: Athlone Press, 1959.

6. Maulana Fazlullah's core group of fighters reportedly consists of Uzbek members of the Islamic Movement of Uzbekistan. Charles P. Blair, 'Anatomzing Non-State Threats to Pakistan's Nuclear Infrastructure: The Pakistani Neo-Taliban'. *Terrorism Analysis Report No. 1*. Federation of American Scientists. June 2011, p. 9.

7. For a good recent treatment of Sayyid Ahmed and his ideas, *see* Ayesha Jalal, *Partisans of Allah: Jihad in South Asia*, New Delhi: Permanent Black, 2008, pp. 58–113.

8. Melvill to C. Allen, Officiating Secretary of the Government of India, 15 October 1852, *Foreign Department, Political* NAI New Delhi; Lt. Lumsden, Commanding the Corps of Guides, to Lt. Col. Lawrence, Deputy Commissioner, Trans-Indus Peshawar, 27 October 1849, *Foreign Department, Secret*, NAI New Delhi.

   For a detailed statement about the composition and state of the colony's recruits, based on the testimony of three captured 'Fanatics', *see* Lylle to Mackeson, 24 March 1853, *Foreign Department, Secret*, NAI New Delhi.

   The Patna connection would be at the center of the so-called 'Wahabi' trials of the 1860s and 1870s.

9. *See for example* Copy of a letter from Commissioner and Superintendent Peshawur Division to Secretary to Government Punjab. No. 165 Dated 10 September 1863, *Foreign Department, Political A*, NAI New Delhi.

10. Colvin went on: 'Touching but little on the metaphysical subtleties of the Sufi opinion, and utterly denouncing such of their professors as are not strict believers, it is still devoted to an exposition of many of the admitted Sufi tenets and practices, and is full of the technicalities of Sufi phraseology. It makes references especially, in its explanations and allusions, to the peculiar divisions which prevail in India, among those who aspire to the honours of religious initiation.... It was one of the peculiar pretensions of Syed Ahmed, that he held himself privileged, instead of confining himself, as is usual, to giving admission to one only of these schools [Chisti, Naqsbandi, Qadiriya], to receive followers at his pleasure into any, or into all of them, and he aimed also at becoming the founder of a school of his own, to which he gave the appellation of the "Tariq-i-Muhammedia."' J.R. Colvin, 'Notice of the Peculiar Tenets Held by the Followers of Syed Ahmed, Taken Chiefly from the "Sirat-ul-Mustaqim," a Principal Treatise of that Sect, written by Moulavi Mahommed Ismail', *Journal of the Asiatic Society of Bengal*, 1, November 1832, p. 480. He also refrained from calling Sayyid Ahmed a 'Wahabi'.

11. *See in particular* William Wilson Hunter, *The Indian Musalmans: Are they Duty Bound in Conscience to Rebel against the Queen?*, London: Trulbner & Co., 1871.

12. This personal connection with Shah Wali Ullah's family has been the basis of a corrupted understanding of his religious teachings as 'Wahabi', misconstruing Shah Abdul Aziz's own teachings, most especially his pronouncement that British India was part of the *dar-al harb*. The assumption

that Sayyid Ahmed 'picked up' Wahabism in the Hijaz during his *hajj* is also guilty of mixing up the chronology. By the time he visited Mecca and Medina in 1821–23, the Wahabis had been expelled by an Ottoman-Egyptian force under Muhammad Ali Pasha. Further, the *Siraj-al Musta-qim*, arguably Sayyid Ahmed's most important work, was written before he undertook the *hajj*. *See* Muhammad Abdul Bari, 'The Politics of Sayyid Ahmad Barelwi', *Islamic Culture: An English Quarterly*, XXXI, April 1957; Harlon O. Pearson, *Islamic Reform and Revival in Nineteenth-century India: The Tariqah-i Muhammadiyah*, New Delhi: Yoda Press, 2008.

13. *See for instance* Translation of a proclamation sent from Kabul for distribution in the Kandahar district, February 1888, *Foreign Department, Secret F*, NAI New Delhi; Extract translation from a report by Raja Jehandad Khan, K. B., Extra Assistant Commissioner, Hazara, May 1883, *Foreign Department, Secret E*, NAI New Delhi. *See generally* Christine Noelle, 'The Anti-Wahabi Reaction in Nineteenth Century Afghanistan', *The Muslim World*, 85, January-April 1995; Metcalf, *Islamic Revival in British India*.

14. For examples of this orthodox position, *see* Peter Robb, 'The Impact of British Rule on Religious Community: Reflections on the Trial of Maulvi Ahmadullah of Patna in 1865' in P. Robb (ed), *Society and Ideology: Essays in South Asian History*, Delhi: Oxford University Press, 1993; Peter Hardy, *The Muslims of British India*, Cambridge: Cambridge University Press, 1972, pp. 81–91.

15. Deputy Commissioner, Huzara, to the Secretary to the Board of Administration, Punjab, 29 September 1849, *Foreign Department, Secret*, NAI New Delhi.

16. Court of the Judicial Commissioner Punjab: The Crown vs. Mahomed Shuffee, Mahomed Jaffir, Abdool Guffoor, Abdool Kurreem, Hooseinee, son of Mahomed Buksh, Hooseinee, son of Mungoo, Yahiya Ali, Abdool Ruheem, Abdool Guffar, Elahee Buksh, Cazee Meean Jan, October 1865, *Foreign Department, Political B*, NAI New Delhi.

17. *See for example* Bunbury to F.D. Cunningham, November 1895, *Foreign Department, Secret F*, NAI New Delhi.

18. *See for instance* Deputy Commissioner, Huzara, to the Secretary to the Board of Administration, Punjab, 29 September 1849, *Foreign Department, Secret*, NAI New Delhi.

19. Alex Padamsee makes a wider argument about the Muslim community of India and Anglo-Indian opinion. Alex Padamsee, *Representations of Indian Muslims in British Colonial Discourse*, Basingstoke: Palgrave Macmillan, 2005, pp. 56–64.

20. Gilgit Agency: Official diary for week ending 2nd June 1890, August 1890, *Foreign Department, Secret F*, NAI New Delhi.

'Mujahidin' had clear implications of religious sanction and pointed towards the adherents' belief that they were engaged in a *jihad* against the powers that be—whether Sikh, British, or indeed sometimes tribal. This was best evidenced by the assumption of the title '*amir-al munimim*' by some of the 'Fanatics' leaders, not least Sayyid Ahmed himself. Marc Gaborieau, 'The *jihad* of Sayyid Ahmad Barelwi on the North West Frontier: The Last Echo of the Middle Ages? Or a Prefiguration of Modern South Asia' in M. Haidar (ed), *Sufis, Sultans and Feudal Orders: Professor Nurul Hasan Commemoration Volume*, New Delhi: Manohar, 2004, p. 34.

21. *See generally* Padamsee, *Representations of Indian Muslims in British Colonial Discourse*.

22. *See for example* Memorandum, October 1865, *Foreign Department, Political B*, NAI New Delhi.

    For a discussion of these movements, *see* Abhijit Dutta, *Muslim Society in Transition: Titu Meer's Revolt (1831)*, Calcutta: Minerva, 1986; Narahari Kaviraj, *Wahabi and Farazi Rebels of Bengal*, New Delhi: People's Publishing House, 1982; Rafiuddin Ahmed, *The Bengal Muslims 1871–1906: A Quest for Identity*, Delhi: Oxford University Press, 1996.

23. *See for example* Memorandum, October 1865, *Foreign Department, Political B*, NAI New Delhi.

24. Nor were the British married to the term. They stopped referring to the *Ahl-i Hadith* as 'Wahabis' in the Punjab in the 1880s because of their protest.

25. *See generally* Kim Wagner, *Thuggee: Banditry and the British in Early Nineteenth Century India*, Basingstoke: Palgrave Macmillan, 2007.

26. It did, however, maintain a close surveillance of 'Wahabis'. *See for instance* 'The Wahabi Sect in India and the Hindustani Fanatics, October 1915', *Foreign & Political Department, Frontier B*, NAI New Delhi; Papers regarding recent activities among Wahabis, 10 January 1916, IOR L/PS/11/111/P4261/1916, London.

27. Minute by the Governor-General 15 October 1852, *Foreign Department, Political*, NAI New Delhi.

28. Hardy, *The Muslims of British India*, p. 69.

29. Court of the Judicial Commissioner Punjab: The Crown vs. Mahomed Shuffee, Mahomed Jaffir, Abdool Guffoor, Abdool Kurreem, Hooseinee, son of Mahomed Buksh, Hooseinee, son of Mungoo, Yahiya Ali, Abdool Ruheem, Abdool Guffar, Elahee Buksh, Cazee Meean Jan.

30. Governor General to Lt. Governor, Punjab, October 1868, *Foreign Department, Political A*, NAI New Delhi.

31. Notes 1870, *Mayo Papers*, Cambridge University Library (henceforth CUL), Add.Ms.7490, Cambridge.

32. '...so long as large classes of people in Bengal, Central India and elsewhere are deceived as to the importance of the Moulvie and his followers, and continue to subscribe for their support as we subscribe for a distant mission (say the Moravian one) I myself despair of extirpating them'. Commissioner, Peshawar, to the Lt. Governor, Punjab, 8 August. Ibid.

Pollock followed Mayo's orders, dealing liberally with Fanatics who sought to return to British territories. He wrote that 'half at least' of them were 'beguiled from their happy homes in Bengal by priestly lies and inventions', including that the British would 'skin and fry' them. Pollock to Burne, 31 July 1869, *Mayo Papers*, CUL Add.Ms.7490, Cambridge.

33. C.U. Aitchison, the Foreign Secretary to the Government of India, wrote, '[t]he very interest that we exhibit in trying to suppress the colony, helps, to my thinking, to keep up a sort of enthusiasm for them among certain classes of our own subjects. They are looked upon as martyrs, men suffering for religion at the hands of the infidel. It therefore become meritorious to keep them. The greater the danger incurred, the greater the merit'. Aitchison to Burne, 12 August 1870, *Mayo Papers*, CUL Add.Ms.7490, Cambridge.

34. *See* Hardy, *The Muslims of British India*.

35. *See* Padamsee, *Representations of Indian Muslims in British Colonial Discourse*.

36. This was undoubtedly a part of what Taylor Sherman has termed the colonial 'spectacle of justice'. *See generally* Taylor C. Sherman, *State Violence and Punishment in India*, London: Routledge, 2010

37. In at least one instance one of the rebuttals was authored by a 'reformed Wahabi'. Hunter's *The Indian Musalmans* was printed by Trubner & Co. in 1871, and went to a second edition with the same press in 1872. Sayyid Ahmed Khan's rebuttal was printed by Medical Hall Press of Benares.

38. C.A. Bayly, 'Ireland, India and the Empire: 1780–1914', *Transactions of the Royal Historical Society (Sixth Series)*, 10, 2000, p. 388.

39. For example, Herbert Edwardes' long-standing connection with the Church Mission Society and post-Mutiny advocacy of Christian proselytization in South Asia undoubtedly affected his attitude towards the 'Fanatics' and 'Wahabis' he prosecuted. T.R. Moreman, 'Edwardes, Sir Herbert Benjamin (1819–1868)', *Oxford Dictionary of National Biography*, 2004. In contrast, A.C. Lyall was a sceptical adherent of high Anglicanism and there is little to indicate that this influenced his attitudes towards Islam, save in a pronounced secularity of thought. Padamsee, *Representations of Indian Muslims in British Colonial Discourse*.

40. Carnact to W.T. Tucker, Officiating Magistrate of Patna, 15 October 1852, *Foreign Department, Political*, NAI New Delhi.

41. Mackeson to Melvill, 28 January 1853, *Foreign Department, Secret*, NAI New Delhi.

42. Edwardes to R. Temple, 31 October 1856, *Foreign Department, Secret*, NAI New Delhi. For a description of their site, *see also* Edwardes to H.B. Urmston, 31 October 1856, *Foreign Department, Secret*, NAI New Delhi. Internal strife and fracturing would become a central feature of the *mujahidin*'s subsequent history.

43. 'Brief Chronology of the Hindustani Fanatics', October 1915, *Foreign & Political Department, Frontier B*, NAI New Delhi.

44. Viceroy to the Secretary of State, 17 March 1864, *Wood Papers*, IOR Mss. Eur.F78/113/1, London.

45. *See for instance* Maj. Hugh James, Commissioner and Superintendent of Peshawur Division, to R.H. Davies, Secretary to Government, Punjab, March 1864, *Foreign Department, Political A*, NAI New Delhi.

46. Taylor to H.R. James, Ibid.

47. Sir Charles Wood, the Secretary of State for India, was outspoken in his criticism of the Ambela campaign. He wrote to John Lawrence that '[W]e never have seen any account of the reasons for doing anything beyond a general statement of necessity of expelling the Sitana fanatics and compelling the tribes to exclude them from our frontier.... Montgomery [Lt. Gov. of Punjab] speaks of a general Mahommedan move against us as a danger looming in the distance, and the course we have taken seems well calculated to accelerate if not to produce it'. Secretary of State to the Viceroy, 23 December 1863, *Wood Papers*, IOR Mss.Eur.F78/LB15, London.

48. The 'Fanatics' also took up arms in 1891, although according to the British, this was done apparently under duress. 'After the lesson taught them at Towarra in the former expedition of 1888, although they were bound by the exigencies of their peculiar position as a band of "irreconcileables" settled among foreigners to take the lead again in opposing the expedition in 1891, they did not dare another open attack by daylight, but resorted to an attempt to effect a night surprise'. Report on the Punjab Frontier Administration for the Year 1891–2, 16 July 1892, *Punjab Administration Reports*, IOR V/10/369B, London. *See also* Cunningham to Maj. Gen. W. K. Elles, Commanding Hazara Field Force, September 1891, *Foreign Department, Frontier A*, NAI New Delhi; Note by the Private Secretary to His Honour the Lieutenant-Governor of the Punjab, dated 10 July 1893, 1893, *Foreign Department*, NAI New Delhi.

49. 'Brief Chronology of the Hindustani Fanatics., October 1915, *Foreign & Political Department, Frontier B*, NAI New Delhi.

50. Appendix C, December 1868, *Foreign Department, Political A*, NAI New Delhi.

51. Abdul Rauf, 'The British Empire and the Mujahidin Movement in the N.W.F.P., 1914–1934', *Islamic Studies*, 44, Autumn 2005, p. 426.

52. *See for instance* Aitchison to Burne, 12 August 1870, *Mayo Papers*, CUL Add.Ms.7490, Cambridge.

53. Edwardes to R. Temple, 31 October 1856, *Foreign Department, Secret*, NAI New Delhi.

54. Jalal, *Partisans of Allah*. *See also* Metcalf, *Islamic Revival in British India*.

55. Davies to the Secretary to the Government of India, Foreign Department, August 1862, *Foreign Department, Political A*, NAI New Delhi.

56. This is a classic model of religious leadership made famous by Ernest Gellner. Ernest Gellner, 'Tribalism and State in the Middle East' in P.S. Khoury and J. Kostiner (eds), *Tribes and State Formation in the Middle East*, Berkeley: University of California Press, 1990.

57. Report on the Hindustani Fanatics, 1895, *Military*, IOR L/MIL/17/13/18, London.

On the issue of Pashtun migrations and their participation at this time in the South Asian military labour market, *see* Nichols, *A History of Pashtun Migration, 1775–2006*, 2008, pp. 24–63.

58. I am not arguing that Sayyid Ahmed was himself a Rohilla Pathan. Although he was born in Rai Bareilly in the lands of Oudh, he spent a considerable amount of time in Barelwi, in the former lands of the Rohilla kingdom.

59. Apparently one of the adherents later ignored the injunction not to approach the cave, only to find a roughly made figure filled with straw. It was obviously in the interest of the colonial state to debunk stories of Sayyid Ahmed's miraculous life on the Frontier. Such a story of disappointment could be a powerful one for the colonial state. Deputy Commissioner, Huzara, to the Secretary to the Board of Administration, Punjab, 29 September 1849, *Foreign Department, Secret*, NAI New Delhi.

60. The British variously referred to the colony as 'Samasti' or 'Smasta' before settling on 'Asmas' in the mid-1920s. At least one commentator asserts this is a corruption of the Pashto word 'Asmas', meaning 'cave'. *See* Rauf, 'The British Empire and the Mujahidin Movement in the N.W.F.P., 1914–1934', p. 411, n. 7. This would have interesting iconographic implications. The Pashtu word for 'cave' or 'cavern' is *'samast'* (سهست).

The British believed 'Asmas' to be a corruption of 'Samasai', roughly translated as 'hill'. Papers regarding recent activities among Wahabis, 10 January 1916, IOR L/PS/11/111/P4261/1916, London.

61. Extract translation from a report by Raja Jehandad Khan, K.B., Extra Assistant Commissioner, Hazara, May 1883, *Foreign Department, Secret E*, NAI New Delhi.

62. Extract from Abstract of Intelligence, Punjab Police, dated 14 April 1883, No. 15, May 1883, *Foreign Department, Secret E*, NAI New Delhi.

63. The Assistant Commissioner, Mardan, to the Deputy Commissioner, Peshawar, May 1883, *Foreign Department, Secret E*, NAI New Delhi.

64. Translation of a letter from Nawab Muhammad Akram Khan of Amb, to the Commissioner and Superintendent, Peshawar Division, dated 20 January 1884, June 1884, *Foreign Department, A Political E*, NAI New Delhi. *See also* Extract from Abstract of Intelligence, Punjab Police, dated 14 April 1883, No. 15.

65. Translation of a letter from Moulvi Abdulla, leader of the Hindustani Fanatics at Palosi, to the Deputy Commissioner of Hazara, dated the 10th Saaban = 23 May 1885, August 1885, *Foreign Department, Frontier A*, NAI New Delhi. *See also* Claim made by the Hindustani colony at Palosi against two British subjects, August 1885, *Foreign Department, Frontier A*, NAI New Delhi.

After this failed attempt in 1885, Maulvi Abdullah again sent out feelers in 1898 corresponding through an intermediary who was a known

British loyalist. Letter from Maulvi Abudulla, sealed with his seal, not dated, but reaching Abdul Kadir of Jhanda on 11 or 12 August, 1897, brought back by Niyamat of Kadra, February 1898, *Foreign Department, Secret F*, NAI New Delhi.

66. One Faiz-ul-Huq, a former state employee of Bhopal and brother of the agent to the consort of the Begum of Bhopal, was allowed to visit the 'Fanatic' colony unhindered. Secretary to the Government of the Punjab to the Secretary to the Government of India, Foreign Department, March 1886, *Foreign Department, Secret F*, NAI New Delhi.

67. Extract from Peshawar Confidential Diary, No. 20, dated the 22 October 1887, March 1888, *Foreign Department, Secret F*, NAI New Delhi.

68. They apparently ignored an entreaty from the Mulla of Hadda, one of the leaders of the revolt. Peshawar Confidential Diary No. 19(a), dated 8 October 1897, November 1897, *Foreign Department, Secret F*, NAI New Delhi.

69. 'Brief chronology of the Hindustani Fanatics', October 1915, *Foreign & Political Department, Frontier B*, NAI New Delhi.

70. Maulvi Abdullah was approached by the Mian Gul, the son of the then late Akund of Swat, to support him against the British. 'The Maulvi is said to have replied that he was unable to put much trust in the people of Swat and Bajour, who might, if the Hindustani fanatics joined them, suddenly make peace and leave them (the Hindustanis) to bear the brunt of the fight, but if Swat and Bajaur really intended to fight, of course he and his party would join'. Peshawar Confidential Diary, No. 6, dated 29 March 1888, April 1888, *Foreign Department, Secret F*, NAI New Delhi.

71. 'It was known that they actually demanded contributions from their supporters throughout India on the strength of the popularity of the expedition'. 'Brief chronology of the Hindustani Fanatics', October 1915, *Foreign & Political Department, Frontier B*, NAI New Delhi.

72. Ibid.

73. Bunbury to F.D. Cunningham, November 1895, *Foreign Department, Secret F*, NAI New Delhi.

One estimate put their strength at the turn of the century at 900 fighting men with nearly 800 Martini-Henry rifles.

'Brief chronology of the Hindustani Fanatics', October 1915, *Foreign & Political Department, Frontier B*, NAI New Delhi. There were various estimates of the strength of the colony during this period, ranging from roughly 500 to upwards of 1,000 fighting men. In 1898, it was reported they numbered 900 and were 'not happy'. Diary of the Political Agent for Dir, Swat and Chitral for the week ending 14 November 1897, January 1898, *Foreign Department, Secret F*, NAI New Delhi. By 1912, their numbers were estimated at 800 fighting men and over 1,200 women and children. Extract from North-West Frontier Provincial Diary No. 15 for the week ending 10 April 1915, October 1915, *Foreign & Political Department, Frontier B*, NAI New Delhi.

74. The Commissioner and Superintendent of the Peshawar Division to the Chief Secretary to the Government of the Punjab, July 1899, *Foreign Department, Frontier A*, NAI New Delhi.

75. Administration report of the Northwest Frontier Province from 9th November 1901 to 31st March 1903, 1903, *NWFP Administration Reports*, IOR V/10/370, London.

76. *See* Chief Commissioner, NWFP, to the Foreign Secretary to the Government of India in the Foreign and Political Department, January 1916, *Foreign & Political Department, Secret F*, NAI New Delhi.

77. Extract from North-West Frontier Provincial Diary No. 15 for the week ending 10 April 1915.

78. Chief Commissioner, NWFP, to the Secretary to the Government of India in the Foreign Department, Ibid.

79. Most of these students eventually proceeded on to Kabul, where they were received by the Amir. Ibid.

80. Roos-Keppel to the Viceroy, 13 February 1915, *Roos-Keppel Papers*, IOR Mss.Eur.D/613/1, London.

81. Chief Commissioner, NWFP, to the Secretary to the Government of India in the Foreign and Political Department, January 1916, *Foreign Department, Secret F*, NAI New Delhi.

82. Lal Baha, 'The Activities of the Mujahidin 1900–1936', *Islamic Studies*, 18, Summer 1979, pp. 104–05. *See also* 'Afghanistan: the Silk Letter Case', 1916–18, *Political & Secret*, IOR, L/PS/10/633, London.

83. *See* 'Statement of "G.B.," a loyal Pathan recorded by an officers of the North-West Frontier Province in October 1915'. Papers regarding recent activities among Wahabis, 10 January 1916, *Political & Secret*, IOR L/PS/11/111/P4261/ 1916, London.

  G. B. was not the only source the British cultivated for information. In the 1920s, the Intelligence Bureau in Peshawar made oblique reference to other sources of information, writing '[d]uring the last 18 months cautious and quite efforts have been sustained to keep closely in touch with this Colony, and with the wishes, ideas and intentions of the two leaders.

  'The sowing has been deep and the plants, when they come up, should be strong and healthy, if they are allowed to remain in the shade, and not exposed the glare of publicity.

  'It has been difficult to break through their triple barrier of suspicion and distrust, and, for a solid year, were unsuccessful.

  'In the last six months, however, we have made a start and I have every hope that, provided the strictest secrecy is maintained, we shall soon know most of what is going on in Chamarkand'. Copy of a report dated 6 July 1925 by the Officer in Charge, Intelligence Bureau, North-West Frontier Province, Peshawar, 6 July 1925, *Political & Secret*, IOR L/PS/11/111/P4261/1916, London.

84. Papers regarding recent activities among Wahabis, 10 January 1916, *Political & Secret*, IOR L/PS/11/111/P4261/1916, London.

85. Lt. Col. Roos-Keppel, Chief Commissioner, NWFP, to A.H. Grant, Foreign Secretary to GoI, 9 May 1917, *Political & Secret*, IOR L/PS/11/111/ P4261/1917, London.

86. For a reprint of his letter to Sir George Roos-Keppel, Chief Commissioner of the North-West Frontier Province, *see* Baha, 'The Activities of the Mujahidin 1900–1936', pp. 156–9.

87. Translation of a letter from Niamatullah, Amir-i-Mujahidin to the Nawab of Amb dated Asmast, the 22nd Rajab 1333 Hijri (corresponding to 15 May 1917), 15 May 1917, *Political & Secret*, IOR L/PS/11/111/P4261/ 1916, London.

88. This was the third distinct episode of communication between the leadership of the 'Fanatic' colony and British authorities. For a copy of the settlement, *see* Lt. Col. Sir George Roos-Keppel, Chief Commissioner of the NWFP, to the Foreign Secretary to the GoI, 1917, *Political & Secret*, IOR L/PS/11/111/P4261/1916, London.

89. Cleveland to Grant, 1917, *Political & Secret*, IOR L/PS/11/111/P4261/ 1916, London.

90. One of the conditions of the peace settlement between Niamatullah and the British was the recall of the Chamarkand *mujahidin*. This was not the only other outpost of the Hindustani fanatics. They also had a small colony in Tirah which sought to stir up trouble amongst the Afridis. The *mujahidin* also established a colony at Makin, in Waziristan, to cause trouble. North-West Frontier Province Intelligence Bureau Diary No. 21 for the period ending 19 November, 15 December 1926, *Political & Secret*, IOR L/PS/10/1137, London; Chief Commissioner, NWFP, to the Foreign Secretary to the Government of India, 1923, *Foreign & Political Department*, *Frontier*, NAI New Delhi; 'Mujahidin: Hindustani Fanatic Colony in Waziristan', 1930, *Foreign & Political Department*, *Frontier*, NAI New Delhi.

As late as 1946, internal rifts within the *mujahidin* led some to establish a breakaway colony 'at Dandar (Surai-Amazai) on the south bank of the Chamla River, about 1 1/2 miles south west of Asmas'. Weekly summary no. 30, dated Peshawar, 27 July, 1946, *Political & Secret*, IOR L/PS/12/ 3200, London.

91. Chief Commissioner, NWFP, to the Foreign Secretary to the Government of India, 1923, *Foreign & Political Department*, *Frontier*, NAI New Delhi.

92. Chamarkand was a colony in Bajuar on the Afghan border. The first mention of the *mujahidin*'s presence there, though not by name, is in November 1916 when it was estimated there were 290 *mujahidin* present. Extract of the North-West Frontier Provincial Diary No. 45, for the week ending 4 November 1916, April 1917, *Foreign & Political Department*, *Secret—Frontier*, NAI New Delhi.

93. His assassination was largely blamed on two emerging leaders of the movement, Maulvi Fazl-i Ilahi and Maulvi Bashir. NWF Provincial Diary No. 38, for week ending 7 October, 1922: The two factions, 1923, *Political & Secret*, IOR L/PS/11/111/P4261/1916, London.

For a description of Maulvi Fazl-i Ilahi, *see* Supplement to the North-West Frontier Province Intelligence Bureau Diary No. 4 for the period ending 12 February 1926, 1926, *Political & Secret*, IOR L/PS/11/111, London.

Fazl-i Ilahi had a penchant for ordering books from booksellers in British India. His orders included: '(1) A brief history of the Punjab; (2) A brief history of Jammu and Kashmir; (3) A geography of Jammu and Kashmir; (4) "The NWFP and the War"; (5) A history of Chitral; [and] (6) "History of the Khyber", by Saida Khan, Shinwari'. North-West Frontier Province Intelligence Bureau, Diary No. 18 for the period ending 10 Sepetmber, 11 October 1928, *Political & Secret*, IOR L/PS/10/1137, London.

He also ordered: '1. "The N.W.F. Province and the War", by Lieutenant-Colonel J. W. Keen; 2. "Outline of Russo-Japanese War, 1904–5", by Colonel C. Ross; 3. "The United Services" Magazine; 4. "Whittaker's Almanack"; 5. "Pear's Encyclopaedia"; 6. Journal of the U.S. Institution of India for 1890; 7. Histories of Afghanistan, China, Chitral, and the Khyber'. This penchant for reading prompted one official to quip, '[t]his will perhaps enlarge the Maulvi's outlook' in the margin of the report. North-West Frontier Province, Intelligence Bureau, Diary No. 16, for the period ending 13 August, 12 September 1928, *Political & Secret*, IOR L/PS/10/1137, London. *See also* North-West Frontier Province Intelligence Bureau Diary No. 34 for the period ending 12 October 1929, 13 November 1929, *Political & Secret*, IOR L/PS/10/1137, London.

94. It was thought these weapons passed through Asmas. The British thought it unlikely that 'established members' of the colony were either active in, or profiting from such activity, and believed that 'a considerable number of them appear to be seriously thinking of abandoning the role of "Muja-hidin" and seeking opportunities to settle down in British territory'. Supplement to the Intelligence Bureau Dairy No. 8 for the week ending 21 January 1924, 1923, *Foreign & Political Department*, *Frontier*, NAI New Delhi.

95. North-West Frontier Province Intelligence Bureau Diary No. 23 for the week ending 15 June 1922, 1923, *Political & Secret*, IOR L/PS/11/111/P4261/1916, London.

For a description of the various *mujahidin* factions along the Frontier, *see* North West Frontier Province Intelligence Bureau Diary No. 12 for week ending 23 March 1922, 1923, *Political & Secret*, IOR L/PS/11/111/P4261/1916, London.

96. Copy of a report dated 6 July 1925 by the Officer in Charge, Intelligence Bureau, North-West Frontier Province, Peshawar. *See also* North-West Frontier Province, Intelligence Bureau, Diary No. 4, for the period ending 18 February, 28 March 1928, *Political & Secret*, IOR L/PS/10/1137, London.

97. Supplement to North-West Frontier Province Intelligence Bureau Diary No. 11 for the period ending 7 May, 2 June 1925, *Political & Secret*, IOR

L/PS/10/1137, London. *See also* Extract from the North West Frontier Province Intelligence Bureau Diary No. 42, for the period ending the 28 October 1931, *Foreign & Political Department, Frontier*, NAI New Delhi.

The Soviet legation reputedly attempted to supply the *mujahidin* colony in Waziristan in 1927 with £300 in gold which was intercepted by Afghan authorities. North-West Frontier Province Intelligence Bureau, Diary No. 23 for the period ending 20 November, 28 December 1928, *Political & Secret*, IOR L/PS/10/1137, London.

98. Copy of a report dated 6 July 1925 by the Officer in Charge, Intelligence Bureau, North-West Frontier Province, Peshawar.

99. Supplement to the North-West Frontier Province Intelligence Bureau Diary No. 8 for the week ending 26 March, 16 April 1925, *Political & Secret*, IOR L/PS/10/1137, London.

100. Supplement to North-West Frontier Province Intelligence Bureau Diary No. 30 for the period ending 10 December, 12 January 1926 1925, *Political & Secret*, IOR L/PS/10/1137, London.

101. Secret note by Intelligence Bureau on the proposal contained in Political Agent, Malakand's Confidential Letter No. 105, dated 30 March 1925, 1923, *Foreign & Political Department, Frontier*, NAI New Delhi.

102. Supplement to North-West Frontier Province Intelligence Bureau Diary No. 7 for the period ending 26 March 1926, 1926, *Political & Secret*, IOR L/PS/11/111/ 4261/1916, London.

Chamarkand remained small. In 1927 it was thought to number only '49 Hindustanis and 14 Punjabis under Maulvi Siraj-ud-din, Bengali, a representative of the Asmas Amir, Rahmatullah [and] 4 Punjabis with Maulvi Fazal Ilahi'. North-West Frontier Province Intelligence Bureau Diary No. 26 for the period ending 29 October, 30 November 1927, *Political & Secret*, IOR L/PS/10/1137, London.

103. On British efforts to interfere with attempts by the Chamarkand *mujahidin* to collect subscriptions in British India, *see* North-West Frontier Province Intelligence Bureau Diary No. 18 for the period ending 24 September, 20 October 1926, *Political & Secret*, IOR L/PS/10/1137, London.

104. Supplement to North-West Frontier Province Intelligence Bureau Diary No. 1 for the period ending 7 January 1926, 10 February 1926, *Political & Secret*, IOR L/PS/10/1137, London. Note, 1927, *Foreign & Political Department, Frontier*, NAI New Delhi.

105. This injunction was particularly aimed at an offshoot colony in Waziristan. North-West Frontier Province, Intelligence Bureau, Diary No. 8, for the period ending 11 April, 23 May 1928, *Political & Secret*, IOR L/PS/10/1137, London.

106. Weekly summary no. 9, dated Peshawar 3 March, 1941, *Political & Secret*, IOR L/PS/12/3195, London. Weekly summary no. 13, dated Peshawar, 31 March, 1945, *Political & Secret*, IOR L/PS/12/3199, London.

107. One was in Swat and the other in Bajaur. Minute: NW Frontier—The Chamarkand and Samasta colonies, 23 April 1923, *Political & Secret*, IOR L/PS/11/111/P4261/1916, London; North West Frontier Province Intelligence Bureau Diary No. 12 for week ending 23 March 1922.

Schools appear to have been a perennial concern of the *mujahidin*. As late as 1947, they were soliciting Afghan contributions for a school in the Chamarkand colony itself. Weekly summary no. 9, dated Peshawar, 1 March, 1947, *Political & Secret*, IOR L/PS/12/3201, London.

108. Supplement to North-West Frontier Province Intelligence Bureau Diary No. 11 for the period ending 7 May.

109. Weekly summary no. 18, dated Peshawar 29 April 1940, *Political & Secret*, IOR L/PS/12/3194, London.

110. North-West Frontier Province Intelligence Bureau Diary No. 18 for the period ending 24 September.

111. The issue for 10 December 1927 held up the Albanian fight for independence as a model to be emulated by the Frontier tribesmen. North-West Frontier Province, Intelligence Bureau, Diary No. 7, for ther period ending 31 March, 2 May 1928, *Political & Secret*, IOR L/PS/10/1137, London.

112. Extract from North-West Frontier Province Intelligence Bureau Diary No. 40 for the week ending 1 November 1923, 1923, *Foreign & Political Department, Frontier*, NAI New Delhi.

113. Sir John Maffey, Chief Commissioner, NWFP, to the Secretary to the Government of India in the Foreign and Political Department, 25 April 1923, *Political & Secret*, IOR L/PS/11/111/P4261/1916, London.

114. Weekly summary no. 47, dated Peshawar 24 November, 1941, *Political & Secret*, IOR L/PS/12/3195, London.

115. North-West Frontier Province, Intelligence Bureau, Diary No. 6, for the period ending 17 March, 25 April 1928, *Political & Secret*, IOR L/PS/10/1137, London.

116. 'Mujahidin: Hindustani Fanatic Colony in Waziristan', 1930.

117. Weekly summary no. 36, dated Peshawar, 7 September, 1942, *Political & Secret*, IOR L/PS/12/3196, London.

118. Weekly summary no. 17, dated Peshawar, 22 April, 1940, *Political & Secret*, IOR L/PS/12/3194, London.

119. Weekly summary no. 14, dated Peshawar 5 March, 1947, *Political & Secret*, IOR L/PS/12/3201, London.

120. It simply reads 'Jemadar Muhammad Ayub Mujahiddin [leader of Chamarkand] has been touring Bajaur collecting harvest money (*zakat*)'. Weekly summary no. 25, dated Peshawar 21 June, 1947, *Political & Secret*, IOR L/PS/12/3201, London.

121. Rauf, 'The British Empire and the Mujahidin Movement in the N.W.F.P., 1914–1934', p. 420, n. 42.

4. THE PAST BECOMES PRESENT

1. For a discussion of the multiple meanings and manifestations of 'modernity', *see* Cooper, *Colonialism in Question*.
2. *See especially* Chapter 1.
3. *For example* Scott Atran, *Talking to the Enemy: Violent Extremism, Sacred Values and what it Means to be Human*, Allen Lane: London, 2010, pp. 256–8.
4. According to Daniel Benjamins who 'tracked Bin Laden during the Clinton administration' and is now 'of' the Brookings Institute, Chitralis have 'a code of hospitality for guests and they have probably gotten a fair amount of money from Bin Laden' http://www.cbsnews.com/stories/2007/09/07/eveningnews/main3243560.shtml. Last accessed on 8th March 2010.
5. For excellent accounts of the importance of hospitality (*melmastia*) and refuge (*nanawatia*) to the moral worlds of Pukhtuns, *see* Charles Lindholm, *Generosity and Jealousy: the Swat Pukhtun of Northern Pakistan*, New York: Columbia University Press, 1982. For a theoretical treatments of tribal understandings of hospitality in Jordan *see* Andrew Schyrock 'The New Jordanian Hospitality: House, Host and Guest in the Culture of Public Display', *Comparative Studies in Society and History*, 46 (1), 2004, pp. 35–62, and Andrew Schyrock, 'Thinking about Hospitality, with Derrida, Kant and the Balga Bedouin', *Anthropos*, 103, 2007, pp. 405–421.
6. For example Islamudin, 'Chitralis perceive discrimination', *Chitral Times*, 30 August, 2010. http://www.chitralnews.com/Letter-30–8–10.htm. Last accessed on November 5 2010.
7. Nigel J.R. Allan, 'Defining Place and People in Afghanistan', *Post-Soviet Geography and Economics*, 42, 2001.
8. One need look no further than Sandeman's use of the *jirga* amongst the Baluch tribesmen.

5. A TOUR NOT SO GRAND: MOBILE MUSLIMS IN NORTHERN PAKISTAN

1. E. Simpson and K. Kresse, *Struggling with History*, p. 27.
2. J. Gray, 'Open Spaces and Dwelling Places: Being at Home on Hill Farms in the Scottish Borders' in S.M. Low and D. Lawrence-Zúñiga (eds), *The Anthropology of Space and Place: Locating Culture*, Oxford: Blackwell, 2003, pp. 225, 27.
3. Bayly, *Asian Voices in a Postcolonial Age*, p. 122.
4. *See* Devji, *Landscapes of Jihad*.
5. *See for instance* Arjun Appadurai, *Modernity at Large: Cultural Dimensions of Globalization*, Minneapolis: University of Minnesota Press, 1996. Marc Augé, *Non-places: Introduction to an Anthropology of Supermodernity*, London, New York: Verso, 1995; James Clifford, *Routes: Travel and Translation in the Late Twentieth Century*, Cambridge, Mass.: Harvard

University Press, 1997; Ulf Hannerz, *Transnational Connections: Culture, People, Places*, London: Routledge, 1996.

6. Engseng Ho, *The Graves of Tarim: Genealogy and Mobility across the Indian Ocean*, Berkeley: University of California Press, 2006, p. 10. Compare Anna Lowenhaupt Tsing, *In the Realm of the Diamond Queen: Marginality in an Out-of-the-way Place*, Princeton: Princeton University Press, 1993.

7. *See for example* Dale F. Eickelman and James P. Piscatori, *Muslim Travellers: Pilgrimage, Migration, and the Religious Imagination*, Berkeley: University of California Press, 1990; Roxanne Leslie Euben, *Journeys to the Other Shore: Muslim and Western Travelers in Search of Knowledge*, Princeton: Princeton University Press, 2006.

8. Muzaffar Alam and Sanjay Subrahmanyam, *Indo-Persian Travels in the Age of Discoveries, 1400–1800*, Cambridge: Cambridge University Press, 2007. For an account of travel's importance to Persianate modernities, see Nile Green, 'Swiss Hill Walkers and Afghan Submariners: Conflicting Modernities in the Literature of Afghan Travel' in Nile Green and Nushin Arbabzadah (eds), *Afghanistan in Ink: Afghan Literatures between Diaspora and Nation*, London: C. Hurst and Co., forthcoming.

9. Javed Majeed, *Autobiography, Travel and Postnational Identity: Gandhi, Nehru and Iqbal*, Basingstoke: Palgrave Macmillan, 2007, pp. 5, 25.

10. *Cf.* Mary Louise Pratt, *Imperial Eyes: Travel Writing and Transculturation*, London: Routledge, 1992.

11. On the pilgrimage to Mecca, *see* Carol Delaney, 'The "Hajj": Sacred and Secular', *American Ethnologist*, 17, 1990; Abdellah Hammoudi and Pascale Ghazaleh, *A Season in Mecca: Narrative of a Pilgrimage*, New York: Hill and Wang, 2006. For work on shrine visitation, *see* Nancy Tapper, 'Ziyaret: Gender, Movement, and Exchange in a Turkish Community' in D.F. Eickelman and J.P. Piscatori (eds), *Muslim Travellers*; Pnina Werbner, *Pilgrims of Love: the Anthropology of a Global Sufi Cult*, Bloomington: Indiana University Press, 2003. Metcalf explores the significance of preaching tours organized by worldwide movements of 'Islamic reform', such as the Tabligh-e Jama'at. Barbara D. Metcalf, 'Living Hadith in the Tablighi Jama'at', *The Journal of Asian Studies*, 52, 1993.

12. Saba Mahmood, *Politics of Piety: the Islamic Revival and the Feminist Subject*, Princeton: Princeton University Press, 2005.

13. Saba Mahmood, 'Part III—Individual, Family, Community, and State—Ethical Formation and Politics of Individual Autonomy in Contemporary Egypt', *Social Research*, 70, 2003, p. 861.

14. Matt Waggoner, 'Irony, Embodiment, and the 'Critical Attitude': Engaging Saba Mahmood's Critique of Secular Morality', *Culture and Religion*, 6, 2005, p. 248. *See also* Lara Deeb, *An Enchanted Modern: Gender and Public Piety in Shi'i Lebanon*, Princeton: Princeton University Press, 2006; Heiko Henkel, 'The Location of Islam: Inhabiting Istanbul in a Muslim

Way', *American Ethnologist*, 34, 2007; Charles Hirschkind, *The Ethical Soundscape: Cassette Sermons and Islamic Counterpublics*, New York: Columbia University Press, 2006. Henkel brings a consideration of place making to the constitution of Muslim subjectivity in Istanbul.

15. Heiko Henkel, 'The Location of Islam: Inhabiting Istanbul in a Muslim Way', *American Ethnologist*, 34, 2007, pp. 57–8.

16. Pakistani labour migrants are rarely documented as exhibiting any curiosity in their worlds, but rather as being concerned above all else by 'working' and 'saving'. *See* Francis Watkins, '"Save There, Eat Here": Migrants, Households and Community Identity among Pakhtuns in Northern Pakistan', *Contributions to Indian Sociology*, 1 February 2003.

17. J. Gray, 'Open Spaces and Dwelling Places, pp. 224–44.

18. Michael Gilsenan, *Lords of the Lebanese Marches: Violence and Narrative in an Arab Society*, London: I.B. Tauris, 1996.

19. Caroline Humphrey, 'Chiefly and Shamanist Landscapes in Mongolia' in E. Hirsch and M. O'Hanlon (eds), *The Anthropology of Landscape: Perspectives on Place and Space*, Oxford: Clarendon Press, 1995, p. 134; Eric Hirsch, 'Landscape: Between Place and Space' in E. Hirsch and M. O'Hanlon (eds), *The Anthropology of Landscape*.

20. Henkel, 'The Location of Islam: Inhabiting Istanbul in a Muslim Way', p. 58.

21. *See* Marsden, *Living Islam*.

22. Anthropologists have noted the ways in which pilgrimage shapes personal and collective experiences of space on different scales. In the case of Hinduism, for example, these scales may include those of India and the village or involve complex modes of time-space compression as Hindu diasporic communities map India's sacred landscape elsewhere. Patrick Eisenlohr, *Little India: Diaspora, Time, and Ethnolinguistic Belonging in Hindu Mauritius*, Berkeley: University of California Press, 2006.

23. Waggoner, 'Irony, Embodiment, and the 'Critical Attitude', p. 238.

24. Ibid., p. 239.

25. Such mosques are found even in Chitral's most remote villages where they stand in contrast to older, mud-brick, flat-roofed village mosques decorated with Chitrali wooden carvings.

26. Shi'a Isma'ilis are taught to believe in the spiritual leadership of the Aga Khan. *See for example* Farhad Daftary, *The Ismailis: their History and Doctrines*, Cambridge: Cambridge University Press, 1990. They are often declared non-Muslim infidels by the region's Sunni 'men of piety', and there have also been moments of communal sectarian violence between the region's two communities.

27. Ussama Samir Makdisi, *The Culture of Sectarianism: Community, History, and Violence in Nineteenth-century Ottoman Lebanon*, Berkeley: University of California Press, 2000, p. 134.

28. *See for instance* Henkel, 'The Location of Islam'.

29. Many Chitralis living and working in labour camps in the Gulf often talk about yearning to visit villages and valleys on their return home. They also

say that they find life in Gulf labour camps more difficult than their fellow workers: 'we are accustomed to travel and freedom', I am often told, 'and this makes life in the camp very difficult'.

30. For scholarly debates on the role played by circulatory forms of mobility in the historical constitution of Indian society, *see* Claude Markovits *et al.*, *Society and Circulation: Mobile People and Itinerant Cultures in South Asia, 1750–1950*, Delhi: Permanent Black, 2003.

31. Juan R. Cole, 'Iranian Culture and South Asia, 1500–1900' in N.R. Keddie and R.P. Matthee (eds), *Iran and the Surrounding World: Interactions in Culture and Cultural Politics*, Seattle: University of Washington Press, 2002. Alam and Subrahmanyam, *Indo-Persian Travels in the Age of Discoveries, 1400–1800*; Alam and Subrahmanyam, 'Discovering the Familiar: Notes on the Travel-Account of Anand Ram Mukhlis, 1745'; Alam and Subrahmanyam, 'The Making of a Munshi', *Comparative Studies of South Asia, Africa and the Middle East*, 24, 2004.

32. Alam and Subrahmanyam, *Indo-Persian Travels in the Age of Discoveries, 1400–1800*, pp. 65–6.

33. Cole, 'Iranian Culture and South Asia, 1500–1900'; Robert L. Canfield (ed), *Turko-Persia in Historical Perspective*.

34. Alam and Subrahmanyam, *Indo-Persian Travels in the Age of Discoveries, 1400–1800*, p. 177.

35. M. Nazif Shahrani, 'Local Knowledge of Islam and Social Discourse in Afghanistan and Turkestan in the Modern Period' in R. Canfield (ed), *Turko-Persia in Historical Perspective*, Cambridge: Cambridge University Press, 1991.

36. One poem that is particularly popular in the region today, for example, describes the experiences of a Chitrali man who was recruited to the local militia, the Chitral Scouts. The poem depicts the love-sick poet as having been robbed of his ability to glimpse his 'beloved' because of the constraints imposed on his mobility on his recruitment to the Chitral Scouts. On the Chitral Scouts, *see* Ghulam Mirza Murtaza, *New History of Chitral Based on the Original Persian Text of Mirza Muhammad Ghufran. Revised and Enlarged with Additional Research of Late His Highness Sir Nair-ul-Mulk by Mirza Ghulam Martaza. Translated from the Urdu-version into English by Wazir Ali Shah*, Chitral: 1982; Rahmat Karim Baig, *Hindu Kush Study Series*, Peshawar: Rehmet Printing Press, 1997; Charles Chenevix Trench, *The Frontier Scouts*, London: J. Cape, 1985.

37. For the significance of images of the prisoner to local concepts of sovereignty in another heterogeneous historic region, see Grant, Bruce, 2009, *The Captive and the Gift: Cultural Histories of Sovereignty in Russia and the Caucasus*, Cornell University Press: Ithaca.

38. Paul Stoler, 'Embodying Colonial Memories', *American Anthropologist* 96 (3), 1994, pp. 634–43.

39. Waggoner, 'Irony, Embodiment, and the 'Critical Attitude', p. 239.

40. *See generally* Gilsenan, *Lords of the Lebanese Marches*.

41. Paul A. Silverstein and Ussama Makdisi, 'Introduction: Memory and Violence in the Middle East and North Africa' in U. Makdisi and P.A. Silverstein (eds), *Memory and Violence in the Middle East and Africa*, Bloomington: Indiana University Press, 2006, p. 9.

42. C. Tilly, 'Introduction: Identity, Place and Landscape', *Journal of Material Culture*, 11, 2006, p. 25.

43. Eric Hirsch, 'Landscape, Myth and Time', p. 154.

44. Michael Lambek, 'The Sakalava Poiesis of History: Realizing the Past Through Spirit Possession in Madagascar', *American Ethnologist*, 25, 1998, p. 108.

45. Eric Hirsch, 'When was Modernity in Melanesia ', *Social Anthropology*, 9, 2001, p. 133.

46. Gray, 'Open Spaces and Dwelling Places'.

47. Majeed, *Autobiography, Travel and Postnational Identity*, p. 24.

48. M. Marsden, 'Love and elopement in northern Pakistan', *Journal of the Royal Anthropological Institute*, 13, 2007.

49. Eric Hirsch, 'Landscape: Between Place and Space', p. 4.

50. Marsden, *Living Islam*.

51. For an excellent treatment of Chitrali relations to the spirit world *see* John Staley, *Words for my Brother: Travels between the Hindu Kush and the Himalayas*, Karachi: Oxford University Press, 1982.

52. Paul A. Silverstein and Ussama Makdisi, 'Introduction', p. 9.

53. Hirsch, 'Landscape: Between Place and Space', p. 4.

54. *See for instance* Muhammad Qasim Zaman, *The Ulama in Contemporary Islam: Custodians of Change*, Princeton: Princeton University Press, 2002.

55. Henkel, 'The Location of Islam', p. 58.

56. *Compare* Hirsch, 'Landscape: Between Place and Space', p. 4; D. Parkin, *Sacred Void: Spatial Images of Work and Ritual amongst the Giriama*, Cambridge: Cambridge University Press 1991.

57. On the importance of sound and listening to Muslims' subjectivity in Cairo, *see* Hirschkind, *The Ethical Soundscape*.

58. Villages also make distinctions between men whose status allows them to spend their days in leisurely travel and others whose tours are a reckless 'waste of expenses' (*fuzul kharj*); these distinctions about the appropriateness of travel are often made on the basis of a person's status and genealogy.

59. Joshua White, *Pakistan's Islamist Frontier*.

60. *See* J. Pouchepadass, 'Itinerant Kings and Touring Officials: Circulation a Modality of Power in India, 1700–1947' in C. Markovits, J. Pouchepadass and S. Subrahmanyam (eds), *Society and Circulation*; A. Sauli, 'Circulation and Authority: Police, Public Space and Territorial Control in the Punjab, 1861–1920' in C. Markovits, J. Pouchepadass and S. Subrahmanyam (eds), *Society and Circulation*.

61. *See for example* Ghulam Mirza Murtaza, *New History of Chitral Based on the Original Persian Text of Mirza Muhammad Ghufran*.

62. On Kalasha society, *see* Peter Parkes, 'Alternative Social Structures Foster Relations in the Hindu Kush: Milk Kinship Allegiance in Frontier Mountain Kingdoms of Northern Pakistan', *Comparative Studies in Society and History*, 43, January 2001.

63. Unsurprisingly, many Kalasha people complain about the intrusive curiosity of Chitralis who are accused of disturbing the peace of life in their remote valleys, staring at their unveiled women and pestering them to sell bottles of 'grape water' made for important ceremonial gatherings.

64. M. Candea, 'Arbitrary Locations: in Defence of the Bounded Field-site', *Journal of the Royal Anthropological Institute*, 13, 2007, p. 25.

65. Claude Markovits, 'Introduction' in C. Markovits, J. Pouchepadass and S. Subrahmanyam (eds), *Society and Circulation*, p. 20.

66. Martin Sökefeld, 'Debating Self, Identity, and Culture in Anthropology', *Current Anthropology*, 40, 1999.

67. Peter G. Mandaville, *Transnational Muslim Politics: Reimagining the Umma*, London, Routledge, 2001, p. 186, 79.

68. Veena Das, *Life and Words: Violence and the Descent into the Ordinary*, Berkeley: University of California Press, 2007, p. 158.

69. Georgi M. Derluguian, *Bourdieu's Secret Admirer in the Caucasus: a World-system Biography*, Chicago: University of Chicago Press, 2005.

70. Deeb, *An Enchanted Modern: Gender and Public Piety in Shi'i Lebanon*; Henkel, 'The Location of Islam'; Hirschkind, *The Ethical Soundscape*; Mahmood, 'Part III—Individual, Family, Community, and State—Ethical Formation and Politics of Individual Autonomy in Contemporary Egypt'.

71. Oskar Verkaaik, *Migrants and Militants: Fun and Urban Violence in Pakistan*, Princeton: Princeton University Press, 2004, pp. 6–7.

72. *See especially* Martha Mundy, *Domestic Government: Kinship, Community and Polity in North Yemen*, London: I.B. Tauris, 1995.

6. MUSLIM COSMOPOLITANS?: TRANSNATIONAL VILLAGE LIFE ON THE FRONTIERS OF SOUTH AND CENTRAL ASIA

1. *See for instance* Olivier Roy, *Globalized Islam: the Search for a New Ummah*, London: C. Hurst and Co., 2004; Gilles Kepel, *Jihad: the Trail of Political Islam*, Cambridge, Mass.: Harvard University Press, 2002.

2. This trip has been supplemented by further visits to Badakhshan in the summers of 2007, 2009 and 2010. One joint trip was also made with Hopkins in February 2007.

3. Vinay Gidwani and K. Sivaramakrishnan, 'Circular Migration and Rural Cosmpolitanism in India', *Contributions to Indian Sociology*, 37, 2003, pp. 339–67.

4. W. van Schendel, 'Geographies of Knowing, Geographies of Ignorance: Jumping Scale in Southeast Asia', *Environment and Planning D: Society & Space.*, 20, 2002, p. 647.

The legacies of the Cold War are as important in considering the region's present as are their colonial antecedents. *See generally* Heonoik Kwon, *The Other Cold War*, New York: Columbia University Press, 2010.

5. Ibid.

6. Yael Navaro-Yashin, *Faces of the State: Secularism and Public Life in Turkey*, Princeton: Princeton University Press, 2002, p. 74.

7. Roy, *Globalized Islam*.

8. Anthropological studies of transnational life in a range of culturally fractured border zones often deploy their ethnographic findings in order to question the 'naturalness' of the nation as a category of analyses. Akhil Gupta, 'The Song of the Non-AlignedWorld: Trans-National Identities and the Reinscription of Space in Late Capitalism', *Cultural Anthropology* 7 (1), 1992, pp. 63–79. Willem van Schendel, 'Stateless in South Asia: The Making of the India-Bangladesh Enclaves', *Journal of Asian Studies*, 61, 2002.

9. I build on Mathijs Pelkmans' call in his study of the Turkey-Ajaria border for the need to 'move beyond the discussion of whether borders are best defined in terms of fluidity or rigidity and examine how these aspects are ultimately interconnected'. Mathijs Pelkmans, *Defending the Border: Identity, Religion, and Modernity in the Republic of Georgia*, Ithaca, NY: Cornell University Press, 2006, p. 13. Other excellent studies of people's experiences of borders and the theoretical insights these offer into the study of the state and the paradoxes of globalization include M. Reeves, 'Unstable Objects: Corpses, Checkpoints and "Chessboard Borders" in the Ferghana Valley', *Anthropology of East Europe Review*, 25 (1), 2007, pp. 72–84.

10. Akhil Gupta, 'The Song of the Non-aligned World'. *See also* Susan Bayly, 'Vietnamese Intellectuals in Revolutionary and Postcolonial Times', *Critique of Anthropology*, 24, 2004; Susan Bayly, 'Imagining 'Greater India': French and Indian Visions of Colonialism in the Indic Mode', *Modern Asian Studies*, 38, 2004; Engseng Ho, 'Names beyond Nations: The Making of Local Cosmopolitans', *Etudes Rurales*, 2002.

11. Anna Lowenhaupt Tsing, 'Conclusion: The Global Situation' in J.X. Inda and R. Rosaldo (eds), *The Anthropology of Globalization: a Reader*, Oxford: Blackwell Publishers, 2002, p. 469.

12. C. Humphrey, M. Marsden and V. Skirvskaja. 'Cosmopolitanism and the City: Interaction and Coexistence in Bukhara', in S. Mayaram (ed), *The Other Global City*, New York: Routledge, 2008, pp. 202–32; A. Appadurai, *Modernity at Large: Cultural Dimensions of Globalization*. Compare James Ferguson, *Expectations of Modernity: Myths and Meanings of Urban Life on the Zambian Copperbelt*, Berkeley: University of California Press, 1999; Hannerz, *Transnational Connections: Culture, People, Places*. *See also* Veena Das and Deborah Poole, *Anthropology in the Margins of the State*, Santa Fe, NM: School of American Research Press, 2004; Gidwani and Sivaramakrishnan, 'Circular Migration and the Spaces of

Cultural Assertion'; Gupta, 'The Song of the Non-aligned World'; Anna Lowenhaupt Tsing, *Friction: an Ethnography of Global Connection*, Princeton: Princeton University Press, 2005; van Schendel, 'Stateless in South Asia'; Hastings Donnan and Thomas M. Wilson, *Borders: Frontiers of Identity, Nation and State*, Oxford: Berg, 1999; Pnina Werbner, 'Global Pathways: Working Class Cosmopolitans and the Creation of Transnational Ethnic Worlds', *Social Anthropology*, 7, 1999.

13. Gidwani and Sivaramakrishnan, 'Circular Migration and the Spaces of Cultural Assertion'.

14. F. Osella and Caroline Osella, '"I am Gulf": The Production of Cosmopolitanism in Kozhikode, Kerala, India' in K. Kresse and E. Simpson (eds), *Struggling with History*.

15. E. Simpson and K. Kresse, 'Introduction' in K. Kresse and E. Simpson (eds), *Struggling with History*, pp. 14.

16. Ho, *The Graves of Tarim*, p. 68. See also Sheldon I. Pollock, 'Forms of Knowledge in Early Modern South Asia: Introduction', *Comparative Studies of South Asia, Africa and the Middle East*, 24, 2004, pp. 19–20.

17. David Gilmartin, 'A Networked Civilization', in B. Lawrence and M. Cooke, *Muslim Networks:from Hajj to Hip Hop*, Chapel Hill: University of North Carolina Press, 2003, pp. 51–68. *Compare* John R. Bowen, 'What is "Universal" and "Local" in Islam?', *Ethos*, 26, 1998, p. 7. For comparative studies of other transregional spaces that cut across more conventional representations of cultural 'areas', *see* Bruce Grant, 'The Good Russian Prisoner: Naturalizing Violence in the Caucasus Mountains', *Cultural Anthropology*, 20, 2005; Ho, *The Graves of Tarim*; Engseng Ho, 'Empire through Diasporic Eyes: A View from the Other Boat', *Comparative Studies in Society and History*, 46, 2004; Ho, 'Names beyond Nations: The Making of Local Cosmopolitans'; Seteney Khalid Shami, 'Prehistories of Globalization: Circassian Identity in Motion', *Public Culture*, 12, 2000; Edward Simpson, *Muslim Society and the Western Indian Ocean: the Seafarers of Kachchh*, New York: Routledge, 2006; van Schendel, 'Geographies of Knowing, Geographies of Ignorance'. For considerations of transregional Muslim identities in West Africa, *see* Benjamin F. Soares and René Otayek, *Islam and Muslim Politics in Africa*, New York: Palgrave Macmillan, 2007; Robert Launay, *Beyond the Stream: Islam and Society in a West African Town*, Berkeley: University of California Press, 1992.

18. Pnina Werbner, *Pilgrims of Love*; Werbner, 'Global Pathways'.

19. Mandaville, *Transnational Muslim Politics*; Barbara D. Metcalf, 'Nationalism, Modernity, and Muslim Identity in India before 1947' in P.v.d. Veer and H. Lehmann (eds), *Nation and Religion: Perspectives on Europe and Asia*, Princeton: Princeton University Press, 1999.

20. Ho, *The Graves of Tarim*.

21. Judith Scheele 'Shurafâ' as Cosmopolitans: Islam, Genealogy and Hierarchy in the Central Sahara', paper presented at conference 'Thirty Years of the Anthropology of Islam: Retrospect and Prospect', London, 1 July 2009.

22. Brian J. Didier and Edward Simpson, 'Islam along the South Asian Littoral', *International Institute for the Study of Islam in the Modern World Review*, 16, 2005, p. 43.

23. By focusing on an expansive mountain range that cross-cuts nation-states, is connected by networks of overland trade routes, and is made up of doctrinally and linguistically diverse valley communities, I aim to show that mountain as well as coastal regions afford complex opportunities for the instantiation of forms of sociality that are highly attuned to the negotiation of religious plurality.

24. On camp-based refugees in Pakistan, *see* M. Nazif Shahrani, 'Afghanistan's Muhajirin (Muslim "Refugee-Warriors"): Politics of Mistrust and Distrust of Politics' in E.V. Daniel and J.C. Knudsen (eds), *Mistrusting Refugees*, Berkeley: University of California Press, 1995; *cf.* Michael Hutt, *Unbecoming Citizens: Culture, Nationhood, and the Flight of Refugees from Bhutan*, New Delhi: Oxford University Press, 2003, on Bhutan's refugee community in Nepal. For a notable exception, *see* David B. Edwards, 'Afghanistan, Ethnography, and the New World Order', *Cultural Anthropology*, 9, 1994; David B. Edwards, 'Frontiers, Boundaries and Frames: The Marginal Identity of Afghan Refugees' in A. Ahmed (eds), *Pakistan: The Social Science Perspective*, Karachi: Oxford University Press, 1990. My work differs from Edwards' work on Pakistan-based Afghan refugees in Pakistan in that I focus on the interactions between Afghan refugees and Pakistani Muslims in a local setting.

25. There is an expanding body of literature by development-focused researchers based in Afghanistan. Mohammad Jalal Abbasi-Shavazi *et al.*, *Continued Protection, Sustainable Reintegration: Afghan Refugees and Migrants in Iran*, Kabul: Afghanistan Research and Evaluation Unit, 2006; Research Afghanistan and Unit Evaluation, *Afghans in Pakistan: Broadening the Focus*, Kabul: Afghanistan Research and Evaluation Unit, 2006; Research Afghanistan and Unit Evaluation, *Afghans in Peshawar: Migration, Settlements, and Social Networks*, Kabul: Afghanistan Research and Evaluation Unit, 2006; Gulbadan Habibi *et al.*, *Afghan Returnees from NWFP, Pakistan, to Nangarhar Province*, Kabul: Afghanistan Research and Evaluation Unit, 2006; Elca Stigter and Afghanistan Research and Evaluation Unit, *Transnational Networks and Migration from Herat to Iran*, Kabul: Afghanistan Research and Evaluation Unit, 2005. There have also been more analytical treatments of the problems associated with the 'repatriation' of Afghan refugees to the country today. David Turton and Peter Richard Valentine Marsden, *Taking Refugees for a Ride?: the Politics of Refugee Return to Afghanistan*, Kabul: Afghanistan Research and Evaluation Unit (AREU), 2002; Monsutti *Afghan Transnational Networks: Looking beyond Repatriation.*, 2006. The focus of these studies, however, is concerned more with the livelihood strategies of refugees than with the implications that such forms of mobility have for understanding the interconnected cultural and religious dynamics of life in Afghanistan and neighbouring countries today.

26. Kepel, *Jihad*; Roy, *Globalized Islam*; Olivier Roy, *The Failure of Political Islam*, Cambridge, Mass.: Harvard University Press, 1994; Mariam Abou Zahab and Olivier Roy, *Islamist Networks: the Afghan-Pakistan Connection*, New York: Columbia University Press, 2004.

27. See Hopkins, *The Making of Modern Afghanistan*; Hanifi, *Connecting Histories in Afghanistan*.

28. I last heard of Sulton in a village in southern Tajikistan where a man told me that whilst living as a refugee in Chitral he had known Sulton. This man said he was now sure that Sulton would never return to Tajikistan because he would be arrested by the security services, and, indeed, he imagined him being pursued in the future by Interpol. The conversation underscored the degree to which local actors conceptualize their world both in relationship to global and national policing organizations.

29. Ho, *The Graves of Tarim*, p. 314.

30. A notable exception is Hermann Kreutzmann's sophisticated exploration of the changing economic and political fortunes of the region's high mountain farmers and pastoralists. Hermann Kreutzmann, 'Ethnic Minorities and Marginality in the Pamirian Knot: Survival of Wakhi and Kirghiz in a Harsh Environment and Global Contexts', *The Geographical Journal*, 169, Sep. 2003.

31. Cole, 'Iranian Culture and South Asia, 1500–1900', pp. 15–35; Farina Mir, 'Genre and Devotion in Punjabi Popular Narratives: Rethinking Cultural and Religious Syncretism', *Comparative Studies in Society and History*, 48, 2006.

32. Muzaffar Alam, *The Languages of Political Islam: India, 1200–1800*, Chicago: University of Chicago Press, 2004; Alam and Subrahmanyam, 'The Making of a Munshi'.

33. These mountain kingdoms also existed on the frontiers of the Mughal Empire, and, like other dry zones in Iran, Afghanistan, and Central Asia have long been intimately connected with the history of India. See Gommans, *Mughal Warfare: Indian Frontiers and High Roads to Empire, 1500–1700*. For an overview of Chitral's historiography, see Wolfgang Holzwarth, 'Chitral History, 1540–1660: Comments on Sources and Historiography' in E.L. Bashir, and Israruddin (eds), *Proceedings of the Second International Hindukush Cultural Conference*, Karachi: Oxford University Press, 1996.

34. Seymour Becker, *Russia's Protectorates in Central Asia: Bukhara and Khiva, 1865–1924*, Cambridge, Mass.: Harvard University Press, 1968. See also M. Kossiakof and E. Delmar Morgan, 'Notes on a Journey in Kareteghin and Darwaz in 1882', *Proceedings of the Royal Geographical Society and the Monthly Record of Geography*, 8 (1), 1886, pp. 32–7.

35. Christine Noelle, *State and Tribe in Nineteenth Century Afghanistan: the Reign of Amir Dost Muhammad Khan, 1826–1863*, London: Curzon, 1997.

36. John Biddulph, *Tribes of the Hindu Kush*, Lahore: Ali Kamran, 1972; IUCN Pakistan, *Chitral: A Study in Statecraft, 1320–1969*, IUCN Pakistan, 2004.

37. Parkes, 'Alternative Social Structures Foster Relations in the Hindu Kush'. The realm as a whole may be compared to Stanley J. Tambiah's model of Southeast Asian 'galactic polities': Stanley Jeyaraja Tambiah, *World Conqueror and World Renouncer: a Study of Buddhism and Polity in Thailand against a Historical Background*, Cambridge: Cambridge University Press, 1976. Court histories of Chitral document the criss-crossing migration of men and their families descended from the ruling families of neighbouring states, especially Badakhshan. Murtaza, *New History of Chitral Based on the Original Persian Text of Mirza Muhammad Ghufran*, p. 302. *See also* Kreutzmann, 'Ethnic Minorities and Marginality in the Pamirian Knot', p. 220.

38. Murtaza, *New History of Chitral Based on the Original Persian Text of Mirza Muhammad Ghufran*, p. 319.

39. The Norwegian linguist Georg Morgenstierne said that he had met a man from Yamg, an predominantly Isma'ili village that is now a part of Tajikistan, in the Chitral bazaar in 1929, pointing towards interactions between Chitralis and Pamiri Isma'ilis. Georg Morgenstierne, *Report on a Linguistic Mission to North-western India*, Oslo, Cambridge, Mass.: H. Aschehoug & Co., Harvard: Harvard University Press, 1932, p. 68.

40. Nazif M. Shahrani and N. Shahrani, *The Kirghiz and Wakhi of Afghanistan: Adaptation to Closed Frontiers*, Seattle: University of Washington Press, 1979, p. 41.

41. John Staley, *Words for my Brother: Travels between the Hindu Kush and the Himalayas*, Karachi: Oxford University Press, 1982.

42. B.D. Hopkins, 'Race, Sex and Slavery: "Forced Labour" in Central Asia and Afghanistan in the Early Nineteenth Century', *Modern Asian Studies*, 42, 2007.

43. Daud Ali, *Courtly Culture and Political Life in Early Medieval India*, Cambridge: Cambridge University Press, 2004, p. 3; Peter Parkes, 'Unwrapping Rudeness: Inverted Etiquette in an Egalitarian Enclave', *An Anthropology of Indirect Communication*, 2001; Staley, *Words for my Brother*, pp. 153–4.

44. Cole, 'Iranian Culture and South Asia, 1500–1900', p. 31.

45. A. Pandian and D. Ali, 'Introduction', in A. Pandian and D. Ali (eds), *Ethical Life in South Asia*, Bloomington: Indiana University Press, 2010, p. 12. *See also for example* Bayly, *Origins of Nationality in South Asia*; Dirks, *Castes of Mind*.

46. Christophe Jaffrelot, *Pakistan: Nationalism without a Nation?*, New Delhi: Manohar, 2002.

47. Chitralis are conscious of the differences between the types of Farsi spoken in Afghanistan, Tajikistan, and Iran and are also aware of the national linguistic categories 'Dari' and 'Tajiki'. On the whole, however, they say that they are able to speak and read 'Farsi'; this is why I refer to Persian, Farsi, Tajiki, and Dari interchangeably throughout this and other chapters of this book. On the complexities of the scholarly usage of the terms

'Persian', 'Farsi', 'Dari' and 'Tajik', *see* Brian Spooner, 'Are we Teaching Persian? Or Farsi? Or Dari? Or Tojiki?' in M. Marashi and M.A. Jazayery (eds), *Persian Studies in North America: Studies in Honor of Mohammad Ali Jazayery*, Bethesda, MD.: Iranbooks, 1994.

48. Seyyed Vali Reza Nasr, 'National Identities and the India Pakistan Conflict' in T.V. Paul (ed), *The India-Pakistan Conflict: an Enduring Rivalry*, New York: Cambridge University Press, 2005.

49. Marsden, *Living Islam*, Chapter 5.

50. *See* Calvin R. Rensch *et al.*, *Sociolinguistic Survey of Northern Pakistan*, Islamabad: National Institute of Pakistan Studies, Summer Institute of Linguistics, 1992; Morgenstierne, *Report on a Linguistic Mission to North-western India*; Staley, *Words for my Brother*.

51. Daftary, *The Ismailis*. Shi'a Isma'ilis came into being as a result of a schism over succession to the imamate in 1094, and Isma'ilis differentiate themselves from *Ithna 'ashariyya* Shi'a Muslims. There have also been a number of doctrinal splits during the course of Isma'ili history. Farhad Daftary, *A Short History of the Ismailis: Traditions of a Muslim Community*, Edinburgh: Edinburgh University Press, 1998, p. 2.

The Nizari Isma'ilis are the largest Isma'ili doctrinal cluster. The other Isma'ili community in South Asia is the Tayyibi Isma'ilis, known as the Bohras. *See* Asgharali Engineer, *The Muslim Communities of Gujarat: an Exploratory Study of Bohras, Khojas, and Memons*, Delhi: Ajanta Publications, 1989; Jonah Blank, *Mullahs on the Modernity among the Daudi Bohras*, Chicago: University of Chicago Press, 2001.

Isma'ilis in Chitral and, indeed, northern Pakistan, are all Nizari Isma'ilis. In Chitral, Shi'a Isma'ilis contrast their modes of theological understanding and experience with those of the region's Sunnis. At one level, what distinguishes them from Chitral Sunnis is that they are taught to believe that the Aga Khan or 'Present Imam' is the center of Shi'a Isma'ili belief and cosmology, imbued with a special form of spiritual insight and power, and considered to be able to interpret the Qur'an in a way that is impossible for ordinary Muslims. At the same time, they also emphasize the ways in which the Shi'a Isma'ili tradition of Islam focuses particularly on the need to understand the inner (*batin*) meanings of the Qur'an. Isma'ili Qur'anic interpretation (*tafsir*) emphasizes the importance of esoteric hermeneutics (*ta'wil*) in which the surface words of the Qur'an are understood as having a deeper meaning than the doctrines they elicit. In contrast, the region's Sunnis are often said to be above all concerned with 'surface level' (*tanzil*) forms of Quranic interpretation (*tafsir*). The historiography of Shi'a Ismai'li forms of knowledge, identity, and devotion in Chitral remains contested, although some authors suggest Ismai'li forms of thought and identity may have been important in the region from the early seventeenth century. W. Holzwarth, 'Chitral History, 1540–1660, pp. 116–34.

52. *See* Marsden, *Living Islam*.

53. *See* Hafizullah Emadi, 'Minority Group Politics: the Role of Ismailis in Afghanistan's Politics', *Central Asian Survey*, 12, 1993; Hafizullah Emadi, 'The End of Taqiyya: Reaffirming the Religious Identity of Ismailis in Shughnan, Badakhshan—Political Implications for Afghanistan', *Middle Eastern Studies*, 34, 1998.

54. On the Afghan Badakhshan's *mujahidin* and their role in the anti-Soviet resistance movement, *see* M. Nazif Shahrani, 'Causes and Contexts of Responses to the Saur Revolution in Badakhshan' in M.N. Shahrani and R. Canfield (eds), *Revolutions and Rebellions in Afghanistan: Anthropological Perspectives*, Berkeley: University of California Press, 1984.

55. Marsden, *Living Islam*.

56. The influences of transnational forces on Isma'ili ways of being Muslim in Chitral today are complex and often have a more apparently 'global' dimension. The Aga Khan is a UK citizen based in Paris, while the offices of the Aga Khan Foundation (a major international nongovernmental organization) are located in Geneva. Both of these places form an important part of the religious and geographical horizons of the region's Isma'ili Muslims. The Aga Khan makes relatively frequent visits to Chitral (most recently in December 2003) and other regions of Pakistan, Tajikistan and Afghanistan with significant Isma'ili populations. During the Aga Khan's visit in December 2003, for example, the family of Chitrali Isma'ili s with whom I stay hosted Isma'ili guests from Tajikistan, Afghanistan and Iran.

57. The religious offices of the Aga Khan, in particular, have sought to 'reform', according to global Isma'ili standards, the practice of funerary rituals in Tajikistan's Badakhshan Province. These reforms have excited debate and opposition amongst Isma'ili s from within the region, and also amongst religious scholars from Badakhshan working in Isma'ili offices elsewhere.

58. Seyyed Vali Reza Nasr, *The Shia Revival: how Conflicts within Islam will Shape the Future*, New York: Norton, 2006.

59. *See* F. Devji, 'Preface', in Marc Van Grondelle, *The Ismailis in the Colonial Era: Modernity, Empire and Islam, 1839–1969*, London: Hurst and Co., 2009. Isma'ilis in Badakhshan and Chitral, however, explain these differences that divide them from their Khoja brethren as being a product of their affiliation to an Isma'ili spiritual tradition said to be a legacy of the preaching activities of the eleventh-century mystical poet Nasir-e Khusraw. Alice C. Hunsberger, *Nasir Khusraw, the Ruby of Badakhshan: a Portrait of the Persian Poet, Traveller and Philosopher*, London: I.B. Tauris, 2000. A complex funeral ritual, the *chiragh-e roshan*, widely said by Isma'ilis throughout the region to be a direct legacy of the preaching activities of Nasir-e Khusraw, is one especially important diacritical mark deployed by the region's mountain Isma'ilis to define themselves in relation to their co-religionists in different settings within and beyond South Asia. *Compare* John R. Bowen for the ways in which Muslims in Sumatra distinguish themselves on the basis of distinctions they make between different modes

of performing Islamic daily prayers. John R. Bowen, 'Salat in Indonesia: The Social Meanings of an Islamic Ritual', *Man*, 24, 1989.
60. E. Simpson and K. Kresse, 'Introduction', in *Struggling with History*, p. 26.
61. For detailed accounts of Tajikistan's civil war, *see especially* Shirin Akiner, *Tajikistan: Disintegration or Reconciliation*, London: Royal Institute of International Affairs, 2002; Adeeb Khalid, *Islam after Communism: Religion and Politics in Central Asia*, Berkeley: University of California Press, 2007, pp. 148–53; Mohammad Reza Djalili *et al.*, *Tajikistan: the Trials of Independence*, New York: St. Martin's Press, 1997. For a recent study of the textual expressions of the Isma'ili Islamic tradition in the Pamirs during the late nineteenth century, *see* Abdulmamad Iloliev, *The Isma'ili-Sufi sage of Pamir: Mubarak-i Wakhani and the Esoteric Tradition of the Pamiri Muslims*, Youngstown, NY: Cambria Press, 2007.
62. Bryna Goodman, 'Improvisations on a Semicolonial Theme, or, How to Read a Celebration of Transnational Urban Community', *Journal of Asian Studies*, 59, 2000; Shu-Mei Shih, 'Gender, Race, and Semicolonialism: Liu Na'ou's Urban Shanghai Landscape', *Journal of Asian Studies*, 55, 1996.
63. The villages and small towns of the Badakhshan Province did not see major fighting, yet they were subjected to a blockade by Tajik government forces. Pamiris (the term widely used to refer to Isma'ilis living in Badakhshan) were involved in the civil war. Some Pamiris fought and became commanders for the opposition Islamic Movement for Tajikistan against pro-government forces. Mariam Abou Zahab and Olivier Roy, *Islamist Networks*. As a result, Pamiris living in Dushanbe were the targets of widespread violent attacks. Consequently, many Dushanbe-based Pamiris sought to escape to their ancestral villages in the Pamirs during the war. Yet the people of Badakhshan, a region that had hitherto largely depended on Soviet subsidies, were starving as a result of the government blockade of traffic to the region, including humanitarian aid convoys. It was during these years that hundreds of ethnic Pamiris from post-Soviet Tajikistan migrated as seasonal labourers and refugees to the villages of Chitral and Pakistan's major cities, especially Karachi, which is also home to a wealthy and vibrant Isma'ili community.
64. These modern-day forms of 'barter' thus invoked older memories of transregional trade in the era before the hardening of the colonial boundaries. See M. Nazif Shahrani, *The Kirghiz and Wakhi of Afghanistan*.
65. During the same period, many Afghans from Badakhshan and elsewhere in the north of the country also moved to Tajikistan. Some of these men, as we shall explore in the book's final chapter, were *mujahidin* commanders. Most, however, were one-time state officials from the pro-Soviet government of the 1980s, who made their living as traders and merchants in Dushanbe, Khorog and Khujand.
66. The next chapter considers the lived experience of heightened border control on the Afghanistan-Tajikistan frontier. Scholars have recognized how

international perceptions of the risk of weapon smuggling that outweigh the empirical threat of such smuggling to the political stability of Central Asian countries contribute to stances regarding the apparent need to strength the region's borders. See, for example, S. Neil MacFarlane and S. Torjesen, 'Awash with Weapons?': the Case of Small Arms in Kyrgyzstan', *Central Asian Survey*, 24 (1), 2005, pp. 5–19. Both the Afghanistan-Pakistan and Afghanistan-Tajikistan borders have, for obvious reasons, been an especially powerful breeding ground for such discourses of risk and danger.

67. These included the closure of established refugee camps in Pakistan, the relocation of Afghan refugees living in urban settings such as Peshawar to more remote and rural locations elsewhere in the frontier, and the offering of financial incentives by the UNHCR designed to encourage the return of Afghans to Afghanistan. *See for example* Turton and Marsden, *Taking Refugees for a Ride?*, p. 3.

68. Most 'Chitrali Afghans', as they often refer to themselves, have now returned to their country; the nature of their experiences of return is the focus of the next chapter. Chitrali development professionals working in Afghanistan also talk of the affectionate friendships they have built with Khowar-speaking Afghan men whom they knew as refugees in Chitral.

69. Villagers also joked with me that whilst they had once been compelled to take their livestock for sale at cheap prices in Chitral, now villagers from Chitral brought their livestock for sale in the Wakhan, where the price of meat was higher than in Pakistan.

70. Such arguments were contested in a meeting I attended involving Soviet-trained Afghan security officials, the former *mujahid* Governor of Badakhshan, and local politicians who had also worked for the Aga Khan Foundation. The security officials argued that Afghanistan's future depended on its people thinking and acting nationally and internationally, rather than in narrow, sectarian and local ways. They argued that Ahmed Shah Massoud, once their enemy, had both defeated the Soviet occupation of Afghanistan and liberated Central Asia's Muslims, yet now Afghans just acted in relation to 'districts'. Thus, interestingly, Soviet-derived forms of internationalism and 'global' expressions of Sunni Islam not only exist side by side but also compete to encompass one another. This adds another ideological dimension to this book's attempts to understand the ways in which the Frontier's fragments simultaneously come together yet are also pulled apart.

71. Magnus Marsden, *Opportunities and Constraints in Central and South Asian Trade Flows: Perspectives from Afghan Traders in Tajikistan*. Project Report, Norwegian Institute of International Affairs, 2010.

72. Peter Parkes, 'Enclaved Knowledge: Indigent and Indignant Representations of Environmental Management and Development among the Kalasha of Pakistan' in R.F. Ellen, P. Parkes and A. Bicker (eds), *Indigenous Environmental Knowledge and its Transformations: Critical Anthropological Perspectives*, Amsterdam: Harwood Academic, 2000.

73. The role played by the Aga Khan Foundation in cultivating a transcultural world is particularly important. Many of the Chitralis currently employed in development posts in Afghanistan are employed by the Aga Khan Foundation. At the same time, I have met women from Tajikistan's Badakhshan region who have been sponsored by the Aga Khan Foundation to undergo courses in health and education training in Chitral. Constraints of space prevent a detailed exploration of the institutional dimensions of transregional space-making here.

74. Devji, *The Terrorist in Search of Humanity*, pp. 118–19.

75. Liisa H. Malkki, *Purity and Exile: Violence, Memory, and National Cosmology among Hutu Refugees in Tanzania*, Chicago: University of Chicago Press, 1995.

76. Aihwa Ong, *Buddha is Hiding: Refugees, Citizenship, the New America*, Berkeley: University of California Press, 2003, pp. 78–9. The problems with conceptualizing refugee movements without considering their relationship to older forms of migration and mobility have also been challenged by refugee specialists working on Afghan refugees in Pakistan, *see* Kerry M. Connor, 'Factors in the Residential Choices of Self-Settled Afghan Refugees in Peshawar, Pakistan', *International Migration Review*, 23, 1989.

77. Tsing, *Friction*.

78. Victor de Munck, 'Sakhina: A Study of Female Masculinity in a Sri Lankan Muslim Community', *South Asia Research*, 25, 2005; Peggy Froerer, 'Emphasizing "Others": the Emergence of Hindu Nationalism in a Central Indian Tribal Community', *The Journal of the Royal Anthropological Institute*, 12, 2006.

79. Depictions of Pukhtuns as child kidnappers are of particular historical significance in South Asia, especially in urban settings such as Bombay, where 'Pathans' also have a reputation for being especially brutal moneylenders and strikebreakers. *See* Rajnarayan Chandavarkar, *Imperial Power and Popular Politics Class, Resistance and the State in India, c. 1850–1950*, Cambridge: Cambridge University Press, 1998; Neeladri Bhattacharya, 'Predicaments of Mobility: Peddlers and Itinerants in Nineteenth-century Northwestern India' in C. Markovits, J. Pouchepadass and S. Subrahmanyam (eds), *Society and Circulation*. On the complexity of this category in Afghanistan, see Tapper, 'Who are the Kuchi: Nomad Self-identities in Afghanistan', *Journal of the Royal Anthropological Institute* 14 (1), 2007, pp. 97–116. On the specific role played by the Kuchi in trading between Peshawar and Kabul in the late nineteenth century, and thus their role in the 'making of Kabul', *see* Hanifi, *Connecting Histories in Afghanistan*. Some of the petty traders in Rowshan bazaar identified themselves as being Sheikh Mohamadi, *see* A. Olesen, 'Peddling in Afghanistan: Adaptive Strategies of the Sheikh Mohamadi' in A Rao (ed), *The other Nomad: Peripatetic Minorities in Cross-cultural Context*. Cologne: Boehlau Verlag, 1985, pp. 35–64.

80. Kreutzmann, 'Ethnic Minorities and Marginality in the Pamirian Knot', pp. 220–21. About 50,000 Wakhi-speaking peoples live on both sides of the Afghanistan-Tajikistan border along the Wakhan corridor, in Pakistan's northern areas (especially the upper zones of the Ishkoman and Hunza valleys), in northern Chitrali villages, and in the town of Tashkurgan in China's Xinjiang region. On the Wakhan, *see* Shahrani, *The Kirghiz and Wakhi of Afghanistan: Adaptation to Closed Frontiers.* For an account of life in a Wakhi community in northern Pakistan, *see* Sabine Felmy, *The Voice of the Nightingale: a Personal Account of the Wakhi Culture in Hunza*, Karachi, New York: Oxford University Press, 1996.

81. For a comparative study of the importance of tropes concerning the differences between city folk and upcountry hicks in Afghan storytelling, *see* Margaret Ann Mills, *Rhetorics and Politics in Afghan Traditional Storytelling*, Philadelphia: University of Pennsylvania Press, 1991.

82. There is also a convergence of both older traditions of Persianate miniature painting that were historically important in Tajikistan's Badakhshan region and newer forms of Soviet-inspired 'Tajik' national art forms. *See* Iloliev, *The Isma'ili-Sufi Sage of Pamir.*

83. It is important to note as well that such extranational forms of identity imaginings have thrived in a broader national setting in which the Pakistan 'state' has consistently sought to homogenize national identity along both ethnic and religious lines. *See* Jaffrelot, *Pakistan*, 2002.

84. Chandavarkar, *Imperial Power and Popular Politics.*

85. Michael Herzfeld, *Cultural Intimacy: Social Poetics in the Nation-state*, New York: Routledge, 1997, pp. 47–8.

86. Ong, *Buddha is Hiding.*

87. Ibid., p. 79.

88. Navaro-Yashin, *Faces of the State.*

89. The Pakistan-Afghanistan border (known as the Durand Line) was established in 1893, while the Wakhan corridor (intended as a buffer zone between Russia and British India) was mapped in 1895. For an account of the mapping of these borders, *see* Algernon George Arnold Durand, *The Making of a Frontier: Five Years Experiences and Adventures in Gilgit, Hunza, Nagar, Chitral and the Eastern Hindu Kush*, Karachi: Oxford University Press, 2001.

90. Shami, 'Prehistories of Globalization', p. 189.

91. *Cf.* R.C.F. Schomberg, *Between the Oxus and the Indus*, London: M. Hopkinson Ltd, 1935, p. 268; Shahrani, *The Kirghiz and Wakhi of Afghanistan.* The Norwegian linguistic scholar Georg Morgenstierne also documented the continuing influx of Wakhiks into Chitral during his first visit to the region in 1929. *See* Morgenstierne, *Report on a Linguistic Mission to North-western India*, p. 68.

Wakhi-speaking people I met in Tajikistan also told me that families from their villages had fled to Chitral on their region's incorporation into the Soviet Union. Douglas Northrop also highlights the importance of movements of people, things, and ideas across the Soviet-Afghanistan border in the early years of the Soviet Union. Douglas Taylor Northrop, *Veiled Empire: Gender & Power in Stalinist Central Asia*, Ithaca, NY: Cornell University Press, 2004.

92. The colonial state may have played an active role in persuading the rulers of Chitral and other princely states in modern-day northern Pakistan to gift land to Afghans who emigrated from their home regions after both the third Afghan war and the expansion of Soviet Union into southern Tajikistan. This chapter's focus on the present-day modes of understandings deployed by Chitralis to think about their transregional pasts prevents a more detailed exploration of this issue. Ghulam Murtaza also documents Chitral's Mehtar, between 1856 and 1892, granting Isma'ili Seyyids from Badakhshan 'asylum' and property following an 'onslaught' by Amir Abdur Rahman Khan. Murtaza, *New History of Chitral based on the Original Persian Text of Mirza Muhammad Ghufran*, p. 223.

93. For studies of the complex, changing and dynamic ways in which premodern Persianate influences have shaped modern Iran, *see* Afsaneh Najmabadi, 'SPECIAL SECTION—Reorienting Sexuality: Reflections on the Study of Sexuality in the Middle East and North Africa—Mapping Transformations of Sex, Gender, and Sexuality in Modern Iran', *Social Analysis.*, 49, 2005; Babayan, *Mystics, Monarchs and Messiahs: Cultural Landscapes in Early Modern Iran.*

94. Alam and Subrahmanyam, 'The Making of a Munshi'.

95. On travel and mobility in the Muslim world, *see* Eickelman and Piscatori, *Muslim Travellers.*

96. Ho, *The Graves of Tarim*, p. 115.

97. Ibid.

98. Ibid., p. 198.

99. Ossman, Susan, 'Introduction', in S. Ossman (ed), *Places We Share: Migration, Subjectivity, and Global Mobility*. Lanham, MD: Lexington Books, 2007, p. 8.

7. GEOGRAPHIES OF PROFIT AND SECURITY: 'RETURN' TO AFGHANISTAN AND BEYOND

1. M. Rieker and K. Ali, 'Introduction', in M. Rieker and K. Ali, *Comparing Cities: the Middle East and South Asia*: Karachi: Oxford University Press, 2009, pp. xvi-xvii.

2. On the interplay of ethnic diversity across the Frontier's national boundaries, *see especially* Fariba Adelkhah and Zuzanna Olszewska, 'The Iranian Afghans', *Iranian Studies*, 40, 2007; Monsutti, *War and Migration*; Kreutzmann, 'Ethnic Minorities and Marginality in the Pamirian Knot'.

3. Adelkhah and Olszewska, 'The Iranian Afghans'.

4. The asphalting of the road between Kabul and the Afghanistan-Tajikistan border post at Sher Khan Bandar means that it is possible to travel between

Dushanbe and Kabul in about eight hours. The growing importance of the Taliban insurgency in northern Afghanistan, however, has also meant that travelling along this route is increasingly considered dangerous. As a result, several airlines owned and run by Afghans—including the national carrier—now also offer regular flights between Dushanbe and Kabul. Our current research focuses on the changing nature of these routes and peoples' experiences of them.

5. Ho, *The Graves of Tarim*, p. 227.

6. *Cf.* Bayly, *Asian Voices in a Postcolonial Age*.

7. Nile Green, 'Tribe, Diaspora, and Sainthood in Afghan History', *The Journal of Asian Studies*, 67, 2008.

8. Ibid. For an excellent study of the importance of Pushtun migration in the making of Afghanistan and Pushtun self-identities in a wide variety of contexts ranging from northern India to Dubai, *see* Nichols, *A History of Pashtun Migration, 1775–2006*.

9. Monsutti, *War and Migration*, p. 248.

10. David Gilmartin, 'A Networked Civilization?' in M. Cooke and B.B. Lawrence (eds), *Muslim Networks from Hajj to Hip Hop*, Chapel Hill: University of North Carolina Press, 2005.

11. Alessandro Monsutti, 'The Impact of War on Social, Political and Economic Organization in Southern Hazarajat' in M.R. Djalili, A. Monsutti, A. Neubauer (eds), *Le monde turco-iranien en question*.

12. Edwards, *Heroes of the Age*.

13. J.F. Bayart, 'Africa in the World: a History of Extraversion', *African Affairs*, 99, 2000, p. 216.

14. Ibid., p. 228.

15. Ibid., p. 252. For a case-study of food's importance to Hazara understandings of morality and identity in the context of their lives as workers and sojourners in Iranian cities, see A. Monsutti, 'Food and Identity among Young Afghan Refugees and Migrants in Iran', in D. Chatty (ed), *Deterritorialized Youth: Sahrawi and Afghan Refugees at the Margins of the Middle East*, Oxford: Berghahn, 2010, pp. 213–47.

16. K. Ali and M. Rieker, *Comparing Cities: the Middle East and South Asia*. Karachi: Oxford University Press, 2009.

17. Ho, *The Graves of Tarim*, p. 348.

18. Ibid.

19. '[T]he expansion of trade, religion and geostrategic diplomatic alliances across an even larger, connected surface, the separate regimes of value embedded in these distinct hierarchies came into close proximity, creating potentials that allowed mobile actors to profit from a kind of geographical arbitrage between them. … the cumulative results of such actions and movements in the Red Sea and Indian Ocean reshaped this space, the relative positions within it, and the distribution of diasporas around it'. Ibid., pp. 121–2.

20. For other, detailed consideration of long-term fieldwork in the Frontier, *see* Benedicte Grima, *Secrets from the Field: an Ethnographer's Notes from Northwest Pakistan*, Karachi: Oxford University Press, 2005. *Compare* Steven Charles Caton, *Yemen Chronicle: an Anthropology of War and Mediation*, New York: Hill and Wang, 2005.

21. As noted in the previous chapter, Badakhshan and Panjshir are provinces of Afghanistan that are home to predominantly Dari-speaking populations. It would be tempting—for the sake of simplification—to lump them together for the purpose of this study into the category of north-east Afghanistan or of Afghan Tajiks, both labels they used to identify themselves. Yet there are significant cultural, social and political differences that distinguish these two provinces and their populations from one another, and these are also registered by 'Badakhshis' and 'Panjshiris', who say that they differ from one another in a variety of ways. I continue to use Badakhshi and Panjshiri as identity labels, seeking where possible to also indicate where the differences between these lie. More broadly, all of this relates to one of the central themes of this book: that belonging and being a 'fragment' of the Frontier is a position even within 'ethnic groups' such as Afghanistan's 'Tajiks'.

22. I am able to converse and conduct interviews in Dari, although not as fluently as in Khowar. Some of my one-time Chitral-based Afghan informants say they prefer to speak to me in Khowar as they fear losing their fluency in it.

23. For an excellent treatment of belonging in another mountainous yet very different community in Pakistan's North-West Frontier, *see* Are J. Knudsen, *Violence and Belonging: Land, Love and Lethal Conflict in the North-West Frontier Province of Pakistan*, Copenhagen: NIAS, 2009.

24. This is a point made especially well by Ho: *The Graves of Tarim*.

25. *See for example* Ulf Hannerz, 'Studying Down, Up, Sideways, Through, Backward, Forward, Away and at Home: Reflections on the Field Worries of an Expansive Discipline', in Simon M. Coleman and Peter J. Collins (eds), *Locating the Field*, Oxford: Berg, 2006.

26. After the fall of the Taliban government Ahmed preferred to take his father to hospitals in Delhi as opposed to Chitral, staying in houses in the city owned by wealthy and influential politician-soldiers from Panjshir.

27. December-January 2007, December-January 2008, March-April 2008, March-April 2009, September 2009.

28. Kunduz province has been central to the emergence of the Taliban insurgent in northern Afghanistan, especially in predominantly Pushtun communities. On the 'new' Taliban, *see* Antonio Giustozzi, *Koran, Kalashnikov, and Laptop: the Neo-Taliban Insurgency in Afghanistan*, London: C. Hurst and Co., 2008; Giustozzi, *Decoding the New Taliban: Insights from the Afghan Field*, London: C. Hurst and Co., 2009. On Pushtun-speaking communities in northern Afghanistan *see* Nancy Tapper, 'The Advent of Pashtūn Māldārs in North-Western Afghanistan', *Bulletin of the School of*

Oriental and African Studies, 36, 1973, pp. 55–79 and *Bartered Brides*, Cambridge: Cambridge University Press, 1990.

29. George E. Marcus, 'Ethnography in/of the World System: The Emergence of Multi-Sited Ethnography', *Annual Review of Anthropology*, 24, 1995.

30. Joanna Cook *et al.*, 'What if there is no Elephant? Towards a Conception of an Un-sited Field' in M.-A. Falzon (ed), *Multi-sited Ethnography: Theory, Praxis and Locality in Contemporary Research*, Farnham, UK: Ashgate, 2009, pp. 65–6.

31. Antonio Giustozzi, *Empires of Mud: War and Warlords in Afghanistan*, London: C. Hurst and Co., 2009; Olivier Roy, 'The Origins of the Islamist Movement in Afghanistan', *Central Asian Survey*, 3, 1984; Gilles Dorronsoro, *Revolution Unending: Afghanistan, 1979 to the Present*, New York: Columbia University Press, 2005.

32. Jonathan Goodhand, *Bandits, Borderlands and Opium Wars: Afghan State-building Viewed from the Margins*, Copenhagen: Danish Institute for International Studies, 2009.

33. Antonio Giustozzi, *Decoding the New Taliban*.

34. Ritu Birla, 'Vernacular Capitalists and the Modern Subject in India: Law, Cultural Politics and Market Ethics', in A. Pandian and D. Ali (eds), *Ethical Life in South Asia*, p. 88.

35. My focus here is on the experience of Panjshiri traders in rural societies in Pakistan. As is the case with trading minorities elsewhere, securing access to live and remain in rural spaces involves complex processes of strategizing on the part of Panjshiris. Cf. Anthony Reid, 'Introduction' in D. Chirot and A. Reid (eds), *Essential Outsiders: Chinese and Jews in the Modern Transformation of Southeast Asia and Central Europe*, Seattle: University of Washington Press, 1997. This is not the entire story of trade's importance to Panjshiri patterns of mobility and identity—some of Afghanistan's most well-known traders and bankers are Panjshiris who made their money in the Soviet Union and its successor states, and were involved in the sale of arms and precious stones, as well also as the money exchange business. Given my focus on networks in Pakistan's and Afghanistan's northern villages and valleys, however, I focus here on small traders because they are especially important for understanding the sociology of regional integration presented in this book.

36. A. Reid, A. 'Introduction'. *See also* Charles Lindholm, *Generosity and Jealousy amongst the Swat Pukhtun*.

37. Many Panjshiris and Badakhshanis, especially those living in the largely Sunni Chitral Town, did take Chitrali wives, yet none of the Panjshiris I knew in Rowshan married into a Chitrali family. On their return to Afghanistan, men who had married in Chitral took their Chitrali wives with them. Talking about such marriages and the 'fate' of Chitrali women is a sensitive issue for Chitrali men. One Chitrali, now working as an NGO employee in Khorog, told me, 'We did not give our wives to the Afghans because we were greedy, it was because we were sharing the same

streets and lanes of the villages and we had to engage in relations with one another to make sure that communal life was possible'. As the last chapter showed, it would be wrong to think of the Rowshan Panjshiris as not having taken wives there because they were either unable or unwilling to ingraitiate themselves in local social structures. Many Panjshiri and Badakhshani Afghans, as noted above, did take wives in Chitral Town. The lack of such relations in Rowshan reflects rather, we suggest, an important principle of commercial life there and in other comparable rural settings— monetarized exchange is often preferred with people outside a moral community. As a result, maintaining boundaries between insiders and outsiders while also being able to navigate these boundaries through displays of linguistic and cultural skill and competence facilitates economic agency.

38. On the distinction between 'traders' and 'merchants' *see* Jon Middleton, *The World of the Swahili: an African Mercantile Civilization*, New Haven: Yale University Press, 1994.

39. In return for being married to the daughter without paying the usual bride price (*kelin*), he would also work as a shepherd for his father-in-law for a period of time to be stipulated in the contract. After completeing his duties as a shepherd for that time period, he would then be provided a plot of land upon which to build his own house by the father-in-law, and be free to travel with his wife elsewhere.

40. This line, indeed, was also part of a well-known poem in Chitral describing Chitralis' experience of life with 'the refugees'.

41. On the role of minorities in the hotel and inn business in Central Europe and South East Asia, *see* Reid, 'Introduction', p. 42. For a comparative study of the importance of hotel and restaurant business to refugee/traders in another context, namely Burma *see* W.C. Chang, 'Venturing into "Barbarous" Regions'.

42. Roitman, *Fiscal Disobedience*.

43. Such smuggling was carried out in a relatively open manner. On one occasion I was sitting with Chitrali friends and having lunch in an Afghan hotel, whilst also listening to a conversation on the neighbouring platform between a Chitrali arms smuggler and a man from the Punjab who wished to purchase guns from him.

44. As noted in Chapter 4, Chitral's role in the transregional economy of northern Afghanistan, Tajikistan and beyond continues to be an important source of local discussion, especially in relation to the construction of a road through the region to Central Asia. The changing significance of Chitral's bazaar to regional trade routes is explored in Kreutzmann, 'The Chitral Triangle: Rise and Decline of Trans-montane Central Asian Trade, 1895–1935', *Asien-Afrika-Lateinamerika* 26 (3), 1988, pp. 289–327.

45. On the importance of this process to understanding the significance of 'borderlands' to state-building in Afghanistan, see Goodhand, *Bandits, Borderlands and Opium wars Afghan State-building Viewed from the Margins*.

46. The networks were made even more complicated because many Panjshiri refugees in Chitral had also travelled—by way of smuggling routes—to the West as refugees. Thus Farid, a Panjshiri who was a refugee in Chitral for fifteen years, was smuggled to London in 2001 where he now lives and rents a shop front from a Panjshiri owned shop for his flat-cap selling business. He has one brother who maintains the family shop (now referred to as a supermarket) in Chitral, one in Peshawar who trades in gemstones, and a final brother in Kabul. Farid himself returns to Kabul each summer, where he hopes one day to make a lucrative deal as a contractor for the American base at Bagram.

47. The Tajikistan-Afghanistan border is a closely regulated international boundary. The weekly border or 'joint' bazaars (*bazaar-e mushtarak*) that are held each Saturday on the bridges that cross the river Pyanj and were built with the support of the Aga Khan Foundation are indications of this border's rigidity rather than any open fluidity. These bazaars are used as meeting points for Afghan and Tajik traders as well as the security and intelligence agencies of each country, and their highly regulated nature sends a clear signal to those who visit them that state authorities regulate and control cross-border movement. Those involved in the policing of this border, moreover, have enjoyed funding from international sources, especially the US government, over the past ten years. New border posts on the Afghan side of the border have been constructed and vehicles have been especially procured for border control. The border also extends spatially upwards. The region's airspace is also carefully monitored by a squardron of French air force planes. Passport officers who work on the border have also attended 'border strengthening' courses held in Khorog, where they have been led by KGB-trained Tajikistan officials, and in Mazar-e Sharif, where they belonged to organized security companies, including the notorious Blackwater, now known as XE. Whilst some villagers occasionally cross the Tajikistan-Afghanistan border without documents, some are arrested and detained by officials, and almost all traders must procure passports and visas if they wish to travel to the other side.

48. For an in-depth consideration of the importance of markers of race and ethnicity in shaping the everyday experices of 'transborder' people on the US-Mexico frontier see L. Stephen, *Transborder Lives: Indigenous Oaxacans in Mexico, California, and Oregon,* Durham, NC: Duke University Press, 2007.

49. Metcalf, *Islamic Revival in British India.*

50. Asta Olsesen, *Islam and Politics in Afghanistan*, London: Curzon, 1995.

51. On the complexity and diversity of the intellectual worlds of Deobandi *madrasa*s in Pakistan, see Qasim Zaman, 'Tradition and Authority in Deobandi Madrasas of South Asia', in R.W. Hefner and M.Q. Zaman (eds), *Schooling Islam: The Culture and Politics of Modern Muslim Education.* Princeton: Princeton University Press, 2007.

52. *See for example* Dietrich Reetz, 'The Deoband Universe: what Makes a Transcultural and Transnational Educational Movement of Islam', *Comparative Studies of South Asia, Africa and the Middle East* 2007, 27 (1), 2007.

53. See A. Giustozzi, 'The Taliban beyond the Pashtuns'. *The Afghanistan Papers* (no. 5). Center for International Governance Innovation, 2010; A. Giustozzi and C. Reutter, 'The Northern Front: an Afghan Insurgency Spreading beyond the Pashtuns'. *Afghan Analysts Network*, 2010.

54. Karin Barber, *The Anthropology of Texts, Persons and Publics: Oral and Written Culture in Africa and beyond*, Cambridge: Cambridge University Press, 2007.

55. Lila Abu-Lughod, *Dramas of Nationhood: the Politics of Television in Egypt*, Chicago: University of Chicago Press, 2005.

56. Mills, *Rhetorics and Politics in Afghan Traditional Storytelling*; Maria Eva Subtelny, 'Scenes from the Literary Life of Timurid Herat' in G.M. Wickens, R. Savory and D.A. Agius (eds), *Logos Islamikos: Studia Islamica in Honorem Georgii Michaelis Wickens*, Toronto: Pontifical Institute of Mediaeval Studies, 1984. The more violent of the country's political elite, moreover, have often been characterized by their lack of wit and agility in verbal exchange. *See for example* David B. Edwards, *Before Taliban: Genealogies of the Afghan Jihad*, Berkeley: University of California Press, 2002.

57. I have seen the importance of mimesis in many other contexts and dimensions of life in the Frontier as well. One of my Panjshiri friends, for example, bought a US army uniform in a second-hand shop and wore it one day to work. He claimed that the US soldiers saluted him as he entered the base, until they eventually realized who he was and forced him violently to hand over the uniform. He insisted, however, that they pay him a 'fair price' for the piece of clothing that he had bought not just to keep himself warm, but also because it was invested with unique forms of value as a fashion item. I have, indeed, spent time with many young men who delight in wearing military-style uniforms and telling me that their neighbours have mistaken them for American soldiers.

59. Rane Willerslev, *Soul Hunters: Hunting, Animism, and Personhood 8mong the Siberian Yukaghirs*, Berkeley: University of California Press, 2007, p. 191.

50. Ibid., p. 25.

60. I use the term 'commander' here because the Dari term *commandon* is how Afghans I know refer to the men of power and authority that this part of the chapter is concerned with.

61. Election campaign pamphlets are produced that show such candidates pictured both with *jihadi* commanders such as Ahmad Shah Massoud and with US military officials. For treatment of Badakhshan's political elite and their complex connections to Kabul, and the insights this provides into the understanding of the Afghan state in the post-Taliban period, *see* Giustozzi and Orsini, 'Center-periphery Relations in Afghanistan.

62. In the same way that these *jihadi* commanders treated Chitral as a safe haven during the *jihad* and the Taliban government, their grandfathers had often moved their families to Chitral earlier in the twenetieth century, when they came into conflict with Afghanistan's modernizing king, Ammanullah. During these stays in Chitral, kinship ties were re-established—the grandfathers of today's warlords married the daughters of their lordly hosts. As a result, both Khowar and Dari were spoken in the houses of such families. Thus, the bodyguard of one such commander with close ties to Chitral told me, as we sat underneath the Chinese Plane tree of his boss who is now an influential MP, that the commander's grandfather had 'come to the village from Chitral, Pakistan, and taken the very best piece of land—look, you can see it with your very own eyes—have you seen a better piece of land here'.

63. Judith Scheele, 'Shurafâ' as Cosmopolitans'.

64. One such descendant of the Chitrali princely family sat as an MP in the Afghan parliament for the largely Pushtun province of Kunar until 2010. Another served in the Ministry of Tribal Affairs during both the pro-Soviet and *mujahidin* governments. A further power holder in the north tied through maternal kin to Chitral's ruling family is also an MP in Kabul.

65. Goodhand offers an account and analysis of the opium trade in Badakhshan. Goodhand, *Bandits, Borderlands and Opium Wars*.

66. *See* Olsesen, *Islam and Politics in Afghanistan*, pp. 48–51.

BIBLIOGRAPHY

Archival sources

India Office Records
   Board Collections: F/4
   Political & Secret
      L/P&S/5
      L/P&S/7
      L/P&S/10
      L/P&S/11
      L/P&S/12
   Maps Collection: X9972
   Crown Representative's Records: R/1
   Punjab Administration Reports: V/10
   NWFP Administration Reports: V/10
   European Manuscripts
      Goldsmid Papers—MSS.Eur.F134
      Bruce Papers—MSS.Eur.F163
      Jacob Papers—MSS.Eur.F75
      Roos-Keppel Papers—MSS.Eur.D613
      Wood Papers—MSS.Eur.F78

British Library (London)
   Ripon Papers—Mss.Add.43613

National Archives (London)
   Foreign Office Records: FO/60—Persian Files

National Library of Scotland (Edinburgh)
   Sir Douglas Haig Papers—Acc.3155

Cambridge University Library (Cambridge)
   Mayo Papers—Add.Ms.7490

National Archives of India (New Delhi)
Foreign Department Records

Maharasthra State Archives (Mumbai)
Political Department

Primary Sources: Published works

Bruce, R.I. 'Administration Report of the Baluchistan Agency for 1885–86'. In *Selections from the Records of the Government of India, Foreign Department*, 22–7. London, 1888.

Bruce, Richard Isaac. *The Forward Policy and Its Results: Or Thirty-Five Years Work Amongst the Tribes on Our North-Western Frontier of India*. London: Longmans, Green and Co., 1900.

Goldsmid, Frederic John. *Eastern Persia: An Account of the Journeys of the Persian Boundary Commission 1870–71–72. Vol. I: The Geography with Narratives by Majors St. John, Lovett, Euan Smith and an Introduction by Major-General Sir Frederic John Goldsmith*, London: Macmillan, 1872.

Jacob, A. Le G. 'Waziristan'. *Journal of the Royal Central Asian Society* XIV, no. iii (1927): 238–57.

Mason, A.H. 'Report on the Hindustani Fanatics'. London, 1895.

Mason, A.H., and W.H. Paget. 'A Record of the Expeditions against the North-West Frontier Tribes, since the Annexation of the Punjab'. Whiting & Co. Limited, 1884.

Reynolds, E.S. 'Appendix B: Administration Report of the South-Eastern Baluchistan Agency for the Year 1887–88'. In *Administration Report of the Baluchistan Agency for 1887–88*, 23–4, 1890.

St. John, Oliver. 'Administration Report of the Baluchistan Agency for 1886–87'. In *Selections from the Records of the Government of India, Foreign Department*. London, 1888.

Sandeman, R.G. 'Administration Report of the Baluchistan Agency for 1888–89'. Edited by Foreign Department: Superintendent of Government Printing, 1891.

Temple, H. M. 'Appendix C: Administration Report of the Baluchistan Agency for 1888–89'. Edited by Foreign Department: Superintendent of Government Printing, 1891.

Tupper, C.L. *Punjab Customary Law*. IV vols. vols. Vol. I–III. Calcutta: Office of the Superintendant of Government Printing, 1881.

Yate, C.E. 'Appendix B: Administration Report of the Thal Chotiali Agency for the Year 1889–90'. Edited by Foreign Department, 76–93: Superintendent of Government Printing, 1891.

Secondary Literature

'Afghanistan: The Problem of Pashtun Alienation'. In *ICG Asia Reports*. Kabul/Brussels: International Crisis Group, 2003.

Abbasi-Shavazi, M.J. and D. Glazebrook. 2006. *Continued Protection, Sustainable Reintegration: Afghan Refugees and Migrants in Iran*. Kabul: Afghan Research and Evaluation Unit.

Abu-Lughod, Lila. 2004. *Dramas of Nationhood: The Politics of Television in Egypt*. Chicago: University of Chicago Press.

Ahmed, Rafiuddin. 1996. *The Bengal Muslims 1871–1906: A Quest for Identity*. 2nd ed. Delhi: Oxford University Press. Reprint, 1996.

Akiner, Shirin. 2002. *Tajikistan: Disintegration or Reconciliation*. London: Royal Institute of International Affairs.

Akiner, Shirin, Mohammad-Reza Djalili and Frederic Grare. 1996. *Tajikistan: The Trials of Independence*. London: RoutledgeCurzon.

Alam, Muzaffar. 2004. *The Languages of Political Islam: India, 1200–1800*. London: C. Hurst and Co.

Alam, Muzaffar and Sanjay Subrahmanyam. 1996. 'Discovering the Familiar: Notes on the Travel Account of Ananad Ram Mukhlis'. *South Asia Research* 16(2): 131–54.

———— 2004. 'The Making of a Munshi', *Comparative Studies of South Asia, Africa and the Middle East* 24(2): 61–72.

———— 2007. *Indo-Persian Travels in the Age of Discoveries, 1400–1800*. Cambridge: Cambridge University Press.

Alavi, Seema. 2001. 'The Makings of Company Power: James Skinner in the Ceded and Conquered Provinces, 1802–1840'. In *Warfare and Weaponry in South Asia, 1000–1800*, edited by Jos Gommans and Dirk H.A. Kolff, 275–310. New Delhi: Oxford University Press.

Algar, Hamid. 1969. *Religion and State in Iran, 1785–1906*. Berkeley: University of California Press.

———— 1991. 'Religious Forces in Eighteenth and Nineteenth Century Iran'. In *The Cambridge History of Iran: From Nadir Shah to the Islamic Republic*, edited by Peter Avery, Gavin Hambly and Charles Melville. Cambridge: Cambridge University Press, 703–31.

Ali, Daud. 2004. *Courtly Culture and Political Life in Early Medieval India*. Cambridge: Cambridge University Press.

Ali, Kamran Asdar. 2005. 'Courtesans in the Living Room'. *Institute for the Study of Islam in the Muslim World Review* 15: 32–3.

Ali, Shaheen Sardar, and Javaid Rehman. 2001. *Indigenous People and Ethnic Minorities of Pakistan: Constitutional and Legal Perspectives*. Richmond: Curzon Press.

Allan, Nigel. 2001 'Defining Place and People in Afghanistan'. *Post-Soviet Geography and Economics* 42, no. 8: 545–60.

Amanat, Abbas. 1991. 'The Downfall of Mirza Taqi Khan Amire Kabir and the Problem of Ministerial Authority in Qajar Iran'. *International Journal of Middle East Studies* vol. 23, no. 4: 577–99.

Appadurai, Arjun. 1996. *Modernity at Large: Cultural Dimensions of Globalization*. Minneapolis: University of Minnesota Press.

Atran, Scott. 2010. *Talking to the Enemy: Violent Extremism, Sacred Values and what it Means to be Human*, London: Allen Lane.

Augé, M. 1995. *Non-places: Introduction to an Anthropology of Supermodernity*. London: Verso.

Babayan, Kathryn. 2002. *Mystics, Monarchs and Messiahs: Cultural Landscapes in Early Modern Iran*, Harvard Middle Eastern Monographs. Cambridge, Mass.: Harvard University Press.

Baha, Lal. 1978. *N.-W.F.P. Administration under British Rule, 1901–1919*, Historical Studies (Muslim India) Series. Islamabad: National Commission on Historical and Cultural Research.

——— 1979. 'The Activities of the Mujahidin 1900–1936'. *Islamic Studies* 18, no. 2: 97–168.

Baig, R.K. 1994. *Hindu Kush Study Series: Volume 1*. Peshawar: Rehmat Printing Press.

——— 1997. *Hindu Kush Study Series: Volume 2*. Peshawar: Rehmat Printing Press.

Banerjee, Mukulika. 2000. *The Pathan Unarmed: Opposition and Memory in the North West Frontier*. Oxford: James Currey.

Banga, Indu. 1997. 'Formation of the Sikh State, 1765–1845'. In *Five Punjabi Centuries: Polity, Economy, Society and Culture, c. 1500–1990*, edited by Indu Banga, 84–111. New Delhi: Manohar.

Barber, K. 2007. *The Anthropology of Texts, Persons and Publics: Oral and Written Culture in Africa and Beyond*. Cambridge: Cambridge University Press.

Bari, Muhammad Abdul. 1957. 'The Politics of Sayyid Ahmad Barelwi'. *Islamic Culture: An English Quarterly* XXXI, no. 2: 156–64.

Barth, Fredrik. 1959. *Political Leadership among Swat Pathans*. London: Athlone Press.

——— 1981. *Features of Person and Society in Swat*. London: Routledge & Kegan Paul.

Bashir, Elena. 1996. 'The Areal Position of Khowar: South Asian and Other Affinities'. In *Proceedings of the Second International Hindukush Cultural Conference*, edited by Elena Bashir and Israruddin, XXX . Karachi: Oxford University Press.

Bayart, Jean-François. 2000. 'Africa in the World: a History of Extraversion', *African Affairs* 99: 217–67.

Bayly, C.A. 1989. *Imperial Meridian: British Empire and the World, 1780–1830*. London: Longmans.

——— 1998. *Origins of Nationality in South Asia: Patriotism and Ethical Government in the Making of Modern India*. New Delhi: Oxford University Press.

——— 2002. *Empire and Information*. New Delhi: Cambridge University Press.

——— 2004. *The Birth of the Modern World, 1780–1914: Global Connections and Comparisons*. Oxford: Blackwell.

Bayly, C.A. and Susan Bayly. 1988. 'Eighteenth Century State Forms and the Economy'. In *Arrested Development in India: The Historical Dimension*, edited by Clive Dewey, 66–90. New Delhi: Manohar.

Bayly, Susan. 2004a. 'Imagining 'Greater India': French and Indian Visions of Colonialism in the Indic Mode'. *Modern Asian Studies* 38(3): 703–44.

——— 2004b. 'Vietnamese Intellectuals in Revolutionary and Postcolonial Times'. *Critique of Anthropology* 24(3): 320–44.

Beattie, Hugh. 2002. *Imperial Frontier: Tribe and State in Waziristan*. London: Curzon Press.

Becker, Seymour. 1968. *Russia's Protectorates in Central Asia: Bukhara and Khiva, 1865–1924*. Cambridge, Mass.: Harvard University Press.

Benton, Lauren. 1999. 'Colonial Law and Cultural Difference: Jurisdictional Politics and the Formation of the Colonial State'. *Comparative Studies in Society and History* 41, no. 3: 563–88.

Bhattacharya, Neeladri. 2006. 'Predicaments of Mobility: Peddlers and Itinerants in. Nineteenth-Century Northwestern India'. In *Society and Circulation: Mobile People and Itinerant Cultures in South Asia, 1750–1950*, edited by Claude Markovits, Jacques Pouchepadass, and Sanjay Subrahmanyam, XXX. New Delhi: Permanent Black.

Biddulph, John. 1972 [1880]. *Tribes of the Hindu Kush*. Lahore: Ali Kamran.

Blank, Jonah. 2001. *Mullahs and the Mainframe: Islam and Modernity among the Daudi Bohras*. Chicago: University of Chicago Press.

Bowen, John R. 1989. 'Salat in Indonesia: The Social Meaning of an Islamic Ritual'. *Man* 24(4): 600–619.

——— 1998. 'What Is Universal and Local in Islam?' *Ethos* 26(2): 258–61.

Burghart, Richard. 'The Formation of the Concept of Nation-State in Nepal'. *The Journal of Asian Studies* vol. 44, no. 1 (1984): 101–25.

Candea, M. 2007. 'Arbitrary Locations: in Defence of the Bounded Field Site'. *Journal of the Royal Anthropological Institute*. 13(1): 167–84.

Canfield, Robert L. (ed). 1991. *Turko-Persia in Historical Perspective*. Cambridge: Cambridge University Press.

Chandavarkar, Rajnarayan. 1998. *Imperial Power and Popular Politics: Class, Resistance, and the State in India, c. 1850–1950*. Cambridge: Cambridge University Press.

Chang, W.C. 2009. 'Venturing into Barbarous Regions: Transborder Trade between migrant Yunnanese between Thailand and Burma, 1960s-1980s'. *The Journal of Asian Studies* 68(2): 543–72.

Chaucer, Geoffrey. 1992. *The Canterbury Tales*. London: Everyman's Library.

Christensen, Peter. 1987. 'The Qajar State'. In *Contributions to Islamic Studies: Iran, Afghanistan and Pakistan*, edited by Christel Braae and Klaus Ferdinand, 4–58. Aarhus: Aarhus University Press.

Christensen, R.O. 1988. 'Tribesmen, Government and Political Economy on the North-West Frontier'. In *Arrested Development in India: The Historical Dimension*, edited by Clive Dewey, 170–87. New Delhi: Manohar.

Clarke, Graham. 1996. 'Blood, Territory and National Identity in Himalayan States'. In *Asian Forms of the Nation*, edited by Stein Tonnesson and Hans Antlov, 205–36. London: Curzon.

Clifford, J. 1997. 'Travelling Cultures'. In *Routes: Travel and Translation in the Late Twentieth Century*. Cambridge, Mass.: Harvard University Press.

Cohn, Bernard S. 1961. 'From Indian Status to British Contract'. *The Journal of Economic History* 21, no. 4: 613–28.

———— 1996. *Colonialism and Its Forms of Knowledge: The British in India*. Princeton Studies in Culture/Power/History. Princeton: Princeton University Press.

Cole, Juan R. 2002. 'Iranian Culture and South Asia, 1500–1900'. In *Iran and the Surrounding World: Interactions in Culture and Cultural Politics*, edited by Nikki R. Keddie and Rudi Matthee, 15–35 . Seattle: University of Washington Press.

Collective for Social Science Research. 2006a. *Afghans in Pakistan: Broadening the Focus*. Kabul: Afghanistan Research and Evaluation Unit.

———— 2006b. *Afghans in Peshawar: Migration, Settlement and Social Networks*. Kabul: Afghanistan Research and Evaluation Unit.

Connor, Kerry M. 1989. 'Factors in the Residential Choices of Self-Settled Refugees in Peshawar, Pakistan'. *International Migration Review* 23(1): 904–32.

Cook, J., J. Laidlaw, and J. Mair. 2009. 'What if there is no Elephant? Towards a Conception of an Un-sited Field' in *Multi-sited Ethnography: Theory, Praxis and Locality in Contemporary Research*, edited by M.-A. Falzon and Association of Social Anthropologists of the UK and the Commonwealth Conference, 47–72. Farnham, England, Burlington, VT: Ashgate.

Cooper, Frederick. 2002. *Colonialism in Question: Theory, Knowledge, History*. Berkeley: University of California Press, 2002.

Copland, I.F.S. 1968. 'The Baroda Crisis of 1873–77: A Study of Governmental Rivalry'. *Modern Asian Studies* 2, no. 2: 97–123.

Crews, Robert D. 2006. *For Prophet and Tsar: Islam and Empire in Russia and Central Asia*. Cambridge, Mass.: Harvard University Press.

Daftary, Farhad. 1990. *The Ismailis: Their History and Doctrines*. Cambridge: Cambridge University Press.

———— 1998. *A Short History of the Ismailis*. Edinburgh: Edinburgh University Press.

Das, V. 2007. *Life and Worlds: Violence and the Descent into the Ordinary*. Berkeley: University of California Press.

Das, Veena and Deborah Poole (eds). 2004. *Anthropology in the Margins of the State*. Oxford: James Currey.

Decker, Kendall D. 1992. *Languages of Chitral*. Islamabad: National Institute of Pakistan Studies, Quaid-i-Azam University, and Summer Institute of Linguistics.

Derluguian, G. 2005. *Bourdieu's Secret Admirer in the Caucasus: a World-system Biography*. Chicago: University of Chicago Press.

Deeb, L. 2006. *An Enchanted Modern: Gender and Public Piety in Shi'a Lebanon*. Princeton: Princeton University Press.

Delaney, C. 1990. 'The Hajj: Sacred and Secular'. *American Ethnologist* 17(3): 513–30.

Devji, Faisal. 2005. *Landscapes of Jihad: Militancy, Morality, Modernity*. London: C. Hurst and Co.

———— 2009. *The Terrorist in Search of Humanity: Militant Islam and Global Politics*. London: C. Hurst and Co.

de Munck, Victor C. 2005. 'Sakhina: A Study of Female Masculinity in a Sri Lankan Muslim Community'. *South Asia Research* 25(2): 141–63.

Didier, Brian J. and Edward Simpson. 2005. 'Islam along the South Asian Littoral'. *International Institute for the Study of Islam in the Modern World Review* 16: 42–3.

Dirks, Nicholas. *Castes of Mind: Colonialism and the Making of Modern India*. Princeton: Princeton University Press, 2001.

Dorronsoro, G. 2005. *Revolution Unending: Afghanistan, 1979 to the Present*. New York: Columbia University Press.

Durand, Algernon. 2001. *The Making of a Frontier: Five Years' Experiences and Adventures in Gilgit, Hunza, Nagar, Chitral, and the Eastern Hindu Kush*. Karachi: Oxford University Press.

Dutta, Abhijit. 1986. *Muslim Society in Transition: Titu Meer's Revolt (1831)*. Calcutta: Minerva.

Edney, Matthew. 1990. *Mapping an Empire: The Geographical Construction of British India, 1765–1843*. Chicago: University of Chicago Press.

Edwards, David B. 1990. 'Frontiers, Boundaries and Frames: The Marginal Identity of Afghan Refugees'. In *Pakistan: The Social Science Perspective*, edited by Akbar S. Ahmed, 61–99 . Karachi: Oxford University Press.

———— 1994. 'Afghanistan, Ethnography, and the New World Order'. *Cultural Anthropology* 9(3): 1–16.

———— 1996. *Heroes of the Age: Moral Faultlines on the Afghan Frontier*. Berkeley: University of California Press.

———— 2002. *Before Taliban: Genealogies of the Afghan Jihad*. Berkeley: University of California Press.

Ehmadi, Hafizullah. 1993. 'Minority Group Politics: The Role of Ismailis in Afghanistan's Politics'. *Central Asian Survey* 12(3): 689–716.

———— 1998. 'The End of Taqiya: Reaffirming the Religious Identities of Ismailis in Shughnan, Badakhshan Political Implications for Afghanistan'. *Middle Eastern Studies* 32(3): 687–716.

Eickelman, Dale F., and James Piscatori. 1990. *Muslim Travellers: Pilgrimage, Migration, and the Religious Imagination*. Berkeley and Los Angeles: University of California Press.

Eickelman, Dale F., and J. Anderson (eds). 1999. *New Media in the Muslim World: The Emerging Public Sphere*, Bloomington: Indiana University Press.

Eisenlohr, P. 2007. *Little India: Diaspora, Time and Ethno-linguistic Belonging in Hindu Mauritius*. Berkeley: University of California Press.

281

Embree, A.T. (ed). 1977. *Pakistan's Western Borderlands: The Transformation of a Political Order*, 1–23. Durham: Carolina Academic Press.

Endressen, Rolf Thiel and Knut Kristiansen. 1981. 'Khowar Studies'. In *Monumentum Georg Morgenstierne*. Leiden: Brill.

Engineer, Asghar Ali. 1989. *The Muslim Communities of Gujarat: An Exploratory Study of Bohras, Khojas, and Memons*. Delhi: Ajanta.

Englund, Harri. 2007. 'Pentecostalism beyond Belief: Trust and Democracy in a Malawian Township'. *Africa: Journal of the International African Institute* 77: 477–99.

Euben, R. 2006. 'Journeys to the Other Shore: Muslim and Western Travellers in Search of Knowledge'. Princeton: Princeton University Press.

Falzon, M. 2005. *Cosmopolitan Connections: the Sindhi Diaspora, 1860–2000*. New Delhi: Oxford University Press.

Felmy, Sabine. 1997. *The Voice of the Nightingale: A Personal Account of the Wakhi Culture in Hunza*. Oxford: Oxford University Press.

Ferguson, James. 1999. *Expectations of Modernity: Myths and Meanings of Urban Life on the Zambian Copperbelt*. Berkeley and Los Angeles: University of California Press.

Fisher, Michael. 1987. *A Clash of Cultures: Awadh, the British and the Mughals*. New Delhi: Manohar.

Fraser, F. 1992. 'Rethinking the Public Sphere: a Contribution to the Critique of Actually Existing Democracy'. In *Habermas and the Public Sphere*, edited by C. Calhoun, 109–42. Cambridge, Mass.: MIT Press.

Freitag, Sandra. 1985. 'Collective Crime and Authority in North India'. In *Crime and Criminality in British India*, edited by Anand Yang, 140–64. Tucson: University of Arizona Press.

Froerer, Peggy. 2006. 'Emphasising 'Others': The Emergence of Hindu Nationalism in a Central Indian Tribal Community'. *Journal of the Royal Anthropological Institute* 12: 39–59.

Gaborieau, Marc. 2004. 'The *Jihad* of Sayyid Ahmad Barelwi on the North West Frontier: The Last Echo of the Middle Ages? Or a Prefiguration of Modern South Asia'. In *Sufis, Sultans and Feudal Orders: Professor Nurul Hasan Commemoration Volume*, edited by Mansura Haidar, 23–44. New Delhi: Manohar.

Geiss, Paul Georg. 2003. *Pre-Tsarist and Tsarist Central Asia: Communal Commitment and Political Order in Change*. London: Routledge Curzon.

Gellner, Ernest. 1981. *Muslim Society*. Cambridge: Cambridge University Press.

——— 1990. 'Tribalism and State in the Middle East'. In *Tribes and State Formation in the Middle East*, edited by P.S. Khoury and J. Kostiner, 109–26. Berkeley: University of California Press.

Ghani, Ashraf. 1978. 'Islam and Statebuilding in a Tribal Society'. *Modern Asian Studies* XII, no. 2: 269–84.

Gidwani, Vinay and K. Sivaramakrishnan. 2003. 'Circular Migration and Rural Cosmopolitanism'. *Contributions to Indian Sociology* 37 (1–2): 339–67.

Giersch, C. Patterson. 2010. 'Across Zomia with Merchants, Monks, and Musk: Process Geographies, Trade Networks, and the Inner-East-Southeast Asian Borderlands', *Journal of Global History*, 5.

Gilmartin, D. 2004. 'A Networked Civilization?' In M. Cooke and B. Lawrence, *Muslim Networks: from Hajj to Hip Hop*, 51–68. Chapel Hill: University of North Carolina Press.

Gilsenan, M. 1996. *Lords of the Lebanese Marches: Violence and Narrative in an Arab Society*. London: I.B. Tauris.

Giustozzi, A. 2007. *Koran, Kalashnikov and Laptop: the Neo-Taliban Insurgency in Afghanistan 2002–2007*. London: C. Hurst and Co.

———— 2009. *Empires of Mud: Wars and Warlords in Afghanistan*. London: C. Hurst and Co.

Giustozzi, A. (ed). 2009. *Decoding the Taliban: Insights from the Afghan Field*. London: C. Hurst and Co.

Gold, A. 1988. *Fruitful Journeys: The Ways of Rajasthani Pilgrims*. Berkeley: University of California Press.

Goldsmid, F.J., and James Falkner. 'Merewether, Sir William Lockyer (1825–1880)'. Oxford: Oxford University Press, http://www.oxforddnb.com/view/article/18586.

Gommans, Jos. 2002. *Mughal Warfare: Indian Frontiers and High Roads to Empire, 1500–1700*. London: Routledge.

Gonzalez, R. 2009. 'Going Tribal: Notes on Pacification in the 21st Century'. *Anthropology Today* 25: 15–19.

Goodhand, J. 2009. *Bandits, Borderlands and Opium Wars: Afghan State Building Viewed from the Margins*. DIS working paper 26.

Goodman, Bryna. 2000. 'Improvisations on a Semicolonial Theme, or, How to Read a Celebration of a Transnational Urban Community'. *Journal of Asian Studies* 59(4): 889–926.

Goody, Jack. 1987. *The Interface between the Written and the Oral*, Studies in Literacy, Family, Culture and the State. Cambridge: Cambridge University Press.

Gopalakrishnan, R. 1982. *The Geography and Politics of Afghanistan*. New Delhi: Concept Publishing Company.

Gordon, Stewart. 1998. 'Legitimacy and Loyalty in Some Successor States of the Eighteenth Century'. In *Kingship and Authority in South Asia*, edited by J.F. Richards, pp. 327–47. New Delhi: Oxford University Press.

Gordon, Stewart (ed). 2003. *Robes and Honour: Khil'at in Pre-Colonial India and Colonial India*. New Delhi: Oxford University Press.

Grant, Bruce. 2005. 'The Good Russian Prisoner: Naturalising Violence in the Caucasus Mountains'. *Cultural Anthropology* 20(1): 39–67.

———— 2009, *The Captive and the Gift: Cultural Histories of Sovereignty in Russia and the Caucasus*. Ithaca: Cornell University Press.

Gray, J. 2003. 'Open Spaces and Dwelling Places: Being at Home on Hill Farms in the Scottish Borders'. In *The Anthropology of Space and Place:*

Locating Culture, edited by S.M. Low and D. Lawrence-Zúñiga, 224–44. Oxford: Blackwell.

Green, N. 2008. 'Trade, Diaspora and Sainthood in Afghanistan History'. *Journal of Asian Studies* 67: 171–211.

Gump, James. 1988. 'The Subjugation of the Zulus and Sioux: A Comparative Study'. *The Western Historical Quarterly* 19, no. 1: 21–36.

Gupta, Akhil. 1992. 'The Song of the Non-AlignedWorld: Trans-National Identities and the Reinscription of Space in Late Capitalism'. *Cultural Anthropology* 7(1): 63–79.

Habibi, Gulbaden and Pamela Hunte. 2006. *Afghan Returnees from NWFP, Pakistan, to Nangarhar Province.* Kabul: Afghanistan Research and Evaluation Unit.

Hall, Charles Joseph. 1981. 'The Maharaja's Account Books. State and Society under the Sikhs: 1799–1849'. Doctoral Thesis, University of Illinois.

Hammoudi, A. 2005. *A Season in Mecca: Narrative of a Pilgrimage.* London: Polity Press.

Hannerz, Ulf. 1996. *Transnational Connections: Culture, Peoples, Places.* London: Routledge.

Henkel, H. 2007. 'The Location of Islam: Inhabiting Istanbul in a Muslim Way'. *American Ethnologist* 34(1): 57–70.

———— 2005. 'Between Belief and Unbelief Lies the Performance of Salāt: Meaning and Efficacy of a Muslim Ritual'. *Journal of the Royal Anthropological Institute.* 11(3): 487–507.

Herzfeld, Michael. 1997. *Cultural Intimacy: Social Poetics in the Nation-State.* London: Routledge.

Hirsch, E. 1995. 'Landscape: between Place and Space'. In *The Anthropology of Landscape: Perspectives on Place and Space*, edited by E. Hirsch and M. O'Hanlon, 1–30. Oxford: Oxford University Press.

———— 2001. 'When was Modernity in Melanesia?' *Social Anthropology* 9: 131–46.

———— 2006. 'Landscape, Myth and Time'. *Journal of Material Culture* 11: 151–65.

Hirschkind, C. 2006. *The Ethical Soundscape: Cassette Sermons and Islamic Counterpublics.* New York: Columbia University Press.

Ho, Engseng. 2002. 'Names beyond Nations: The Making of Local Cosmopolitans'. *Études Rurales*, 163–64, 215–32.

———— 2004. 'Empire through Diasporic Eyes: A View from the Other Boat'. *Comparative Studies in Society and History* 46: 210–46.

———— 2006. *The Graves of Tarim: Genealogy and Mobility across the Indian Ocean.* Berkeley and Los Angeles: University of California Press.

Holdich, T.H. 1916. *Political Frontier and Boundary Making.* London: Macmillan and Co.

Holzwarth, Wolfgang. 1996. 'Chitral History, 1540–1660: Comments on Sources and Historiography'. In *Proceedings of the Second International*

Hindukush Cultural Conference, edited by Elena Bashir and Israrudddin: 116–34. Karachi: Oxford University Press.

Hopkins, B.D. 2008. *The Making of Modern Afghanistan*. Basingstoke: Palgrave Macmillan.

Hopkirk, Peter. 1990. *The Great Game: On Secret Service in High Asia*. London: John Murray.

Hull, M. 2008. 'Rule by Records: the Expropriation of Land and the Misappropriation of Lists in Islamabad'. *American Ethnologist* 35(4): 501–518.

Humphrey, C. 1995. 'Chiefly and Shamanist Landscapes in Mongolia'. In *The Anthropology of Landscape: Perspectives on Place and Space*, edited by E. Hirsch and M. O'Hanlon, Oxford: Oxford University Press.

Hunsberger, Alice C. 2000. *Nasir Khusraw, The Ruby of Badakhshan: A Portrait of the Persian Poet, Traveller and Philosopher*. London, York: I.B. Tauris/Institute of Ismaili Studies.

Hutt, Michael. 2005. *Unbecoming Citizens: Culture, Nationhood, and the Flight of Refugees from Bhutan*. New Delhi: Oxford University Press.

Iloliev, Abdul. 2006. 'Poetic Expression of Pamiri Ismāīlism: The Life and Thought of Mubārak-i Wakhānī, a Nineteenth-Century Mystic Poet and Religious Scholar'. Doctoral Thesis, Cambridge University.

Ingram, Edward. 1992. 'India and the North-West Frontier: The First Afghan War'. In *Great Powers and Little Wars: Limits of Power*, edited by Jane Errington and Hamish Ion. New York: Praeger.

IUCN Pakistan. 2004. *Chitral: A Study in Statecraft (1320–1969)*. Karachi: IUCN Pakistan. http://www.iucn.org [accessed October 10, 2007].

Jaffrelot, Christophe (ed). 2002. *Pakistan: Nationalism without a Nation*. London: Zed Books.

Jalal, Ayesha. 2008. *Partisans of Allah: Jihad in South Asia*. New Delhi: Permanent Black.

Janson, M. 2005. 'Roaming about for God's sake: the Upsurge of the Tablīgh Jamā'at in The Gambia'. *Journal of Religion in Africa* 35, 4, 450–81.

Kandiyoti, Deniz. 2002. 'Post-Colonialism Compared: Potentials and Limitations in the Middle East and Central Asia'. *International Journal of Middle East Studies* 34(2): 279–97.

Kashani-Sabet, Firoozeh. *Frontier Fictions: Shaping the Iranian Nation, 1804–1946*. Princeton: Princeton University Press, 1999.

Kasprowicz, Michael D. '1857 and the Fear of Muslim Rebellion on India's North-West Frontier'. *Small Wars and Insurgencies* 8, no. 2 (1997): 1–15.

Kaviraj, Narahari. *Wahabi and Farazi Rebels of Bengal* New Delhi: People's Publishing House, 1982.

Kepel, Gilles. 2002. *Jihad: The Trail of Political Islam*. London: I.B. Tauris.

Khaldun, Ibn. 1958. *The Muqaddimah: An Introduction to History*. Translated by Franz Rosenthal. 3 vols, Bollingen Series. New York: Pantheon Books.

Khalid, Adeeb. 2007. *Islam after Communism: Religion and Politics in Central Asia*. Berkeley and Los Angeles: California University Press.

Klaits. A. and G. Gulmanadova-Klaits. 2004. 'Love and War in Afghanistan'. New York: Seven Stories Press.

Kreutzmann, Hermann. 2003. 'Ethnic Minorities and Marginality in the Pamirian. Knot: Survival of Wakhi and Kirghiz in a Harsh Environment and Global Contexts'. *Geographical Journal* 169(3): 215–35.

Lambek, Michael. 1990. 'The Practice of Islamic Experts in a Village on Mayotte'. *Journal of Religion in Africa* 20(1): 20–40.

——— 1998. 'The Sakalava Poiesis of History: Realizing the Past through Spirit Possession in Madagascar'. *American Ethnologist* 25(2): 106–127.

Lange, Matthew K. 2004. 'British Colonial Legacies and Political Development'. *World Development* 32, no. 6: 905–22.

Larkin, B. 2008. 'Ahmed Deedat and the Form of Islamic Evangelism'. *Social Text* 26(3): 101–121.

Launay, Robert. 1992. *Beyond the Stream: Islam and Society in a West African Town*. Berkeley and Los Angeles: University of California Press.

Lindisfarne, N. 2008. 'Culture Wars'. *Anthropology Today* 24(3): 3–4.

Lugard, Frederick. 1965 [1922]. *The Dual Mandate in British Tropical Africa*. 5th ed. London: Frank Cass & Co. Ltd.

Mahmood, S. 2004. *Politics of Piety: the Islamic Revival and the Feminist Subject*. Princeton: Princeton University Press.

——— 2003. 'Ethical Formation and the Politics of Individual Autonomy in Contemporary Egypt'. *Social Research* 70(3): 1501–1530.

Major, Andrew. 1999. 'State and Criminal Tribes in Colonial Punjab: Surveillance, Control and Reclamation of the "Dangerous Classes"'. *Modern Asian Studies* 33, no. 3: 657–88.

Majeed, J. 2007. *Autobiography,Travel and Postcolonial National Identity: Gandhi, Nehru and Iqbal*. Basinsgtoke: Palgrave Macmillan.

Makdisi, U. 2000. *The Culture of Sectarianism: Community, History and Violence in Nineteenth-century Ottoman Lebanon*. Berkeley: University of California Press.

Makdisi, U. and P. Silverstein. 2006. 'Introduction: Memory and Violence in the Middle East and North Africa'. In *Memory and Violence in the Middle East and North Africa*, edited by U. Makdisi and P. Silverstein, 1–24. Bloomington and Indianapolis: Indiana University Press.

Malkki, Liisa H. 1995. *Purity and Exile: Violence, Memory, and National Cosmology among Hutu Refugees in Tanzania*. University of Chicago Press.

Mamdani, Mahmood. 1996. *Citizen and Subject: Contemporary Africa and the Legacy of Late Colonialism*. Princeton Studies in Culture/Power/History. Princeton University Press.

Mandaville, Peter G. 2004. *Transnational Muslim Politics: Reimagining the Umma*. London: Routledge.

Marcus, G. 1995. 'Ethnography in/of the World System: the Emergence of Multi-sited Ethnogrophy'. *Annual Reviews in Anthropology* 24: 95–117.

Markovits, C., J. Puchepadass and S. Subrahmanyam. 2006a. *Society and*

Circulation: Mobile People and Itinerant Cultures in South Asia, 1750–1950. New Delhi: Permanent Black.

———— 2006b. 'Introduction'. In *Society and Circulation: Mobile People and Itinerant Cultures in South Asia, 1750–1950*, edited by C. Markovits, J. Puchepadass and S. Subrahmanyam, 1–22. New Delhi: Permanent Black.

Maroya, Alex. 2003 'Rethinking the Nation-State from the Frontier'. *Millenium: Journal of International Studies* 32, no. 2: 267–92.

Marsden, Magnus. 2005. *Living Islam: Muslim Religious Experience in Pakistan's North-West Frontier.* Cambridge: Cambridge University Press.

———— 2007a. 'Islam, Political Authority and Emotion in Northern Pakistan'. *Contributions to Indian Sociology* 41(1): 41–80.

———— 2007b. 'Love and Elopement in Northern Pakistan'. *Journal of the Royal Anthropological Institute* 13(1): 91–108.

———— 2010. *Opportunities and Constraints in Central and South Asian Trade Flows: Perspectives from Afghan Traders in Tajikistan.* Project Report, Norwegian Institute of International Affairs.

Masquelier, A. 2007. 'Negotiating Futures: Islam, Youth and the State in Niger'. In *Islam and Muslim Politics in Africa*, edited by B. Soares and R. Otayak, 243–254. London and New York: Palgrave Macmillan.

McFate, Montgomery. 2005, 'Anthropology and Counterinsurgency: The Strange Story of their Curious Relationship', *Military Review*, March/April.

Metcalf, Barbara. 1982. *Islamic Revival in British India: Deoband 1860–1900.* Princeton: Princeton University Press.

———— 1993. 'Living Hadith in the Tabligh-i Jamaat'. *Journal of Asian Studies* 52: 584–608.

———— 1999. 'Nationalism, Modernity, and Muslim Identity in India before 1947'. In *Nation and Religion: Perspectives on Europe and Asia*, edited by Peter van der Veer and Hartmut Lehmann. Princeton: Princeton University Press.

Mills, Margaret A. 1991. *Rhetorics and Politics in Afghan Traditional Storytelling.* Philadelphia: University of Pennsylvania Press.

Mir, Farina. 2006. 'Genre and Devotion in Punjabi Popular Narratives: Rethinking Cultural and Religious Syncretism'. *Comparative Studies in Society and History* 48(3): 727–58.

Mojtahed-Zadeh, Pirouz. 2004. *Small Players of the Great Game: The Settlement of Iran's Eastern Borderlands and the Creation of Afghanistan.* London: Routledge.

Monsutti, Alessandro. 2005. *War and Migration: Social Networks and Economic Strategies of the Hazaras of Afghanistan.* Translated by Patrick Cammiler. London and New York: Routledge.

———— 2006. *Afghan Transnational Networks: Looking beyond Repatriation.* Kabul: Afghan Research and Evaluation Unit.

———— 2008. 'The Impact of War on Social, Political and Economic Organization in Southern Hazarajat'. In *Le Monde Turco-Iranien en question*, edited by M. Djalili, A. Monsutti, Alessandro and A. Neubauer, 195–210. Geneva: Karthala.

Morgenstierne, Georg. 1932. *Report on a Linguistic Mission to North-Western India*. Cambridge, Mass.: Harvard University Press.

———— 1936. 'Iranian Elements in Khowar'. *Bulletin of the School of Oriental Studies* 8 (2–3): 657–71.

Mundy, M. 1995. *Domestic Government: Kinship, Community and Polity in North Yemen*. London: I.B. Tauris.

Murtaza, Ghulam Mirza. 1982. *New History of Chitral*. Based on the Original Persian Text of Mirza Muhammad Ghufran. Revised and enlarged with additional research of Late His Highness Sir Nasir-ul-Mulk by Mirza Ghulam Murtaza. Translated from the Urdu version into English by Wazir Ali Shah. Chitral.

Najmabadi, Afsaneh. 2005. 'Mapping Transformations of Sex, Gender and Sexuality in Modern Iran'. *Social Analysis* 49(2): 54–77.

Nasr, Vali. 2005. 'National Identities and the India Pakistan Conflict'. In *The India-Pakistan Conflict: An Enduring Rivalry*, edited by T.V. Paul, 178–201. Cambridge: Cambridge University Press.

———— 2006. *The Shia Revival: How Conflicts within Islam Will Shape the Future*. New York: W.W. Norton.

Navaro-Yashin, Yael. 2002. *Faces of the State: Secularism and Public Life in Turkey*. Princeton: Princeton University Press.

Newbury, Colin. 2003. *Patrons, Clients and Empire: Chieftancy and Over-rule in Asia, Africa and the Pacific*. Oxford: Oxford University Press.

Nichols, Robert. 2001. *Settling the Frontier: Law, Land and Society in the Peshawar Valley, 1500–1900*. Oxford: Oxford University Press.

———— 2008. *A History of Pashtun Migration, 1775–2006*, Oxford: Oxford University Press.

Noelle, Christine. 1995. 'The Anti-Wahabi Reaction in Nineteenth Century Afghanistan'. *The Muslim World* 85, no. 1–2: 23–48.

———— 1997. *State and Tribe in Nineteenth Century Afghanistan: The Reign of Amir Dost Muhammad Khan, 1826–1863*. London: Curzon.

Norris, J.A. 1967. *The First Afghan War, 1838–1842*. Cambridge: Cambridge University Press.

Northrop, Douglas. 2004. *Veiled Empire: Gender and Power in Stalinist Central Asia*. Ithaca, NY: Cornell University Press.

O'Connor, Damian. 2002. *The Zulu and the Raj: The Life of Sir Bartle Frere*. Knebworth: Able Publishing.

Olesen, Asta. 1995. *Islam and Politics in Afghanistan*. Nordic Institute of Asian Studies Monographs. London: Curzon Press.

Ong, Aihwa. 2003. *Buddha Is Hiding: Refugees, Citizenship, the New America*. Berkeley and Los Angeles: California University Press.

Osella, F. and Caroline Osella. 2007. '"I am Gulf": The Production of Cosmopolitanism in Kozhikode, Kerala, India'. In *Struggling with History: Islam and Cosmopolitanism in the Western Indian Ocean*, edited by K. Kresse and E. Simpson. 323–56. London: Hurst and Co., 2007.

Ossman, Susan. 2007. 'Introduction'. In *Places We Share: Migration, Subjectivity, and Global Mobility*, edited by S. Ossman. Lanham, MD: Lexington Books.

'Pakistan's Tribal Areas: Appeasing the Militants'. 2006. In *Asia Report*. Islamabad/Brussels: International Crisis Group.

Parkes, Peter. 2000. 'Enclaved Knowledge: Indigent and Indignant Representations of Environmental Management and Development among the Kalasha of Pakistan'. In *Indigenous Environmental Knowledge and Its Transformations: Critical Anthropological Perspectives*, edited by Roy Ellen, Peter Parkes and Alan Bicker, 253–91. Amsterdam: Harwood Academic.

———— 2001a. 'Alternative Social Structures and Foster Relations in the Hindu Kush: Milk Kinship and Tributary Alliance in Former Mountain Kingdoms of Northern Pakistan'. *Comparative Studies in Society and History* 43(1): 4–36.

———— 2001b. 'Unwrapping Rudeness: Inverted Etiquette in an Egalitarian Enclave'. In *An Anthropology of Indirect Communication*, edited by Joy Hendry and C.W. Watson, 232–51. London: Routledge.

Parkin, D. 1991. *Sacred Void: Spatial Images of Work and Ritual amongst the Giriama*. Cambridge: Cambridge University Press.

Parvin, Manoucher and Maurie Sommer. 1980. 'Dar Al-Islam: The Evolution of Muslim Territoriality and Its Implications for Conflict Resolution in the Middle East'. *International Journal of Middle East Studies* vol. 11, no. 1: 1–21.

Pearson, Harlon O. 2008. *Islamic Reform and Revival in Nineteenth-Century India: The Tariqah-I Muhammadiyah*. Edited by Saurabh Dube, New Perspectives on Indian Pasts. New Delhi: Yoda Press.

Pelkmans, Mathijs. 2006. *Defending the Border: Identity, Religion. and Modernity in the Republic of Georgia*. Ithaca, NY: Cornell University Press.

Pollock, Sheldon. 2000. 'Cosmopolitan and Vernacular in History'. *Public Culture* 12(3): 591–625.

———— 2004. 'Forms of Knowledge in Early Modern South Asia: Introduction'. *Comparative Studies of Africa, South Asia and the Middle East* 24(2): 19–21.

Pouchepadass, J. 2006. 'Itinerant Kings and Touring Officials: Circulation and a Modality of Power in India, 1700–1947'. In *Society and Circulation: Mobile People and Itinerant Cultures in South Asia, 1750–1950*, edited by C. Markovits, J. Puchepadass, and S. Subrahmanyam, 240–74. New Delhi: Permanent Black.

Pratt, M. 1992. *Imperial Eyes: Travel Writing and Transculturation*. London: Routledge.

Quddus, Syed Abdul. 1990. *The Tribal Baluchistan*. Lahore: Ferozsons Ltd.

Ratanapruck, P. 2007. 'Kinship and Religious Practices as Institutionalization of Trade Networks: Manangi Trade Communities in South and Southeast

Asia'. *Journal of the Economic and Social History of the Orient*, 50 (2–3), 325–46.

Rauf, Abdul. 2005. 'The British Empire and the Mujahidin Movement in the N.W.F.P., 1914–1934'. *Islamic Studies* 44, no. 3: 409–39.

Reetz, Dietrich. 2007'.The Deoband Universe: what Makes a Transcultural and Transnational Educational Movement of Islam', *Comparative Studies of South Asia, Africa and the Middle East*, 27(1).

Reid, A. 1997. 'Introduction'. In *Essential Outsiders: Chinese and Jews in the Modern Transformation of Southeast Asia and Central Europe*, edited by Daniel Chirot and Anthony Reid. Seattle and London: University of Washington Press.

Robb, Peter. 1997. 'The Colonial State and Constructions of Indian Identity: An Example of the Northeast Frontier in the 1880s'. *Modern Asian Studies* 31, no. 2: 245–83.

Roitman, J. 2005. *An Anthropology of Economic Regulation in Central Africa*. Princeton: Princeton University Press.

Roy, Olivier. 1994. *The Failure of Political Islam*. London: I.B. Tauris.

——— 2000. *The New Central Asia: The Creation of Nations*. London: I.B. Tauris.

——— 2004. *Globalized Islam: The Search for a New Ummah*. London: C. Hurst and Co.

Roy, Olivier and Mariam Abou Zahab. 2004. *Islamist Networks: The Afghan-Pakistan Connection*. London: C. Hurst and Co.

Rzehak, L. 2008. 'Remembering the Taliban'. In *The Taliban and the Crisis of Afghanistan*, edited by R. Crews and A. Tarzi. Harvard: Harvard University Press.

Sauli, A. 2006. 'Circulation and Authority: Police, Public Space and Territorial Control in the Punjab, 1861–1920'. In *Society and Circulation: Mobile People and Itinerant Cultures in South Asia, 1750–1950*, edited by C. Markovits, J. Puchepadass and S. Subrahmanyam, 215–39. New Delhi: Permanent Black.

Schetter, Conrad *et al.* 2007. 'Beyond Warlordism. The Local Security Structure in Afghanistan'. *Internationale Politik und Gesellschaft* 2: 136–52.

Schomberg, R.C.F. 1935. *Between the Oxus and the Indus*. London: M. Hopkinson.

Scott, David. 1995. 'Colonial Governmentality'. *Social Text* 43: 191–220.

Scott, James. 2009. *The Art of not being Governed: an Anarchist History of Upland South-East Asia*. New Haven: Yale University Press.

Shahrani, M. Nazif. 1984. 'Causes and Contexts of Responses to the Saur Revolution in Badakhshan'. In *Revolutions and Rebellions in Afghanistan: Anthropological Perspectives*, edited by M. Nazif Shahrani and Robert L. Canfield, 139–69 . Berkeley: Institute of International Studies, University of California, Berkeley.

——— 1991. 'Local Knowledge of Islam and Social Discourse in Afghanistan and Turkistan in the Modern Period'. In *Turko-Persia in Historical Perspec-*

tive, edited by Robert L. Canfield, 132–60. Cambridge: Cambridge University Press.

———— 1995. 'Afghanistan's Muhajirin (Muslim "Refugee-Warriors"): Politics of Mistrust and Distrust of Politics'. In *Mistrusting Refugees*, edited by E. Valentine Daniel and John Chr. Knudsen, 187–206. Berkeley and Los Angeles: University of California Press.

———— 2002. [1979] *The Kirghiz and Wakhi of Afghanistan: Adaptations to Closed Frontiers and Wars*. Seattle: Washington University Press.

Shalinsky, Audrey. 1993. *Long Years in Exile: Central Asian Refugees in Afghanistan and Pakistan*. Washington: University Press of America.

Shami, Seteney. 2000. 'Prehistories of Globalization: Circassian Identity in Motion'. *Public Culture* 12(1): 177–204.

Sharma, Sunil. 2004. 'The City of Beauties in Indo-Persian Poetic Landscape'. *Comparative Studies of South Asia, Africa and the Middle East* 24(2): 73–81.

Sherman, Taylor Corpus. 2010. Taylor C. Sherman, *State Violence and Punishment in India*, London: Routledge, 2010

Shih, Shu-Mei. 1996. 'Gender, Race and Semicolonialsm: Liu Na'ou's Urban Shanghai Landscape'. *Journal of Asian Studies* 55(4): 934–56.

Simpson, Edward. 2006. *Muslim Society and the Western Indian Ocean: The Seafarers of Kachchh*. London: Routledge.

Simpson E. and K. Kresse, 'Introduction', in *Struggling with History: Islam and Cosmopolitanism in the Western Indian Ocean*, London: C. Hurst and Co., 2007.

Sökefeld, M. 1999. 'Debating Self, Identity, and Culture in Anthropology'. *Current Anthropology* 40.4, 417–47.

Soares, Benjamin F. 2005. *Islam and the Prayer Economy: History and Authority in a Malian Town*. Edinburgh: Edinburgh University Press.

Soares, B. and R. Otayek. 2007. 'Introduction'. In *Islam and Muslim Politics in Africa*, edited by B. Soares and R. Otayek, 1–24. London and New York: Palgrave Macmillan.

Spain, James W. 'Political Problems of a Borderland'. In *Pakistan's Western Borderlands: The Transformation of a Political Order*, edited by A.T. Embree, 1–23. Durham: Carolina Academic Press, 1977.

Spear, Thomas. 2003. 'Neo-Traditionalism and the Limits of Invention in British Colonial Africa'. *Journal of African History* 44: 3–27.

Spooner, Brian. 1989. 'Baluchistan: Geography, History and Ethnography'. *Encyclopedia Iranica Online* (1989), www.iranica.com.

———— 1993. 'Are We Teaching Persian? Or Farsi? Or Dari? Or Tojiki?' In *Persian Studies in North America: Studies in Honor of Mohammad Ali Jazayery*, edited by Mehdi Marashi, 175–90. Salt Lake City: University of Utah Press.

Staley, John. 1982. *Words for My Brother: Travels between the Hindu Kush and the Himalayas*. Karachi: Oxford University Press.

Stein, Burton. 1977. 'The Segmentary State in South Indian History'. In *Realm and Region in Traditional India*, edited by Richard G. Fox, 3–51. New Delhi: Vikas.

Stigter, Elca. 2005. *Transnational Networks and Migration from Herat to Iran*. Kabul: Afghan Research and Evaluation Unit.

Swidler, Nina. 1992. 'Kalat: The Political Economy of a Tribal Chiefdom'. *American Ethnologist* 19, no. 3: 553–70.

Subtelny, Maria Eva. 1984 'Scenes from the Literary Life of Tīmurīd Herāt'. In *Logos Islamikos: Studia Islamica in Honorem Georgii Michaelis Wickens*, edited by R. Savory and D.A. Agius, 137–55. Toronto: Pontifical Institute of Mediaeval Studies.

Tambiah, Stanley J. 1976. *World Conqueror and World Renouncer: A Study of Buddhism and Polity in Thailand against a Historical Background*. Cambridge: Cambridge University Press.

Tapper, N. 1990. '*Ziyaret*: Gender, Movement, and Exchange in a Turkish Community'. In *Muslim Travellers: Pilgrimage, Migration, and the Religious Imagination*, edited by D. Eickelman and J. Piscatori, 236–55. London: Routledge.

Tilly, C. 2006. 'Introduction: Identity, Place and Landscape'. *Journal of Material Culture* 11: 7–32.

Titus, Paul. 1998. 'Honor the Baloch, Buy the Pushtun: Stereotypes, Social Organization and History in Western Pakistan'. *Modern Asian Studies* 32, no. 3: 657–87.

Trench, C. 1985. *The Frontier Scouts*. London: Cape.

Tripodi, Christian. 2009. 'Good for One but Not the Other: The 'Sandeman System' of Pacification as Applied to Baluchistan and the North-West Frontier 1877–1947'. *Journal of Military History* 73, no. 3: 767–802.

Tsing, Anna. 1993. *In the Realm of a Diamond Queen: Marginality in an Out-of-the-way Place*. Princeton: Princeton University Press.

—— 2002. 'Conclusion: The Global Situation'. In *The Anthropology of Globalization*, edited by Jonathan Xavier Inda and Renato Rosaldo, 453–486. Oxford: Blackwell.

—— 2005. *Friction: An Ethnography of Global Connection*. Princeton: Princeton University Press.

Turton, David, and Peter Marsden. 2002. *Taking Refugees for a Ride: The Politics of Refugee Return to Afghanistan*. Kabul: Afghanistan Research and Evaluation Unit.

Van Schendel, Willem. 2002a. 'Geographies of Knowing, Geographies of Ignorance: Jumping Scale in Southeast Asia'. *Environment and Planning D: Society and Space* 20: 647–68.

—— 2002b. 'Stateless in South Asia: The Making of the India-Bangladesh Enclaves'. *Journal of Asian Studies* 61(1): 115–47.

Verkaaik, O. 2004. *Migrants and Militants: Fun and Urban Violence in Karachi*. Princeton: Princeton University Press.

Waggoner, M. 2005. 'Irony, Embodiment, and the 'Critical Attitude': Engaging Saba Mahmood's Critique of Secular Morality'. *Culture and Religion* 6(2): 237–61.

Wagner, Kim. 2007. *Thuggee: Banditry and the British in Early Nineteeth Century India.* Basingstoke: Palgrave Macmillan.

Warduk, Ali. 2002. '*Jirga*: Power and Traditional Conflict Resolution in Afghanistan'. In *Law after Ground Zero,* edited by John Strawson, 187–204. London: Glasshouse Press.

Watkins, F. 2003. '"Save There, Eat Here": Migrants, Households and Community Identity among Pukhtuns in Northern Pakistan'. *Contributions to Indian Sociology,* 37 1&2, 59–81.

Werbner, Pnina. 1999. 'Global Pathways: Working Class Cosmopolitans and the Creation of Transnational Ethnic Worlds'. *Social Anthropology* 7(1): 17–37.

——— 2004. *Pilgrims of Love: The Anthropology of a Global Sufi Cult.* London: C. Hurst and Co.

Wilkinson, J.C. 1983. 'Traditional Concepts of Territory in Southeast Arabia'. *The Geographical Journal* vol. 149, no. 3: 301–15.

Willersley, R. 2007. 'Soul Hunters: Hunting, Animism and Personhood among the Siberian Yukaghirs'. Berkeley: University of California Press.

Wilson, Thomas M. and Hastings Donnan. 1998. 'Nation, State and Identity at International Borders'. In *Border Identities: Nation and State at International Frontiers,* edited by Thomas M. Wilson and Hastings Donnan, 1–30. Cambridge: Cambridge University Press.

Winichakul, Thongchai. 1994. *Siam Mapped: A History of the Geo-Body of a Nation.* Honolulu: University of Hawaii Press.

Woodruff, Philip. 1954. *The Men Who Ruled India: The Guardians.* London: Jonathan Cape.

Yang, Anand. 1985. 'Dangerous Castes and Tribes: The Criminal Tribes Act and the Magahiya Doms of Northeast India'. In *Crime and Criminality in British India,* edited by Anand Yang, 108–27. Tucson: University of Arizona Press.

Yapp, M.E. 1980. *Strategies of British India: Britain, Iran and Afghanistan 1798–1850.* Oxford: Clarendon Press.

——— 1987. 'British Perceptions of the Russian Threat to India'. *Modern Asian Studies* 21, no. 4: 647–65.

Zaman, Qasim. 2002. *The Ulama in Contemporary Islam: Custodians of Change.* Princeton: Princeton University Press.

——— 2005. 'The Scope and Limits of Islamic Cosmopolitanism and the Discursive Language of the "Ulama"'. In *Muslim Networks: From Haj to Hip Hop,* edited by M. Cooke and B. Lawrence, 84–104. Chapel Hill and London: University of North Carolina Press.

INDEX

Abdullah, Maulvi: 89; death of (1903), 90

Afghanistan: 7, 17, 49, 61–2, 102, 139, 146, 157, 161; Afghan National Army, 155, 171, 200; Badakhshan, 157–8, 163, 169, 172, 180, 184, 190, 194, 197, 206; borders of, 1, 3–8, 10–11, 18, 23–5, 33, 47, 49, 62, 114, 139, 145, 153, 155, 157–8, 165, 180, 195–6; economy of, 199; Government of, 90–1, 96; Hazarajat, 181; Helmand, 209; Herat, 30–1; Hindu Kush, 153, 216; Isam'ili population of, 150, 152, 169; Jalalabad, 143, 201; Kabul, 5, 36, 41, 91, 95, 147, 151, 154–5, 160, 168, 179–80, 184, 192, 198–203, 205–6, 210–11, 217; Kandahar, 155, 201; Kunduz, 180, 186, 194, 201, 203, 212; *Madrasas* in, 211; Mazar-e-Sharif, 180, 187, 201, 203; Operation Enduring Freedom, 6, 169, 193; Panjshir Valley, 162, 194, 197; People's Democratic Party of Afghanistan (PDPA), 209; River Pyanj, 152; Soviet Invasion of (1979–89), 164, 167–8, 187, 192, 204–5, 207; Sunni population of, 152; territory of, 195; Wakhan corridor, 162, 207

Aga Khan Development Network: 158, 163; activity in Chitral, 156

Aga Khan Health Programme: hospitals built by, 186

Ahmed, Sayyid: 98; death of (1831), 78, 87; followers of, 80, 85, 87; *jihad* led by, 19, 76, 78, 87; *Siraj-al Mustaqim*, 80

Algeria: 1

Ali, Maulvi Barakat: former Extra Assistant Commissioner and Subjudge in Lyallpur District, 93

Ali, Maulvi Muhammad: former head of Habibia College Kabul, 93

Anglo-Persian War (1856–57): 34; impact of, 33

Aziz, Shah Abdul: family of, 80

Badakhshan: 147; population of, 102; territory of, 120, 146

Badakhshi: support for Taliban, 197–8

Baghola: concept of, 127

Baluch: 72; territory inhabited by, 72–3; tribal structure of, 70

Baluchistan: issue of Frontier Crimes Regulation (1890), 72; Pishin, 60; Sibi, 60; Zhob, 60